BLAIR INC.

To our partners, Linda, Margaret and Laura.

BLAIR INC.

THE MONEY, THE POWER, THE SCANDALS

Francis Beckett
David Hencke
Nick Kochan

JOHN BLAKE

Published by John Blake Publishing Limited,
3 Bramber Court, 2 Bramber Road,
London W14 9PB, England

www.johnblakepublishing.co.uk

www.facebook.com/johnblakebooks [f]
twitter.com/jblakebooks [t]

First published, as *Blair Inc.: The Man Behind the Mask*, in hardback in 2015.
This paperback edition published in 2016.

ISBN: 978-1-78418-998-3

British Library Cataloguing-in-Publication Data:
A catalogue record for this book is available from the British Library.

Design by www.envydesign.co.uk

Printed in Great Britain by CPI Group (UK) Ltd

3 5 7 9 10 8 6 4 2

Papers used by John Blake Publishing are natural, recyclable products made from
wood grown in sustainable forests. The manufacturing processes conform to
the environmental regulations of the country of origin.

Every attempt has been made to contact the relevant copyright-holders, but some were
unobtainable. We would be grateful if the appropriate people could contact us.

CONTENTS

ACKNOWLEDGEMENTS

The authors are grateful to several excellent freelance journalists who did some specific pieces of research, without which the book would be much poorer. They are Jeff Apter, Paris stringer for magazines throughout the English-speaking world; Lynne Wallis, freelance for national papers; and three talented young journalists, Natalie Illsley, Chris Pitchers, and Naomi Westland.

We also wish to thank Andrew Lownie, an energetic and creative literary agent, without whom this book would not have happened.

We were also given access to the excellent research done by Sasha Joelle Achilli for the *Dispatches* programme about Blair, and we thank her for it.

A number of journalists have passed us ideas or tips, or helped us with their knowledge and contacts, and we thank them all. We are immensely grateful to Sam Greenhill of the *Daily Mail* and his colleagues James Chapman, Guy Adams and Alex Brummer. We would also like to thank the researcher Richard Cookson. For information on the Middle East, we thank especially Harriet Sherwood (*Guardian*), Don Macintyre

(*Independent*) and freelance journalists Jonathan Cook, Kieran Kaufman, Lawrence Joffe and Lidia Kurasinska. We would finally like to thank Chris Mitchell at John Blake Publishing for the care and thought which has gone into editing this book.

DRAMATIS PERSONAE

Tim Allan

Former adviser to Tony Blair between 1992 and 1998, went on to found Portland Communications. Allan and his PR company are part of the caravan of consultants that supported Blair in advising jurisdictions such as Kazakhstan.

Sir Mark Allen

Former British spy (head of MI6 Middle East Bureau), once close to Gaddafi's son Saif al-Islam Gaddafi. Allen facilitated Blair's trips to Libya during the Gaddafi regime. Blair cleared him to join the board of the oil major BP immediately after quitting the civil service.

Dr Hanan Ashrawi

Palestinian political leader and outstanding advocate who has been a severe critic of Blair's role in the Quartet. A Palestinian legislator, activist and scholar.

Nick Banner
Former Foreign Office official who became Blair's chief of staff in the office of the Quartet Representative; facilitated Blair trips to Libya.

Cherie Blair QC
Blair's wife and mother of his four children: Euan (born 1984); Nicholas (born 1986); Kathryn (born 1988); and Leo (born 2000). Blair – a barrister – founded Omnia Strategy, a law firm that provides consultancy to governments on legal issues. Founder of the Cherie Blair Foundation for Women, and owner (with Euan) of twenty-four flats.

Tony Blair
Born 6 May 1953, Member of Parliament for Sedgefield from 1983 to 2007 and Leader of the Labour Party from 1994 to 2007. Prime Minister from 1997 to 2007. Consultant and philanthropist from 2007 to present. Said to be worth £90 million.

Lauren Booth
Cherie Blair's half-sister, and outspoken critic of Blair's role in the Middle East.

Martin Bright
Former political editor at *New Statesman* and political editor for the *Jewish Chronicle*, hired by Blair to edit the 'Faith and Globalisation' website of the Tony Blair Faith Foundation. Left after five months saying that he lacked independence.

Stephen Byers
Byers, a former Labour Secretary of State for Trade and Industry, quit the Commons after being caught on television describing himself as a 'cab for hire'. He is unwilling to discuss clients, which includes Consolidated Contractors International.

DRAMATIS PERSONAE

Charles Clarke

Former Education Secretary and Home Secretary under Blair; old friend of Blair and long-standing Labour MP. Runs a 'Religion and Society' course at Lancaster University.

Tim Collins

US billionaire, founder of Ripplewood investment company, who introduced Blair to Yale Schools of Management and Divinity where he taught a course. Collins served on the board of the Tony Blair Faith Foundation and Blair consulted Collins about his business prospects and tactics but ignored the advice. Collins accompanied Blair on a trip to Libya.

Wendi Deng Murdoch

American businesswoman, former wife of News Corporation boss Rupert Murdoch (his third). Murdoch filed for divorce in 2013 after allegations, denied by Blair, that he had had an affair with her.

Colonel Muammar Gaddafi

Libyan dictator, killed during battle of Sirte in 2011, following which his country collapsed. Despite being discredited for his funding of Irish terrorism, he was courted by Blair, both in office and afterwards. Blair flew at least twice to Tripoli on a jet paid for by the Gaddafi regime.

Rachel Grant

Former Head of Communications at Tony Blair Associates, now at the management consultant McKinseys.

President Paul Kagame

Rwandan head of state whom Blair advises. Kagame's party has been accused of genocide. In the 2010 general election Kagame received 92 per cent of the vote. Blair wrote a panegyric of praise for Kagame and his regime at the twentieth anniversary of the start of the Rwandan genocide.

Michael Klein

US banker, formerly with Citigroup, and strategic adviser to both parties in Xstrata's merger with Glencore. Blair himself persuaded Qatar Holdings to vote their shares in favour of the deal. Blair introduced Klein to President Condé of Guinea with a view to the government of Guinea hiring him.

Denis MacShane

Europe Minister in Blair's government who supported Blair's candidacy for Presidency of the European Union. Subsequently fell foul of the parliamentary expenses law and received a prison sentence.

Peter Mandelson

Mandelson founded consultancy firm Global Counsel which has consultancy interests directed towards Russia and the Eastern bloc. Former Labour Party communications chief, then Minister under Blair, as well as EU Trade Commissioner.

Shruti Mehrotra

Worked for Monitor before joining Blair. Managed humanitarian relief for international NGOs. Represented AGI in Guinea and then worked for Blair in Burma.

Ed Miliband

Leader of the Labour Party whose proposals, including the Mansion Tax, increased funding for the National Health Service, and caps on energy pricing, have been targeted by Blair and his political supporters.

DRAMATIS PERSONAE

Crown Prince of Abu Dhabi

His Highness Sheikh Mohammed bin Zayed al-Nahyan oversees the Mubadala Development Company, the sovereign wealth fund of Abu Dhabi, which is a client of Tony Blair Associates. Blair is a regular visitor to Abu Dhabi.

President Nursultan Nazarbayev

Hired Blair and the caravan of Blairite consultants including Jonathan Powell, Alistair Campbell and Portland Communications to burnish the image of Kazakhstan. Reputedly paid Blair £13m for two years' consultancy.

Victor Pinchuk

Ukrainian oligarch who has donated $500,000 to the Tony Blair Faith Foundation. Pinchuk founded Interpipe – a maker of pipes sold to Russia. Blair has visited his factories, and described the company as 'an outstanding creation'.

Jonathan Powell

British diplomat who served as the Downing Street chief of staff under British Prime Minister Tony Blair from 1995 to 2007. Powell, a managing director of American bank Morgan Stanley, became part of the Blair consultancy caravan, appointed senior adviser to Tony Blair Associates. Brother of Charles Powell, Baron Powell of Bayswater, former adviser to Margaret Thatcher and Blair's envoy to Brunei.

John Rentoul

Author of a biography of Tony Blair, *Tony Blair: Prime Minister*. Rentoul, (now a professor and part-time chief political commentator to the *Independent on Sunday*) started as a critic of Blair and is now a trusted and uncritical admirer.

Haim Saban

Israeli businessman living in the US. Reportedly the 104th richest person in America and has long supported the Israeli cause. Says 'I'm a one issue guy and my issue is Israel.'

Baroness Elizabeth Symons

Daughter of the former head of the Inland Revenue, Liz Symons was general secretary of the First Division Association, a civil service trade union. Symons served as a Minister for State for the Middle East under Blair; she later became rich through consultancy, including to US law firm DLA-Piper.

She is linked to Consolidated Contractors Company, a massive Middle Eastern construction firm. She is married to Phil Bassett, former *FT* journalist and Blair adviser.

Ruth Turner

Former Downing Street official whom Blair brought into the Tony Blair Faith Foundation. Turner, whose father is a Catholic theologian and a former member of Opus Dei, is a devout Roman Catholic, who facilitated Blair's Faith Foundation deal with Yale Divinity School, in conjunction with businessman Tim Collins.

Sunny Varkey

Member of the Tony Blair Faith Foundation's strategic board, wealthy Dubai-based founder of the GEMS private educational company.

John Watts

Former Downing Street official under Blair who joined lobbyists Brown Lloyd James. BLJ, of which Watts is the managing director, represents the Tony Blair Faith Foundation as well as numerous Qatari clients; it is close to the Qatari government. BLJ has been credited with securing the controversial choice of Qatar for the 2022 Football World Cup.

Benjamin Wegg-Prosser

Mandelson's research assistant in the Labour Party who went on to become his special adviser when he was Trade and Industry Minister. On Mandelson's resignation, he worked for a number of media companies before teaming up with Russian oligarchs. Wegg-Prosser is managing partner of Mandelson's consultancy Global Counsel. He lives round the corner from Blair's Connaught Square address.

James Wolfensohn

Former President of the World Bank. Preceded Blair as Representative of the Quartet for developing the Palestinian territories.

COMPANIES

Africa Governance Initiative

Blair's pro-bono organisation with staff in London and Africa, advising governments of varying ideologies on governance.

Consolidated Contractors Corporation

Palestinian-owned construction company, linked to many Blair activities. Stephen Byers, former Trade and Industry Secretary under Blair, is chairman of British subsidiary AKWA.

DLA-Piper

US law firm with global network to whom Liz Symons was an international consultant. Blenheim Capital Partners, a defence company with which Symons is connected, also has links to DLA-Piper.

Firerush Ventures
A limited and limited liability partnership set up for Tony Blair which is also registered by the Financial Conduct Authority to be able to trade on stock markets. Also offers investment advice.

Global Counsel
Strategic management advice company, set up by Peter Mandelson and Benjamin Wegg-Prosser to handle overseas and British clients. WPP, run by Sir Martin Sorrell, also has a stake in the company. It keeps its client list secret.

JP Morgan Chase
US investment bank which employs Blair at a reputed $2 million per year on a part-time advisory basis. Blair said he expected to advise the bank on global 'political and economic changes'.

Monitor
Set up by Michael Porter, the business guru and academic. The consultancy failed in November 2012. Many Monitor consultants joined Blair's consultancy, Tony Blair Associates.

Tony Blair Associates
An umbrella organisation covering all Tony Blair's commercial activities. Work includes advising governments and multinational corporations across the world.

Tony Blair Faith Foundation
Charitable organisation rooted in faith. Apparently designed to portray faith as a positive force in the world and counter extremism.

Willbury

Company set up by Peter Mandelson to handle all income from books and speeches. Mandelson is the sole shareholder.

Windrush Ventures

Commercial limited and limited liability partnership set up for Tony Blair which could be used to attract investors backing the former PM. Accounts provide very little information about its activities.

INTRODUCTION

Blair Inc.: The Money, the Power, the Scandals has not been easy to research. The secrecy that surrounds his companies and employees – forced to sign long, ferocious confidentiality agreements – indicate Blair's unwillingness to level with the public and answer the question: Who are you, Tony Blair?

It would be hard to find another organisation with such a strong culture of secrecy. Blair's employees, friends and political allies tended to be either outraged that we were making impertinent enquiries about matters that were no concern of ours, or terrified of what might happen to them if they were known to have spoken to us.

The outraged category was headed by the former Home Secretary Charles Clarke, who wrote to one of the authors (Beckett), 'Dear Francis, I'm afraid your mind really does work in a corkscrew way and you are simply unable to avoid insults.'

This odd sentence, which reminded us of the old schoolboy joke, 'Stop bloody swearing', was the opening salvo in Clarke's alarmingly vituperative email declining to help us with this book. For, although Tony Blair is far less popular than he was, the few who still support him do so with much greater intensity than before, and become baffled and angry that people should question his activities or motives.

Yet those activities are of enormous, and legitimate, public interest. Tony Blair has deliberately stayed in public life: accepting an important and high-profile international role as Middle East envoy and unsuccessfully seeking another one, as President of the European Council; founding high-profile charities that bear his name; as well as advising governments all over the world, both publicly and privately.

We asked for help from Blair's organisations and his friends, and made the point to them that secretiveness builds suspicion. We added, truthfully, that we were not out to write a hatchet job, but to understand how one of the century's leading politicians, arguably one of its most successful, has conducted himself after leaving office and the nature of the influence he still wields.

Very occasionally, one encounters a public figure who is evidently affronted that any person should seek to write about them whom he has not authorised to do so, and who instructs his employees and adherents to give no assistance at all to so disrespectful a project. We have only once come across a case as extreme as Tony Blair, and that was when we sought to interview Arthur Scargill for an earlier book.

We approached Blair's media spokespeople, many of his senior staff, many former senior members of his staff (all of whom have signed the savagely worded confidentiality agreements already mentioned – as does everyone who works for Blair, even unpaid interns) and many of his old political allies, like Clarke.

The majority refused to talk to us or tell us anything on the record – some, like Clarke, rudely and splenetically so, some, like the former Blair head of communications Matthew Doyle, with elaborate, almost wistful courtesy. Even ordinary, harmless pieces of information, often already in the public domain, were treated as though they were state secrets.

This gave us a few comical moments. We asked the press officer at the

Tony Blair Faith Foundation (Blair's religious organisation, supposedly aimed at getting religious groups to work together and respect each other) – more as an icebreaker than as a serious question – where the TBFF's office was. When she abruptly changed the subject, we suddenly became really interested in the location of the office, and eventually the acutely unhappy press officer said she was not authorised to disclose it on the telephone. She could only, she said, give us the address on the website, which is PO Box 60519, London W2 7JU.

So could we write in and ask, and be given it? This, apparently, was a matter way above her pay grade. We should write to her boss, the director of communications and strategy, Parna Taylor – and, no, it wasn't possible to speak to Ms Taylor on the telephone.

So we emailed Ms Taylor, and the response was: 'The address for all correspondence to TBFF is public on our website – this is the PO Box address.'

We asked Ian Linden, then TBFF director of policy – we got him on his mobile because they wouldn't put us through at the office – and he hung up on us rather than tell us.

We asked Rupert Shortt, a former employee, who twisted and turned in abject misery and said he supposed they had to be careful about terrorists finding out the address. 'There's a bulletproof screen on the ground floor and all the post has to be scanned,' he added by way of explanation.

Then we saw some letters sent to various folk by Tony Blair's office. The heading was simply 'The Office of Tony Blair' – no address, no contact details at all. The 'signature', too, was 'The Office of Tony Blair' – no name, no actual signature. They were even keeping secret the name of the person writing the letter.

In the hope of some cooperation, we sent several emails to Ciaran Ward, media officer for the Office of Tony Blair – the hub round which Blair's charities, his commercial consultancy and his work as Middle East envoy revolves. On the fourth try we got an answer. It looked quite hopeful:

Apologies for the delayed reply.

It would be great to get some more detail on the book. Specifically, what are you looking to cover in the book? What would you like to speak to Mr Blair about? What stage of the writing process are you at? What's the timescale for publication and also, when would you need to do an interview with Mr Blair by?

The only omen of what was to come was that it arrived in an email with no contact details. Still, we gave him the information he wanted, and back came an offer of a meeting with him and his boss, the head of communications Rachel Grant.

'We're happy to come to you,' he said. But we don't have a central London office and they do, so, we asked, could we meet in their office? Apparently not. Mr Ward wrote back to offer a meeting in a coffee bar.

It occurred to us to say that we already knew where their office was, so they might as well let us come to it, but things seemed to be going so well that we thought better of it.

It was a friendly discussion. They said, sorry the TBFF press office seemed unhelpful, we've got nothing to hide, why don't you put everything through us in future? We said, fine, and, by the way, what *is* the address of the TBFF? And they looked at each other, and Mr Ward said, 'I think it's been in *The Sunday Times*,' and Ms Grant said, 'All right, then,' and Mr Ward said, 'Well, it's in Marble Arch,' though he avoided giving the exact address. (It's 1 Great Cumberland Place, London W1H 7AL, and it's the last building on the right as you come towards Marble Arch, since you ask.)

We said, 'Can we have an interview with Mr Blair?' And they said they'd ask. We said, 'Can we have an interview with the new director of the TBFF?' And they said they'd ask. We said, 'We've got some questions,' and they said, 'Put them in writing.'

They asked whether we would like two of Mr Blair's speeches on Europe emailed to us, and we said yes, please. And, when Mr Ward sent them, lo!

he'd put in his telephone numbers, both landline and mobile. We were in now, we thought.

And that's almost the last we ever heard of them. We emailed Mr Ward half a dozen times after that, asked questions, said we hoped we'd get that interview with the chief executive of the TBFF, and there was no reply. So we phoned both the numbers we'd been given several times. Our calls were never answered and there was no voicemail.

We told our troubles to Matthew Taylor, once chief of staff to Blair in Downing Street and the partner of former TBFF chief executive Ruth Turner, and he promised to see if he could persuade his old colleagues to talk to us properly. He couldn't.

Taylor expanded on a theory he held, which he hoped we'd explore: that, unlike the USA, Britain gives former prime ministers no role at all in the state. Former US presidents are still known as President – we still talk of President Bush and President Clinton – and they have their foundations and their libraries. Former British PMs have nothing, and that – he seemed to be saying – was why Blair has floundered, uncertain what direction to go in.

Similarly, the Conservative MP for Kensington Malcolm Rifkind told us that 'the only official role he has is as the Representative of the Quartet. Everything else he does is as a private citizen. He has exactly the same rights as any other private citizen. If he wants to spend his time flying around the world like the Flying Dutchman, that is his sacred right. It is something we had better get used to, we have the cult of youth. Prime ministers are in their forties or fifties when they retire. You can't expect people who have had full-time occupations to simply go into gentle retirement playing golf from forty or fifty onwards.'

It seemed a promising area for investigation, though we felt a little sceptical. Our prime ministers leave office financially secure from years of well-paid work and the very best pension arrangements, and with international reputations and bulging contacts books should they wish to work. It seems enough, and we're not convinced they need further cosseting.

But Taylor hoped we would explore the thesis. So we tried, even though no one close to Blair was willing to offer us any evidence. It led us to the conclusion that there was some significance to the way Blair had created for himself as near a replica as he could of the life he once lived in 10 Downing Street. This idea is pursued in some detail in this book.

A few people spoke off the record, but these were always edgy, difficult conversations in which they were evidently terrified that the smallest piece of information might be traced back to them.

Some edged towards us flirtatiously, then rushed away, some disappearing suddenly and refusing to pick up the phone, others apologising profusely and lingeringly with what seemed like genuine regret, as though they would speak if they dared.

Others were less polite, though none were quite as determined to be unpleasant as our old friend Charles Clarke, who wrote to us of 'your pleasure in a rather unpleasant and very unjournalistic reputation which you try and promote,' adding, 'You have a set of views (to which you're entitled even when they're miles off course).'

We did eventually meet the official press officers again. Towards the end of this project, there appears to have been a partial rethink. One of us went to the same coffee bar to meet Rachel Grant, who was personable and professional and dealt with some queries. Mostly, her answers were along the lines of, 'We never give the amounts of our fees'; 'We never give names of donors' – but they were answers. At a late point in our researching process, the Africa Governance Initiative did also provide us with an account of its contribution to the international effort to counter the Ebola outbreak in West Africa

Meanwhile, the TBFF got a new press officer, William Neal, who didn't seem unremittingly hostile, which was an advance. We had a civilised coffee with him, and he, too, dealt with a few queries for us. He even finally managed to get an answer to our year-old request for an interview with chief executive Charlotte Keenan. The answer was no.

So we've done the book the hard way.

INTRODUCTION

GETTING RICH: BLAIR'S SECOND
CAREER CHOICE

Tony Blair is the first British prime minister in history whose life after he left power has merited a book of its own. Most people pursue second careers to do more of what they enjoy with less stress. This is not the case with Tony Blair. He struts the world stage, travelling, we understand, for a third of the year, constantly on and off private jets and in and out of splendid hotel suites. He seems confused about his goals and conflicted in his responsibilities and interests.

How comfortable can the businessman in pursuit of excessive wealth be with the Labour Party politician who once protected Thatcher's legacy? Successful by the standards of a businessman, Blair still haunts the screens, giving his opinions on the lives of the ordinary folk who once voted for him in droves. Contradictions haunt him at every stage. He once asked a stranger at a garden party, 'Why don't people like me?'

How can the poor of the Middle East rationalise the international salesman, in his expensive suits, his salesman's smile at the ready to greet a dictator or oligarch, with the 'Representative of the Middle East Quartet' supposed to bring investment into the Palestinian economy?

How does he answer the charge of many distinguished public figures that those he solicits for funds for the Palestinians are confused about whether he is also seeking funds for Tony Blair and his sponsors and companies?

This book will seek to answer these questions. Our conclusions are both shocking and disturbing for British public life and for the political class that Blair damages.

The story begins on 27 June 2007. That was the day Tony Blair officially resigned as prime minister, was appointed Middle East peace envoy, and set about making himself seriously rich.

CHAPTER ONE

A HANDS-OFF ENVOY: BLAIR IN THE MIDDLE EAST

'For Tony Blair to say, "I would like to talk to you about the peace process" is a very different entry point from saying, "I would like to get an oil concession in the east of your country for a client or I would like to become an adviser to your country."'
– JAMES WOLFENSOHN, BLAIR'S PREDECESSOR AS MIDDLE EAST ENVOY.

'Jim Wolfensohn resigned because he is a man of great principle and courage who did not want to be used. They had to find someone who would play the game, and Tony Blair accepted the role.'
– DR HANAN ASHRAWI, PALESTINIAN NEGOTIATOR.

At 8 a.m. on 27 June 2007, a big white removal van drew up outside 10 Downing Street. A man stood at the corner where Downing Street meets Whitehall – the nearest the public can get to No. 10 – with a placard saying, in huge capitals: 'GOOD RIDDANCE'. Around him were a large number of protestors against the Iraq War. As far as anyone knows, there was no one there to support the outgoing PM.

But if Tony Blair noticed the stark contrast between his last day as Prime Minister and the day, ten years earlier, when he had entered the building in triumph, he gave no sign of it. In Parliament at midday he gave his standard non-apology for Iraq, saying of Britain's soldiers, 'I am truly sorry for the dangers they face in Afghanistan and Iraq. I know some people think they face these dangers in vain. I don't and I never will.'

There was something for MPs to congratulate him on. That day he was stepping down not just as Prime Minister, but also – unusually for a retiring PM – as Member of Parliament for Sedgefield, and he announced that he had accepted an invitation to become Special Envoy of the Quartet on the Middle East. The Quartet is an international diplomatic group consisting of the United Nations, the European Union, the United States and Russia. Its website spells out Blair's mission:

> Tony Blair is charged with implementing a development agenda in line with the Quartet's mandate: promoting economic growth and job creation in the West Bank and the Gaza Strip and supporting the institution-building agenda of the Palestinian Authority (PA). The goal is to produce transformative economic change on the ground, underpinning the top-down political process.

In the House of Commons, the Rev. Ian Paisley said, 'He has entered upon another enormous task. I hope that what happened in Northern Ireland will be repeated, and that at the end of the day he'll be able to look back and say: it was well worth while.'

As we write, seven years later, Tony Blair, with his magnificent Jerusalem offices, his armour-plated car, his Jerusalem staff, would be a fantasist indeed if he were looking back with the satisfaction that Ian Paisley hoped for. Peace in the Middle East looks further away than ever, and the Quartet envoy seems entirely irrelevant to what is going on in the region.

Could he have made a difference? Could a different Quartet envoy have made a difference? It's hard to say. It's hard even to say what success might look like. All you can ask is that the envoy should put his heart and soul into it. Did Blair do that?

Blair's appointment was not straightforward. The Bush administration in Washington drove the appointment. According to a well-placed

Washington source, the State Department opposed the appointment, but Bush insisted, saying, 'Blair sacrificed his political career for me.'

The new British government under Gordon Brown may have been privately pleased that Blair might be spending a lot of time abroad, but EU leaders were lukewarm and the Russians positively hostile – they endorsed the appointment unwillingly. The Israeli government welcomed the appointment and the Palestinian Authority was not consulted.

As the Quartet Representative (QR), Blair has to ensure that the group's mandate and primary aim is met. The position is unpaid. He says he spends about a week a month in the region, but all of our sources – including diplomats and Middle East correspondents of British newspapers, who monitor his activities as closely as he will allow – tell us that this is an overgenerous estimate. 'About two or three days a month' is the assessment given to us by a veteran British Middle East correspondent, while Middle East-based journalist Jonathan Cook, who has excellent Palestinian sources, says, 'It's widely known that he spends as little time as he can get away with in the region.' The typical pattern of his one week a month in the Middle East, according to a diplomat quoted by Jonathan Cook, is, 'He'll arrive on a Monday evening and leave Thursday morning.'[1]

The French journalist Jean Quatremer, Brussels correspondent for *Liberation*, talks of his 'rare appearances' in the Middle East, and the appearance of being more interested in making money.[2]

A Palestinian negotiator, Dr Hanan Ashrawi, told us, 'He is very part-time. His presence is not intrusive. It does not feel like a week a month. He certainly doesn't report to me once a month.' If he were spending any time with Palestinian negotiators, Ashrawi would either be there or at least know all about it.

Blair's office does not give any indication of how much time he spends in the region, but told us that journalists would not be aware of all his visits, so their estimates would, we were told, not be reliable. However, the office declined to offer its own estimate.

MATCHING UP TO WOLFENSOHN

There is no doubt that his predecessor in the job, James Wolfensohn – for whom Ashrawi had much more respect – spent much more time in the region than Blair does. Wolfensohn, former president of the World Bank, did the job for a year, from April 2005, after being appointed by the four partners.

Wolfensohn told us that, to do any good for the peace process, you have to put a lot of time into the work. 'The point about the Israel–Palestinian thing is that there is an important job to do. To a degree it is a full-time job and you cannot do that on a timetable of two or three days. You cannot do anything in a rushed manner in the Arab world. Condi [Condoleezza Rice, then US Secretary of State] found this; I found this.'

Wolfensohn worked on the job of QR almost full time. By contrast, Alex Brummer, city editor of the *Daily Mail*, who ghostwrote Wolfensohn's autobiography, said on his newspaper's website that 'far from being embroiled in his mission of deepening economic and security ties between Israel, the PA and other parties, [Blair's] feet rarely touch the ground in Jerusalem'. According to Brummer, 'Blair's approach to the job has been a stark contrast to that of his predecessor as Quartet negotiator the former World Bank president James Wolfensohn …

'The former head of the World Bank used to be in non-stop negotiations between the Israelis and Palestinians, shuttling between Gaza, Jerusalem and Ramallah.'

Brummer says that Wolfensohn addressed issues such as the removal of rubble left by Israeli bulldozers when, at the request of the Palestinian Authority, they destroyed the settlements inside Gaza, and organised openings at the road crossings between Israel and Gaza so there could be free movement of buses for the Arab population and goods between the West Bank and Gaza.

Brummer adds,

4

What the Wolfensohn experience demonstrated is that the quartet's work was not about great geopolitical thinking or the war on terror, familiar territory for Blair's high-flown rhetoric, but about detailed on the ground negotiations.

There is nothing exciting about bus routes, Gaza border openings and security barriers in the West Bank. But this is what being the Quartet negotiator was meant to be about. It is a job to which Blair, with his once over lightly, butterfly approach to diplomacy was entirely unsuited.

That has not bothered the former Prime Minister. The Quartet sinecure may pay him no money directly but has been a godsend for his broader ambition of making as much money for Blair Inc. as quickly as possible.

So while the Middle East has lived through some of its most traumatic and bloodiest modern episodes – the aftermath of the second Israel–Lebanon war of 2006 and Israel's Gaza campaigns of 2009 and 2014 – Blair was hardly to be seen.

Instead of continuing with the effort to bring Israel and Palestine together, through economic and security cooperation, on the former PM's watch the situation worsened dramatically …

Blair seemed to think that occasionally turning up at the region's most exotic hotel – the mosaic-clustered British-owned American Colony in Arab East Jerusalem – and consulting with his negotiating team and a few local leaders and journalists was sufficient.[3]

Is all this a little over the top? Brummer, after all, is known to have a low opinion of Blair, as does the newspaper he writes for. It's worth examining how much of this is confirmed elsewhere, and what Wolfensohn himself thinks; and we were able to get this from Wolfensohn himself.

Wolfensohn resigned partly because the work was so hard and unrelenting and was damaging his health, but also because he was frustrated at the lack of progress, because he thought his mandate was inadequate, and because he felt he did not have the support from the Bush administration that he should have had.

Alvaro de Soto, former UN envoy to the Quartet, says Wolfensohn was lured with a proposed job description that would have given him a writ 'essentially covering the entire peace process'. But his final terms of reference were much narrower and were quickly whittled down further still, according to de Soto.[4]

James Wolfensohn arrived full of enthusiasm in May 2005. It was a turbulent time, but a time of hope. Israel was disengaging from Gaza and parts of the West Bank, which was a step in the right direction; but, in January the next year, Hamas won the Palestinian elections, and Israel refused to talk to the organisation. All the building blocks were in place for the conflict that erupted in 2014.

Wolfensohn was to monitor the Israeli disengagement from Gaza and to help heal the dismal Palestinian economy, for which he raised $9 billion. He donated money of his own to help the Palestinians buy Israeli-owned greenhouses in Gaza. He 'devoted his considerable clout to bringing about some semblance of co-ordination between Israel and the Palestinians so as to ensure a smooth disengagement,' according to de Soto. 'He also worked to set out the preconditions for economic growth in the post-disengagement period.'

But it soon started to go wrong, and Wolfensohn lasted in the job only eleven months, resigning when it became clear that he had no room for manoeuvre and no power to change anything. He was a prisoner of the US and Israeli governments. 'I was stupid for not reading the small print,' he told the Israeli daily *Ha'Aretz* in an interview a year after his resignation. He might have had a minimal role in partially relieving the worst effects of the Israeli occupation on the Palestinians, and he might have been able to take small steps towards reviving the Palestinian economy through high-level fundraising, but none of that was going to make a real difference.

De Soto noted that Wolfensohn tried hard and often to get his mandate broadened, but 'this was resisted perhaps most strongly by the US State Department, which had proposed his appointment in the first place'.

To make a real difference, Wolfensohn was clear that he needed a different mandate. He says that his attempts to expand his mandate quickly made him enemies in the State Department, most notably with the neoconservative official Elliott Abrams, as well as with Israeli leaders. He told *Ha'Aretz*, 'The basic problem was that I didn't have the authority. The Quartet had the authority, and within the Quartet it was the Americans who had the authority ... I would doubt that in the eyes of Elliott Abrams and the State Department team, I was ever anything but a nuisance.'

Eventually, according to de Soto, he painstakingly cobbled together an Agreement on Movement and Access which, Wolfensohn and de Soto agreed, was wrecked by State Department interference. And that, for Wolfensohn, signalled that the end was near. Sure he could not achieve much without a better mandate, he was ready to go. De Soto wrote, 'An attempt by Secretary General Annan late in 2006 to revive his mission met with Russian support but was received with little enthusiasm in Washington and shunned by Wolfensohn himself.'

Wolfensohn had played a useful role, nonetheless. He had helped the Gaza disengagement to go as smoothly as it could go. He also, says de Soto, 'helped to carve out arrangements concerning the fate of Israeli infrastructure left behind by the [Gaza] settlers'. He made a 'clever deal to buy, then transfer to the Palestinians, most of their lucrative greenhouses.'

But Gaza remained what de Soto called 'an open-air prison controlled directly by Israel on all borders, including the sea which is tightly patrolled by the Israeli navy, and indirectly the border with Egypt.' And, on 4 January 2006, the architect of Gaza disengagement and towering figure in Israeli politics, Ariel Sharon, fell into a coma from which he never recovered. His successor, Ehud Olmert, refused to negotiate with the Palestinians while Hamas was part of the government, and the Quartet supported this decision.

De Soto was one of many diplomats who thought that finally and irrevocably shutting the door on talks with Hamas was the short way to endless war. He pleaded for a flexible approach that would not set impossible demands on the Palestinians as a precondition of negotiations, but others in the Quartet – principally the Americans, but also the EU – refused.

That was how things stood when Wolfensohn resigned and, several months later, Blair arrived.

The *Ha'Aretz* interview took place after Wolfensohn's resignation and shortly before Blair was due to take up his appointment, and Wolfensohn did not sound as though he hoped for much from the Blair mission: 'My worry for Tony Blair is that if you read the mandate he has – it's exactly the same as mine. It talks about helping both sides, helping the Palestinians, but there's nothing there about negotiating peace.'[5]

He was in no doubt about the size of the problem facing Blair. 'Just pretending that 1.4 million people can live in a sort of prison is not a solution at all. So I think it's going to require, on the part of Tony Blair or someone, some real negotiations to try and get this started.'

Blair's mandate, like Wolfensohn's, confined him to promoting improved conditions for Palestinians by boosting their economy, as well as security coordination with Israel, humanitarian issues and institution-building. In practice he has mostly concerned himself with economic issues, and with trying to get investment into Palestine.

His work was supposed to reduce violence on both sides, but the Quartet's concern under Blair has been almost exclusively confined to Palestinian violence. Officially at least, the goal is Palestinian statehood as envisioned in the 2003 document known as the Road Map.[6]

Wolfensohn told us that the mandate that Blair has as QR is identical to his own, and confirmed that this weak mandate was one of the main reasons why he resigned. He says that Blair tried to get an expanded mandate, but it was not allowed.

Dr Hanan Ashrawi told us that the mandate issue is crucial. 'The mandate is very limiting,' she told us. 'It is just about the economy. The envoy should have a political mandate. It can be quite counterproductive for the envoy to work with such a limiting mandate, because it can give the illusion of motion, while not approaching the real issue.'

She thinks Wolfensohn was right to refuse to continue to work with it. 'Jim Wolfensohn resigned because he is a man of great principle and courage who did not want to be used,' she said. 'They had to find someone who would play the game, and Tony Blair accepted the role.'

Blair, she says, occupies himself with the peripheral issue of getting a few checkpoints lifted, 'But, while he gets a few checkpoints lifted, three times as many are established in other places. The point is not to get a few checkpoints lifted but to ask: why should there be checkpoints?'

Wolfensohn, talking to us shortly before his eightieth birthday, said he did not want to get into a conflict with Blair, whom he knows well. But he wondered aloud whether much could be achieved by the QR with the present mandate. The only way to solve this process is at the head-of-state level, as US President Bill Clinton did when he brought together Israeli PM Yitzhak Rabin and Palestinian leader Yasser Arafat, said Wolfensohn. 'I am not sure how much power the position [of QR] has, and that is why I got out.'

Blair's office has told the *Guardian*'s Harriet Sherwood that the mandate issue is a red herring, saying it is irrelevant to the mission's actual achievements. Among these, say officials, are double-digit growth in the Palestinian economy; lifting checkpoints that severely restricted movement in the West Bank; assisting the development and training of Palestinian security forces; the easing of Israel's blockade on Gaza in 2010; securing an additional 10,000-plus permits for Palestinian labourers to work in Israel; and persuading Israel to release a share of the radio spectrum to allow a second mobile-phone company to operate in Palestine.[7]

The last of these was of great interest to US investment bank JP Morgan Chase, to whose board Blair was appointed on 10 January 2008. His role seems to be to lobby governments on behalf of the bank. He became senior adviser to the bank as well as a member of its international advisory board, and JP Morgan Chase pays him £2 million a year.

James Wolfensohn told us, 'I would guess he was very helpful [to JP Morgan Chase] because he kept in touch with a lot of his buddies and was probably in a position to give informed talks to the international board when they were interested in some particular subject. I have no doubt that to give effective responses to questions, he could utilise his excellent network and could find out what kinds of things were going on in response.

'That job would suit him and, given that his observations were not on the front pages of the newspapers, he did something that a lot of former heads of state have done with great effect. He has helped, especially, bankers and their clients who want to see the rulers or the leaders. It has allowed him to be very well compensated. That is fair game, that is what a lot of former politicians and leaders do.'

Wolfensohn also reported a perception held, he said, by many people, that Blair may be using the post of QR to increase his general exposure to the Middle East, as distinct from having a serious focus on the peace process. You can start a conversation about the intractable subject of peace in the Middle East, but, once it is begun, other things that are rather less intractable might well come up, he told us. It's possible to get in the door by talking about the Middle East, and, once in, to advance your business interests.

He said, 'For Tony Blair to say, "I would like to talk to you about the peace process" is a very different entry point from saying, "I would like to get an oil concession in the east of your country for a client or I would like to become an adviser to your country."'

Wolfensohn is careful to point out that he has not been present during Blair's meetings with the leaders of oil-rich states, nor with potential client states, and cannot therefore say with any certainty what occurred in their discussions.

Ashrawi, too, told us tersely, 'The role gives him access all across the region. I have no proof that he uses this to feather his own nest.'

Journalist Alex Brummer dispenses with the careful diplomatic language of Wolfensohn and Ashrawi. He has written in the *Daily Mail* that Blair's role as envoy is 'no more than a ticket to making ever more millions' and that it 'has been a godsend for his broader ambition of making as much money for Blair Inc. as quickly as possible'.

He added,

> His big selling point as he offers himself as a deal maker around the Middle East and as a lecturer in the banking parlours of New York and Chicago is his continuing role as an international mediator. He is not just a former PM, collecting his cheques, but an active big hitter who could open the door of foreign ministries and palaces.[8]

It's a theme that is echoed by several of those who have watched Blair from close quarters. An American businessman who was once close to Blair, and advised him to prioritise doing good rather than making money, has discreetly moved out of Blair's life as he watched the progress of his work with the Quartet. He feels that Blair treats the job as a 'calling card'. He says, 'I have seen the whole Quartet thing not make progress; he doesn't have much of a relationship with the Palestinians and yet he travels round the world as the Quartet Representative. My impression is that the Quartet thing is a calling card.

'But when he meets the Sultan or the Emir … do they think they are going to talk about the Quartet or getting investment advice from him?'

Brummer told us, 'It's a job for a person who is interested in negotiating on details, and who is willing to work hard to do so, not for someone broad-brush like Blair. Blair should step aside and let someone with experience of dealing with low-level economic development do the job. It needs someone with practical skills.'

But Blair does not step down. Why? Brummer is sure he knows the reason. 'The job has given him amazing access across the Middle East.'

Malcolm Rifkind offers a slightly different analysis of the reason that Blair remains. He admits that 'being realistic about it, it gives him an entry elsewhere in the Middle East in a way that would not be so automatic otherwise.' However, he told us that, 'I don't think that's why he does it. I think he does it because he likes to continue to feel like an international statesman and not just a businessman.'

PALESTINIANS SAY NO TO BLAIR

Blair's usefulness as QR is limited by the fact that the Palestinians have no trust in him at all. In this he differs from Wolfensohn, who worked hard and successfully to gain the trust and respect of the Palestinian negotiators, who still speak affectionately and respectfully of him.

'Useless, useless, useless,' the Palestinian Authority has called Blair.[9]

Many people – including leading Palestinians – question whether Blair has brought about any significant, useful or lasting change. Nabil Shaath – a former foreign minister, chief negotiator and senior associate of Mahmoud Abbas, President of the Palestinian National Authority – told us that, when Blair took on the role of Quartet envoy, 'we thought he would be a real support to the Palestinians. But he gradually reduced his role to that of asking the Israelis to take down a barrier here or a barrier there … He really escaped all the political requirements of his job as representative of the Quartet. He is not involved in the politics now; he comes and goes. He is confined to economic issues and the illusion of prosperity.'

Blair might argue that he did not *escape* the political requirements but that there were none, according to his mandate. But you can hardly expect to make a difference in the Middle East if you regard the politics as above your pay grade. He cannot escape the politics – and of course, he does not. He is simply seen as hopelessly one-sided about them. Shaath told us that Blair acted as Israel's 'defence attorney' in the face of Abbas's application to the UN for a Palestinian state to be admitted as a full member, which Shaath says gave cause for 'serious doubt' that Blair could carry on his duties as a neutral.

He said that the former PM told the Palestinians 'to forget about the Road Map [which he created] and the Oslo Agreement, to forget about a settlement freeze [one of the key terms]. He has never resisted Israel changing the terms of reference, and he has gone along with the insistence on us dropping basic requirements. He is citing the Israeli position as a matter of fact, telling us to be "realistic".'

Ashrawi told us, 'He always tries to accommodate [Israeli Prime Minister Binyamin] Netanyahu.'

This suggests that Blair's role as Middle East envoy is compromised, given that the QR's guiding principle is that 'political negotiations can only fully succeed if there is broad support on both the Israeli and the Palestinian side and if the parties perceive that a peace agreement is possible.'[10]

He is not neutral: he has sided with the big battalions, with those who control what he calls the realities of the situation. Yet, oddly, it is this area he chooses to highlight in his own publicity, claiming on the Tony Blair Associates website that 'he represents the United States of America, United Nations, Russia and the European Union, working with the Palestinians to prepare for statehood as part of the international community's effort to secure peace.'

Dr Abdul Wahid, chairman of Hizb ut-Tahrir UK, told us, 'Blair's role with the Quartet is extraordinary. His is one of the most hated names in the region. He could not be seen as an honest broker.' Jerusalem-born Dr Ghada Karmi, a fellow and lecturer at the Institute of Arab and Islamic studies at Exeter University, has said, 'He is – at best – a total irrelevancy.'[11]

Since he took on the role, Blair has, at the time of writing, visited Gaza only twice. He says the security situation prevents him from visiting more often, but he speaks 'regularly' with people from Gaza. When he visited the West Bank city of Hebron in 2009, shoes were thrown at him, demonstrating clearly that he is not welcome.

Cherie Blair's half-sister Lauren Booth, who is now an activist on behalf of the Palestinians, was in Hebron the day her brother-in-law's cavalcade passed through the town and he met local leaders. She saw the local community leaders afterwards. 'The sense of disgust and disappointment was thinly veiled,' she told us. 'They said, he is simply not on top of his brief. Also, they wanted to show him the narrow corridor the Israelis force them to pass through in order to go to the mosque and pray. He said no, he wouldn't look. They said, "You have come to see the Hebronites but you do not want to see this side of the story."'

She says that Blair threw away the trust of the Palestinians while he was Prime Minister, and needs to make an effort to recover it. Booth first went to Palestine as a journalist for the *Mail on Sunday* in 2005, when her brother-in-law was still in Downing Street. 'They loved him then,' she says.

But in January 2006 came the Palestinian Authority elections, which Hamas won with seventy-four of the 132 seats, while the ruling Fatah won just forty-five, and Blair was soon calling for new elections and backing Israeli sanctions. That year the Israelis imposed a land, sea and air blockade on the Gaza Strip, after Hamas militants seized an Israeli soldier named Gilad Shalit. A heightened blockade was imposed in 2007 by Israel in an attempt to reduce support for Hamas and pressure the authorities into returning Shalit (who was subsequently released in November 2011) after it seized power in Gaza.

Prime Minister Blair and his Israeli counterpart Ariel Sharon had demanded free elections so that the Palestinians could choose a government that could speak for them, but were now saying they did not accept the choice the Palestinians had made. It was remembered with bitterness when Blair became the QR. If he was to be effective, Blair needed to do something to show the Palestinians that he was even-handed. He has not done this, and most of what he has done reinforces the Palestinians in their view of him.

This was certainly true of his behaviour after the killing by the

Israeli Defence Force of nine Turkish activists on an aid ship, the *Mavi Marmara*, in 2010. Israel consequently came under huge pressure to lift its blockade of the Gaza Strip. It was a moment that the QR could have used to good effect.

Nabil Shaath told us that Blair's worst moment as QR was at this point: 'As a result [of the killing], public opinion was enraged and [US President] Barack Obama and [the EU's foreign affairs representative] Catherine Ashton were talking about lifting the siege. I personally presented to Obama a suggestion to open the harbour of Gaza by leasing two piers in Limassol, Cyprus, and all ships proceeding to Gaza could be searched by international apparatus, and then escorted by military launch, to end all claims that Israel security will be infringed.

'The US and EU were interested and this was the moment for Blair to use the momentum. Instead he swallowed Israeli Premier Ehud Barak's argument completely that ending the siege should become a voluntary Israeli easing. I think for him it was a personal-risk calculation, thinking about his ability to continue in the job. His statements are so benign that they are irrelevant.'

Despite huge international pressure to lift the blockade, Blair managed nothing more than to get the Israelis to agree to allow a few more previously banned items into Gaza. But he made the best of it, taking a high-profile PR role in promoting the arrangement in the world's media as a victory. Whatever effect this may have had in the rest of the world, in Palestine it was taken as confirmation that there was nothing to be hoped for from Tony Blair.

All of this happened before Blair finally blew any hope of gaining the respect and cooperation of the Palestinians. He did it by doing something at once so simple and so crass that it is hard to see how a man with years of political experience and a well-tuned political antennae could do it by accident. What he did was to appoint, as a consultant in the Office of Tony Blair, an Israeli intelligence official.

INTELLIGENCE OFFICER JOINS BLAIR TEAM

Lianne Pollak worked as an officer in the Israeli Army in intelligence analysis, where, according to her public profile on the professional networking website LinkedIn, she 'led intelligence teams and intelligence processes in volatile periods, working with senior generals on a daily basis.' After that she worked for Israeli Prime Minister Binyamin Netanyahu – the Israeli politician more loathed by Palestinians than any of his predecessors – 'in the negotiation team with the Palestinians.'

She worked for Blair between October 2012 and May 2013, and he claims that her role in his organisation was on a project not related to the Middle East, and that he also has Palestinians working for him. This is entirely unverifiable, because of the secretive nature of Blair's businesses. It may be true. It may also be true that she had no influence on her boss in matters related to the Middle East conflict; she did, after all, work for Tony Blair Associates, not for the Quartet. But that is the problem with wearing so many different hats: what you do wearing one hat yesterday will not be forgotten just because you are wearing a different hat today.

It was obvious to anyone – it must surely have been obvious to Blair – that Palestinians would see her appointment as an indication of how he thinks about them; that her appointment would be taken as confirmation of their worst suspicions about him. It does not seem possible that he made such an appointment without realising the devastating effect that it would have on the effectiveness of his mission in the Middle East.

Today, it would be impossible to persuade any Palestinian leader, even a moderate and sophisticated negotiator such as Dr Ashrawi, that Blair was anything but an Israeli mouthpiece. Blair seems to have accepted this; certainly there seems to be no attempt to be even-handed. After a meeting with Israeli PM Binyamin Netanyahu on 18 June 2014 he told the media 'The only way forward will be when Hamas understands that the only proper choice to make if you want peace is to engage in solely peaceful means to achieve political ends.'

There was no balancing suggestion that Israel needed to do anything. Blair made his comments shortly after three religious Israeli teenagers were kidnapped and killed. This event led to the launch of the seven-week long Israeli assault on Gaza in the summer of 2014 which resulted in the deaths of some 2,200 Gazans and 66 Israeli soldiers.

While Palestinian politicians say he has done very little to promote peace with Israel, its business leaders say that he has not persuaded Israel to lift blockades of necessary goods, which stifles economic growth; and they question whether he has tried to do so.

BUSINESSMAN CRITIC

Businessman Lord (Clive) Hollick went on a fact-finding mission to Palestine in 2013 with trade union leader Hugh Lanning and Labour peer Tessa Blackstone. He told us, 'We were told by the UN that the Palestinian economy was operating at between 20 and 25 per cent of its potential capacity. Palestinian businesses are unable to grow and realise their potential because of measures imposed by Israel such as the back-to-back arrangements which require the goods to be exported through Israel. Much-needed machinery cannot be imported into Palestine because of its alleged potential for military use.

'If you sell software it must go through Israel. Palestinian companies therefore become subcontractors and suppliers of services to Israeli software companies, who extract the lion's share of the profit. All this smothers entrepreneurial activity in Palestine and makes the country more dependent on international aid than it needs to be.

'And aid goes to the Palestinian Authority and does not trickle down properly. This means that the European taxpayer is filling in the hole left by the profits, which have gone to Israel.

'I have subsequently been told by sources close to the Israeli government that it is a matter of policy to suppress the growth of the Palestinian economy and that is only going to change as part of a wider peace negotiation.'

We understand that Blair commissioned some research on the Palestinian economy from the management consultancy firm McKinsey & Company, focusing especially on how to bring in outside investors. But Hollick believes this commissioned research misses the point. Investors will not lead the way to peace. He says that, as things stand, outside investors will not come in without having the whole profit pool; and that will not change until the political situation changes. Investment will follow political stability. You cannot expect investment to come first and create political stability, he says.

Part of Blair's mandate as QR is to 'support the development of the Palestinian economy and institution-building in preparation for eventual statehood'. None of this, says Hollick, will work if you start by trying to attract investment without solving, or beginning to solve, the politics. On this front, Hollick, though anxious to avoid directly criticising Blair, made it clear he was unable to detect any Blair input.

This is confirmed by those sympathetic to Blair. One of these, academic Dr Toby Greene, research director at the pro-Israeli organisation Bicom, wrote on 14 October 2013 in the *Jewish Chronicle*, 'Mostly, Blair has accepted that his role is not to broker final-status negotiations, but to facilitate the bottom-up development of Palestinian security, economic and political institutions.'

An expanded mandate, of course, would have required Blair to do what Wolfensohn had done: convince the Palestinians that his mind was not closed to their grievances.

ISRAELI MOUTHPIECE?

For Blair this was always going to be uphill work, because he started with a reputation among the Palestinians for being an Israeli mouthpiece. Greene's supportive book on Blair's work in the region convincingly makes the case that, as Prime Minister, he 'showed far greater sympathy for Israel, as a democratic state at threat from extremism, than many of his European counterparts, much to the dismay of many of his colleagues in his own party.' Greene says Blair, 'in increasingly strident terms during his time in office, rejected the idea that Western foreign policies caused [Muslim] radicalisation as "nonsense".'[12]

In Britain, Blair became close to the Jewish community, but there has always been dislike and distrust between him and British Muslims, and he seems never to have tried to change that. Journalist Alex Brummer is also a vice president of the Board of Deputies of British Jews, and he says, 'The Jewish community in Britain has good relations with Blair. Lord Levy [Labour peer and leading figure in several Jewish organisations in the UK] was the original link. Blair was the speaker at the Board of Deputies in 2010, speaking about the Middle East peace process.'

The board of advisers of his Faith Foundation includes the Chief Rabbi, but the only Muslim it contained at its beginning was a Kuwaiti politician of whom leading British Muslims have never heard, Dr Ismail Khudr Al-Shatti, an adviser to the Prime Minister of Kuwait – a politician, not a cleric or theologian. Either Blair did not trust or approve of any Muslim religious leaders, or they were not willing to work with him – or both. (We come back to the makeup of the Faith Foundation in Chapter 12: 'Doing God'.)

This had important implications for his work as QR, for a perceived enemy of Islam is bound to find it hard to persuade the Palestinians of his good faith or even-handedness.

ENTER HAIM SABAN

Getting the trust of the Palestinians will be made even harder now it is known that one of the main funders of the Tony Blair Faith Foundation is Haim Saban, an American Israeli billionaire and one of the most prominent pro-Israeli lobbyists in America. 'I'm a one-issue guy and my issue is Israel,' Saban told the *New York Times*.[13] He joins several other campaigners for Israel among the Faith Foundation's donors, but there are no Muslims as far as anyone knows. This, says a TBFF insider, is perceived as a problem by the Faith Foundation, but there is not much it can do about it.

It's again a question of too many hats. The TBFF could argue convincingly that accepting Saban's money was fine. But for the QR to be so deeply indebted to Saban, even though wearing another hat, is a serious problem.

Any lingering chance that the Palestinians might grow to see Blair as even-handed vanished with this revelation, for pro-Israeli lobbyists in the USA are considered – generally with justice – to be anti-Palestinian. Palestinians cannot realistically be expected to say, 'Ah, but this donation was in his role as sponsor of his Faith Foundation, and it does not mean that he is in hock to the Israeli lobby.' They are bound to see Blair's involvement with Saban as another indication that they cannot expect fairness from him.

What Blair does as sponsor of his Faith Foundation, what he does as a businessman through Tony Blair Associates and what he does as QR are sure to affect each other. He has limited his effectiveness as QR by taking Saban's money for his Faith Foundation and by appointing Lianne Pollak to work for Tony Blair Associates. He has probably also limited the effectiveness of his Faith Foundation by his work as QR, since he seemed to have trouble getting any prominent Muslim to sit on its board, though other faiths have senior representatives there. If Blair had wanted to spend his post-PM years doing some good in the world, he would have been well advised to limit the number of activities he engaged in.

He might also have been better advised not to make a stream of speeches and statements over the years that mark him as one of Islam's fiercest and most intractable critics.

CRITIC OF ISLAM

There is of course no reason why Blair, as a prominent citizen and former Prime Minister, should not say what he sincerely believes to be the case. But the QR is not just a prominent citizen and former Prime Minister: he holds an important and sensitive public office, and must consider to what extent his public statements curb his effectiveness. It does seem as though

Blair's effectiveness as QR is a matter of very little concern to him, since he issues a stream of statements that he knows the Muslim community will find hostile and deeply insulting.

One typical statement was made at the time of the murder of the British soldier Fusilier Lee Rigby in London in May 2013. As leading British Muslims were rushing to condemn the murderers, saying that their faith deplored such acts, Tony Blair weighed in with this: 'There are two views of its significance. One is that it was an act by crazy people, motivated in this case by a perverted notion of Islam, but of no broader significance. Crazy people do crazy things, so don't overreact. The other view is that the ideology that inspired the murder of Rigby is profoundly dangerous. I am of the latter view.' He added, 'There is a problem within Islam – from the adherents of an ideology which is a strain within Islam. We have to put it on the table and be honest about it … I am afraid this strain is not the province of a few extremists.'[14]

This is, of course, a view that a former prime minister is entitled to express. But it is not a view that a QR interested in making a difference in the Middle East should have expressed.

BLAIR'S SECURITY: A COST TO BRITAIN
Blair as QR is a considerable drain on the public purse – in Britain, in the UN, and in Palestine.

As a former prime minister, he receives a ministerial pension of £64,000 and a further £84,000 to run his office. He gets a car, a police driver and round-the-clock Special Branch protection. As well as this, his personal security guards claim £250,000 a year in expenses alone from the taxpayer.[15]

As QR, until 2011 he and his team occupied an entire floor of the luxury American Colony Hotel in Jerusalem at a cost of £1 million a year, for he has expanded his staff massively since Wolfensohn did the job with (on Alex Brummer's estimate) six or seven staff. However, in 2011, as part of a cost-saving exercise, he moved to a purpose-built, seven-storey building on Sheikh Jarrah, East Jerusalem's millionaires' row, where most of the diplomatic missions are. This costs the Quartet £750,000 a year in rent. He also requires finance from the UN Programme of Assistance to the Palestinian People. In 2007 this programme spent more than $400,000 on rarely used armoured cars for Blair.

FINDING FUNDS FOR PALESTINIANS

Blair's most obvious achievements as QR have been to facilitate large economic projects. Two such projects include a gas-extraction deal for Gaza and securing the Israeli release of electromagnetic frequencies in November 2009 for the commercial launch of a second Palestinian mobile-phone operator Wataniya (investments worth $150 million and $350 million respectively). According to an investigation for the Channel 4 programme *Dispatches* broadcast in September 2011, both these deals benefited the corporate clients of JP Morgan.

The gas-extraction deal saw Blair champion the development of a gas field off the coast of Gaza as a priority for the territory. The owner of the rights to operate the field is BG Group, a client of JP Morgan. A spokesman for Blair has claimed that the former PM had no idea that BG Group was connected to JP Morgan and has said any suggestion of a conflict of interest is defamatory.[16]

Tony Blair exerted a great deal of effort to get Israel to release the necessary mobile-phone frequencies to allow telecommunications company Wataniya International to operate a new 3G service in the West Bank city of Ramallah.

Wataniya had paid the Palestinian government £181 million for the deal, but Israel controls the radio frequencies and refused to allow them to be used. The deal appeared to be dead, until Blair stepped in. For over a year he lobbied the Israeli government, speaking to Prime Minister Ehud Barak on the subject several times. It finally agreed to release the frequencies in November 2009.

More that half of Wataniya – 54 per cent – is owned by the Qatari telecoms giant Q-Tel, which bought the company in 2007 with a $2 billion loan arranged by the bank JP Morgan, according to the *Dispatches* programme about Blair. Q-Tel is a JP Morgan client, and JP Morgan pays Blair £2 million a year for providing 'strategic' advice. JP Morgan stood to make 'substantial profits' if the deal went through, the documentary said.

After a year of negotiations and two delayed launch dates, on 29 November 2009 Wataniya launched its service. JP Morgan stood to profit from the original setup fee, ongoing management and advice fees, and interest on the loan to Q-Tel that facilitated the deal.

For JP Morgan to expose itself to this degree of capital risk in such a volatile area when the frequency deal was not permanent was highly unusual. Its original exposure was thought to be around $200 million.

Before the deal could go ahead, Blair had to break a deadlock. The problem was that Israel had tied approval of Wataniya's frequencies to the Palestinian Authority dropping efforts to pursue the Goldstone report on Israeli war crimes in Gaza during its December 2008 war. This was a report into human-rights violations during an earlier Gaza conflict, which left 1,400 Palestinians dead, from a team led by South African judge Richard Goldstone. The team was set up by the United Nations in April 2009, and Israel refused to cooperate with it. The report accused both the Israeli forces and the Palestinian militants of war crimes, and suggested Israel might also be guilty of crimes against humanity.

Blair succeeded in breaking the deadlock. The Palestinian Authority postponed for six months its draft UN resolution on the Goldstone Report, and Wataniya got its frequencies. Wataniya International's chief executive officer Bassam Hanoun told *Dispatches* that Blair 'played a significant role' in breaking the monopoly in the telecommunications sector in Palestine.

The Wataniya phone network had been built but was not operational until Tony Blair's intervention with Israeli ministers. Israel expected the Palestine communications group Paltel to share its 900-range frequency with the competitor Wataniya. Paltel was refusing to agree and Tony Blair had again to intervene to push for a 'creative solution'.

'I would say his prime contribution to Wataniya was negotiating the release of the frequencies. That was a milestone, obviously,' says Bassam Hanoun. It made Wataniya's shareholders very rich. 'November 2009, we were nothing … And since then we have done fantastically well. We have captured 23 per cent of the market.'

Blair says that he raised the issue of Wataniya with the Israelis at the request of the Palestinian Authority. He has said that there was no conflict of interest at all, and that he did not know that JP Morgan, the bank he works for, helped finance the deal he rescued.

The extent of this lobbying was revealed in a previously undisclosed confidential letter Blair sent to Hillary Clinton on 17 September 2009, using the notepaper of the 'Office of the Quartet Representative'. The letter was obtained using US Freedom of Information provisions and was declassified on 9 August 2012.

The letter from Blair, which is also copied to Ban Ki-moon, Secretary General of the United Nations, Sergei Lavrov, Foreign Minister of the Russian Federation, Carl Bildt, Swedish Minister of Foreign Affairs, Benita Ferrero-Waldner, member of the European Commission and Javier Solana, High Representative of the European Union, Brussels, Belgium, was sent in advance of a meeting that the Quartet principals were holding in Trieste.

The letter starts by referring to a 'transformative change agenda' which embraces 'economic development including a number of "flagship projects".' The 'transformative change agenda' is referred to many times in the letter, suggesting a Blairite, third-way mantra. The letter proceeds to give a round-up of some of the more mundane work that Blair's office has been doing, in terms of improving the flow of trade through the checkpoints between Israel and the West Bank, and the state of relations between the Palestinian government at the time and the government of Israel. The letter up to this point is relatively low-key. At the end of the second page, we then read, 'below I set out some of the key issues which, if delivered on soon, can give impetus to the change agenda.'

What are these projects that can radically change the economic, and implicitly political situation in the Middle East conflict? The first is bringing in a second mobile telephony operator for the Palestinian market. The second, the proposal to build a new town in the West Bank.

The letter cannot over-emphasise the significance of bringing in Wataniya as the second mobile operator. Clinton is told that this is a 'major project, which if successful would entail the largest investment in the Palestinian economy to date.' The price of failure, says the letter, would be grave indeed, no less than the collapse of the entire 'transformative change agenda'. The letter reads, 'Conversely, its failure would send entirely the wrong signal about the prospects for the transformative change agenda, and would deter sustained foreign investment in the Palestinian territories.'

Blair admitted that the Wataniya project was encountering some resistance at that time from the Israeli government, which appeared reluctant to give Wataniya a mobile bandwidth. But he said he had everything under control. 'The Government of Israel has yet to allocate the necessary 4.8MHz bandwidth ... I have recently received an assurance from Minister Barak that the necessary bandwidth will be allocated and I hope we can now resolve this on that basis.'

Why does Blair emphasise to Clinton the importance of Wataniya? He may feel strongly that the people of the Palestinian territories deserve a second mobile operator, and it is a matter of adding to their choice. By the same token, he may feel that his 'transformative change agenda' needs a trophy project to sell to the Quartet, to show his level of activity – which otherwise may be less than impressive – and Wataniya is it. Or could he be a little less confident than he claims about getting Israeli support for the bandwidth and he wants Clinton's support for the bandwidth allocation, perhaps to put in a word with Jerusalem? The more Machiavellian interpretation sees Blair serving his paymasters' interests, and indirectly his own, in the pushing of Wataniya, and the profound 'transformative' impact it will have on the Palestinian territories.

Aside from the mobile phone project, we hear about Blair's support for the creation of a new town in the West Bank called Rawabi. The letter referred to above describes it also as a 'major project...the first new Palestinian town in modern times.' It continues, 'Investors are ready to back an estimated $1 billion investment.' Some roads are needed to enhance access to the site and this requires Israeli re-designating land for Palestinian use, previously reserved for Israel. The letter cites Rawabi as a case where 'transferring designation of small, limited areas of land would unlock progress on the change agenda. My team have identified a number of specific examples ...' Rawabi is the largest private sector project in Palestinian history. It was initiated at the Palestine Investment Conference, which took place in Bethlehem in 2008. Rawabi's development, near Ramallah, is linked to a $500 million affordable mortgage scheme. The *Washington Post* reported that Rawabi 'is specifically designed for upwardly mobile families.' The total cost of the development, mostly funded by the Qatari company LDR and Palestinian multimillionaire Bashar al-Masri, is estimated at $850 million. Al-Masri is the founder and managing director of Bayti Real Estate Investment Company. Bayti, jointly-owned by Qatari Diar Real Estate Investment Company and Massar International, was created to build Rawabi. Blair has spoken approvingly of Masri in a publication issued by Lloyds Bank. 'It is his combination of resilience, commitment and refusal to bow to the forces of cynicism that makes his work so valuable.'

The Rawabi project involves a public-private partnership with the Palestinian Authority responsible for providing off-site infrastructure, while Bayti is tasked with the design and development of the city. The Rawabi economic growth strategy has the aim of creating 3,000 to 5,000 new jobs in 'knowledge economy' industries including information technology, pharmaceuticals and health care.

Blair's letter to Hillary Clinton ends with an extraordinary incursion by the Quartet representative Tony Blair into Middle Eastern politics. Breaching his mandate to reserve his activities to the economic development of the West Bank and Gaza, Blair makes some overt references to the political situation.

> On the issue of security sector control and strengthening the rule of law, there continues to be notable improvement in Palestinian security capacity. But the PA's capacity to deliver a coherent Rule of Law effort remains more limited. Progress on reform in the security and justice sectors has been slow, as has legal reform within both sectors. Israeli Defence Forces continue to mount incursions into West Bank urban centres and maintain curfews on movement of PA security personnel. Nor can PA security and criminal justice personnel move freely between Areas A, B and C. The United States Security Coordinator and the EUPOL COPPS mission [the European Union Co-ordinating Office for Palestinian Police Support] continue to provide invaluable support to the security and rule of law sector. My primary task here is to put the arguments to the PA and the GoI on enabling actions each must take to allow the Rule of Law sector to thrive.
>
> The situation in Gaza remains unsustainable in the medium term and highly combustible. Yet there appears to be no prospect of a substantive change in GoI policy, so long as Corporal Shalit remains in captivity. While there appeared to be a prospect of limited easing over the summer, including by allowing reconstruction materials through crossings, this has not happened.

The letter ends with some further references to the Blairite mantra of the 'transformative change agenda' and signs off with a reference to a meeting he is having with Hillary Clinton in New York.

GAZA'S GAS AND BG GROUP

Another client of JP Morgan is British Gas. While Blair was still Prime Minister, he promoted the purchase of a gas field off the coast of Gaza by British Gas. Then, as Middle East envoy (and as a JP Morgan board member), he lobbied the Israelis to allow development of the site, to the potential benefit of both British Gas and JP Morgan. How far Palestine stood to benefit is hotly disputed, and it is by no means clear that the proposed deal was fair to Palestine.

British Gas owns the rights to operate the field – thanks to the Blair deal – but Israel, which controls Gaza's waters, refused to allow any further development. In Gaza – the only Palestinian territory with access to the sea – Israel has prevented the Palestinians from developing their fields, and the gas continues to lie, undisturbed, under Palestinian waters.

In November 1999, Yasser Arafat signed a twenty-five-year contract for gas exploration with British Gas. BG had discovered a large gas field between seventeen and twenty-one nautical miles from the Gaza coast, three-quarters of it in Palestinian waters. The Oslo accords gave the PA maritime jurisdiction over its waters up to twenty nautical miles from the coast.

In July 2000, Israeli Prime Minister Ehud Barak authorised BG to drill the first well, although companies in the Yam Thetis consortium, which was set up to operate in adjacent Israeli gas fields, petitioned the Israeli government to stop the Palestinians from developing the fields.

On 27 September 2000, on the eve of the second intifada, Arafat, accompanied by Palestinian businessmen and the media, lit the flame proving the presence of gas at the BG offshore exploration platform. Arafat declared that the gas was 'a gift from God to us, to our people, to our children. This will provide a solid foundation for our economy, for establishing an independent state with holy Jerusalem as its capital.'

Barak's authorisation to drill the second well, and the successful gas strikes at both, seemed to promise a potential windfall for the PA. According to the 1999 contract, BG holds 90 per cent of the licence shares and the PA 10 per cent until gas production begins, at which point the PA's share increases to 40 per cent, of which 30 per cent would be held by Consolidated Contractors Company (CCC), a very big, privately owned construction firm (and a client of Tony Blair Associates). We shall meet CCC again.

To reduce the investment risk – since Palestine is only a small gas consumer – BG sought long-term advance gas purchase commitments from other clients, starting with Israel. In June 2000, BG proposed to supply gas from Egypt, Gaza and Israel to the state-owned Israel Electric Corporation (IEC). But the IEC refused to buy gas from Gaza, saying that it was more expensive than Egyptian gas. The real reason for the refusal, according to Israeli newspapers at the time, is more likely to have been political. Israel's new (as of spring 2001) Prime Minister, Ariel Sharon, had vetoed purchase of Palestinian gas.

In May 2002 the veto on Gaza gas was lifted, at least partly at the urging of British Prime Minister Tony Blair. But the next year there was another Israeli veto: Sharon refused to allow funds to flow to the PA lest they be used to support terrorism. Yet it had been agreed, and Israel had announced, that gas revenues to the Palestinians would be transferred to the special account that was already being used for international aid and tax-clearance revenues remitted by Israel to the PA.

Arafat died in November 2004. Mahmoud Abbas was elected PA President in January 2005, and Ariel Sharon was replaced by Ehud Olmert as Israeli Prime Minister a year later. A PA reform cycle that won Israeli and international acceptance was implemented, and, on 29 April 2007, the Israeli cabinet approved Olmert's proposal to authorise renewed discussions with BG. Abbas and the Israeli government secretly agreed that the PA share of the revenues would be transferred through an international account that would be inaccessible to the official PA government, dominated by Hamas since the PA legislative elections in January 2006. So the government the Palestinians had elected would not be able to touch a penny of it.

On 14 June 2007, Hamas seized power in the Gaza Strip. The new government in Gaza declared that it would change the terms of the contract, and in particular ensure that the Palestinian share, 10 per cent, was increased.

Negotiations between Israel and the PA in Ramallah continued, bypassing Hamas. But, in the end, BG and the Israeli government announced that they would delay any signing until the end of the year. In December 2007, BG officially announced the end of the negotiations with Israel on grounds of insurmountable disagreements, and just over a year later BG closed its office in Israel, while keeping its office in Ramallah and retaining its concession for the gas fields.

However, Egypt's cuts in the volume of gas being sold to Israel following the Egyptian Revolution of 2011 showed the Israeli government that it needed to have more sources of energy, to lessen its dependence on Egyptian gas. So Prime Minister Binyamin Netanyahu revived talks with Mahmoud Abbas about a possible gas purchase contract.

On 4 February 2011, Netanyahu announced, with Tony Blair (in his new incarnation as QR) at his side, that the time had finally come to develop Palestinian gas. He said, 'There is a Palestinian Authority gas field adjacent to an Israeli gas field. We need to develop both simultaneously.' A new round of negotiations between the PA and Israel began in September 2012, with Hamas reiterating its rejection of any agreement on Gaza gas reached without its participation. But the negotiations went nowhere. The military occupation enables Israel to prevent Palestinians access to their offshore resources, including their gas fields. This makes civil or commercial navigation to or from the Gaza Strip impossible.

Within months of the disengagement, Hamas won the Palestinian legislative elections, which led ultimately to the political separation of the West Bank and the Gaza Strip under rival Palestinian governments. Israel therefore felt the need to tighten its stranglehold on Gaza's maritime access. From the twenty nautical miles established by Oslo, the area was reduced to twelve nautical miles, to six nautical miles following the Hamas electoral victory in 2006, and finally to three nautical miles in the aftermath of Israel's assault on Gaza in 2008–9.

The Israeli navy controls all maritime routes, and over the years has killed a number of Palestinian fishermen who strayed beyond the three-mile limit and within range of its gunboats. Such rules clearly make any Palestinian access to the wells impossible.[17]

In 2013 and 2014 there was talk of reviving the project yet again, according to the *Financial Times* (*FT*). It would have been the largest yet of several big economic projects in Secretary of State John Kerry's $4 billion plan to lift the Palestinian economy out of its dependency on foreign aid and Israeli energy, which was to be overseen by Tony Blair.

Blair was furious that this activity was questioned in the Channel 4 *Dispatches* programme. It pointed out that JP Morgan advised the British Gas Group – which, as we have seen, had an interest in the Gaza Marine gas development – which he was promoting as QR. Blair told the *FT*'s Lionel Barber that JP Morgan advised BG elsewhere in the world, that he had never discussed the matter and that Gaza Marine was potentially a vital source of energy to the occupied territories: 'That ridiculous Channel 4 programme that should never have been made and was a complete waste of public money …' he said.[18]

But, whatever he says, many Palestinians think the deal is to the benefit of everyone except them. It has been described as an 'act of theft' by Ziad Thatha, the Hamas economy minister, who claims it should be up to the Palestinians alone to decide what to do with the gas, and who should benefit.[19]

One significant beneficiary will be Kurdish tycoon Mohammed Rashid, who has already made millions from the deal. Blair dealt with Rashid while still PM, when promoting the British Gas purchase of the gas field. Rashid has excellent connections across the Middle East, and was also financial adviser to Arafat.

Arafat appointed Rashid head of the Palestinian Investment Fund (PIF), a £1 billion company set up to make use of Palestine Liberation Organisation (PLO) funds. Rashid brokered the Gaza gas consortium – composed of British Gas, which holds 60 per cent of the shares, the PIF (10 per cent) and the construction multinational CCC, which has subsidiary firms in the Middle East, Britain and America.

Security and political issues blocked progress on the development of the field, but, by the time Blair left office, the gas deal had given him access to Mohammed Rashid, and, through him, a route to Libya – and his relationship with the Libyan leader the late Colonel Muammar Gaddafi.

As so often with Blair, one activity impinges upon another, and it is not always easy to see where each fits into the overall pattern; Blair's dealings with Libya will be unravelled in a separate chapter.

The Mohammed Rashid story comes to a sticky end. The man who was Mr Ten Per Cent in the Gaza gas deal between Israel, British Gas, the Palestinian Authority and the CCC, was sentenced to fifteen years in prison by a court in Ramallah in 2012 for embezzling millions of euros. He and two other businessmen were ordered to return 33.5 million in stolen funds.[20]

Blair also regularly visits Abu Dhabi for the Quartet. At the same time, his consultancy company, Tony Blair Associates, was and is providing 'global strategic advice' to the Crown Prince's sovereign wealth fund, Mubadala, which invests Abu Dhabi's oil profits.[21]

THE KUWAIT DIMENSION

Perhaps the most serious potential for a conflict of interest comes in Blair's dealings with Kuwait. These also properly belong to a later chapter about his commercial activities, and will be covered there; but, as so often happens with Blair, it is not entirely clear when one role ends and another begins, and the *start* of the Kuwait contract needs to be reported here.

On 26 January 2009, when Blair was in Kuwait for the Quartet, he met with the Emir. The former British PM was accompanied by his new senior adviser Jonathan Powell, which was odd because Blair was there officially on behalf of the Quartet, and Powell – who had been Blair's chief of staff during the Iraq war – did not work for the Quartet: he worked for Blair's personal consultancy.

There is a very revealing photograph showing Blair surrounded by the Emir and the Emir's advisers, and, on a sofa a little way away, sits Powell.

Even though the Emir has a large number of advisers with him, Blair has no one from the QR's office. He is entirely alone. Except for Powell.

What came out of the meeting from the point of view of the Quartet we do not know. We do know that Tony Blair Associates picked up a stunningly lucrative consultancy contract. Kuwaiti sources familiar with the deal told *Dispatches* that Blair's firm stood to earn more than 12 million dinars, the equivalent of £27 million.[22]

ACCOUNTABILITY ISSUES

An American businessman who was once close to Blair says, 'There are two issues. One is getting his financial interests, which are paramount, mixed up in things like the Quartet, which should be a very high priority and have nothing to do with his business.'

Robert Palmer of the campaigning group Global Witness says, 'There seems to be growing evidence that Tony Blair's business activities across the Middle East may be in conflict with his peace-envoy role. It is time he came clean about all of his interests in the region and who they are benefiting.'

It is possible for Blair to have all of these potentially conflicting interests because no code of conduct applies to him. Anis Nacrour, a senior French diplomat who worked directly for Blair at the Quartet's Jerusalem office for three years as a political and security adviser, revealed this to *Dispatches*, saying, 'I think he makes his own rules depending on the experience he has as a former prime minister for over ten years.'

If Blair was still an MP or sat in the House of Lords, or worked for the World Bank or the IMF or even directly for the United Nations, he would be bound by a strict and publicly available code of conduct that demanded he set out in full all his commercial interests. But he is none of these, and, as a result, his commercial interests and those in his role as QR envoy appear to overlap significantly. Ask a question about Blair as QR and the answer – if you get one – is quite likely not to come from the Quartet's Jerusalem office, but from a completely different Blair operation.

British journalists reporting from the Middle East have remarked with surprise on the fact that the Quartet's press officer, Ruti Winterstein, appears to have been sidelined. They are not expected to go to her, but to Blair's personal head of communications in London – Matthew Doyle until 2011, then Rachel Grant until 2014. Both Doyle and Grant often travelled with him to the Middle East.

Dr Nicholas Allen, a specialist in parliamentary ethics and standards in public life at the University of London, has told us that Blair's role as Middle East envoy is not transparent. 'Clearly, if he was holding a ministerial office in Britain, that kind of conflict, even the *appearance* of that kind of conflict, the appearance of that influence, wouldn't be tolerated.' When asked how many of the seven Nolan principles – the code of ethics for public servants enforced by Tony Blair when he was PM – appear to be undermined by Blair's conduct and behaviour, Allen said, 'I think there's a good case for saying that six of the principles appear to be undermined by Blair's conduct and Blair's behaviour.'

Allen told us that no code of conduct applies to Blair's role as QR because of 'the nature of the Quartet itself. A sort of weird international governmental anomaly.' Additionally, he said, 'If he was really serious about bringing peace to the Middle East, you might say that it would be expedient not to have those kinds of connections. It's going to be harder to get the trust of certain groups if they know that your own Faith Foundation is massively funded by a pro-Israeli lobby.'

He continued, 'The question is, is this really just window dressing? Is this him just doing a jobs-for-the-boys network that's really a cushy feather in his cap, or is it something really substantial? My horrible sneaking suspicion is that it's possibly slightly more of a feather in the cap than anything else, but I say that on the basis of no detailed knowledge of what he's been up to there.

'The question is – do the people he's dealing with mind? And that's one of the key elements in terms of his effectiveness. Does he have regular meetings with the various sides in the Middle East? If he does and they mind, then he should stop. If he does and they don't mind, then it's probably not a problem. If he doesn't meet them at all, it begs the question: what the hell is he actually doing?

'In one sense, yes, he's obviously in breach of them [the Nolan principles], if you take them as general ethical values, because he is clearly mixing interests, I think. That is unambiguous – there is a potential conflict of interest in some of his work.'

John Kerry's $4 billion investment in the Palestinian economy could be the very last attempt to breathe life into the Blair mission. But where was the money? Where were the details? Max Blumenthal, journalist and specialist in Israeli politics, wrote, 'Nearly all that is known is that Tony Blair, the Special Envoy of the Quartet, had been placed in charge of the initiative. My email and telephone queries to Ruti Winterstein, Blair's political and media adviser at the Quartet offices in Jerusalem, have not been answered.' We know how he feels.

Blumenthal goes on: 'The few Jerusalem and Ramallah based reporters who requested particulars about the initiative were unable to get any answers either, with one correspondent telling me they were being stonewalled by Blair and Kerry's people.'[23]

Which is not surprising, because the truth was that there was no money. The key to the whole deal, Kerry admitted, was Tony Blair; as he said this to a press conference, hardened Middle East correspondents discreetly closed their notebooks, clear at last that this was a story that was unlikely to have legs. It was all going to turn out to be smoke and mirrors.

David Horovitz, editor-in-chief of the *Times of Israel*, wrote that, at last,

Kerry – a veteran of four Middle East shuttle missions in his less than four months in office – unveiled the fruits of his diplomatic labours. No, he hadn't cut a peace deal … In fact, no, he hadn't even managed to arrange a meet between Abbas and Prime Minister Benjamin Netanyahu.

So what magic had he wrought? What did he have to present to us all? An economic plan. Bigger and better and bolder and brighter than anything hitherto attempted for the Palestinians.

What? Foreheads furrowed. Fingers went to clean out eardrums. Were we hearing this right? The secretary was proposing a financially driven path to Israeli-Palestinian peace and happiness? …

How? What? Who? Where? The answer to all such questions, it seemed, was: Tony Blair. The indefatigable former British prime minister, shaking hands with those sheikhs at the side of the hall, he was going to fix it. Somehow, Tony the economic tiger was going to rustle up the necessary $4 billion in investment and – presto! – all our problems would be solved …[24]

Once again, it all ignores a harsh truth – the truth that Lord Hollick alerted us to – which Horowitz sums up like this: 'Potential private investment is out there. And it can certainly flow into the Palestinian territories. But it will only flow – as opposed to trickle – *after* the conditions are created for long-term stability, not as the means to create those conditions.'[25]

The French daily *Le Monde*'s Jerusalem correspondent, Laurent Zecchini, came to the same conclusion:

This 'Marshall Plan' remains today in its box, because its implementation – which supposes a mobilisation of the private sector – requires a significant advance in Israel-Palestine peace talks … The distance separating the objectives proposed by Mr Blair from the reality of the Palestinian economy was apparent on Wednesday at the conference of Palestinian donors, held in New York.[26]

But, in June 2014, Tony Blair was still chasing the illusion that private-sector investment will flow in sufficient quantities to change the politics. His office was now referring to the idea as the Initiative for the Palestinian Economy, or IPE, and it is the main focus of his work as QR. This is supposed to 'effect transformative change and substantial growth in the

Palestinian economy and create hundreds of thousands of new jobs' according to the Quartet's website. It's entirely separate from 'the political negotiations between Israel and the Palestinian Authority (PA), led by US Secretary of State John Kerry'.

The office said, 'The ambitious plan was drafted by a team of policy advisers, external economic analysts and international domain experts under the leadership of Quartet Representative Tony Blair in support of renewed Palestinian–Israeli negotiations.' It 'focuses on catalysing private-sector-led growth in the West Bank, the Gaza Strip and East Jerusalem'. And it relies on 'the inflow of new financing into the Palestinian economy, in particular from the private sector'. [27]

There's a lot more like this, but no mention of where this 'inflow of new financing' is going to come from.

The fact is that it is not peace, but money – both real money and pretend money – that is at the heart of what Tony Blair does in the Middle East. And that makes it all a chimera, because private-sector money is not going to flow into Palestine without real political progress towards peace. This progress can only be hustled along by someone who is trusted by both sides – and Blair has thrown away the trust of the Palestinians.

He appears to be trying to juggle various roles. 'In the morning he is the big Middle East negotiator,' writes the American journalist Jacob Heilbrunn in the American publication *The National Interest*. 'In the afternoons, he's the businessman trying to lubricate connections between big shots. In essence, Blair has turned himself into a mini-corporation. He's cashing in on his former job.'[28]

This is a tragedy. Tony Blair left Downing Street in 2007 with huge international prestige, and walked straight into the QR's job. If he had devoted himself to it, heart and soul, history might have remembered the man credited with peacemaking in Northern Ireland as one of the few people in the world to have made a real difference in the Middle East, which would be enough for most of us to say: well done, Tony. His international reputation would have soared. If he wanted the European presidency – a job that, in the event, he did want, and it was denied to him – it would probably have been his for the asking.

Why did he not do so? He does not need money. He already owned several properties (though not as many as he owns now). He can command six-figure sums for speeches pretty well whenever he chooses, and so can his wife. He can be sure that his family will never want for anything. A man, however rich, can wear only one suit at a time, and sleep in only one house at a time. To be sure, the envoy's job is unpaid, but if he had felt, for any reason at all, that it ought to be paid, the Quartet would surely have agreed a very good salary, and no one would have begrudged him that, for he would have been demonstrably earning it.

Instead, he has irrevocably contaminated the QR job with his other activities. He often takes his personal staff, not QR staff, to meetings, and his personal staff, not QR staff, often speak for him in his role as QR. His personal business and politics – whether it is being a hard-line opponent of Islam, taking money from Israeli lobbyists, appointing Israeli spies to his personal staff, or taking well-paid work from Middle Eastern potentates – have been allowed to overshadow his work in the Middle East.

Maybe he really is putting in the effort, spending far more time in the region than observers are aware of. If that's the case, why not demonstrate it, rather than needlessly allow the perception to grow that he does not? If he actually spends far more time there than journalists and the top people in the Palestinian Authority realise, it would be sensible to make himself more visible, to them and to everyone else, instead of simply saying that all the estimates we have heard are wrong. Otherwise, the Palestinians are bound to believe either that he is too busy elsewhere or that he arrives in secret and talks only to Israelis. Both these perceptions are poison to his mission.

Today as QR he is a passenger at best, a liability at worst. He is still in the job partly because the Israelis are quite sure he will never bring them unwelcome news, but, much more importantly, because he symbolises a comforting untruth to which American and Israeli negotiators are clinging: that private-sector investment in Palestine can be used as a path to peace. The truth is the one that businesspeople such as Hollick and well-informed journalists such as Zecchini and Blumenthal have been telling anyone who would listen: that progress in peace talks come first, and only when they have delivered some sort of stability will private investment follow.

We know from private sources that some old political friends have spoken privately to Blair about his role in the Middle East, and urged him to do it full time. They have said: no one can blame you if you don't bring peace to the Middle East, but you should avoid the criticism that you haven't tried hard enough; you should do it full time or not at all.

But we're way beyond that stage now. Today, it's impossible not to have some sympathy for the Palestinian view, shared now by several key people in Europe, that Blair – to paraphrase what the Tory politician Leo Amery said of Prime Minister Neville Chamberlain in 1940, quoting Oliver Cromwell – has been there too long for any good he can do, and that he should go.

CHAPTER TWO

THE BLAIR RICH PROJECT

'Blair is very interested in money and it takes precedence over other
things. There is no evidence that he has done anything positive, other than
make money. My advice to him was that he can make a lot of money as long
as it's a by-product of what you're doing.'
– AMERICAN BUSINESSMAN AND FORMER FRIEND OF
TONY BLAIR, SPEAKING TO AUTHORS.

After Tony Blair's last Prime Minister's Questions on 27 June 2007, he headed back to his constituency with Cherie and the children. Outside Darlington Station there was a sharp reminder of his swiftly changed status. The family headed straight towards a smart BMW – and, just in time, someone arrived to whisper to the former PM that that was not his car. Would he kindly head towards the Vauxhall in the far corner?

Perhaps it was at that moment that Blair decided he would never be humiliated like that again; that the car waiting for him would always be the best in the place; that he would recreate the life he had lived as Prime Minister. More likely, the decision had been made many years earlier.

Months earlier he had been advised by a leading American businessman that, when he gave up the premiership, he should focus on rehabilitating his reputation, on doing good works, and business should be secondary. The businessman said that Blair should do a few things that are important. If there was money to be made as a by-product of doing something good for the world, fine. The model, he said, should be Paul Volcker, who made a fair amount of money, but as a consequence of doing something good and not as a principle focus.

Blair had asked to meet this businessman, who is, like himself, an active Christian, through an intermediary. The businessman, who has since broken off his relationship with Blair, now says that the former Prime Minister did not take any of his advice. He told us that Blair privately thought it was absurd advice. He says Blair is 'very interested in money and it takes precedence over other things. It is also clear he has done a horrible job in all the assignments he has taken. There is no evidence that he has done anything positive, other than make money.

'My advice to him was that he can make a lot of money as long as it's a by-product of what you're doing. James Wolfensohn built greenhouses using his own money. He was a wonderful man. There is nothing wrong with a politician making money, but you have to be prepared to sacrifice some money to do the higher thing.'

Blair's interests have centred on the Tony Blair financial empire, the most impenetrable financial body that is legally possible in the United Kingdom. The structure of his companies makes it impossible to know who is paying him, or where the money goes, and ensures that no one can find out what he is worth.

Extremely clever tax accountants and lawyers have devised a scheme that breaks no rules but means that Tony Blair can deny any public claim disclosing his income because no one can prove it. When journalists and others make estimates, Blair representatives invariably say the estimates are wrong, but provide no information.

Except once. Blair was asked about his net worth during the razzmatazz on 21 July 2014, occasioned by the twentieth anniversary of his taking the leadership of the Labour Party. Asked if he was worth £100 million, he replied that he was worth just a fifth of that. £20 million? Our estimate is quite a lot more – we'll come to that – but he has set up a system that makes it virtually impossible to work out his wealth; even *he* might have difficulty calculating it.

ORIGINS OF A FINANCIAL EMPIRE

Blair's financial empire dates from 2009, when Tony Blair Associates (TBA) was established. Curiously, it just postdates a remarkable turnaround in the Blairs' property fortunes (for more on Blair's property interests, see Chapter 14, 'The Property Portfolio'). He moved from being overburdened with mortgage debt on his grand house in Connaught Square to being able to splash out on new properties for himself and his wife in the country in 2008, and then to finance homes for his own children. The only explanation for this remarkable reversal in fortunes is that he must have big new sources of income from new clients and access to much more credit to bankroll this.

TBA's website has changed since it was originally set up, but in early 2015 it read,

> Tony Blair Associates is the umbrella organisation for our commercial operations.
>
> We work with governments on the path of reform providing advice and support on key areas of governance, modernisation and implementation.
>
> We provide geopolitical and strategic advice to multinational corporations.
>
> We bring together institutional investors with potential investment opportunities.
>
> Tony Blair's commercial activities provide important funding for his philanthropic work.
>
> Tony Blair Associates is entirely separate from the Foundations which are independent charitable entities accountable to their own boards and trustees and subject to applicable charity regulations.[1]

When he started out, it was said in the *Sunday Times* that the company would 'allow him to provide, in partnership with others, strategic advice on a commercial and *pro bono* [free, as a public service] basis, on political and economic trends and governmental reform'.[2] Since then we have heard little about TBA doing *pro bono* work, and the home page now says, 'Tony Blair's commercial activities provide important funding for his philanthropic work.' But how much of the profit from TBA goes into the Blair charities is a closely guarded secret.

What exactly does it do? Ken Silverstein, in his book *The Secret World of Oil*, points out that there are several governments and companies all over the world who need better relationships with the USA, and hire lobbying and PR firms to manage their relationship with the American public and policymakers.

But, says Silverstein,

[L]obbying is subject to disclosure laws, and hence in recent years foreign governments and interests seeking influence in Washington have increasingly turned to other means, which are largely unregulated and don't always require public disclosure. These include: making contributions to think tanks, universities, and non profit groups; setting up business associations that advocate for better political ties with the US but aren't legally defined as lobbying organizations; and offering huge consulting contracts and speaking fees to politically prominent Westerners. These financial flows have helped recruit many prominent Western cheerleaders, including retired politicians (and their offspring), corporate titans, college professors, think-tank fellows, and countless former senior government officials …[3]

Blair ticks all the boxes. He is as prominent a former statesman as you're likely to be able to hire. He has philanthropic bodies such as the Tony Blair Faith Foundation to which his clients can contribute. And, most important of all, he has the best possible contacts in the USA.

From former employees, we understand that originally there were to be two businesses – one offering advice to governments, the other offering advice to companies. However, the companies that make up TBA are structured to be impenetrable and Blair was persuaded by the business experts he hired to simplify the structure and put them under one body, TBA. Even then, his own internal business experts thought what he ended up with was too complicated, with its two similar private companies, Windrush and Firerush, which were originally intended to cater for the two different sorts of client – governments and companies.

'Tony's organisation has been in my personal and very confidential view a bit too complex in terms of the entities,' says one of them. 'The trading names of the company sound very much like off-the-shelf companies, which they are. There is a structure that looks unnecessarily complex and those names do not mean much in terms of trading. You know, the president of Kazakhstan doesn't say, "Gosh I want to be advised on governance by Windrush or Firerush." He says, "I want to be advised by Tony Blair."'

TBA has similarities in its work with Kissinger Associates, which was set up in 1982 by Henry Kissinger, the former American secretary of state and national security adviser and both generates cash through consultancies and does some philanthropic work.

TBA has almost no public profile and its finances are shrouded in secrecy too. There exists a complex web of structures involving twelve different legal entities.[4]

They almost certainly handle some of the large amounts originally coming in from Blair's six-figure speaking fees – according to one charity, the minimum fee is £500,000 – and from his banking and insurance consultancies, and his pay from Middle Eastern regimes. This would not include his memoirs though, as he gave away the advance to the Royal British Legion.

OPAQUE CORPORATE STRUCTURES

Blair has set up a complex, opaque corporate structure that makes it impossible to know how much money he is making. 'He's willing to spend good money to keep it hidden,' said Richard Murphy, an accountant and founder of the London-based Tax Justice Network. Blair has thus far declined to accept a peerage, which he is entitled to, and which Murphy suspects is due to the fact that he would have to disclose his income to the House of Lords if he did so.[5]

Murphy is an expert in this area. He explained how Blair set up such a structure to handle his money. He points out that Blair has used a very arcane structure based not on the more common limited-liability partnership – as used by Peter (Lord) Mandelson (a minister in the Blair government and a former European Commissioner for Trade) to set up his company – but on the little-known partnership regulations set up in 1907 by the Campbell Bannerman Liberal government.

As we have seen, Blair has two sets of companies: the Windrush companies and the Firerush companies. As they are partnerships under the 1907 Act, they are not taxed themselves like a limited-liability partnership or a limited company, but, instead, the owners of all their investments are taxed individually. The great thing is that the owners don't have to be declared. It all goes back to Bircham and Company Nominees Ltd – organised through a leading private-wealth specialist lawyer, Bircham Dyson Bell – or BDB, as it now calls itself. The structure is said to have been set up by Alex Harle, Blair's lawyer. The nominee company is called BDBCO No. 819 Ltd.

Set up as a nominee company to act as a trustee or an executor of a will, this entity does not reveal its ownership on records at Companies House. Instead, its shares are listed as held by a second off-the-shelf entity, BDBCO No 822. This company in turn conceals its true ownership. Its shares are listed as held by the lawyers, acting as nominees. Even the details of the accounts are private.

There is also one important difference between the two sets of companies – Windrush and Firerush – set up for Blair to receive his income. Firerush, unlike Windrush, is registered with what was then the Financial Services Authority, now the Financial Conduct Authority (FCA). Firerush offers investment advice in a number of low-tax and lowly regulated jurisdictions, including Gibraltar, Lithuania and Romania. This allows two things: people can invest in Blair's Firerush companies without its being declared who they are; and the Firerush companies, unlike the Windrush companies, can start trading and investing on the world's stock markets.

And the latter is certainly what has happened, as the *Sunday Telegraph* revealed in January 2013.[6]

The newspaper reported that:

- a trading desk was now operating at Blair's London headquarters;
- five employees at one of his companies, Firerush Ventures, had obtained licences from the Financial Services Authority;
- the team was led by David Lyon, formerly managing director at Barclays Capital;
- the FCA (formerly FSA) licences gave Blair's staff the power to advise clients and invest money on their behalf.

So why on earth would Blair want to be registered with the FCA? One of his former financial specialists told us, 'They don't trade. They are registered with the Financial Services Authority, just in case. What Tony didn't want to do was inadvertently do something unauthorised, so they had a counsel's opinions to what would be the safest way to make sure they never did anything that would look like they have crossed the line.

'There is a category called arranging deals and investments, or something like that. Now, Tony said, if I had to give financial advice I'd start making people very poor. He absolutely did not give financial advice; he doesn't really do anything that you could call financial services at all; he wouldn't want to.'

So why the FCA authorisation? There is a clue in the fact that Blair is close to sovereign wealth funds – the biggest intact pools of capital in the world. 'Tony happens to know the rulers of the countries who have the biggest funds,' we were told, 'whether it's Malaysia, Brunei or whatever. Let's say a company comes to him and says, I'm setting up a new venture and we need funding for this, whatever it is, and Tony introduces them to some sheikh, let's say over lunch.

'That's absolutely fine. Tony is not giving financial advice; he's not saying to the person providing the money, I have evaluated this opportunity and the return structure is excellent or whatever, this is a good investment for you. He's absolutely not doing that; he's never wanted to. However, just possibly, he could be interpreted to be in this category of arranging deals and investments, simply by making an introduction, even if he had no role in the financial advice.

'So, just to be absolutely on the safe side, you haven't strayed into financial services without meaning to, and therefore performed financial services without being under the requirement of regulation.'

It is complex and costly to become FCA-authorised, and you need to employ clerical and legal people, just to keep your authorisation up to date. It is a lot of trouble to go to on the off-chance. But we are assured: 'Tony does not give financial advice. Tony's best advice is, as you can imagine, about global political trends; it is about, for companies, how to deal with governments, and for governments, how to govern better.'[7]

A posting on LinkedIn discloses details of Blair's operation. It was written by an IT consultant called Matt Walsh, who worked for Blair for just over a year until May 2011. Some of the clues to the Blair operation were given on the LinkedIn pages by Walsh and former Blair employee Scott Macpherson as part of their knowledge and experience to attract new clients.

Walsh discloses that he provided support for the IT operations for Blair's possible trading system. He listed all the IT systems he oversaw during his time with Blair, including two types of trading system. This included systems used by Reuters and Bloomberg – used by expert City traders.

Macpherson discloses that he worked for Blair between 2009 and 2011 and was involved in setting up new offices for his Africa Governance

Initiative.[8] On his profile, Macpherson said his duties included 'planning and implementation of satellite sites, primarily consulting on and implementing sites in Kuwait, Sierra Leone, Toronto, Liberia, Yale NY, Rwanda as well as other locations.' Like Walsh, he said he provided 'Bloomberg support for a small trading team.'

In September 2011 it was reported that high-profile banker Mark Labovitch had resigned as chief operating officer of Blair's Firerush Ventures. His resignation came little more than a year after he was appointed – along with a former Lehman Brothers banker, Varun Chandra – and just days before the broadcast of the Channel 4 *Dispatches* documentary we speak about in Chapter 1, which revealed Blair's incredibly lucrative business dealings across the Middle East.[9]

Labovitch had worked for the Irish newspaper magnate Tony O'Reilly, who at that time owned the *Independent*, and was an old friend and colleague of the *Independent*'s John Rentoul, the only journalist writing for national newspapers who remains slavishly uncritical of Blair. It was O'Reilly who introduced Labovitch to Blair, at one of several lunches Blair had in O'Reilly's boardroom while he was Prime Minister. Blair wanted him to set up financial systems for dealing with clients who were companies, rather than governments. He wanted him to help build a commercial business. Blair was working for governments but he was seeking to approach companies.

Labovitch was there to provide a commercial office discipline, to make sure contracts were written properly. He never thought Blair needed help with setting himself up in businesses – someone would always want to pay for Blair's help, his advice, his name. But he did want banking contacts and expertise, and part of Labovitch's role was to show Blair the sorts of ways in which he might be useful to corporate clients.

Labovitch presented Blair with six options (not all of which are known), one of which was setting up an asset-management operation, because asset management was more rewarding than pure advice. One of Labovitch's options was ruled out because it would compete with JP Morgan.

Blair also asked Labovitch to check out Oman, suggesting he visit Sir Erik Bennett, a former air force officer who was in charge of the Oman air force, to see if there was some business they could do there.

The departure of Labovitch, who has connections to some of the world's richest investors, threatened to leave a hole in Blair's business empire. There was a lot of damaging speculation about the reasons for Labovitch's departure, but we understand it was simply that Labovitch is interested in dealing with commercial clients, and the business was veering towards government clients.

It did also raise questions about the ways in which the empire is run.

As we have seen, Blair's initial income goes into a limited partnership (under 1907 partnership regulations) in both Windrush and Firerush, called Windrush and Firerush No. 3. This limited partnership is not required to publish accounts, so we cannot see where the money comes from or how much it is.

This money is then transferred to a limited-liability company, Windrush or Firerush No. 2, in a lump sum – but we don't know whether any of the money from the No. 3 companies is channelled elsewhere. It is perfectly possible, though there is not the slightest evidence, that it could be transferred to offshore trusts.

The money is then passed from there to a No. 1 company or Windrush Ventures company, also a limited partnership under the 1907 regulations, which does not have to declare tax. But nobody knows how much of the original money that went into No. 3 company ends up in the ventures company or No. 1 company. The only information publicly available is in the abbreviated accounts of the limited-liability partnership – the No. 2 company.

In 2009 Richard Murphy did this analysis of the No. 2 company on his blog post,[10] which provides the most comprehensive information we have, even though it is six years out of date:

Its members are Windrush Ventures Limited and Windrush Ventures

No. 1 Limited (they certainly exercised their imaginations when naming this lot).

KPMG audited it, which leaves me overflowing with confidence.

It turned over £6.8 million and made a profit of £350,000 from December 2007 to April 2009. We know from the accounts of Windrush Ventures Limited that just £12,000 of this was due to Windrush Ventures Limited to April 2008 but in the period from, presumably, December 2007 to April 2008 (when the limited company accounts were made up) some £1,463,000 was paid to Windrush Ventures for management services to Windrush Ventures No. 2 LLP. That's about £365,000 a month. If that continued to April 2009 another £4.4 million or so of the income of the LLP would have gone to the Limited company in this way. That's most of its reported expenses. It would be interesting to know why tax relief might be granted on this sum, and what transfer pricing enquiry it might give rise to (and yes, transfer pricing rules do apply internally in the UK) but I leave that aside for now.

Tony Blair is the controlling party of the whole structure. This is despite the fact that the recorded owner of the one share in issue in both Windrush Ventures Limited and Windrush Ventures No. 1 Limited is a nominee company – Bircham and Co. Nominees Limited. We have to assume they act for Tony Blair.

Windrush Ventures No. 1 Limited simply seems to hold a 50% interest in Windrush Ventures No. 2 LLP – from which it received £12,000 profit in the period to 30 April 2008. It seems to have no other activity.

Windrush Ventures Limited does have a trade, and an odd balance sheet which seems inflated by both large long term debts and liabilities for the size of probable activity it is undertaking, but from which no firm conclusions can be drawn as abbreviated accounts have been filed.

Murphy's conclusion was,

> First, there is an obvious desire for secrecy in this structure and a willingness to pay for it. The use of nominees to own the companies at the bottom of the pile is a start. Add to that the fact it is hard to find Blair in the set-up even though he owns it. Is it tax efficient? Not particularly. True, the profits all end up in UK limited companies – and the number of them means that the use of the small companies rate might be restricted – increasing the tax bill in the year to 30 April 2009 in all likelihood.

He also thinks Blair has been able to do this because of a loophole in the regulations for limited partnerships when they were updated – ironically by the then Chancellor Gordon Brown under Labour in 2000. The regulations said: 'The partnership regulations will apply to most limited partnerships that have limited companies as their general partners and are registered under the Limited Partnerships Act 1907, as these partnerships must have their principal place of business in Great Britain on registration.'

Murphy comments in his blog,

> Note the key point in the last paragraph: if the general partner is a limited company then the limited partnership must file accounts. And that is also true if the general partner is an unlimited company or Scottish partnership with members who are limited companies. But someone, somewhere, clearly forgot to update the regulation for the creation of UK limited liability partnerships in 2000. And some lawyer somewhere has noticed this. The result is the whole structure that has been created for Tony Blair.

Blair himself was known by colleagues to be a pretty good employment and tax lawyer, but there is no evidence, and it is extremely unlikely, given Gordon Brown's reputation for probity, that this loophole was created by

Gordon Brown to help Blair in the future. The only official justification came from a written statement by Matthew Doyle, then political director of the Office of Tony Blair, to the *Guardian*: 'Why we set it up … was in order to allow Mr Blair's office sensibly to administer his different projects, in accordance with relevant regulations and company law in the UK. He has an operation that has over 80 people working for it around the world. This was done on the basis of advice.' It employs considerably more now.

However, a similar conclusion to Richard Murphy's has come from a tax lawyer who pointed out that this structure is used by private-equity companies. The same structure allows them to manage their investments from overseas in the UK without paying additional tax, and also means they do not have to pay corporation tax on all the companies, as do most UK-based corporations. They benefit from the lowering of capital-gains tax by successive governments. And, if they pay out dividends, they get taxed at a lower rate. This structure has become more common as private-equity and alternative financing structures have been developed in the UK.

Blair's new secretive companies also follow the rapidly developing offshore world of capitalism, outlined by business journalist Nicholas Shaxson in his book *Treasure Islands*,[11] where secretive firms based in high-tax countries, such as the UK, load huge administrative expenses to avoid tax without proper transparency, while often operating through trusts and tax havens and offshore banks.

Indeed our researches produced a rather interesting offshore riddle. Firerush and Windrush were set up in Gibraltar in 2010 on the same day. They were created by accountants Baker Tilly and run from a nameplate office in Gibraltar with the main shareholders being BT (Baker Tilly) Nominees and BT (Baker Tilly) Corporate Services Ltd.

Tony Blair's office says this has nothing to do with him. It is a remarkable coincidence that someone has chosen to use the same names Blair has chosen for his companies in an offshore country.

Blair keeps control over the companies he does own in the hands of people he has trusted for years. One is Jonathan Powell, Tony Blair's chief of staff during the Iraq War, who was appointed senior adviser to TBA and also works for JP Morgan, which, as we have seen, pays Blair. He also, interestingly, took exams so that he has the necessary qualifications from the FCA to look over Blair's interests in Firerush.

Official accounts show that a company set up by Blair to manage his business affairs paid just £315,000 in tax in 2011 on an income of more than £12 million. In that time, he employed 26 staff and paid them total wages of almost £2.3 million. The documents also reveal that, in the two years to 31 March 2013, Blair's management company had a total turnover of nearly £15 million and paid tax of about £653,000.[12]

According to these accounts, in 2013 he was sitting on a cash pile of £13 million after paying out large sums to cover his overseas visits – often in a leased private jet and with very expensive hotel bills.

TBA clients are of course confidential. From public sources, these include:

- Louis Vuitton Moet Hennessy, the iconic luxury handbag, luggage manufacturer, and cognac and champagne company, which employed Euan Blair at one stage;
- Zurich Insurance, thought to bring in £0.5 million a year;
- JP Morgan, thought to bring in £2 million a year – or $4 million according to the *FT*;
- Emir of Kuwait, thought to have paid £27 million for consultancy advice;
- Abu Dhabi government, thought to bring in £1 million a year;
- Government of Kazakhstan, which, according to the Kazakh press, pays £8 million a year for economic and governance advice;
- UI Energy, a Korean oil company, for which Blair admitted he had done some consultancy work but declined to publish the details, despite being pressed by the Advisory Committee on Business Appointments (the watchdog body) to do so;[13]
- International Sanitary Supply Association, for which Blair addressed a conference for a £50,000 fee;[14]

- Wataniya, the Palestinian phone company owned by Qtel, itself a
  client of JP Morgan.

Blair has also made substantial sums of money from speeches in China
and now advises the Mongolian government under a two-year consultancy
agreement.[15] He also got involved in the row over the Glencore and
Xstrata merger. His recent role as peacemaker is said to have won him
£620,000.[16]At a meeting in Claridge's in 2012, the *Mail* reported that
he acted 'as a mediator in negotiations between Glencore mining boss
Ivan Glasenberg and Qatari Prime Minister Sheikh Hamad bin Jassim
bin Jaber al-Thani.' Finally, in 2012 Blair's Government Advisory Practice
(GAP) pulled in a contract with the state government of São Paulo in
Brazil, worth almost £4 million a year.[17]

So how much money does Tony Blair make from all this? Some of
the money (we do not know how much) is said to be routed towards
his charitable activities. Cherie Blair also makes profit from her own
business and law practice. And the charities, in particular the Blair Faith
Foundation, also have their own secret donors, as we shall see. He also has
to pay some 200 employees now, a figure he's set his sights on growing to
500 over the coming years.

Depending on whom you believe, he is now worth around £60 million
or possibly more.

Sources close to Blair have told us that the model for his growing
organisation is the equally secretive US global management consultancy
McKinsey. 'There was a great New Labour love affair with McKinsey
when Blair was Prime Minister,' says one senior banking source close to
Blair. 'There are lot of McKinsey alumni on the government advisory side
of Blair's business, and always have been.'

The vast company, which advises world governments and business
leaders, refuses to name the people it does business with, or discuss its
multibillion-pound deals.

Staff lists of the ex-PM's Africa Governance Initiative (AGI) – the charity he set up in 2008 – as well as Tony Blair Associates, the umbrella operation for his GAP, read like a Who's Who of former McKinsey executives. They include German-born Dr Stephan Kriesel, the GAP head; Joe Capp, who runs Blair's South American organisation; and Nnaemeka Okafor, who is the AGI's head in Nigeria. Kriesel appears to enjoy his role. His Facebook page, which is open to public viewing, shows him in various locations, often wearing flamboyant clothing, including a bright white suit and gold turban, or else photographed on a camel wearing Arab dress.

Blair, who has links to McKinsey going back to his time in office, has also copied the US firm's policy of hiring bright young graduates from Oxbridge, Harvard, Princeton and the Massachusetts Institute of Technology, instead of relying on experienced business managers.

McKinsey had a lot of input into the Blair business model, too, according to TBA insiders. Blair says that when you come to power for the first time, even though you're called Prime Minister, you don't have a lot of levers in your office, and you pull them only when things happen. He found this when he first came into office. So he created one in Downing Street, and now exports his model, according to one of the people who have helped him create the TBA business, 'forming the policy unit, the delivery unit and the way you monitor what each department is doing so that it actually is responsive to the centre – this kind of structured methodology was created, I think there was lots of McKinsey input into that.'

Increasingly, Tony Blair Associates' UK headquarters – in a Georgian townhouse in London's Grosvenor Square, for which he pays £550,000 a year in rent – resembles the seat of power of a president or prime minister. The headquarters – the base for his three directors of Windrush Ventures – employs 35 people on an average salary of £86,000 a year, almost £1 million more than in 2012.

The company's highest-paid director receives £273,000 – up from £200,000 the previous year, according to the accounts submitted to Companies House for 2012–13. This director is thought to be either

Catherine Rimmer, Blair's chief of staff and a former Downing Street aide, or David Lyon, a former Barclays investment banker who was recruited by Blair in 2012 to 'grow and develop' his business activities. The other two directors share £307,000 between them – nearly double the £175,000 paid in 2012.

The most accurate assessment of the wealth generation of Blair's companies' can be shown in this table.

Payment schedule					
	30 April 2008	30 April 2009	31 March 2010	30 April 2011	31 March 2012
Windrush	£000	£000	£000	£000	£000
A: Income of No. 2 LLP from No. 3 LP		6,436	5,152	9,837	10,588
B: Profit Share of No. 3 LP to No. 2 LLP		350	437	646	2,954
C: Remuneration from No. 2 LLP to Windrush Ventures Limited	1,463	6,436	5,152	9,837	10,588
Profit Share of No. 2 LLP					
D: to Windrush Ventures Limited	12	163	218	426	1,177
E: to No. 1 Ltd	12	163	218	223	1,777
Firerush					
A: Income of No. 2 LLP from No. 3 LP			438	802	1,603
B: Profit Share of No. 3 LP to No. 2 LLP			–	–	–
C: Remuneration from No. 2 LLP to Firerush Ventures Limited			438	802	1,603
D: Profit Share of No. 2 LLP			–	–	–
E: to Firerush Limited			–	–	–
F: to No. 1 Ltd			–	–	–

Altogether, this suggests that, up to 2012, Blair's companies – not the Blairs themselves – generated some £40.7 million. If you add figures up to 2013, the money generated by Blair's companies increased by another £13 million taking it to nearly £54 million.[18] What is clear from these figures is that Blair's financial empire is growing by the day, and the money he is making – whether for his charities or his family – continues to rise. He may not be in the league of Bill Clinton yet but he certainly aspires to be. Indeed, he is said to have told one of the people guarding him that he would love to be worth as much as the former American President.

His finances in the decade ahead could make him one of the most powerful global figures – advising companies and governments, from China to large swathes of Africa, Eastern and Central Europe and the Middle East. Whether he will be doing any good in the world, given the many brutal dictators whose image he is burnishing, is another matter.

CHAPTER THREE

EUROPE: BLAIR'S
FAILED AMBITIONS

'The EU might not be able to afford Tony Blair.'
– FORMER FOREIGN SECRETARY
DAVID MILIBAND.

Tony Blair hoped to be the first president of the European Council. It would have crowned a luminous political career to have taken a big international job just two years after stepping down as Prime Minister, and it seemed entirely achievable. From 2007, when he ceased to be Prime Minister, almost until the appointment was made in 2009, it looked almost as though the job was his for the asking.

Blair had been British Prime Minister for ten years. He had huge international prestige, despite Iraq. As Prime Minister he had been a dominant force in European politics. He had a prestigious international job as Middle East envoy. He had the enthusiastic support of an admirer in the Élysée Palace, French President Nicolas Sarkozy, who, according to the Brussels correspondent of *Liberation*, Jean Quatremer, 'has never hidden his admiration for the Anglo-Saxon model in general and for Tony Blair in particular'.[1]

And so he should have done. Almost Blair's last act as Prime Minister was to broadcast in French to the French people, congratulating them and Sarkozy on the latter's election as President. He admired Sarkozy, '*que je considére un ami* ' ('whom I consider a friend'). Interestingly, these words were left out of the English version, which he recorded at the same time; considering Sarkozy a friend might not have gone down a storm in the Labour Party. (Blair's French, incidentally, is quite good, but not as good as it's cracked up to be. After resigning as PM he risked an interview in French. He's fairly fluent and understands what's said to him, but his accent is dreadful, and, when he's not sure of a word, he has the Englishman's tendency to use the English word and give it a French intonation. The French for leadership is not 'lidairsheep'.)

In May 2012, when Sarkozy lost the presidency, he seems to have gone down the path already trodden by Blair, charging £100,000 for speeches and being frequently seen in Qatar. He now faces accusations that his 2007 campaign was aided by funds from Blair's old contact, the late Libyan dictator Colonel Muammar Gaddafi.[2]

In fact, Blair had looked like an obvious candidate from the moment the job was first mooted, and he had been a key player in devising the job description. In December 2001, two years after the euro was introduced to world financial markets, he had been one of the leaders of the European Council at Laken, which established the Convention on the Future of Europe, with former French President Valéry Giscard d'Estaing as its president. The Convention was to draft the treaty establishing a constitution for Europe.

It was this convention that, in July the next year, produced what was intended to become the European Constitution. But, in April 2004, Blair unexpectedly promised the UK a referendum on the EU Constitution, having previously rejected the idea. The next year the French and the Dutch rejected the Constitution in referenda, and the thing was effectively dead.

Blair was a key player in the process of picking up the pieces, and salvaging what there was to be salvaged. An informal group was set up to draft a replacement which was to fall short of being a constitution. This was chaired by the former Italian PM Giuliano Amato and included the former British EU commissioner Chris Patten. In June 2007 they produced a draft treaty, and Blair, already on the way out as PM, said this would not require a British referendum since it was not a constitution. This treaty, later known as the Lisbon Treaty, was agreed.

One of the provisions of this treaty was for an EU president to chair EU summits, represent the EU on common foreign and security policy and take on some of the functions of the presidency of the Council of the European Union, which is held on a rotating six-month basis by EU heads of government. It was not as big a job as had been envisaged in the constitution, but it was still quite substantial. It had the potential for its holder to be a major player on the world stage, if held by someone with the status and political skill to make it so.

Blair was a strongly fancied candidate. 'He is the most European of Britons … it would be intelligent to think of him,' said Sarkozy on 23 June 2007, just four days before Blair left Downing Street.

The only doubt in most people's minds was: did Blair want the job? As his post-premiership career took shape and it became clear that he was going to make himself seriously rich, former Foreign Secretary David Miliband was heard to say, perhaps in jest, that the EU 'might not be able to afford him.' However, Sir Malcolm Rifkind is in no doubt of what his intentions were, telling us that 'His main aspiration was to hold onto some public office in the hope that he would be asked to take on some more fundamental responsibility on the international stage. He had hoped to be President of the European Council. If somebody had asked him to do something of that kind, he would jump at it.'

In January 2008, Sarkozy invited him to the national council of his party, the UMP, to mark his support for Blair's candidature and to 'sell' Blair to his party colleagues. Shortly afterwards, Sarkozy invited Blair to be one of the two keynote speakers at a conference on the global financial crisis, held at the École Militaire – the other was Sarkozy himself.

John Monks, general secretary of the European Trade Union Confederation and the former British TUC chief, was there to take part in a panel discussion, and remembers watching Sarkozy and German Chancellor Angela Merkel, side by side, as Blair spoke. Sarkozy nudged Merkel and whispered something – it looked like appreciation of Blair's performance. Merkel looked sceptical.

There was a difference between Sarkozy's speech and Blair's, Monks told us. Sarkozy saw the crash as a major heart attack for modern capitalism and argued for big changes. Blair was much more cautious and was not critical of the banks and other financial institutions whose recklessness and greed had caused the crisis.

During the coffee break, Monks asked Blair whether he had regrets about the light-touch regulation – verging (said Monks) on adulation for the City – that had often characterised New Labour in government.

Blair replied, 'You have seen what the prime-ministerial in-tray looks like – heavy files on foreign policy, Iraq, the NHS, Northern Ireland and a host of others. With all these subjects demanding urgent attention, why would you transfer the City from the asset pile to the problems one? The City was contributing huge tax revenues that paid for much social expenditure, and no one saw the impending problems.' Before Monks could question him further, Sarkozy, working tirelessly to promote Blair for President of the European Council, interrupted the conversation.

Not everyone, even in Sarkozy's own Party, was as enthusiastic about Blair as Sarkozy would have wished. 'Blair cannot symbolise the Europe we want' said former Prime Minister Edouard Balladur, while Valéry Giscard d'Estaing, former President and architect of the now-dead constitution, thought the president should come from a country that respected all the European rules.

At the time, these were minority voices. It still looked good for Blair. But, in May 2008, it started to unravel, with Sarkozy wondering aloud if Blair was the right person after all. Blair, he recalled, was, after all, the architect of the Iraq War, and he had kept Britain out of the euro and the so-called Schengen zone of passport-free travel (named after the Luxembourg town where the agreement was signed).

But what had changed? All these things had been just as true eleven months earlier, when Sarkozy endorsed him, and four months earlier, when Sarkozy sold him to the UMP. What had changed was that Sarkozy no longer felt confident he could deliver. For the previous month, April 2009, Prime Minister Gordon Brown, President Sarkozy and Chancellor Angela Merkel agreed that they would all have a veto on the appointment. It became clear that Merkel might well veto Blair.

If he could not have the presidency, Blair was now reported to be interested in the other permanent position created under the Lisbon Treaty, the high representative for foreign affairs, effectively the EU's foreign minister, which he felt – probably rightly, so long as he did not have a strong president – could be turned into the real powerhouse of EU affairs.

But this put the British government in a bind. It already had a potential candidate for that job – the Foreign Secretary, David Miliband. Of course, if Blair was the president, Britain could not hope to have the foreign-affairs post as well. So Miliband's potential candidacy was on ice while Blair was frontrunner for the presidency.

If he were to hope to deliver the foreign-affairs brief to Miliband, Gordon Brown would have to give up backing Blair for president. But he did not feel he could safely do that. Brown led a parliamentary Labour Party that contained a large number of vengeful Blairites who thought Brown had pushed their man out of No. 10, and who stood ready to tear the new Prime Minister to pieces if he appeared not to be giving Blair his full support.

Sarkozy had not given up. He soon decided to give it another go, partly because he felt that the strongest alternative candidate to Blair, Luxembourg Prime Minister and Finance Minister and Eurogroup President Jean-Claude Juncker, had failed to act decisively during the economic crisis. Sarkozy was determined to block Juncker, as David Cameron was in 2014.

Blair's old friend Silvio Berlusconi backed him. Ireland and Czechoslovakia backed the Lisbon Treaty, the last two nations to do so.

Gordon Brown and David Miliband endorsed him. Sarkozy seemed to have grounds for optimism. But he badly underestimated the growing opposition to Blair. Juncker told a meeting of European finance ministers, 'I will do anything to prevent a certain person becoming president of the European Council.' The Brussels press pack knew exactly whom he meant: Tony Blair.[3]

This started a bandwagon. Smaller EU countries – Poland, Belgium, the Netherlands, Luxembourg, Sweden, Austria – began ranging themselves against Blair, and suggesting that the first president should come from one of the smaller countries. Some key German politicians agreed with them, though Angela Merkel kept her options open.

Brown's government became nervous about the outcome, with Brown himself ramping up the rhetoric in support of Blair's candidature and assigning civil servants to lobby for Blair, and former EU commissioner and Blair's old friend Lord Mandelson reassuring everyone that Blair really did want the job.

But the campaign they were trying to revive was failing. On 24 October, *Newsweek* published an article by Blair's former Europe Minister, the ultra-loyal Denis MacShane, which constituted a desperate last-minute attempt to shore up the Blair candidature. Blair personally encouraged MacShane to write the article, and suggested lines to him. MacShane wrote that Blair did the EU a favour by not holding a referendum on the euro in the UK, because he would have lost it and thereby set back the cause of European integration. He poured scorn on Blair's opponents: 'old European grandees like former French president Valéry Giscard d'Estaing, who craves the post for himself.' And, as for that old canard that Blair was too fond of money, 'Blair has spent his whole life in public service, turning down more lucrative options as a young man to spend years in opposition before finally winning power.' This sanitised Blair's early career and ignored his post-prime-ministerial one.

The story has a strange postscript. MacShane was a longstanding ally and emissary. In the last years of Blair's premiership he had been engaged in a frenetic round of European travel, seeing key people on Blair's behalf, but unable to present his expenses to his master; and he remained active on Blair's behalf after Blair left Downing Street, travelling European capitals and shoring up Blair's crumbling support.

But he had no one to whom he could present the substantial expenses he incurred in air travel, as well as buying books and journals in foreign capitals. He was travelling on Blair's behalf, but at no time did Downing Street offer to pick up the tab. So he claimed them from Parliament. If they had been UK travel, or if they had been limited to three trips in a year, this would have been OK. But it wasn't, and he invented a shadow research company to pick up the bills.

This was catastrophic for MacShane, who has served time in a high-security prison for wrongly claiming them from Parliament. While he was in prison (from December 2013 to mid-2014), Blair sent him a handwritten letter:

Dear Denis

I have been trying to track down how to contact you.

I just wanted to say how sorry I am about the situation you find yourself in. You were always a good supporter of mine and a thoroughly sympathetic colleague who contributed a huge amount to the government.

I can only imagine how ghastly this is. But please come and see me after you emerge and I will do whatever I can to help.

You still have a lot to give and you should know you have a friend in me.

Yours ever
Tony

Blair had fired MacShane from the government job he loved and was good at, as Europe Minister, and had then continued to allow MacShane to use his unofficial services as an emissary around Europe, without bothering his head about how Denis might pay for all this globetrotting. But MacShane's loyalty to his old master is absolute. He was deeply touched by the letter, and if (as we hope he has) Blair has made good the implied promise in the last couple of paragraphs, MacShane is far too loyal to tell us.

However, even MacShane's eloquence could not save the doomed Blair candidature. Just three days after MacShane's article, on 29 October 2009, Sarkozy and Merkel indicated they were not backing Blair. 'The *on dit* [rumour] was that Merkel gently told Sarko that Blair wouldn't fly,' MacShane tells us. They had done a political deal – the presidency for the Christian Democrats, the foreign-affairs job for the social democrats. This ruled out Blair, who came from a social democratic party, even though most of Europe recognised that ideologically he was a Christian Democrat.

Gordon Brown fought on for his old rival, continuing to demand the presidency for Blair, and in doing so badly undermined his own credibility among European leaders. Brown gave way only on condition that Britain obtain the foreign-policy job, which he intended for Miliband.

On 19 November the Belgian Prime Minister Herman van Rompuy was chosen as President unanimously. Then the rest of Brown's strategy unravelled. David Miliband ruled himself out as foreign-affairs representative. He was saving himself for the top job in British politics – he thought he would succeed Brown as Labour leader and become Prime Minister. Blair was no longer interested in the second job – and perhaps no longer acceptable for it.

So Brown got an important job for Britain, but the frantic last-minute wheeling and dealing meant that he had to scratch around for a last-minute candidate to take it on. The little-known (though reputedly able) Baroness (Catherine) Ashton got the job. Ashton's political career had begun only a decade earlier, when she was created a life peer and then Parliamentary Undersecretary of State in the Department for Education and Skills in 2001, and subsequently in the Department for Constitutional Affairs and Ministry of Justice in 2004. She became Leader of the House of Lords in Gordon Brown's first cabinet in June 2007, and in 2008 she succeeded Peter Mandelson as Commissioner for Trade in the European Commission. She has never held elected office, and was hardly a political big hitter.

Ashton's appointment was the peace offering Europe made to Britain. Announcing it, Commission President José Manuel Barroso said, 'We believe it's so important that Britain remains at the heart of our project.'

Brown felt he had to keep on fighting for Blair to the last ditch, for he was still terrified that the vengeful Blairites would turn on him and drive him out. But it did him real damage in Europe. In the long term, Ashton herself, by proving to be able and diligent, helped reverse some of that damage.

But Brown was not forgiven in Europe. In Germany, Martin Winter of the daily *Süddeutsche Zeitung* reflected much official thinking:

> The fact that Brown backed Blair for so long has not done Europe any good. For too long, petty arguments dominated the debate. Too many byzantine-seeming intrigues were hatched to either get Blair into office or to keep him out of it. That prevented the Europeans from looking for the most competent and politically best-suited candidates for the two tasks.[4]

Why did it all go wrong for Blair? If you asked his opponents at the time, they would have said, smoothly and emolliently, that they thought it better to have someone from a small country, but no one can doubt that if a candidate they really liked had emerged from Britain, France or Germany, they would not have blocked them. They blocked him because the candidate was Blair.

If you had pressed them on why they opposed Blair personally, they might have mentioned events in his premiership: mainly the Iraq War, but also European matters such as the euro and the Schengen agreement. John Monks thinks the biggest single reason for Blair's failure to get the presidency was Iraq. Much of the EU leadership, while often admiring Blair, was strongly critical of British intervention in Iraq alongside US President George W. Bush, made worse by the fact that the intelligence about Saddam Hussein's weapons of mass destruction was unravelling just at the time that the manoeuvrings for the European Council presidency were taking place.

Another factor damaged Blair: the fact that he did not cultivate 'a strong left constituency' in Europe, according to Monks. Most of his support came from the centre right, with whom he was more comfortable than with the social democrats. It looked bad that he had no support and few friends on what was nominally his side. 'That's the choice he made,' says Monks.

All these things played their part. But these were all known right from the start of the presidency debate, when Blair was clear favourite and almost no one seemed to want to stand in his way. What tipped the scales was that Blair was getting a reputation as a man who was more interested in money than in anything else. His Middle East contracts in particular alienated key political support in Europe, as well as reminding European politicians of the Iraq War; and there was a growing feeling that he was not performing well in his one big international job, as Middle East envoy.

As Jean Quatremer put it in 2009, 'He is blamed also for his inactivity as Quartet Representative in the Middle East, where he makes only rare appearances, despite the sumptuous fitting-out he has demanded for his place there.' People were asking themselves, reports Quatremer, whether he was really interested in the European job, which 'will bring him much less than he gets as a consultant'.[5]

European politicians were still asking the half-humorous David Miliband question: can Europe afford Blair? Neither did Blair's countrymen's hostility help. Conservative foreign-affairs spokesman William Hague, who was to become Foreign Secretary the next year, told Europe's decision makers that a Blair presidency was 'the best way of turning Britain against the EU', and it turns out to have been wise advice.

Blair has not given up on a European future for himself. When we approached his office in 2013, the one thing it did give us, without our even needing to ask for them, was his two major speeches on the future of Europe, and they make very interesting reading. They are thoughtful, aimed at a European audience and studded with graceful compliments to Angela Merkel, whose opposition originally sank his hopes of the presidency.

The first, delivered to the Council for the Future of Europe in Berlin on 29 October 2012, calls for a 'grand bargain' to rescue Europe, and a part of this would be a directly elected president:

> A Europe-wide election for the Presidency of the Commission or Council is the most direct way to involve the public. An election for a big post held by one person – this people can understand. The problem with the European Parliament is that though clearly democratically elected, my experience is people don't feel close to their MEPs. This could change but only if the European Parliament and National parliaments interact far more closely.

No prizes at all for guessing who the former Prime Minister thinks might do the job.

The second, delivered on 28 November 2012, is a call for Britain to stay in Europe, play her full part in the Union and help to overcome the euro crisis, ending with this:

> Europe is a destiny we will never embrace easily. But it is an absolutely essential part of our nation remaining a world power, politically and economically. It would be a monumental error of statesmanship to turn our back on it and fall away from a crucial position of power and influence in the 21st Century.

Almost unnoticed in Britain, he criticised David Cameron's threat to leave the EU if his old enemy Jean-Claude Juncker was appointed President of the Commission, and he did so in terms that sound as though they were carefully calculated to appeal to Angela Merkel: 'It would be more convincing if he spoke of what is good for Europe, and not only of what is good for Great Britain.'

But it did no good. No one suggested Blair's name for the job, and eventually he told *Le Monde*, 'I am not a candidate for any post, formal or informal, in the EU. It is just a subject about which I care passionately.'[6]

Blair is a hero to many Americans and Kuwaitis, but this does not help him to gain trust in EU countries. That is why so much of Tony Blair Associates' business is among Middle Eastern sheikhs. But he does do some business in the EU, though its governments have not employed him. On 28 January 2008, while still pressing for the EU presidency, he signed a six-figure contract with Swiss insurer Zurich to help with its climate initiative and advise chief executive officer James Schiro on general political trends and developments.

The company said at the time that Blair was to advise on the best way to adapt its policies for businesses to take account of climate change, as well as providing Schiro with 'general guidance on developments and trends in the international political environment.'[7] No one was willing to say how much Blair was getting, but the company did not deny that it was in six figures. Schiro left the company the following year to go to Goldman Sachs.[8]

Then, after the EU presidency campaign had failed, a six-figure contract for the luxury-goods firm Louis Vuitton Moët Hennessey (LVMH) came along. Blair owed this to a contact he made during his premiership, when he became close friends with France's richest man and LVMH's head, Bernard Arnault, the richest person in France and one of the richest twenty people in the world. The two became such good friends that Blair's children were invited to do work experience with

Arnault while their father was still in office, and stayed at Arnault's Paris residence.

It started with an invitation for Arnault to Chequers, the Prime Minister's official country house in Buckinghamshire. Soon afterwards, in the summer of 2004, Blair's son Nicky did work experience at LVMH's Krug vineyard in the Champagne region of France, and a year later Blair's other son Euan did work experience at a French radio station owned by Arnault, and lived in a luxury apartment paid for by him.

In February 2007, when Blair was still PM, his daughter Kathryn stayed in Arnault's Parisian mansion while undertaking a three-month language course at the Sorbonne. In September 2007, soon after Blair had left Downing Street, the Blairs stayed aboard Arnault's yacht, *Amadeus*, in the Mediterranean. Arnault accompanied the Blairs when they had an audience with the Pope at the Vatican. So did Blair's former chief of staff Jonathan Powell, his closest aide during the Downing Street years. Powell's brother Lord Powell is chairman of the LVMH offshoot LVMH Services Ltd.[9]

As we've seen, Powell followed Blair out of office to become a senior adviser in Tony Blair Associates. He was the only person with Blair when he visited the Emir of Kuwait on behalf of the Quartet, and picked up his most lucrative contract.

Bernard Jean Étienne Arnault, according to the Forbes World Billionaires List in 2012, was the fourth richest person in the world, with a net worth variously estimated at between $24.1 billion and $41 billion.

He is known for his collection of contemporary art and privately owns a $35 million oasis in the Bahamas. The 133-acre estate features several hilltop villas, pristine beaches, tennis courts and a marina. He owns a villa in the island of St Tropez, and jointly owns a 150-year-old castle surrounded by a 41-hectare vineyard, Chateau Cheval Blanc, in the furthest corner of northwest Saint-Emilion in Bordeaux.

Arnault supported Sarkozy in his successful presidential election bid in 2007, but one year later the new president attacked tax havens, earning

Arnault's severe displeasure. He is criticised in France for parking money in Belgium, away from the French tax man.[10]

He sparked an uproar by seeking Belgian citizenship, just as President François Hollande planned to impose a 75 per cent tax on incomes of more than 1 million euros. Belgian income and inheritance taxes are significantly lower than in France, and unlike France, Belgium does not impose a tax on personal wealth.

On 10 April 2013, Arnault announced he had decided to abandon his application for Belgian citizenship, saying he did not want the move to be misinterpreted as a measure of tax evasion at a time when France faced economic and social challenges.

CHAPTER FOUR

ADVISER TO OIL-RICH SHEIKHS

'Part of the discussion might be about the Quartet; part of it might be about making a relationship with the Faith Foundation; part of it might be about business, something for JP Morgan. I think Tony himself probably thinks, "Do you remember the very early quote, that everyone knows I'm a straight kind of guy?"'

– FORMER FINANCIAL ADVISER TO TONY BLAIR,
SPEAKING TO AUTHORS.

When Tony Blair led a government, he had an army of diplomats, known as the Foreign Office, to keep him posted about the state of world events, about politicians who carried clout, about future trends and risks. Her Majesty's diplomats are famous for their contacts and their analyses.

When Blair left government, he sought to build a global consultancy not unlike the government he had left. He turned himself into an international outsourcing company, doing at an international level something very similar to what companies such as Capita and Serco do at the domestic level. He looked to persuade governments that functions traditionally carried out by civil servants could with advantage be outsourced to him.

To do this, he sought the assistance of those in the private sector who could give him insight into the world. Just as Capita recruits former local-authority education administrators, many of these Blair thought he could use were former diplomats; and a surprising number worked, and indeed work, for one of two secretive consultancies. One is the private-investigative and due-diligence consultancy bearing the name Hakluyt. The second is the now defunct American agency called Monitor, a US financial consultancy founded by the management guru Michael Porter; its name crops up frequently in the Blair story. Those connected to these outfits are familiar with the murkier parts of Whitehall, the Pentagon or the State Department.

Former Blair employees now working for Hakluyt include Nick Banner, a former diplomat who worked for Tony Blair Associates; Varun Chandra, a financial expert who assisted Blair to set up his asset-management business, which was stillborn; and Jonathan Powell, Blair's former chief of staff who is also described as a senior adviser to the spooks.

Cherie Blair and her law firm Omnia Strategy are also wedded to the private due-diligence sector for their international knowledge-gathering operations, and Tony Blair Associates has made much use of the US consultancy McKinsey.

Many international advisers to Blair have been sourced from Monitor, which collapsed amid financial mismanagement in 2012. These include Abdullah Al Asousi, a former TBA adviser in Kuwait; Naser Almutairi, who acts as Blair's government consultant in Kuwait; and Khaled Jafar. The Monitor Group employed the retired British spy Sir Mark Allen, who had advised Blair on his dealings with Libya's Muammar Gaddafi.

The reasons for Monitor's failure are interesting to us, because they are an indication of the sort of business strategy the former Prime Minister admires. *Forbes* magazine explained its philosophy and why it fell:

> In the theoretical landscape that Porter invented, all strategy worthy of the name involves avoiding competition and seeking out above-average profits protected by structural barriers. Strategy is all about figuring out how to secure excess profits without having to make a better product or deliver a better service.
>
> It is a way of making more money than the merits of the product

or service would suggest, or what those plain folks uncharitable to the ways of 20th Century business might see as something akin to cheating. However for several decades, many companies were ready to set aside ethical or social concerns and pay large consulting fees trying to find the safe and highly profitable havens that Porter's theory promised …

[Porter's] framework for the discipline of strategy isn't just an epistemological black hole: in its essence, it's antisocial, because it preserves excess profits, and it's bad for business, because it doesn't work. It accomplishes the unlikely feat of goading business leaders to do wrong both to their shareholders and to their fellow human beings …[1]

The importance to Blair of having his alumni in these agencies is that they serve as extensions of his network. Having worked for him, either in government or for TBA, they can be called on by him. They in turn will open to him a network of influential people.

When governments call on Blair, they want not only the man but his contacts. It works both ways, of course, so, when Hakluyt or any other consultancy needs a political door opened, it can call on Blair.

This partly explains the eye-watering amounts corporates and wealthy individuals will pay for Blair's mystique, wrapped round, as it is, his promise of power and access. The fact that Blair does little more than pick up a phone to a contact he has acquired through a consultancy composed of warmed-up executives never reaches the ears of the deep-pocket who wants a call made or a back scratched.

Here's how it could work. A government wants to sell a product to a NATO power, is looking for contacts in that country's government and calls Blair. Blair in turn contacts Nick Banner at Hakluyt. Banner (an old Foreign Office hand who has advised Blair on foreign affairs) in turn picks up the phone to Javier Solana, a former secretary general at NATO. Solana happens to sit on the advisory board of Pelorus Research, part of Hakluyt. Solana knows someone in the relevant country's defence ministry and advises the minister that the CEO of the company with the product will give him or her a call.

The Pelorus board is stuffed with former executives from India, Turkey, Japan, the US and the UK, each with their wealth of connections. If the deal goes through, each party in the chain receives a fee, depending on the time it puts in and the level of authority it holds. If it does not go through, parties remember who helped and how, for the next time they are needed.

Hakluyt makes secrecy its virtue. Its website contains no more than the four addresses of its offices in London, Singapore, New York and Tokyo. The London office is predictably in the West End, at 34 Upper Brook Street, W1K 7QS. The respectability of Hakluyt is little more than paper-thin. Details of its activities that leak out give the lie to the blue-chip consultancy, for the firm has been found spying on Greenpeace (Shell and BP have both admitted they hired the firm) and they worked for Enron, the fraudulent energy company.

KINSHIP WITH KUWAIT

These connections make Tony Blair more valuable than just any old run-of-the-mill former prime minister. The government of Kuwait values him highly. In January 2009, when Blair was in Kuwait as Middle East envoy for the Quartet, he met with the Emir and his advisers. But the former PM did not have anyone with him from the Quartet secretariat. Instead, he was accompanied by the new senior adviser at Tony Blair Associates, Jonathan Powell, although Blair was there on behalf of the Quartet and Powell, as we saw in Chapter 1, does not work for the Quartet but for Blair's consultancy.

Shortly afterwards, TBA won a contract with the Kuwaiti regime to undertake an analysis of the Kuwaiti economy. It helped, certainly, that in Kuwait he was dealing with an old friend. Blair has enjoyed a longstanding relationship with the Emir of Kuwait. As Prime Minister, he held talks with Sheikh al-Sabah in May 2003, just weeks after Saddam Hussein was deposed in Iraq. Sheikh al-Sabah is eternally grateful for Blair's role in bringing about the Iraq War and Saddam's downfall.

Political analyst and economist Nasser Al Abolly, a leading Kuwaiti campaigner for democratic reform, spoke to Peter Oborne for a Channel 4 documentary – a risky thing to do in a country like Kuwait, where criticising the autocratic Emir is illegal. Al Abolly said he had heard from good sources that Blair had been paid 12 million dinars – about £27 million. Oborne asked, 'How do you know he got paid that money?' Al Abolly replied, 'There is always talk about any money spent through the secret funds, circulating in Kuwait through people who are close to the Emir or through those who are involved in confidential transactions.'

Blair's office said that the figure agreed 'at that time' was very significantly less than £27 million, but declined to disclose the lifetime value of the contract. That lifetime value may, of course, be significantly more than was paid for the report itself – as we will see, Blair has staff embedded in the Kuwaiti government.

Oborne asked, 'Would £27 million have been good value for TBA's report?' Al Abolly replied, 'Of course not.'

Whether the report really was worth £27 million or not is hard to judge, because nobody's allowed to see it. But Al Abolly not only considers it exorbitant: he also told Oborne that much of Blair's eventual report was not original and it had come up with many of the same recommendations as earlier reports on the future of Kuwait – an observation echoed by other Kuwaiti politicians.

Kuwait is thought to have commissioned an earlier report on much the same subject from the consultants McKinsey. It is not known whether Blair's team had access to that report.

According to Peter Oborne, writing in the *Daily Telegraph* on 23 September 2011,

Mr Blair's visit to the Emir of Kuwait, part of a wider Middle Eastern tour, was made on January 26, 2009. He was introduced to the Emir – who is said to feel a profound sense of gratitude to the former British Prime Minister because of his role in deposing Kuwait's greatest enemy, Saddam Hussein.

Shortly afterwards, the Emir handed Tony Blair Associates a lucrative consultancy deal to provide advice on the future of the Kuwaiti economy. Nobody knows how much this deal – which was kept secret for two years – is worth. Because the TBA contract was handled by the Emir's personal office, it is exempt from scrutiny by Kuwait's normally rigorous financial regulatory body.[2]

The five-year plan is part of the government's 'Vision Kuwait 2035'. The report proposes reforms to the oil, trade and finance sectors, business environment, and health and education systems. Sheikh Nasser Sabah Al-Ahmad has said the report prepared by Blair's team 'analyses the major issues facing the country and presents detailed proposals' for addressing them.

What came out of the Blair report? We don't, of course, know, because we don't know what was *in* the Blair report. But 798 construction projects worth 4.8 billion dinars were subsequently planned. The five-year plan was based on 330 policies that would be supported by 45 new laws. Five public sectors – housing, electricity, ports, warehouses and health insurance – would be privatised. The new plan will pump billions into prestige megaprojects such as the $77 billion City of Silk Bridge.

The City of Silk is a proposed urban area on the other side of Kuwait Bay from Kuwait City, designed to include a duty-free area beside a new airport, a large business centre, conference areas, environmental areas, athletic areas and areas that concentrate on media, health, education and industry, as well as tourist attractions, hotels, spas and public gardens.

The oil sector will also benefit from projects such as a new $14.5 billion oil refinery that was previously held up in parliament. There will also be a massive skyscraper, planned to top out at 1,001 metres in order to reflect the Arabian folk tale collection *One Thousand and One Nights*. The complex will be linked to Kuwait City by a 23.5-kilometre bridge across Kuwait Bay.

As a result of the contract, TBA has staff permanently based inside the office of the Kuwaiti Prime Minister. One of these has been Haneen Al-Ghabra, a Kuwaiti woman who was the Prime Minister's communications manager. She was recruited by TBA in 2010. 'I am responsible for ensuring message consistency at both a governmental level and for the Prime Minister himself,' Al-Ghabra said. 'Our department is responsible for branding, media relations, public perception and strategic communications.'[3]

After receiving her BA in communication in 2003 and her MA in public communication in 2004 from Washington University's School of Communication – a course that included internships at the World Bank and the Middle East Institute – she worked in strategic communications. Al-Ghabra was recruited and trained for this position by the Office of Tony Blair. She told her alumnae bulletin that communication is a vital industry in society, particularly in her native Kuwait.

'It's an important facet of the world because it tells a certain public or culture what to think and what to perceive,' she said. 'It is a very powerful tool and unfortunately used in the wrong way in the Arab World.'

Al-Ghabra said the struggle she faced between the independence she felt and her return to the traditional values in Kuwait was difficult, and that her education inspired her to pursue a PhD in communication. Although there has been progress for women in the Arab world, such as women gaining the right to vote or serve in Parliament in Kuwait, she said there was still a long way to go.

'We still lag behind, and women here face a vast glass ceiling like no other society,' she said. 'I think women need to be empowered through communication.' Al-Ghabra has since omitted her employment at the Office of Tony Blair from her LinkedIn profile. Quite how helping the autocratic Emir with his PR will help to empower Kuwaiti women is not clear to us. Discrimination against women in the judicial and education sectors is still legally sanctioned, though the Kuwaiti courts seem to be taking a stand against it.

What has not come out of the Blair report is any improvement in the country's lamentable record on democracy and human rights. We have no means of knowing whether the subject was covered in the report.

Blair's old friend the Emir is not, of course, a democrat. This does not seem to trouble Blair – as we shall see in a later chapter, he has an idiosyncratic opinion about democracy.

Freedoms of speech and the press are protected under Articles 36 and 37 of the constitution, but only 'in accordance with the conditions and in the circumstances defined by law.' Under 2006 amendments to the press law, press offences are no longer criminal in nature; offenders now face steep fines instead. However, Kuwaiti law prohibits, and continues to demand jail for, the publication of material that insults God, the Prophet or Islam. The law also forbids criticism of the Emir, as well as disclosing secret or private information, and calling for the regime's overthrow. Any citizen may press criminal charges against an author suspected of violating these bans.[4]

Human Rights Watch (HRW) notes that the elections held on 1 December 2012 were boycotted by Islamists, liberals and nationalists, and that Kuwait continues to exclude thousands of stateless people, known as Bidun, from full citizenship, despite their longstanding roots in Kuwaiti territory. 'Authorities criminally prosecuted individuals for expressing nonviolent political opinions, including web commentary,' says HRW.

On 28 October 2013, the Kuwaiti Court of Appeals upheld a ten-year prison sentence for a local blogger's comments on Twitter. Hamad al-Naqi was sentenced for insulting the Prophet Mohammed and the kings of Saudi Arabia and Bahrain, among other charges.

Whether Mr Blair ever mentions these matters to his friend and client the Emir, we have no means of knowing.

By the normal standards of British public life, Blair would not have been allowed to accept this contract and keep his position as Quartet Representative. It would be seen as a conflict of interest. He is promoting peace in the region on the one hand, and making millions from an autocratic regime in the region on the other. This may be why the deal was kept private for as long as possible. The appointment did not come to light until 2010. It had been declared to the UK's Advisory Committee on Business Appointments (ACOBA) but the committee agreed to keep it quiet at Kuwait's request.

KUWAIT AND THE FAITH FOUNDATION

Meanwhile, Blair was setting up his Faith Foundation, and looking for a Muslim to sit on its advisory board to provide a semblance of balance, since other faiths were well represented. He was hampered by the fact that his many statements condemning Islam have made Islamic theologians wary of him.

It was the Kuwaiti government that provided the solution, by giving him Dr Ismail Khudr Al-Shatti, a prominent Kuwaiti politician. He is head of the Kuwaiti premier's advisory committee at the time of writing, is the former Deputy Prime Minister of Kuwait and a former minister at the Ministry of Communications. Al-Shatti is also an expert in future studies, or trying to predict what the future holds.

He is not a cleric, or a theologian, or in any sense a prominent religious figure, even though, according to the *Global Muslim Brotherhood Daily Watch*, he is a prominent member of the Islamic Constitutional Movement (ICM), the Kuwaiti branch of the Muslim Brotherhood. This carried a story on 16 February 2009 which stated, 'According to his resume, Ismail Khudr Al-Shatti has been a leader in the Islamic Constitutional Movement, the Kuwaiti branch of the Muslim Brotherhood. Mustafa Ceric is tied to the global Muslim Brotherhood through his membership in the European Council for Fatwa and Research (ECFR), headed by Brotherhood leader Youssef Qaradawi and by his participation in the

UK-based "Radical Middle Way", consisting of a wide range of associated scholars representing the global Muslim Brotherhood.'

The invasion of Iraq was the most controversial act of Blair's premiership but it was excellent news for Kuwait. Blair enjoys much prestige in the country as a result, and he regularly visits it and receives a huge amount of money in fees from it for work that seems, to put it mildly, intangible. No doubt the decision to go to war was made from the highest motives, but it has certainly served, incidentally, to help enrich the man who drove through the decision with a level of energy, single-mindedness, ruthlessness and deception that surprised everyone at the time.

ABU DHABI GETS A FREQUENT VISITOR

Critics of the Iraq War say the conflict was over access to oil rather than weapons of mass destruction. Blair has denied that he has any direct business interest in Iraq oil. In one sense, this is true, but it rather depends what you mean by 'direct'. His relationship with the repressive monarchy of Abu Dhabi certainly brings him into close contact with Iraqi oil.

Abu Dhabi is the capital of the United Arab Emirates and the largest of its seven member principalities. Blair regularly visits Abu Dhabi for the Quartet, where he meets the Crown Prince, Sheikh Mohammed bin Zayed Al Nahyan, who succeeded his father in the job in 2004. Al Nahyan is also deputy supreme commander of the UAE armed forces, as well as being a member of the Supreme Petroleum Council and special adviser to the President of the UAE, who is his older brother, Khalifa bin Zayed Al Nahyan. He is also the head of the Mubadala Development Company, the main investment vehicle for the government of Abu Dhabi. And he is a director of the Abu Dhabi Investment Authority – the sovereign wealth fund of Abu Dhabi – head of the UAE offsets programme and head of the Abu Dhabi Education Council.

The Crown Prince is also a client of Tony Blair Associates. TBA provides 'global strategic advice' to Mubadala, which invests Abu Dhabi's oil profits. Blair's 'government consultant' covering Dubai and Abu Dhabi is Khaled

Jafar, who worked for Monitor Consulting until it went bankrupt, and who was first assigned to Blair by Monitor.

Abu Dhabi is just along the Gulf coast from Iraq. The sovereign wealth fund gets most of its income from oil and gas and Blair was signed up while the fund was in talks to help develop a massive oilfield – not in Abu Dhabi, but in Iraq.

About the time Blair was signed up to advise Mubadala, *Trade Arabia* was reporting on 23 October 2009:

Occidental Petroleum Corporation (Oxy) is in negotiations with Abu Dhabi about its government investment fund, Mubadala, sharing in the US oil company's stake in Iraq's massive Zubair field, a top official said. 'We're going to share part of our share probably with Abu Dhabi and there may be others coming along,' chief executive Ray Irani told analysts on a conference call to discuss Occidental's third-quarter earnings.[5]

Oil and gas, aerospace and infrastructure are the three biggest revenue contributors. In 2010, as portfolio diversification continued, oil and gas contributed 38 per cent of the revenue, compared with 81 per cent in 2008. But oil and gas is still the largest revenue contributor of Mubadala.

On 3 January 2010 the *Sunday Times* reported that Mubadala was in negotiations to join a consortium of Western oil companies developing the Zubair oilfield in southern Iraq. More than £6 billion of investment was required for the project.[6]

Mubadala's CEO is Khaldoon Al Mubarak, Emirati businessman and chairman of Manchester City FC.[7] TBA receives a reported £1 million a year[8] for this contract. Critics say it is incompatible with Blair's position as the international peace envoy to the Middle East. Mubadala's interests also include oil exploration contracts in Libya, where, as we shall see, Blair's involvement is close and longstanding.

Blair also drops by Abu Dhabi regularly, apparently to discuss religious affairs and climate change as well as Middle East peace. Those, at any rate, are the only subjects for discussion that are mentioned in his public announcements of his engagements. These do not give any indication of any discussions on business conducted with the Crown Prince on behalf of TBA. However, surely the Crown Prince expects some face time for his £1 million a year. When does he get it, if not when Blair is visiting ostensibly to discuss peace or religion?

He went to Abu Dhabi towards the end of July 2007, meeting the Crown Prince 'as part of a tour of the region.' The Crown Prince hosted a dinner in Blair's honour. *Gulf News* in its announcement gives the Crown Prince his full title: 'His Highness General Sheikh Mohamed bin Zayed Al Nahyan is the Crown Prince of Abu Dhabi, Deputy Supreme Commander of the UAE Armed Forces and Chairman of the Abu Dhabi Executive Council.'[9]

The Crown Prince was trained at the elite British military academy Sandhurst before commanding his country's air force and advising his father, the late Sheikh, on security matters. According to Human Rights Watch, the human-rights situation in the country has worsened under his rule: 'Authorities arbitrarily detain civil society activists, holding them in secret, and harassing and intimidating their lawyers. An independent monitor found significant problems in the treatment of migrant workers on the high-profile Saadiyat Island project in Abu Dhabi, identifying the payment of illegal recruitment fees as a key concern.'

Whether this matter is ever mentioned in Blair's meetings with the Crown Prince, we do not, of course, know. But he's had plenty of chances to mention them. We find him back there four months later, to meet the Crown Prince again 'as part of his regional tour in quest for peace in the region,' reports *Gulf News*.[10]

Towards the end of March 2009 we find him in Abu Dhabi telling an invited audience that now is the moment when the international community must act decisively on the Palestine–Israel conflict.[11] A couple of weeks later, in mid-April, there he was again, urging investors to donate money to the Palestinian economy and saying that the West Bank is ready for business, as well as holding private talks with the Crown Prince.[12]

Then we find him visiting the place not as Quartet envoy but as patron of the Tony Blair Faith Foundation. The TBFF website reports:

> In an historic event, former British Prime Minister, the Right Honourable Tony Blair, gave a speech at Abu Dhabi Men's College today about the ground-breaking multi-faith work the Tony Blair Faith Foundation is undertaking around the world.
>
> Mr Blair announced that the Higher Colleges of Technology is the first associate university partner from the Middle East to join the Tony Blair Faith Foundation's Faith and Globalisation Initiative.[13]

Which Tony Blair keeps visiting Abu Dhabi? The patron of the TBFF? The Middle East peace envoy? Or the principal of Tony Blair Associates? It generally seems to be the last-named who benefits most from his visits.

But it would be unfair to end this chapter without quoting, albeit anonymously, from the only former senior member of the staff of Tony Blair Associates who talked to us about these matters, albeit under conditions of strict anonymity, and defended Blair's role as Quartet Envoy.

This person, whose background is financial, said, 'He wants to be relevant politically more than he wants money. And the Quartet role is very important to him. What people say is, "How can you be doing business with Arab governments, around the Gulf and at the same time do your job in the Quartet?" Now, the way I rationalise that is actually quite simple: his role in the Quartet is an economic development role more than anything else. And the Gulf Arabs have never been particularly fond of the Palestinians, and certainly they have not given them that much money. And it wasn't helped by Arafat making this disastrous call of the First Gulf War by supporting Saddam – do you remember? The Gulf rulers absolutely adore Tony.

'And, you know, he's a very endearing and charming chap, so they're particularly fond of him. Now, his contribution to the development of the economy of the West Bank is he has got Gulf money coming to the West Bank which wasn't there before. Whereas some people might say it's a conflict of interest that you have someone who has business relationships with Gulf rulers as well as having a political role in the Middle East, in practical terms it's been helpful …

'And part of the discussion might be about the Quartet; part of it might be about making a relationship with the Faith Foundation; part of it might be about business, something for JP Morgan. I think Tony himself probably thinks, "Do you remember the very early quote, that everyone knows I'm a straight kind of guy?"'

CHAPTER FIVE

APOLOGIST FOR DICTATORS: CENTRAL ASIA PROVIDES FERTILE PICKINGS

'[Nazarbayev has displayed] the toughness necessary to take the decisions to put the country on the right path.'
– TONY BLAIR IN A KAZAKH VIDEO PRAISING THE PRESIDENT OF THAT COUNTRY.

The former British Prime Minister makes a business out of providing consultancy to mostly unacceptable and disreputable clients. How else to explain the work he does for President el-Sisi in Egypt – who obtained his power by a military coup – or Joseph Kabila of the Democratic Republic of the Congo, not to mention the consultancy he provides, at great expense no doubt, to the unelected leaders of Gulf countries.

But perhaps the best-documented example of this touting of contacts built up over years of running a British government is seen in his consultancy to the Central Asian state of Kazakhstan. This last contract would lead many to ask if a former prime minister of a Western democracy should even be associating with someone with the record for human-rights abuse that Nursultan Nazarbayev has, let alone giving him public-relations advice.

Kazakhstan was gushing oil and gas in the late 2000s, when Tony Blair was building his consultancy. Sources of petrodollars had fallen into the hands of politicians who had varying degrees of illegitimacy to burnish their image. Blair made a beeline for Nursultan Nazarbayev – a politician whom he had cultivated over the previous decade when he was Prime Minister.

The darkness of the deal between Blair and Nazarbayev was set against a historic backcloth of pure innocence. How fitting that, in 2000, Blair entrusted into the arms of Nazarbayev his young son Leo, just six months old at the time, at Downing Street. The press cameras flashed as the thickset Kazakh bruiser, who was then sixty-two and had sired a number of children of his own, cradled the baby, Blair beaming as he looked on. The symbolism is said to have particular resonance for the highly family-conscious Central Asian public. Eleven years later, in 2011, when Blair had moved out of Downing Street, the man who held his child would be hiring him as image maker.

By this stage, Nazarbayev had removed ex-Soviet nuclear weapons from his soil. He may have looked to Blair to win him the Nobel Peace Prize. Moreover, Nazarbayev was showing his country round the world and wanted to be trumpeted as a moderniser. The rehabilitation of an old Soviet fixer as Third Way liberaliser (à la New Labour) was an elusive goal Blair could never deliver.

Nazarbayev also dreamed of his country being seen by the Western world as a Central Asian Singapore, modern and productive. A spokesman for Tony Blair said he was not involved with President Nazarbayev's campaign for the Nobel Prize. He said, 'Tony Blair has helped put together a team of international advisers and consultants to set up an advisory group for the Kazakhs, with a team of people working on the ground. The work they are doing is excellent, sensible and supports the reforms they are making. The Kazakhs also engage with a number of other former European leaders.'

It seems likely that Blair persuaded the Kazakh President he could open his way to the global establishment, to the fabled British establishment and even to the British royal family. While members of the royal family, such as Prince Andrew, have indeed been regular visitors to Astana, the Kazakh capital, and they have done business deals with Kazakh tycoons, the great and the good remain wary of Kazakhstan.

Nazarbayev has been prepared to pay generously for the access afforded by Blair. Needless to say his fee is not disclosed but the *Financial Times*, the *Daily Telegraph* and other newspapers have put it at £7 million a year, and that is almost certainly a good ballpark figure. Our understanding is that Blair was paid £8 million for the first year of the consultancy and £7 to 8 million for the second year. The Blair organisation was not helpful in quantifying the fee. 'We don't and have never confirmed value of contracts – it's commercially confidential information. So the figures bandied about are often wrong,' we were told by Blair's spokeswoman, Rachel Grant. It's a rather more polite expression of the usual Blair formulation: we're not telling you, but, whatever you calculate, you're wrong. But she did confirm that there is a fee. It pays for 'the cost of running the project – including a team of advisers on the ground, who are experts in political, social and economic reform.' She also agreed that the fee does provide a profit for Tony Blair Associates – not, she wanted to point out to us, to Tony Blair personally, but to his company. 'Profits go back into running the business' was how she put it.

While, as of now, Blair continues to receive his pay cheque, rumours surface constantly that the contract may not be or has not been renewed. These may grow louder as those close to the President ask if Blair was a luxury funded by the high price of oil, a luxury that cannot now be afforded as the price collapses and the country's budget feels the strain.

Blair's value is not restricted to his own advice. He also comes with a familiar entourage of public-relations people and fellow travellers. The Kazakh government has hired PR companies including the leading UK firm Bell Pottinger – founded by the arch Thatcherite Lord (Tim) Bell – to present a modern economy and a haven of religious tolerance.

The roles of Blair and Bell are in some ways analogous, albeit their political histories are diametrically opposed. The famous right-wing PR man has helped many clients with difficult histories such as Thaksin Shinawatra, the ousted Thai premier; Asma al-Assad, the wife of the President of Syria; Alexander Lukashenko, the dictator of Belarus;

Rebekah Brooks, after the phone-hacking scandal broke; the repressive governments of Bahrain and Egypt; the polluting oil company Trafigura; the fracking company Cuadrilla; the Pinochet Foundation during its campaign against the former Chilean dictator's British detention; and the much-criticised arms conglomerate BAE Systems.

Other partners in the Blair consulting machine working with Kazakhstan are Tim Allan and the Portland PR company that Allan founded; Alastair Campbell, the former Blair PR chief who famously 'sexed up' the memo on weapons of mass destruction in Iraq; and Jonathan Powell, who we have come across before. Powell runs a mediation charity but has said his work for President Nazarbayev is not part of his charitable activities. Asked about his work for Nazarbayev, Powell said, 'I've got nothing to say about that. I suggest you talk to Tony Blair's office about that.' Blair's office confirmed to Ken Silverstein that Blair had put in a good word for his colleagues at Portland for the Kazakh account, and they got it on his recommendation. Portland, says Silverstein, is also lobbying for Nazarbayev in the United States.[1]

Another player in Kazakhstan from the Blair ménage is his wife Cherie, whose legal firm Omnia Strategy is being paid hundreds of thousands of pounds for a few months' legal work by Kazakhstan's Ministry of Justice. Omnia was hired to conduct a review of the country's 'bilateral investment treaties'. The first stage of the review, which was expected to take as little as three months, is worth £120,000, sources have told the *Sunday Telegraph*. A second phase of the project is understood to be worth a further £200,000 to £250,000 for another three to four months' work. Omnia Strategy also has an option to complete a third stage of the legal project for the Ministry of Justice.

THE CLIENT

So who *is* Blair's friend in Kazakhstan, Nursultan Nazarbayev? The man who sits on the other side of the table when Blair offers his advice and negotiates his fee has been called one of the 'ultimate oligarchs' of the post-Soviet Central Asia states. Bruising, ruthless, visionary and greedy, he was a man with whom Blair could not only work, but openly admire.

Nursultan Äbishuly Nazarbayev was born in 1940 to a poor family in rural Kazakhstan at a time when the country was a Soviet republic. He worked his way up the greasy pole, first in the Young Communist League and then the Communist Party, becoming a full-time worker for the party. He was undoubtedly effective, at one time complaining about bureaucracy and inefficiency. It was a message that resonated with the then Soviet leader Mikhail Gorbachev, who ensured that he became general secretary of the party in Kazakhstan in 1989, when the country was still a Soviet republic but on the brink of independence. He was chairman of the Supreme Soviet (head of state) from 22 February to 24 April 1990. Nazarbayev was elected the nation's first president following its independence from the Soviet Union in December 1991. He was the sole candidate and won no fewer than 91.5 per cent of the votes.

He was determined that things should stay that way. So, when opposition political parties called for the formation of a coalition government in 1992, holding demonstrations, Kazakh security forcibly put down the protest. Opposition parties played little role over the subsequent years. This was democracy more in form than reality.

The election due in 1995 was abandoned, in favour of a referendum in which the electorate extended his presidential term by five years. He was re-elected in January 1999 and again in December 2005 – the election before which the leading opposition candidate Zamanbek Nurkadilov was said to have shot himself twice in the chest before shooting himself in the head.

Nazarbayev duly won another seven-year presidential term by an overwhelming majority of 91.15 per cent (from a total of 6,871,571 eligible participating voters). This incurred criticism from the Organization for Security and Co-operation in Europe as falling short of international democratic standards. It found that an election requires two or more candidates running in opposition. A single candidate is not an election but a referendum.

On 18 May 2007, the Parliament of Kazakhstan approved a constitutional amendment that would allow Nazarbayev to seek re-election as many times as he wished. This amendment applies only to Nazarbayev – the original constitution's prescribed maximum of two presidential terms would still apply to all future presidents of Kazakhstan. This was seen as guaranteeing Nazarbayev a lifetime presidency. One commentator described Kazakhstan as operating a 'soft dictatorship'. He said that that Nazarbayev 'is not himself happy with the arrangement and he was heard saying that it was a mistake. He wanted to be a senior official at the UN, not president.'

In May 2011, the Kazakh Parliament approved a constitutional amendment that made President Nursultan Nazarbayev 'leader of the nation', thereby granting him and his immediate family permanent immunity from prosecution. The amendment also gave him the lifelong right to make final decisions on foreign and security policy matters. Defacing pictures of the 'leader of the nation' and misrepresenting his biography were made criminal offences. In September, Nazarbayev indicated that he would run for another term in office in 2012.

Nazarbayev appeared now to develop grandiose ideas of his importance and employed Blair to make them real. We see *The Economist* commenting, 'When he hired Mr Blair in October 2011, many thought he might be seeking help to win himself a Nobel Peace Prize, on the basis of his having handed over to Russia the nuclear weapons that were stored in the Kazakh Soviet Socialist Republic at the collapse of the Soviet Union.' This idea was reputedly planted by one of Nazarbayev's one-time favourite businessmen, Alexander Maskievitch, the former Kyrgyz academic who jointly founded the partially state-owned company ENRC. *The Economist* went on to observe that, shortly after Blair joined Nazarbayev's team, its security forces opened fire on protesters.

The assumption of a lifetime presidency appears to have been the final straw for his son-in-law, Rakhat Aliyev. He had just been appointed ambassador to Austria and the country's representative to the Organization for Security and Co-operation in Europe (OSCE) when, amid a welter of allegations of corruption, false imprisonment of a journalist, kidnapping of bankers and the like, he was stripped of his position. Kazakhstan requested that Austria extradite him, and the President apparently unilaterally forced him to divorce his daughter Dariga, who had had three children with Aliyev. His daughter subsequently said that Nazarbayev had pressurised her to agree to the divorce. Aliyev wrote a book called *The Godfather-in-Law*, accusing the President of having opposition leaders murdered. He also exposed the corrupt and abusive Nazarbayev household. He later fled to Malta.

The scene was set for a long-running feud between father and former son-in-law and this has been waged in Washington as well as London and elsewhere. Nazarbayev is said (by the *New York Times*) to have paid lobbyists millions to rebut the allegations by Aliyev. Aliyev had occupied high office inside Kazakhstan, including in the tax office, and had made a massive fortune. He had also acquired documents and evidence that he publicised widely, following the breakdown of relations with the President.

Aliyev's public-relations campaign discredited the carefully crafted image of the father of the nation, contrived by the former Soviet heavyweight Nazarbayev as he sought to be loved by his nation. The backdrop for some cosy counterblast, headed by Blair but partnered by many other image-makers, was established. The Kazakhstan's ambassador to the US, Erlan Idrissov, wrote in a letter published in the *New York Times* in response to the newspaper's article, 'Kazakhstan has indeed hired consultants, including in the United States. This is to explain its position, as is accepted practice, and to respond to critics of the President who continue to perpetuate the fiction that Kazakhstan is a dictatorship.'

The country splurged out on PR campaigns in the US with a task force organised by two Washington think tanks – the Center for Strategic and

International Studies and the Institute for New Democracies – receiving $290,000 from the Kazakh government to write a series of reports assessing the country's progress towards democracy, according to Central Asian affairs website eurasianet.org. Another group of lobbyists received $9 million.

The wise leadership of the leader was hailed as worthy of protection from all the slings thrown at it by Aliyev. Margarita Assenova, executive director of the Institute for New Democracies, was quoted as saying that 'the people credit the wise leadership of Nazarbayev for peace, stability, economic development and ethnic harmony in Kazakhstan. They want this to continue.' The OSCE, for its part, criticised the results, saying that 'reforms necessary for holding genuine democratic elections have yet to materialize.'

Blair's place in the Nazarbayev 'family' of deferential cronies was cemented during a state visit to the UK in 2000, when Blair famously gave him Leo to cradle. Nazarbayev, who remarked on the importance of family ties, visited again in 2006 and paid his respects to Blair. But it was not until 2011 that Nazarbayev finally paid his dues to Blair by hiring him as his adviser.

The onset of ill health – as demonstrated by a visit (intended to be kept secret but leaked to the press) to Israel for an operation – has raised the stakes in the selection of a successor to Nazarbayev. The President is not thought to have any intention of naming a successor, let alone handing over power in his lifetime. Individuals who have staked any claim to replace him have suffered severe fates. This ensures a constant guessing game: first, about the President's longevity, and, second, about who is most likely to be sitting when the music stops. The President makes all key political decisions, and Blair's generous contract is undoubtedly one of those. It does not seem likely that Blair will be able to hang on to his contract in the turmoil that seems certain to follow the moment when the President at last steps down.

CAN BLAIR BURNISH SUCH AN IMAGE?

If much of his role is to make the unacceptable acceptable to the sceptical, and in some cases downright hostile, Western world media, what is he having to contend with? The answer is that Nursultan Nazarbayev's tenure on power is held by his complete domination of a system. He doesn't have democratic legitimacy. He has led the country since its independence from the Soviet Union in 1991; in 2011 he was re-elected with 95 per cent of the vote, a percentage that is seldom achieved by strictly democratic means. In accomplishing this he has outmanoeuvred opponents and put many in prison.

His reign of fear is brutal and comprehensive. It is illegal to criticise the President. The police routinely torture opponents, and the use of child labour is widespread. A newspaper that attacked the President has been the target of threats, web-blocking by Kazakhtelecom (the country's largest Internet service provider), libel actions and even arson attacks. In 2002, its offices were burned down and a dead dog left hanging from a ground-floor window in full view of the street. Attached to the carcass was a note stating simply, 'You won't get a second warning.'

The full horror of the authoritarian state was laid open to full view just two months after Blair's appointment, in December 2011, when at least fifteen oil workers were mown down by police. The number is approximate as no official death toll was provided. The massacre occurred in the oil town of Zhanaozen, and it followed a protracted strike for unpaid wages and better working conditions. Local courts outlawed the strike and the state oil company sacked nearly 1,000 employees.

Some eight months after the strike began, police and protesters clashed over attempts to evict them from the square in preparation for an Independence Day celebration. Activists claimed security officers opened fire on unarmed demonstrators in the course of the celebrations. Authorities claimed that 'bandits' infiltrated the protesters and began the riots first, producing video to support their version of events. In the disturbances which followed, local government offices, a hotel and an office of the state oil company were set on fire. Eighty-six people were injured in the clashes, according to officials. Unrest spread throughout Kazakhstan's oil fields as a result of the killings.

OPPONENTS OF THE PRESIDENT

The massacre was widely criticised by civil rights groups across the country as well as by mining unions abroad. In late June 2012, Human Rights Watch issued a report attacking the lamentable state of human rights in Kazakhstan. It also detailed 'significant setbacks' in the country, including the use of criminal charges for 'inciting social discord' (which carries a maximum sentence of twelve years in prison).

In late 2012 Kazakhstan closed an opposition newspaper, *Respublika*. This had been used as the political mouthpiece of Mukhtar Ablyazov, the former head of BTA Bank, who allegedly stole some $11 billion from the bank before going on the run, first to London, then Italy then France. The public-relations company Portland Communications, run by Blair's former press officer Tim Allan with Alastair Campbell on the board, is representing BTA Bank in its multibillion-pound case against Ablyazov. BTA Bank is one the country's largest banks.

In late June 2012, Human Rights Watch issued a report that detailed 'significant setbacks' in Kazakhstan. Former Kazakh Prime Minister Akezhan Kazhegeldin, who was forced into exile in 1997, is dismissive of Blair's alleged efforts. 'He can offer all the advice he wants but you can't have better governance in Kazakhstan without changing the government.'

Corruption is the bane of Nazarbayev's one-party state. In 2004 Transparency International ranked Kazakhstan 122 in its 'corruption perception' listing of 146 countries. This is an annual index of corruption covering most countries, carried out by an authoritative non-governmental organisation. Nazarbayev has paradoxically declared a holy war against corruption and ordered the adoption of 'ten steps against corruption' to fight it at all levels of state and society. Despite his becoming chairman of the Organization for Security and Co-operation in Europe in 2010, little has been done to address human-rights abuses and widespread corruption in the country. Allegations of corruption have been used to keep some leading (and almost certainly blameless) Kazakh officials behind bars, most notably Moukhtar Dzhakishev, the former head of the atomic-energy company Kazatomprom. From all of this, one must wonder how comfortable someone professing transparency in the manner of the former British Prime Minister feels about this assignment.

The Nazarbayev family itself was embroiled in a series of investigations by Western governments into money laundering, bribery, and assassinations, in so-called 'Kazakhgate'. This concerned an oil executive called James Giffen, who worked closely with Nazarbayev in the years prior to Kazakh independence and afterwards. Allegations of impropriety surfaced in 2003 and were resolved only at the conclusion of a trial in 2010. It was disclosed at Giffen's trial that he funnelled some $80 million to Nazarbayev through a complex series of bank accounts. Giffen was brought to trial in the United States for breaches of the Foreign and Corrupt Practices Act. He did not deny the fact that he had paid the money to Nazarbayev as a bribe, but rather that he had paid it in his role as an operative of the Central Intelligence Agency, to which he was providing information about Nazarbayev.

So the payment was justified on the grounds that it was in the US government's interest. Giffen pleaded guilty to one low-level offence and received a nominal penalty. A former minister in the Nazarbayev government, Zamanbek K. Nurkadilov, said that Nazarbayev should answer allegations that Kazakh officials had accepted millions of US dollars in bribes from an intermediary for US oil firms in the 1990s. This openness was a grave mistake, since, as we have seen, three weeks before the 2005 presidential election Nurkadilov was assassinated.

The regime makes no attempt to appear acceptable to its own people, let alone the outside world. An American diplomatic cable in 2010, released by WikiLeaks, reported that in 2007 'President Nazarbayev's son-in-law, Timur Kulibayev, celebrated his 41st birthday in grand style. At a small venue in Almaty, he hosted a private concert with some of Russia's biggest pop-stars. The headliner, however, was Elton John, to whom he reportedly paid one million pounds for this one-time appearance.'[2]

Kazakh state businesses are routinely run by favoured cronies of the President. Two of these businesses are in natural resources, a sector where the country is very rich, and include Eurasian Natural Resources Corporation (ENRC) and the Kazakh mining company Kazakhmys. The former is run by two Kyrgyz oligarchs and one Uzbek, the latter by a Kazakh. Both companies have been listed on the London Stock Exchange, bringing Kazakhstan to the attention of the international capital markets.

Their fates have been very different. ENRC became mired in corruption allegations over African deals, and is now the subject of a probe by the UK's Serious Fraud Office. Its leaders have been forced to drop their listing and throw themselves at the mercy of Nazarbayev in Kazakhstan. The disastrous adventure has tarnished Nazarbayev's dream of a modern Kazakh presence in international markets. Moreover, the President's defensiveness in bringing the company back home to Kazakhstan and out of the public limelight testifies to a fear of scrutiny by democratic agencies. Kazakhmys has kept its nose clean and London continues to invest in this Kazakh poster child.

Nazarbayev meanwhile has been accused of transferring at least $1 billion worth of oil revenues to his private bank accounts in other countries and his family controls many other key enterprises in Kazakhstan. Those working in the country say that the Nazarbayev regime is in thrall to a coterie of wealthy entrepreneurs and friends of the President. One observer, a lawyer advising Kazakh companies, said that no one in the country obtains wealth except by paying him and his retinue a proportion. They must likewise serve his interests.

One Russian adviser to a former senior minister in a Nazarbayev government told us: 'All of the big business people in Kazakhstan are close to the President. They can exist only if they are close to the President. Likewise Mukhtar Ablyazov [the allegedly corrupt former head of BTA Bank] became a billionaire in a few years because he stayed close to the President.'

Nazarbayev is not the only Kazakh leader to use Tony Blair for his political purposes. Blair is also used by Prime Minister Karim Massimov when he wants to sway the President in favour of one of his proposals; Nazarbayev holds Blair in such high esteem that Blair's imprimatur boosts Massimov's standing. Massimov reciprocates the favour, housing Blair's five-strong local team in his offices. He uses them to scrutinise his proposals before forwarding them on to the President as recommended by Blair. Blair was particularly helpful to Massimov when he sought to raise the profile of Islamic banking in Kazakhstan, leading to a presidential visit to the Gulf and increasing amounts of Gulf money flowing to his country.

WHAT DOES BLAIR DO FOR HIS MONEY?

Blair evidently has his work cut out to make the unacceptable acceptable. Yet try it he does. We see Blair acting as an amanuensis for Nazarbayev, writing his speeches, being the door-opener to international leaders who otherwise would not pick up the phone. There are also the consultants with a team of administrators to staff the presidential office and other offices of state.

As Nazarbayev's publicist, Blair appeared in a video, a panegyric of praise for the country's economy and its leader that does not mention once any issues of human rights abuse. In this dreary neo-Stalinist propaganda video, he says that Nazarbayev had displayed 'the toughness necessary to take the decisions to put the country on the right path, but also a certain degree of subtlety and ingenuity that allowed him to manoeuvre in a region that is fraught with difficulties, and frankly wedged between two great powers, China and Russia.'

Blair says, 'It is a country almost unique I would say in its cultural diversity and the way it brings different faiths together, different cultures together.' The film features extensive interviews with Nazarbayev and Western energy executives praising him, as well as fawning interventions from Blair. 'In the work that I do there, I've found them really smart people, capable, very determined, and very proud of their country,' he says.

The film is one hour and seven minutes long and it is hard to see who might have the endurance to view the whole thing. It is an endless parade of talking heads fawning over the great leader. Blair looks pinched and ill, and does not speak with his usual brio; he is looking down, speaking carefully in a hoarse, hushed voice. He looks rather as though he hopes no one he knows will ever see the thing. Several people have pointed out that he seems uneasy rather than displaying the confident and aggressive presence that Nazarbayev must have thought he was buying. He looks ashamed of it. As he should be.

The video, entitled *In the Stirrups of Time* and made by Kazakh satellite channel Caspionet, features photos and moving footage of the President and the country and clips of interviews with international business figures and Kazakh ministers.[3] Blair is also filmed sitting at a long table at Nazarbayev's right-hand side, a position normally reserved for subservient ministers. Blair performed the same publicist role in a speech in Astana in May 2012. This is reported on Blair's website – which does not make clear to whom the speech was made. It puffs up the President again, though in slightly more measured tones:

> The opportunity and the challenge for Kazakhstan in this changing global landscape is very clear. Over the past twenty years since emerging from the Soviet Union, Kazakhstan has grown its income per head of population more than tenfold, taking it from Third World to Second World status, a remarkable achievement. On that day of independence in 1991, it was the world's fourth-largest nuclear-weapons power and it has since renounced and dismantled them, a great example to the world, as President Obama recently noted …
>
> However, the challenge is also clear. As Kazakhstan moves to the next level of development – economic, social and political – it has to

evolve and reform. This is the pattern the world over and also part of that changing geopolitical landscape …

The value to Nazarbayev is buying both Blair's reputation as a moderniser and his connections, even if these are growing colder with each new assignment he acquires. But Blair appears to show the way forward, appears to be impatient with those who block change, appears to be able to sell and fix images.

In his role as a door opener, especially to the British political scene, Blair's hand was seen in the visit made by David Cameron, the first by a sitting British head of government to Kazakhstan. In the course of the visit, which took place on 30 June 2013, Nazarbayev reputedly quipped, in answer to a question about human rights raised by Cameron, that he would have voted for him if he had a vote in Britain.

We see Blair's role as reputation builder and fixer for the unacceptable face of Kazakhstan in glorious Technicolor following the previously discussed killing of at least fifteen striking workers on 16 December 2011. As described above, the massacre was perpetrated by Kazakh police on oil workers at the western town of Zhanaozen and was prompted by unpaid wages and poor working conditions.

The President was apparently beside himself about the damage that would be done to the country's reputation. Nazarbayev was preparing to give a speech at the University of Cambridge that month and wanted a form of words to explain the blot on his record, so sought the advice of Blair. Blair wrote a letter to Nazarbayev in July 2012 on notepaper headed 'Office of Tony Blair' suggesting the President insert several key passages into the speech in order for it to be acceptable to the 'Western media'.

The letter (reported in the *Daily Telegraph*) stated,

Dear Mr President, here is a suggestion for a paragraph to include in the Cambridge speech. I think it best to meet head on the Zhanaozen issue. The fact is you have made changes following it; but in any event these events, tragic though they were, *should not obscure the enormous progress that Kazakhstan has made. Dealing with it* [the massacre] *in the way I suggest, is the best way for the western media. It will also serve as a quote that can be used in the future setting out the basic case for Kazakhstan* [emphasis added].

The *Telegraph* reported that Blair enclosed two paragraphs of about five hundred words for Nazarbayev to insert into his speech. The newspaper said, 'The words written by Mr Blair but spoken by Mr Nazarbayev with some changes were widely picked up at the time. They were used to portray Mr Nazarbayev as a visionary leader who had improved living standards in his homeland.'

In his delivered speech Nazarbayev gave the Blair script, saying, 'These are questions of democracy and human rights, which must be properly addressed and have energy devoted to them … I understand and hear what is being said of us by our critics. But we would like this to be done with a certain sense of balance and an objective valuation of the achievements of my country.'

Blair's letter to Nazarbayev ended with his offering 'very best wishes', saying, 'I look forward to seeing you in London! Yours ever, Tony Blair.'

Blair's letter congratulating the regime on making 'enormous progress' was written just a few months after the show trial began of thirty-seven workers and political activists who were arrested following the massacre. They were accused of participating in mass unrest, the destruction and theft of private property and the use of force against government representatives. Thirteen defendants received multi-year prison terms, with one, Roza Tuletaeva, receiving a sentence of seven years in a prison colony from which she was eventually released in November 2014. Sixteen defendants were given suspended sentences, and five were convicted but pardoned. Just three of those on trial were acquitted.

What we do know is that Blair has many fine words of advice that the President is both happy to have spoken by his consultant and equally happy to ignore himself. In this vein, Blair told Astana university students in 2012,

> The status quo is not an option. There has to be the development of proper systems of democratic participation, with competitive political parties; a responsible but free press; adherence to its hard-won reputation for religious tolerance; judicial and other reforms to enhance the rule of law; and an attack not just on corruption but on the systems in areas like public procurement that sustain it. The recent events at Zhanaozen, with the sharp focus on issues to do with human rights and single-industry towns, emphasise the need for systems that instil confidence. All of these issues have been widely canvassed in speeches and statements by President Nazarbayev and in the interaction with the EU, US and other countries who wish Kazakhstan well and want to see a process of steady political evolution put in place. The challenge is actually to do the reforms – to do them sensibly, preserving the core stability of the country; but do them also in such a way that the reform programme shows a decisive direction of travel.

Blair will frequently refer to the strength of the country's economy, noting that in the twenty-five years since Kazakhstan set up a separate country, its commercial sector has grown dramatically. But Kazakhstan is rich in natural resources such as coal, gas and precious metals, so the collapse in the oil price and in precious metals and commodities will hit it badly. In 2013, Kazakhstan had a gross domestic product of $149 billion and a population of 16.3 million. This is minuscule for a country whose land area is greater than that of Western Europe. In the video mentioned above, *In the Stirrups of Time*, Blair talks about the country's 'extraordinary economic potential'.

Ken Olisa, the former nonexecutive director of ENRC, the Kazakh energy company that was shamed into leaving the London financial market after disclosures of alleged corruption, has noted that 'every element in the periodic table lies under the Kazakh soil.'[4] While prices lie low and the country's economic system is dogged by corruption and bureaucracy, those metals will stay where they are, rather than benefiting the Kazakh people.

While part of Blair's role in Kazakhstan is making the President look good, part is what may be called 'networking'. That is finding and making friends and putting his friends together, on the basis that they will reward him as well as themselves. Hence, we see him putting the Crown Prince of Abu Dhabi with Nazarbayev. It is rumoured that Nazarbayev has invested much of his personal wealth in the oil-rich state.

Sources in Astana have told the *Daily Telegraph* that Nazarbayev has given the Abu Dhabi royal family a ninety-nine-year lease on a huge hunting reserve in the south of Kazakhstan, and the Arab leader has reciprocated with a luxury home on an island off the Gulf coast. President Nazarbayev has been a guest of honour at the Abu Dhabi Grand Prix. As a result of the contact, a regular flight has been established between the two countries. Tony Blair the fixer will have been appreciated.

Blair's contribution to the President is his capacity to buy influence, says Steve LeVine, author of *The Oil and the Glory*, a book about corruption in Kazakhstan. 'Think about the contacts that you get with a former British prime minister. Why wouldn't he want them if he can have them?'

Blair also has a role as matchmaker for friends and clients. This long preceded his consultancy, when he was still Prime Minister, but one might speculate that he had his eye on a future commercial relationship. How else to explain Blair's facilitating the link-up between Sir Dick Evans, the former chairman of the UK defence firm BAE Systems – a company that had been investigated for bribery in Saudi Arabia – and Nazarbayev while the Kazakh was on a state visit to the UK? BAE systems was run by Evans. Two years after Evans ceased to be chairman, Lord Goldsmith, the Attorney General during Blair's administration between 2001 and 2007, pulled the investigation by the Serious Fraud Office into bribes involving the Al-Yamama contract, for $40 billion worth of military plane sales to Saudi Arabia. Blair cited the threat by Saudi Arabia to withhold intelligence about Middle Eastern terrorism from the UK as the reason for closing down the investigation.

Blair answered Nazarbayev's need for an industrialist by putting him together with Evans and, in 2006, the bluff northerner became chairman of the Kazakh state holding company, Samruk, which owns most of the major companies in the country, including the national rail and postal service, the state oil and gas company, the state uranium company, the airline Air Astana and numerous financial groups. In 2008 Evans was replaced as chairman, while remaining the 'independent' director. Evans oversaw the restructuring of Air Astana for the Kazakh government in 2005 using the services of the consultancy McKinsey, with BAE having a significant minority shareholding in the company.

Evans told the *Spectator* magazine in February 2008, 'I was introduced to Nazarbayev on one of his early trips to the UK by Tony Blair while I was still at BAE.' That meeting led to BAE helping to restructure aviation in Kazakhstan and taking 50 per cent of Air Astana, which is a joint venture with Samruk-Kazyna, the country's sovereign wealth fund and investment agency. 'The President was pressing hard for me to come, and he wore me down. I was over here on a review of the airline, we had lunch at the palace and he said, "We want to talk to you again about Samruk," and there and then at that lunch, after a previous nine months' warm-up, I said, "Fine, OK, I'll do it." I don't think I could've said yes had I not seen a lot of them and got to know them quite well.'

Evans is less than flattering about the country's top officials. 'It's a lot easier for guys like myself to question the very senior people here about why they are doing something in a particular way. The whole culture here, for local people, is not to do that. When you go down underneath the top level of government, there's what you might call a permafrost of the Soviet bureaucracy which is alive and very well.' Evans was re-elected as an independent director on the Samruk board in January 2014.

It's not clear what 'reforms' or 'progress' Blair constantly refers to. In 2011 Samruk-Kazyna hired Lord Mandelson, architect of Blair's election victories, to give two speeches at its events. At one of the conferences in Astana, in October 2010, Mandelson reportedly lavished praise on Samruk-Kazyna, saying, 'I want to stress a special role [it] played as a saviour of the world economy.'

Blair's overall goal is to assist Kazakh President Nazarbayev in presenting his country as modern and dynamic. The moderniser who understands international markets and the challenges emerging countries face will lend allure to the little-known '-stan', made famous by Borat, in the person of actor-comedian Sasha Baron Cohen, as lingering in the dark ages. In the public mind, Kazakhstan is easily confused with Azerbaijan, Kyrgyzstan, Turkmenistan, Uzbekistan. The common thread between all these '-stans' is their addiction to despots. These leaders enabled them to surface as independent states from the Soviet Union, but they would be an obstacle to their becoming members of the wider global community. Jonathan Aitken, the writer of a fawning biography of Nazarbayev, *Nazarbayev and the Making of Kazakhstan*, recalls in his book a press conference in November 2006, when the British Prime Minister and the President stood side by side in Downing Street, and Nazarbayev was evidently discomfited by the Borat caricature. When asked to comment, he said, 'The film was created by a comedian, so let's laugh at it … any publicity is good publicity.'[5]

CLAIMS AND COUNTERCLAIMS

Messages claiming to evoke morality emanated from Kazakhstan long before Blair came to the aid of the party. The President, for example, has sought to trumpet his country's religious freedom. He has also boasted about its modernity. One has only to make the journey to the extraordinary recently built political capital of Astana, with its raft of glass-and-concrete buildings. The British architect Norman Foster was part of a team that designed what became a new city. It includes the world's largest tent, the 150-metre-high Khan Shatyr, trumpeted by a leading architectural paper as 'a spectacular architectural and engineering achievement'. The building was designed by Foster + Partners, the well-known architectural practice of Lord Norman Foster. The message is one of hubristic pride at any price, paid for out of the country's massive oil revenues.

Coupled with the modernity and excess is the claim to be tolerant of religious diversity. Nazarbayev even commissioned a £36 million Palace of Peace and Reconciliation, designed by Foster, where religious leaders from around the world could meet and find common ground. The rhetoric does not connect with the reality.

In October 2011, the *Independent* reported that human-rights activists in Kazakhstan were observing an increasingly hostile attitude towards religious groups, and raised serious questions about Nazarbayev's recruitment of Tony Blair as an adviser.[6] Nongovernmental organisations such as Amnesty International and Human Rights Watch, on the other hand, have called on Blair to use his role in Kazakhstan to put pressure on Nazarbayev to stop repression of religious communities and to implement democratic reforms rather than simply to polish the image of an increasingly autocratic state.

Blair's office told journalist Ken Silverstein that he is 'supporting the development of the reforms' under way and that, while he was 'well aware of the criticisms made of the Kazakhstan government … there are also visible signs of progress'. Local journalists seeing the reality of life in the country and who live under Nazarbayev's yoke dispute this vehemently.

Strangely, perhaps, for a country that has the founder of the Tony Blair Faith Foundation as a consultant, Kazakhstan is less than friendly to its Christian minority, although most pressure is exerted on its Muslim minorities, some of whom are revealing alarming fundamentalist tendencies, not something favoured by its President. In a move marking a reversal from claimed religious toleration, in 2011 Nazarbayev proposed a law that was later adopted by the parliament imposing stringent restrictions on religious practices. Religious groups were required to reregister or face closure. The initiative was explained as an attempt to combat Islamic extremism. However, under the new law many minority religious groups, including many Christians, were deemed illegal. In order to exist on a local level, a group must have more than fifty members; on a regional level, more than five hundred; on the national level, more than five thousand. It is estimated that two-thirds of currently existing religious groups have been forced to close down. 'Kazakhstan has repeatedly gone through the motions of introducing restrictions on religion during the two decades since it gained independence. Those efforts have been routinely quashed in the final stages amid vocal international criticism,' wrote Peter Leonard, in the *Huffington Post* in September 2011.

Activists say that minority groups consistently face harassment. 'This new law has simply legalised the current practice … of persecuting unregistered minority religious groups and limiting missionary activity,' said rights activist Ninel Fokina, head of the Almaty Helsinki Committee as quoted in the *World Post* in September 2011. Fokina said authorities had been openly speaking about the need for a purge in the religious sphere. 'I believe that out of the 4,500 religious groups currently in existence, barely 1,500 will remain,' she said. Fokina said the new rules would also greatly complicate the life of even relatively large Christian Protestant communities, such as Lutherans, Baptists, Seventh-day Adventists and Jehovah's Witnesses.

Nazarbayev's repressive activity contradicts Blair's claim in the video *In the Stirrups of Time*, where Blair is filmed saying, 'It's a country that is almost unique I would say in its cultural diversity and the way it brings different faiths together, and cultures together. In the work that I do there, I've found them really smart people, capable, very determined and very proud of their country.'

WHAT EXTERNAL AGENTS COMMENT ON BLAIR IN KAZAKHSTAN

Few people are fooled by Blair's claims and Nazarbayev's boasts. Criticism has followed Blair's role in Kazakhstan. This has come not least from those inside the country.

In January 2012, fifty-two Kazakh youth activists urged Blair to back away from this deal in the opposition newspaper *Respublika*, after the massacre of at least fifteen oil workers referred to above. They told Blair that 'the leadership of Kazakhstan in peacetime opened fire on unarmed citizens. Such methods have been the bloody practice in our country as soon as you became an adviser to President Nursultan Nazarbayev.' Their letter was headed 'Blood of the people on your hands, Blair.'

'You are an adviser to the leadership of Kazakhstan on political issues. Why in the last seven months has power been deaf to the demands of oil workers?' demanded the letter, published on 28 December. 'And now it has opened fire on its citizens. Many were killed and many more are missing.'

None of the fifty-two people who signed the letter were well-known opposition leaders. The authorities responded by saying that police feared for their lives and even then they only fired into the air.

As the number of voices calling for Blair to intervene increases, one would expect that the pressure he feels to encourage Nazarbayev to make democratic reforms does too. Whether he ever attempts to guide the President away from repression, we cannot, of course, know. Bloomberg has called Mr Blair's consultancy in Kazakhstan his 'most controversial, and potentially most lucrative'.

DOES BLAIR GIVE VALUE FOR MONEY?

Blair may be a consummate moderniser and builder of images but are his efforts in Kazakhstan bearing fruit? Cynics, of which there is no shortage inside the country and outside, will say that, as long as Kazakh oil keeps flowing, enabling his bills to get paid, he will remain the salesman of the unacceptable.

Kairat Abusseitov, Kazakhstan's ambassador to Britain, quoted in the *Daily Telegraph*, 29 October 2011, has said,

The former British Prime Minister acts as an adviser to the

Government of Kazakhstan. He [President of Kazakhstan] is relying on Mr Blair and his key advisers to help him show how he is reforming his country and also to emphasise the key strategic and intelligence role his country played during the wars in Iraq and Afghanistan. He hopes they will help him highlight his role encouraging the United Nations General Assembly to adopt August 29 as the International Day Against Nuclear Tests and his initiative to hold two international forums of world and traditional religions in Astana to foster mutual co-operation between faiths.

The former Prime Minister brings years of experience and we have benefited significantly from his strategic vision and deep understanding of the global economy as well as effective government and international policy making.

The project is supporting the reforms the Government is making aimed at furthering democracy, strengthening the rule of law and improving the economic environment in Kazakhstan.'

This is quite odd. The ambassador seems to be saying that Blair is there to burnish the President's image, to 'help him show how he is reforming his country', to 'emphasise the key strategic and intelligence role his country played during the wars in Iraq and Afghanistan', to 'help him highlight his role' in peace and religious-tolerance initiatives. Blair himself, however, describing his role there in a 2012 speech, spoke in very different terms: 'The work my team does within the Policy Advisory Group, and outside experts, focuses on areas such as decentralisation, public procurement, judicial and other reforms to do with the rule of law, precisely those types of things identified by the EU and others as necessary for Kazakhstan's future development. It is important for Kazakhstan that the reform programme set out by President Nazarbayev succeeds. It is important for the world.'

So whose version do we believe? Blair, who says he is doing policy work, or the Ambassador, who says Blair is there to burnish the President's image?

There will be those who point to the closeness between Kazakhstan's wealthy and the British aristocracy and power elite as a sign of a triumph for Blair and his entourage. Rich Kazakhs are increasingly present in London, not least through Prince Andrew, who counts the glamorous energy tycoon Goga Ashkenazi – who lives in a £28 million house in Holland Park, west London – among his friends. She has a young son with Timur Kulibayev, the Kazakh tycoon who bought Prince Andrew's former home Sunninghill Park for £15 million. It has been widely speculated that this was a very generous price for the property, a fact denied by the parties to the deal. Kulibayev also reportedly spent £44 million on a row of four houses in Belgravia, central London. Kulibayev is said to control 90 per cent of the Kazakh oilfields.[7] He stands accused of money laundering, but cannot be prosecuted, having been given immunity in 2011.[8]

The modernisation of Kazakhstan has been a constant preoccupation of the President, and Blair has discussed with Nazarbayev at Davos how the country can meet its 2050 target of putting Kazakhstan into the group of the world's top thirty developed economies. A local press report of the talks said that 'consultation [presumably with Blair] would play an important role' in achieving this target. London is expected to be the financial hub for future Kazakh companies seeking international capital. The country has the challenge of explaining the ignominy of the departure of Eurasian Natural Resources from London amid a corruption scandal. Perhaps Blair will be involved in showing how that happened and why the country's companies have learned their lessons.

The severest criticism has come from Labour supporters who once believed in Blair. Mike Harris, for example, a former Labour political adviser and strong supporter of Tony Blair as PM, even during the Iraq War, feels a sharp sense of betrayal at Blair's activities on behalf of dictators, and especially Nazarbayev. He told us, 'The man who ushered in the post-Westphalian era, the anti-Kissinger who prevented the genocide of Kosovan Muslims and defended the rights of Sierra Leoneans, is now the counsel of oil-rich dictators.' Harris widens his attack to any connections the former Prime Minister makes with other nondemocratic countries. 'Any association, however tangential, with our politicians, is hugely symbolic for authoritarian regimes in helping them legitimise their rule within their countries. That Blair is involved is deeply depressing. The majority of despots are not household names – for a reason. Well-paid lobbyists tempt journalists over to write puff pieces on the burgeoning tourism trade. Or outfits like the European Azerbaijan Society use MPs like Mark Field or Mike Gapes to help promote the country's interests with little reference to human rights violations.'

BLAIR IN AZERBAIJAN

The promise of a role in Azerbaijan's energy boom may be what drew Tony Blair to a country whose President, Ilham Aliyev, locks up his critics and shuts down newspapers. We learn from a WikiLeaked cable in January 2010 that 'observers in Baku, the capital of Azerbaijan, often note that today's Azerbaijan is run in a manner similar to the feudalism found in Europe during the Middle Ages: a handful of well-connected families control certain geographic areas, as well as certain sectors of the economy.'

Blair's interest appears to have been the Southern Gas corridor pipeline, which runs from Azerbaijan through Turkey and across the Mediterranean Sea to Italy. This pipeline, which frees European countries from Russian control of gas distribution, involves Azerbaijan, Turkey, Georgia, Turkmenistan, Kazakhstan, Iraq, Egypt, Uzbekistan and Iran. The pipeline is expected to bring at least 60 billion cubic metres of gas to Europe and is now in the process of being built. One source described the pipeline as 'one of the most complex gas value chains ever developed in the world. Stretching over 3,500 kilometres, crossing seven countries and involving more than a dozen major energy companies, it is comprised of several separate energy projects representing a total investment of approximately US$45 billion.'[9]

It is understood that Blair is involved with an organisation known as the Southern Corridor Advisory Council, whose key interest is protecting

Western emerging and construction companies. The Southern Corridor Advisory Council has three directors, namely Blair, Peter Sutherland and Hans Genscher.

Blair appears here to be acting as a representative – whether formal or informal is not clear – of the British government, one of whose largest energy corporations, BP, is building the project in conjunction with a number of other European companies. Alan Riley, professor of law at London's City University and an expert in international energy law, says that Blair is protecting 'the strategic interest of the British state who regard the pipeline as a "key element in their energy security".' This coincides with the discreet involvement in the committee of Peter Sutherland, a former executive chairman of BP and former chairman of Goldman Sachs. Hans Dietrich Genscher, a former German foreign minister, is thought to be protecting the interests of the German companies participating in the construction of the pipeline.

Azerbaijan has had an allure for Blair since 2009, when he visited the country and met the President. He observed that Aliyev had a 'very positive and exciting vision for the future of the country'. It was noted in the course of a diplomatic cable in 2009 that Azeri foreign policy had a 'helpful bias toward integration with the West'. The same could not be said of the President's internal practice.

Azerbaijan's big presidential election in 2013, according to the *Washington Post*, was 'anticipated to be neither free nor fair'. During the election campaign, President Aliyev, who took over from his father ten years previously, stepped up intimidation of activists and journalists, and they complained about free-speech restrictions and one-sided state media coverage. The BBC's headline for its story on the election read 'Azerbaijan election: the pre-determined president'.[10]

But, said the *Washington Post* on 9 October 2013,

> ... one expects a certain ritual in these sorts of authoritarian elections, a fealty to at least the appearance of democracy, if not democracy

itself. So it was a bit awkward when Azerbaijan's election authorities released vote results – a full day before voting had even started.

The vote counts – spoiler alert: Aliyev was shown as heading toward a landslide – were pushed out on an official smartphone app run by the Central Election Commission. It showed Aliyev as 'winning' 72.76 per cent of the votes, although with only about 15,000 votes cast, as Azerbaijani officials later noted as part of their defense that the results had been partial and a test run. That share is on track with his official vote counts in previous elections: he won ('won'?) 76.84 per cent of the vote in 2003 and 87 per cent in 2008.[11]

This has not fazed Blair, who has visited the country to make well-remunerated speeches for politicians who are close to Aliyev. He was reported to receive £100,000 for one speech in the country. The country has also been a generous supporter of a Westminster-based pressure group called the European Azerbaijan Society.

The final piece of Blair's Central Asian portfolio is Mongolia, where he is reported to have burgeoning business interests. Blair has indeed signed a contract to advise the country's leaders on 'good governance'. Mongolia is a landlocked country, bordered by Russia to the north and China to the south, east and west. Ulaanbaatar, the capital and also the largest city, is home to about 45 per cent of the population.

It was a dirt-poor nation, but it is about to become more like a conventional Blair client – very rich, thanks to vast copper and gold mines in the Gobi Desert.

Wherever one looks in Blair's portfolio of business interests, one encounters the same problem: potential conflicts of interest. When Blair sits on the board of the Southern Corridor Advisory Council is he rooting for Britain – as you might expect a former prime minister to be – or is he rooting for Blair and hoping to receive a fee from a commercial interest such as an oil company? Conflicts in Kazakhstan are not dissimilar: when Blair uses contacts he has made as Prime Minister to promote the interests of a dictatorship – albeit not the world's worst – should the remuneration be scrutinised by the British state that he served? Perhaps the cash-strapped state that Blair led to economic crisis deserves a portion of his earnings.

In any event, the shameless deference Blair shows to politicians who flout every democratic principle and lock up opponents and who are brazenly corrupt is sharply at odds with values he once espoused. Blair's nonchalance about the claims of the striking miners mown down by Kazakh police sits uncomfortably with a man who once laid claim to principle. Autocrats claim the right to use their looted money to buy what advice they can. The seller of such advice must be regarded as a public-relations agent for a disreputable client.

Where Blair is conflicted out of the market is that he wants to be seen as principled to some audiences – namely the Middle Eastern parties – and a mere salesman of messages to another – namely a bunch of corrupt dictators. Cynicism of that kind infects each and every Blair enterprise. Not least his offer of help to Asia's international pariah regime.

CHAPTER SIX

BURMA'S MILITARY GOVERNMENT CALL IN BLAIR

'Blair doesn't seem to have bothered to meet any grassroots or human rights groups before meeting Thein Sein and government representatives.'
– MARK FARMANER OF BURMA CAMPAIGN UK.

One of the many dictators to benefit from Blair's advice is the Burmese military, though it is not paying for it – yet, anyway. In October 2012 the former PM turned up on a quiet visit to Burma with colleagues from TBA, and the British ambassador joined him in his meetings with government ministers.

The Burmese newspaper *The New Light of Myanmar* reported that Blair had 'led a delegation' to Burma, and spoke with the lower house speaker Shwe Mann. It said they discussed 'cooperation in bilateral ties' and parliamentary affairs. The British Embassy said Blair was there on behalf of the Office of Tony Blair – interestingly, not for one of his charities (which would suggest *pro bono* work) and not for TBA (which would suggest paid work), but for the 'Office', which covers everything he does. It looks as though, at that stage, Blair had not decided whether Burma was a potential client for TBA, or a potential case for assistance from the Tony Blair Faith Foundation, or something else.

He was there again in March 2013, according to information obtained from the Foreign Office under the Freedom of Information Act by the

Burma Campaign UK. He met the Vice President Nyan Tun (former commander-in-chief of the navy) and Minister Soe Thein (another former naval commander-in-chief) at the presidential palace in Naypyidaw, the new capital.

The trip was not publicised, but news got out to the independent *Irrawaddy Journal*. When the newspaper approached Blair's office, a spokesperson said, 'At the present time we are simply having wide-ranging discussions with the [Burmese] government on the development of the country because Mr Blair is interested in it.'

He was there for a third time on 3–4 August 2013, and this time he was not accompanied by the ambassador or any of the Embassy staff when he saw the President and other government officials – he had only his own aides with him. This meeting came just a fortnight after Burmese President, General Thein Sein, was in London to meet Prime Minister David Cameron.

This timing cannot have been accidental. It tells us that, at any rate, one of the matters on which Blair is advising Thein Sein is his relationship with Britain, and probably with the West generally. During 2014, journalists who know Burma well noticed that Thein Sein was behaving in a far more sophisticated and media-savvy way with the international community, and have speculated that he is getting advice from someone.

'He's much better with foreign governments and much better with their media than he used to be,' says one close observer. 'He has pre-prepared messages for the media. When he is asked a question that isn't answered by one of his pre-prepared messages, he gives one of these messages anyway. He's been getting some training from somewhere.'

The old team has assembled in Burma. Jonathan Powell has turned up, training politicians in peace-making. He has arranged for Burmese political figures to visit Northern Ireland to meet the IRA and learn how they made peace – an idea suggested to the UK government by the Burma Campaign UK, but the Campaign has now been shut out and Powell entrusted with the implementation. One of Blair's staff, Shruti Mehrotra, is working with one of the Burmese ministers, Soe Thein.

Mehrotra is one of those bright young people whom Blair inherited from his friends in the Monitor Group (see Chapter 4). It is also the same consultancy that provided both of Blair's men in the Emir of Kuwait's office as well as Blair's 'government consultant' covering Dubai and its neighbour Abu Dhabi. Blair began to use Monitor staff in 2008. For a while, TBA and Monitor had a very close relationship. But, in November 2012, Monitor was unable to pay its bills and was forced to file for bankruptcy protection – we shall revisit this episode in the chapter on Libya.

Mehrotra has also managed humanitarian relief for international NGOs and worked for the World Economic Forum. Her first job for Blair was as his representative in Guinea.

Mark Farmaner at Burma Campaign UK says, 'Blair doesn't seem to have bothered to meet any grassroots or human rights groups before meeting Thein Sein and government representatives.'[1] What his motives are for courting Burma's leaders are unclear, for, as Farmaner notes, 'As Prime Minister, Tony Blair showed little interest in Burma.' He promised to introduce tougher sanctions when campaigning for office, but backtracked once in government. 'The most we got was a bland three-line statement on [Burmese opposition politician and democracy leader] Aung San Suu Kyi's birthday,' says Farmaner.[2]

Now he is taking an interest, and the reason is, like most things Blair does, a closely guarded secret. Zoya Phan, one of the Burmese staff of Burma Campaign UK, wrote three times in 2013 to Blair's office on the campaign's behalf, and got no reply.

The fourth time, a letter arrived in reply, which is an exemplar of the Tony Blair way of dealing with requests for information. The address on the notepaper was a PO box, and there was no signature nor even a name at the bottom – it was merely 'signed' 'The Office of Tony Blair'. It was dated November 2013, rather than with an exact date. It read,

Dear Ms Phan

Thank you for getting in touch with your own [sic] enquiry and please accept our apologies for the delayed response.

Tony Blair takes a keen interest in the region. During his visits to Myanmar, he has met a number of political figures, including Ministers and Aung San Suu Kyi, to discuss politics, reform and global issues.

We are currently carrying out governance work on a short term basis, supporting the government to build delivery mechanisms to help deliver their long term strategic goals. This work is being carried out on a *pro bono* basis and is very similar to the work that Mr Blair does in Africa for one of his charities, the Africa Governance Initiative.

> Yours sincerely
> The Office of Tony Blair

'We are currently carrying out governance work on a short[-]term basis, supporting the government to build delivery mechanisms to help deliver their long[-]term strategic goals' is a masterpiece of drafting, designed to give not one scrap of information away. What work? What mechanisms? What strategic goals? Do these goals perhaps involve some moves to democracy, or do they involve finding ways of burnishing the image of the existing undemocratic regime?

Is Blair, as Farmaner hopes, going to try to avert what many observers think is impending genocide? The Burma Campaign, said Farmaner, hoped at first that Blair was there 'on behalf of his Faith Foundation, perhaps in response to the recent anti-Muslim and anti-Rohingya [an ethnic group] nationalism from some Burmese Buddhists. However, he hasn't met with any Rohingya representatives before meeting the government or others, which seems strange.'[3]

The Tony Blair Faith Foundation does take some limited interest in what is happening to the Rohingya. According to its spokesperson, 'We examine all sorts of aspects of religious dynamics in foreign policy and conflicts around the world through our Faith and Globalisation course, run in 23 universities. This includes looking at a wide range of conflicts with a religious dimension such as in Myanmar, where Muslims are facing persecution.' But the issue does not seem to form any part of Blair's intentions in his many visits to the country. So is Blair in Burma, as Farmaner fears, to 'help Thein Sein make the transition from being a pariah dictatorship to being a normal dictatorship'?

Nine out of ten of Burma's 53 million people are Buddhists, including the current president and all heads of state. The generals who imprisoned Aung San Suu Kyi after she won the 1989 election were Buddhists, and the Burmese who stand to profit from the economic opening of the country (a powerful group of military-backed businessmen known as the 'cronies') are nearly all Buddhists. The opposition party, the National League for Democracy, is led almost entirely by Buddhists, and its leader, Aung San Suu Kyi, is famously devout.[4]

In May 2012, three Muslims allegedly raped and murdered a Buddhist girl in southern Arakan.[5] On 4 June , Buddhists stopped a bus and invited non-Muslims to get off. Then they let the bus go on a short distance, stopped it again, dragged about ten Muslim passengers onto the street, and beat them to death.[6]

After that, Buddhists launched coordinated attacks against Muslim neighbourhoods and villages all over Arakan state. Many Muslims were killed. Most of the displaced are in dozens of squalid camps across Arakan state. The penalty for leaving these camps is three months' imprisonment – if a Rohingya is caught by the police. If caught by the wrong civilians, it could be lynching.[7]

The Buddhists burned the Muslims' abandoned homes and possessions. Some Muslims retaliated, and a much smaller number of Buddhists died or were driven into camps of their own after riots across the state. The government has not taken any sort of lead to stop this.

Is this an occasion when the Tony Blair Faith Foundation can start to fulfil what it claims to be its main purpose, and teach those of different faiths to live together in mutual respect? Is Blair there to try to pave the way for democracy, and for the generals to stand down?

Such evidence as we have been able to find suggests neither of these things. It suggests rather that he is assisting the generals to burnish their international image.

Which is very bad news indeed, because former General Thein Sein is a particularly brutal tyrant, even by the standards of Blair clients. Burma's military-backed government has one of the worst human-rights records in the world, and Thein Sein has been personally named in a UN report for human-rights abuses. The Burmese army rapes, loots, burns, tortures and kills. Forced labour is commonplace and the many political prisoners are routinely tortured. The army has child soldiers and uses rape as a weapon against ethnic minorities.

Aung San Suu Kyi spent more than fifteen years under house arrest. Her party, the National League for Democracy, won 82 per cent of the seats in elections held in 1990, but the army refused to transfer power to her. A year after she was released, during a tour of northern Burma in 2003, Aung San Suu Kyi and her supporters were attacked by the Union Solidarity and Development Association (USDA), a government-sponsored militia. Seventy people were killed and more than a hundred were arrested, including Aung San Suu Kyi.

A rigged election was held in November 2010, and a new parliament was created, dominated by pro-military parties, in which the military have 25 per cent of the seats. A clause in the constitution bars anyone from being president who has a child who is not a Burmese citizen – a clause obviously inserted to bar Aung San Suu Kyi, whose son holds British citizenship.

As any change to the constitution requires a majority of more than 75 per cent, the military can veto any efforts in Parliament to try to make the constitution more democratic. Real power lies with the President, the Commander-in-Chief and the new National Defence and Security Council, who are not accountable to Parliament.

Many of the most serious abuses, such as rape, torture, executions, forced labour, use of child soldiers and deliberate targeting of civilians by the Burmese Army since the government broke the ceasefire in Kachin State, have happened after Thein Sein became President in 2011.

As far as the British government is concerned, is Blair a standard bearer or an embarrassment? Derek Tonkin, a former British ambassador to Burma, is of the opinion that he is more of the latter than the former. He notes that the British ambassador was not photographed with Blair in any official record of the visits, indicating that they were private. Tonkin says that Blair may still have received help from the Brititish ambassador with logistics and contacts, but he doubts whether Blair's visits to Burma would be particularly welcome to Whitehall.

The present Government has been remarkably proactive in developing its engagement with the civilianized government in Myanmar and would not want or need any particular input from Tony Blair, who has never taken a strong interest in the country. On matters like the peace process, civil and political rights in Myanmar, the UK's Conservative Government would wish to keep this under their control, though to the extent that Tony Blair was historically involved in the peace process in Northern Ireland, he might have been invited to attend background talks when Burmese Ministers came to London. He would also no doubt as a courtesy have given the Government a brief account of any salient points arising from his visits.

The motive for Blair's visits to this political pariah remains murky. The best guess is that he sees the opportunity to parlay his expertise in image rebuilding to assist a client manifestly in dire need of some cosmetic surgery. The path is open for the prime-minister-as-public-relations man to develop this assignment into a big earner.

A LUCRATIVE KOREAN JOB

Asia provided some wealth-making opportunities for the former prime minister. One was rather lucrative. His appointment to a paid job advising a consortium of investors led by South Korean energy giant UI Energy Corporation in August 2008 stayed under wraps for two years. It came to light in 2010, two years later, when we examined the Advisory Committee on Business Appointments (ACOBA) records. This was the same source that disclosed Blair's Kuwait contract.

UI Energy is one of the biggest investors in Iraq's oil-rich Kurdistan region, which became semi-autonomous in the wake of the Iraq War.[8] It also has extensive interests in the US. What exactly Blair did for the company has never been revealed.

UI Energy, like the UAE's Mubadala, another Blair client, bought up Iraqi oilfields following the Iraq War. These contracts were kept secret by ACOBA. Blair repeatedly claimed to the committee, which assesses jobs taken up by former ministers, that the existence of the deal had to be kept secret at the request of the South Koreans because of 'market sensitivities'.[9]

This claim was first made by Blair in July 2008, when the committee agreed to break its normal rules and postpone publication for three months. In October, Blair's office went back to the committee and asked for a further six months. It promised to let the committee know as soon as the 'market sensitivity' had passed. But it never did.

ACOBA had to chase up Blair's office, and the deal was at last made public in 2010, when the former prime minister was overruled by the chairman of ACOBA, Ian Lang, the former president of the Board of Trade in John Major's government, even though Blair was still claiming the deal was still too sensitive to reveal. About the same time came the news that UI's CEO had been imprisoned for fraud

Blair's fee has not been disclosed, either. A persistent rumour that it was

£1 million is as likely to be an underestimate as an overestimate. When the deal was announced, the then-Tory MP Douglas Carswell, quoted in the *Daily Mail* on 19 March 2010, said, 'It seems that the former Prime Minister of the United Kingdom has been in the pay of a very big foreign oil corporation and we have been kept in the dark about it.

'Even now we do not know what he was paid or what the company got out of it. We need that information now. This is revolving-door politics at its worst. It's not as if Mr Blair has even stepped back from politics, because he is still politically active in the Middle East.'

Liberal Democrat MP Norman Baker said, 'These revelations show that our former Prime Minister is for sale – he is driven by making as much money as possible. I think many people will find it deeply insensitive that he is apparently cashing in on his contacts from the Iraq War to make money for himself.'[10]

Subsequently the CEO of UI Energy, Kyu-Sun Choi, was jailed for bribery in one of his country's most notorious corruption scandals.[11] He made illegal payments to influence the awarding of lucrative contracts to run a national lottery. Korean newspapers have printed pictures of Choi and Blair together, but Blair has refused to say when, or why, he met Choi.

Blair is also advising the China Investment Corporation (CIC), which holds a £700 million share in Thames Water and an £880 million stake in the company that owns Canary Wharf, east London. Thames Water is owned by Kemble Water Holdings, a consortium formed in late 2006 by Australian-based Macquarie Group's European Infrastructure Funds to purchase Thames Water. Other large shareholders in recent years include: the BT Pension Scheme (13%), the Abu Dhabi Investment Authority (9.9%, acquired in 2011) and the China Investment Corporation (8.7%, acquired in 2012). The CIC's investment in Thames Water came a month after the Abu Dhabi Investment Authority (ADIA), a £400 billion sovereign wealth fund, purchased its holding of more than £800 million, in the same company.

Sheik Mohammed bin Zayed al-Nahyan, Crown Prince of Abu Dhabi, is one of ADIA's board directors. He also heads Mubadala, the Abu Dhabi state investment fund, which, as we have seen, employed TBA in 2009. Blair's debt to this sheikh is therefore considerable, for it was the same Sheik Mohammed bin Zayed al-Nahyan who recommended his services to the President of Kazakhstan.

So two sovereign wealth funds known well to Tony Blair made very similar buy-ups of Thames Water at about the same time. The company's board of directors includes Ed Richards, another of the former members of Tony Blair's policy unit at No. 10 – he advised the PM on media, telecoms, the internet and e-government. [12]

Thames Water paid no corporation tax in 2012 despite making profits of more than half a billion pounds. That year the company put up customer bills by 6.7 per cent, awarded its chief executive a £274,000 bonus and made profits of £549 million on a turnover of £1.8 billion. It even managed to get a £5 million credit from the Treasury by writing off investments against the amount it was due to pay the government. [13]

The company's accounts also revealed that it paid £328.2 million interest on 'inter-company loans' to pay external bondholders such as pension funds via a Cayman Islands funding vehicle. [14]

The arrangement is legal; however, the head of industry regulator Ofwat said that the complex tax arrangements and large profits of some water companies were 'morally questionable'. [15]

The CIC is one of the world's largest sovereign wealth funds and oversees part of China's £2 trillion of foreign-exchange reserves. Blair has visited China regularly over many years. His spokesman told the *Daily Telegraph* that Blair and Tony Blair Associates (TBA) 'know CIC well'. But the spokesman denied that they were paid consultants to CIC.

The spokesman also denied claims that Blair had anything to do with advising CIC on its purchase of its 8.68 per cent stake in Thames Water.

The international and increasingly wealthy globe-trotter had a large rolodex of names of potential clients. But no name would prove more sensational and more controversial than that of the late and unlamented Colonel Gadaffi of Libya, whom he embraced with apparent alacrity.

CHAPTER SEVEN

EMBRACING GADDAFI

'Unless Mr Blair can come up with a convincing explanation as to why the Quartet secretariat should have been involved in this visit [to Libya], it would indeed be a reason for legitimate and serious criticism.'
– FORMER FOREIGN SECRETARY MALCOLM RIFKIND.

Papers found in Tripoli after Colonel Muammar Gaddafi's overthrow in 2011 showed that Blair held at least six private meetings with the Libyan dictator in the three years after he left Downing Street, which probably encouraged Gaddafi in his mistaken assumption that the West would not act against him.

As often happens with Blair, it is unclear exactly whom he was representing – even those accompanying him were unclear about that, which led to some bitter recriminations.

Oil may have been a part of it. US oil companies anxious to speed up the pace of rapprochement between Washington and Tripoli had set up a lobbying organisation, which was seeking allies, called the US–Libya Business Association (USLB). The US companies were concerned that European oil companies were getting to Libya ahead of them.[1]

Blair's then head of communications Rachel Grant told Ken Silverstein that the Blair–Gaddafi meetings were 'primarily on the subject of Africa'. But he wrote a note to Gaddafi on Quartet letterhead after one meeting, so did the two men discuss Middle East peace? Or, as sources told the

127

Daily Telegraph, maybe he was there 'sounding out deals for JP Morgan'? Or was he instead sounding out deals for Tony Blair Associates, which might explain why, after one 2008 meeting, he wrote to thank Gaddafi for his 'hospitality during my visit to Libya and for taking the time to meet with me' and to emphasise that he was 'particularly interested in what you said about the funds that will be dedicated to projects in Africa, since you know I am doing a lot of work there and know of good, worthwhile projects for investments.'[2]

At Blair's last meeting with Gaddafi as Prime Minister, a month before his resignation, he was accompanied by BP chairman Peter Sutherland, who subsequently announced the company would return to Libya after a thirty-year absence.

So perhaps oil *was* discussed. It seems certain that investment matters of interest to the bank JP Morgan Chase were discussed.

Tim Collins, the billionaire founder of a Wall Street investment company, Ripplewood Holdings, and a former close friend of Blair, told us, 'I assume what he does for JPM is open doors. He is a complicated character; he is hard not to like. But, when you step back, his business doesn't make much sense to me. The idea that he is giving advice to anyone seems to me a stretch. I have never known much about his business. Whenever he talked about his business, it seemed pie in the sky.'

Five of the meetings with Gaddafi took place in a fourteen-month period before the release of Abdelbaset Ali Mohammed al-Megrahi – the man who went to prison in Scotland accused of being the Lockerbie bomber. On at least two of these occasions Blair flew to Tripoli on a private jet paid for by the Libyan regime.[3]

This did not come out until five years later, in 2013, when the *Daily Telegraph* revealed that, on 2 June 2008, a member of Blair's Quartet staff, Gavin Mackay, wrote on Office of the Quartet Representative-headed paper to Libya's ambassador in London, expressing Blair's gratitude that Libya was providing him with a private jet to fly him from Sierra Leone to Tripoli for a four-hour stopover and then on to the UK.

Former UK Foreign Secretary Malcolm Rifkind commented, 'Unless Mr Blair can come up with a convincing explanation as to why the Quartet secretariat should have been involved in this visit, it would indeed be a reason for legitimate and serious criticism.'[4]

Blair held secret talks with the Colonel in April 2009, four months before al-Megrahi's release. Again he was flown to Libya at Gaddafi's expense, in Gaddafi's private jet. Libya was threatening to cut all business links if al-Megrahi stayed in a British jail.

Blair brought American billionaire Tim Collins to that meeting. Gaddafi seems to have thought Collins was there to advise Gaddafi on building the beach resorts he was planning on the Libyan coast. But a spokesperson for Collins stated, 'Tim was asked to go by Tony Blair in his position as a trustee of Mr Blair's US Faith Foundation.'

In fact, we understand Collins thought he was there to further the Tony Blair Faith Foundation campaign to get bed nets for children in Africa to protect them against malaria; and that they were talking to Gaddafi because he was head of the African Union. Collins was surprised when Blair turned up with some people from JP Morgan in tow.

Whatever the truth, Collins thought Gaddafi quite mad, and has told friends that Blair's deferential attitude towards the dictator made him cringe. Collins himself was clear that he had only come for the Faith Foundation, and to talk about bed nets, but Gaddafi seemed more interested in getting him to help with investment.

As he left, the British ambassador asked Collins if he would help Gaddafi with some business and Collins said that the guy was crazy, and he would not take his money. The beach resort was a non-starter, anyway, because the Libyans would not allow alcohol or gambling at the resorts, apparently. Quite why Blair needed to have with him a trustee of the Tony Blair Faith Foundation is not clear, since bed nets appear hardly to have been discussed, if at all.

Collins, we are told, was never quite sure what Blair had in mind and has told friends that Blair may have set up the meeting for bed nets, but JP Morgan got business from it. Blair, he says, is charismatic; people take his calls, he can set up meetings, as with Gaddafi – but what's it all for?

A friend of Bill Clinton, Tim Collins is no longer a trustee of the Tony Blair Faith Foundation. He is one of the wealthy and well-connected American businessmen on whose advice Blair relied heavily, but he has broken with Blair now.

He is a member of the Yale Divinity School advisory board, and getting to know Collins was one of the benefits that the Yale connection had for Blair. He is also a member of the Yale School of Management board of advisers, and of the United Board for Christian Higher Education in Asia. He attended the 2010, 2011 and 2012 Bilderberg Group conferences in Spain, Switzerland and Chantilly, Virginia, alongside the great and the good in international politics and finance.

Blair's old friends in the now-bankrupt Monitor organisation were also involved with Libya. 'Monitor is not a lobbying organization,' its CEO Mark Fuller and director Rajeev Singh-Molares wrote to their Libyan client in July 2006. 'Our ability to introduce important, influential visitors to Libya's advantage depends on our experience, prestige, networks and reputation for independence. We are deeply committed to helping you with this program.'[5]

Blair's involvement with Libya and its autocratic ruler goes back to his premiership. Mohammed Rashid (whom we met in Chapter 1) became a key figure in a secret intelligence 'back channel' through which MI6 was trying to induce Libya to give up its nuclear-weapons programme. Blair saw the considerable commercial benefits: access to Libya's colossal reserves of oil and gas, as well as huge opportunities for foreign firms to renew its ancient infrastructure.

Blair, as we have seen, also dealt with Rashid (while still PM) over Palestinian gas, when Rashid brokered the Gaza gas consortium. Rashid was the former financial adviser to Yasser Arafat, who appointed him head of the Palestinian Investment Fund (PIF), a £1 billion company set up to make use of PLO funds. He is now on the run, having been sentenced to fifteen years' imprisonment for fraud.

In 2002, Rashid was not only Arafat's financial adviser but also that of Colonel Gaddafi's son Saif al-Islam Gaddafi, and was spending increasing amounts of time in Tripoli. That autumn, as the storm over weapons of mass destruction (WMD) gathered over Iraq, Saif asked Rashid to use his British contacts to open talks. Rashid arranged a secret meeting between Saif al-Islam and three MI6 officers in a hotel room in London's Mayfair in March 2003.

Saif al-Islam quickly agreed that Libya could make a sincere effort to address WMD concerns. Saif says the British reciprocated by immediately obtaining Blair's promise to deal with Libya in good faith. 'When they called 10 Downing Street,' he recalls, 'they said, "Don't fall off your chair. We got something from the Libyans." It was a total surprise to them.'

The next day Saif flew to meet his father, who was on a state visit to Burkina Faso, and received his blessing for the initiative. 'I will see if we can be friends,' he quotes his father as saying over a lamb-and-rice lunch. Gaddafi dispatched his foreign-intelligence chief Musa Kusa to Geneva for a meeting with top MI6 and CIA officials, who then travelled secretly to Tripoli in September to meet Gaddafi himself. The Libyans agreed in principle to throw the country's WMD projects open to an MI6–CIA team of technical experts.

Progress was slow. The Iraq War was in full swing, which complicated negotiations, and Gaddafi wanted some guaranteed incentives – such as military cooperation and a complete end to sanctions – if Libya were to admit to and then dismantle its WMD programmes. When Gaddafi grew nervous, Saif al-Islam says he reassured his father about the West's intentions, telling him, 'Trust me.' Saif's recollection was, 'I could smell it.'

Saif says that Gaddafi's confidence grew as the number of messages from the British and US governments came in via MI6 and the CIA. In September 2003, Gaddafi was handed a personal letter from Prime Minister Blair formally agreeing to Gaddafi's conditions for proceeding.

That paved the way for the visit of the MI6–CIA technical team to inspect all of Libya's secret WMD sites.

'We realised that we were dealing with friends and sincere people,' Saif al-Islam says. He and government officials spent months in secret negotiations with representatives of both the CIA and MI6, working out a deal in which Libya would give up its nuclear ambitions. There was almost a last-minute hiccup when American soldiers captured Iraqi leader Saddam Hussein after the Iraq War. Gaddafi was worried that the humiliating capture of Saddam would be seen as his motive; he wanted to postpone the deal.

According to Saif al-Islam, the Prime Minister pleaded with Gaddafi, 'Please, we are in a hurry. It is a big success for all of us.' Blair's pleading worked. Gaddafi agreed to dismantle his weapons.

After Western agents had worked to remove all the components of Libya's WMD programme and dismantle its long-range ballistic missiles, Blair sent the Libyan leader a friendly letter of congratulation, addressing him as 'Dear Muammar' and signing off 'Best wishes, Yours ever, Tony'.[6]

On 18 December, Blair and Gaddafi talked by telephone and the very next day Blair and Bush announced Gaddafi was ending his WMD programme.

Blair and Gaddafi remained in touch for the rest of Blair's premiership, which ended in 2007, after which they kept contact. In 2004 they had their famous meeting in a tent near Tripoli, the 'deal in the desert', to destroy WMD. The same year, Gaddafi put up £40 billion of cash assets, triggering a war between major investment banks.

The British MI6 officer who conducted the negotiations with Gaddafi alongside his counterpart from the CIA was Sir Mark Allen, a former adviser to Blair and a former head of the MI6 Middle East Bureau, who now works for BP and is a key figure in the Blair story.

Allen is a member of London School of Economics (LSE) Ideas Advisory Board, whose membership reads like a Who's Who of Tony

Blair's friends and business associates. Other members have included Liz Symons, now Baroness Symons, who is, as we shall find, deeply enmeshed in the Libyan business with Blair; Jonathan Powell, who used to be senior consultant with Tony Blair Associates, whom we have already met at meetings with the Sheikh of Kuwait; Sir Nigel Knowles, CEO of DLA Piper, the world's largest law firm, operating across 29 different companies advising business and governments, with which Symons, Blair and other of their business associates have a longstanding relationship; Sir David Manning, British ambassador to the United States from 2003 to 2007, and a key figure in Blair's drive to go to war in Iraq, who was, between 1995 and 1998, British ambassador to Tel Aviv and from 2001 a foreign policy adviser to Prime Minister Tony Blair.

Manning was also, like Allen himself and others of Blair's entourage, a senior adviser with the Monitor Group. Educated at the prestigious Catholic public school Downside and still a devout Roman Catholic, Allen went to Oxford to study classics but quickly changed to Arabic. Today Sir Mark (he was knighted in 2007) is, according to his LSE profile, 'one of Britain's pre-eminent Arabists' who served in British Foreign Service for thirty years and lived for many years in the Middle East.

That's true as far as it goes, but it's a cleaned-up version of the truth: Allen is a former British spy. After studying at the Middle East Centre for Arabic Studies, believed to be a British 'spy school' in a village near Beirut,[7] he was posted to Abu Dhabi in 1974, and spent much of the rest of his operational career in the Middle East.[8]

He fell in love with the sport of falconry, whose best practitioners are to be found among the Bedouin tribes. In the Middle East, Allen was never without his own pet hawks, often peregrine falcons, each worth thousands of pounds.

Allen developed his relationships with the Libyan regime through Saif al-Islam, who studied for a PhD on 'The Role of Civil Society in the Democratisation of Global Governance Institutions' at the LSE, for which he made use of research provided by the Monitor Group – and for which Blair himself offered advice, according to the papers that came to light in Tripoli after Gaddafi's overthrow.

In 2003, as head of MI6's counterterrorism unit, Allen and Stephen Kappes of the CIA led the talks that resulted in an end of support for terrorist activity by Gaddafi, and of international sanctions against Libya. In March 2004, Abdelhakim Belhaj, former leader of the Libyan Islamic Fighting Group, was detained with his heavily pregnant wife in China in 2004. Their friends say MI6 lured the couple to Bangkok with the promise of a UK visa. They were flown in a CIA plane to Tripoli in 2004. His wife was blindfolded, taken to a cell and 'chained to the wall by one hand and one leg' before being 'taped to a stretcher tightly, making her fear for her baby' and forced on board the CIA jet.[9]

Belhaj says he was beaten on arrival in Tripoli, and his wife 'could no longer feel her baby move in her womb and was concerned that he had died.' The couple were taken to Tajoura prison, a detention facility in Tripoli operated by the Libyan intelligence services. They were imprisoned and tortured for six years. British agents visited him.

'They [the British] knew I was being tortured, I have no doubt of that,' he told Kim Sengupta of the *Independent*. 'I hoped they would do something about it. I was too terrified during the meeting to say out loud what was being done to me because I thought the Libyans [secret police] were taping what was going on. When the Libyan guards left I made sign movements with my hands.

'The British people nodded, showed they understood. They showed this understanding several times. But nothing changed, the torture continued for a long time afterwards.'

The papers now disclosed show that the British did nothing to help. Rather, they – and in particular Sir Mark Allen – repeatedly asked the Libyan secret police for information about Belhaj. Allen wrote to his Libyan counterpart, 'I was grateful to you for helping the officer we sent out last week.'

Speaking to the *Independent* in a Tripoli hotel years later, after the fall of Gaddafi, Belhaj described being interviewed by three British agents, one woman and two men, at the headquarters of Musa Kusa, Gaddafi's Minister of Foreign Affairs. The two questioning sessions each lasted about two hours. 'The name of the female officer is known to the *Independent* but it is not being published for security reasons,' wrote the *Independent*'s Kim Sengupta. 'Documents show that she was one of the most frequent visitors to Tripoli under the Gaddafi regime.'

Cori Crider, a lawyer at the anti-death-penalty organisation Reprieve, told the *Guardian* that neither Blair nor his then Foreign Secretary, Mark Allen's chum Jack Straw, was prepared to give the apology that she believed Belhaj was owed. She said, 'Instead they are running a specious and immoral argument that British courts cannot judge British officials when they are said to have conspired with foreign torturers.'[10]

Allen was to be questioned, in secret, by the Gibson Inquiry into allegations of collusion in torture and inhumane practices used by MI5 and MI6 (where they are known as 'enhanced interrogation techniques'). But the inquiry was brought to an abrupt halt in January 2012 when Justice Secretary Kenneth Clarke said that the Crown Prosecution Service's announcement of new criminal investigations to be carried out by the Metropolitan Police meant that the inquiry could not carry out its mandate as envisaged.[11]

In 2004 Allen's bid to become head of MI6 failed, despite support from his friend Jack Straw. Blair appointed instead Sir John Scarlett, head of the Joint Intelligence Committee, who played a leading role in drawing up the Iraq weapons dossier, and we now know from his evidence to the Chilcot Inquiry that Allen was strongly against the invasion of Iraq. Allen resigned the same year and retired from public service.

Prime Minister Blair however cleared him to take work immediately as a special adviser for BP, despite rules that would normally have prevented a former civil servant from taking money from a large corporation so soon after retirement.

As Blair's premiership was coming to an end in 2007, Allen was using his contacts in both the United Kingdom and Libya to resolve the issues surrounding the release of Abdelbaset Ali al-Megrahi. Al-Megrahi had been found guilty by a Scottish court of the bombing of a Pan Am flight over the Scottish town of Lockerbie. We now know that, contrary to what we were told at the time, the British government was closely involved in the decision to release al-Megrahi, and saw it as part of the ongoing negotiations with Gaddafi.

On 29 May 2007, a month before he left Downing Street, Blair visited Libya, meeting Gaddafi and his Prime Minister Al Baghdadi Ali al-Mahmoudi in the then-beautiful city of Sirte, subsequently utterly ruined after the battle in which Gaddafi died. It was one of Blair's last international meetings as PM. He was accompanied by BP chairman Peter Sutherland, who subsequently announced the company would return to Libya after a thirty-year absence. Blair also pledged to provide support for Gaddafi's military, and signed up to 'exchanges of information on NATO and EU military and civil security.'

Part of the meeting's purpose was to try to deal with the al-Megrahi issue, for Gaddafi was very keen to get al-Megrahi home. It seems that, on this trip, a deal was thrashed out that included prisoner transfer (though not necessarily of al-Megrahi), just before BP announced an investment of about £454 million to prospect for £13 billion worth of oil in Libya.

Immediately afterwards, Allen, who had been using his Libyan contacts in BP's drive to win gas and oil contracts in the country, flew with the then-BP boss Lord Browne to meet Gaddafi in the desert and signed a contract with Libya.

But there was a hitch. By November it had still not been ratified because of delays in finalising prisoner transfers, which had been arranged between Blair and Gaddafi in tandem with the BP deal. The sticking point was that the British government still wanted to exclude al-Megrahi from the deal.

What was to be done? Allen could have gone to Blair, who he was sure would have helped, if only he was still Prime Minister, but he wasn't, and his successor Gordon Brown was thought to be a bit too straitlaced for these manoeuvres. Allen made two calls to Jack Straw, asking for the agreement to be speeded up. Within six weeks of his second call in November 2007, Straw had written to Scottish Justice Minister Kenny MacAskill to say al-Megrahi would be included.[12]

The prisoner-transfer agreement was eventually signed in November 2008. Although the UK government originally wanted to exclude al-Megrahi from its provisions, the final version of the agreement included him and could have been used to authorise his return to Libya. However, the Scottish government refused to send al-Megrahi to Libya under the prisoner-transfer agreement. Instead, it allowed his release on compassionate grounds because he was suffering from terminal cancer.

But Lockerbie was not the only airline bombing for which Gaddafi was held responsible, and the very next year – 2008 – another one came back to bite him. Just nine months after Lockerbie, on 19 September 1989, UTA Flight 772 from Chad was blown up, killing all 170 passengers. After a long legal battle by relatives of those who had died, a US court ordered Libya to pay $1.5 billion (£1 billion) to the relatives of the seven Americans killed. This meant that the proceeds of Libyan investment deals in the US, mainly in oil and gas, could be seized.

FORMER PM AT GADDAFI'S SIDE

Whom could Gaddafi turn to in this crisis but his old friend Tony Blair? It was 2008 and Blair was no longer Prime Minister, but he was ready to busy himself in a good cause.

His chief of staff in the Quartet office, Nick Banner, had a word with David Welch, the US official who was negotiating with Libya over compensation. Blair, due to meet Gaddafi on 10 June , was in touch with Sir Vincent Fean, British ambassador to Libya. Fean sent an email to Blair's office, obviously in reply to a request.

TB should explain what he said to President Bush (and what Banner said to Welch) to keep his promise to Col Q [Gaddafi] to intervene after the President allowed US courts to attach Libyan assets. He [Blair] could express satisfaction at the progress made in talks between the US and Libya to reach a govt to govt solution to all the legal/compensation issues outstanding from the 1980s ...

Blair spoke to Gaddafi, and approached Bush. Bush signed the Libyan Claims Resolution Act in August 2008. This meant that Libya made a one-off payment of $1.5 billion for all the bombings – the UTA flight, Lockerbie and a Berlin discotheque bombing – and had immunity thereafter from all terrorism-related lawsuits. The UTA relatives got about $100 million instead of the $1.5 billion they were awarded by the courts.

The American lawyer who represented the UTA relatives said his clients 'got screwed' by the Act. 'It sent the wrong message to terrorist states – don't worry about these lawsuits and judgements as the politicians will eventually fix it.' He said he had heard rumours at the time of Blair's involvement, but did not get the proof until 2013.[13]

Blair met Gaddafi again in January 2009, when JP Morgan was trying to negotiate a deal between the Libyan Investment Authority (LIA) and a company run by the Russian oligarch Oleg Deripaska, a friend of Lord Mandelson (to whom we will return in Chapter 8). The multibillion-dollar deal, which later fell through, would have seen the LIA provide a loan to Rusal (owned by Deripaska), the world's largest aluminium producer.

Blair has denied that he acted as an emissary in this matter. But it came just a few months after Deripaska spent £300,000 co-funding a project set up by Blair – 'Breaking the Climate Deadlock' – which lobbied governments over climate change.[14]

JP Morgan has said Blair had no knowledge of the Rusal proposal. Blair's spokesman said, 'Neither Tony Blair nor any of his staff raised any issue to do with a Russian aluminium company.' He added that the 'bulk of the conversations' with Gaddafi had been about Africa and how Libya could develop infrastructure. More than once Gaddafi raised the issue of the Lockerbie bomber's release, but Blair claims he always repeated, 'It is a matter for the Scottish government.'[15]

Even if all that is true, Blair's links to the LIA, his role as a Middle East peace envoy, a fundraiser in Africa and a business adviser all sit uneasily together.

It is no wonder that Youssef Sawani, executive director of the Gaddafi International Charity and Development Foundation, told the *Washington Times* in 2010 that Gaddafi 'talks regularly to Blair as a friend' and 'consults him on many issues.'

After Blair resigned as Prime Minister, Libya under Gaddafi was a natural place for him to exercise his entrepreneurial talent. Blair's spokesman has said that 'he has not spoken to or met Mohammed Rashid since leaving office'. Then again, he did not need to. The channel Rashid had opened up allowed Blair to develop his own relationship with both Saif al-Islam and his father Gaddafi. Now that Rashid is on the run after his fraud sentence, Blair seems in no hurry to acknowledge his old friend.

It's clear that during Gaddafi's reign, Blair courted the LIA and the National Oil Corporation (NOC) on behalf of British companies, and it is claimed that he performed the same service for JP Morgan clients. Both the LIA and the NOC were massive and corrupt institutions with fabulous wealth. There have been reports of regime figures describing Blair lobbying extensively for clients, and in return he intervened personally to aid the Gaddafi clan on several occasions.

The closeness of the relationship is indicated by a letter of 5 March 2007 from Blair to Saif al-Islam Gaddafi, a personally signed letter on Downing Street headed paper addressed in Blair's own handwriting to 'Engineer Saif', which thanked Saif for showing him 'your interesting PhD thesis'. Blair later denies proofreading the thesis or helping in any way.

He did try to persuade Oxford University to give a place to Saif, and is thought to have been instrumental in the eventual decision of the LSE to admit him. Perhaps his heavy representation on the LSE's Ideas Board may have given him some leverage there.[16]

After he ceased to be PM, Blair kept the relationship in good repair. In June 2008, January 2009 and April 2009, Blair and his entourage visited Gaddafi on a private jet provided by Gaddafi for around £150,000. The *Daily Telegraph* claims a total of six meetings.

Between leaving No. 10 and the revolution that saw the capture and killing of Gaddafi, Blair visited Libya – which has enormous oil reserves – several times, but his spokesman has frequently refused to explain the purpose of his visits. The relationship continued right up to Gaddafi's fall. During the Libyan Revolution, Blair telephoned Gaddafi twice on 27 February 2011, reportedly to ask him to stop the violent crackdown. Gaddafi might reasonably have expected a little help at the time of his greatest need, but that was the last time the two spoke, and a few weeks later Gaddafi was being put to death in the most horrible and humiliating way. Perhaps Blair shed a tear for his old chum. Then again, perhaps he didn't.

BARONESS SYMONS PLAYS HER PART

Blair's old crony Baroness Symons left it even later than Blair himself to disengage from Gaddafi. Symons, whose peerage came at Blair's hands so that he could bring her into his government, left it until March 2011 to sever her links with the National Economic Development Board of Libya, to which she was a paid adviser. In fact, only a matter of days earlier she appeared to praise Gaddafi's 'sound ideology'. She had joined the board shortly before the release of Abdelbaset al-Megrahi.[17]

Liz Symons is one of the most shadowy figures in Blair's wake. Until eight months before the Labour landslide general election victory of 1997 she was a trade union official, working first for the Inland Revenue Staff Federation before becoming general secretary of the First Division Association (FDA), a small trade union for senior civil servants.

Her life took a radically new turn on 7 October 1996 when, on the recommendation of the Leader of the Opposition, Tony Blair, she became Baroness Symons of Vernham Dene, while still in her post at the FDA. Normally, trade union general secretaries were not elevated to the Lords until their retirement, and generally not even then unless they were from unions that had bank-rolled the party, which the FDA did not. But Blair had plans for Liz Symons: she went straight into a ministerial role following the election victory in May 1997.

She is a friend of Blair and is married to Phil Bassett, one of Blair's closest advisers and a former *Financial Times* industrial correspondent. She was Blair and Bassett's type of trade unionist: no one could remember the last time the FDA had even held a strike ballot, let alone taken strike action.

She served as a frontbench spokesperson in the Lords on trade and investment in 2001–3. On 14 September 2001 she addressed the Lords on behalf of the Blair government in the aftermath of 9/11. On 18 October 2001 she told the Lords, after the UK had joined in attacks on terrorist targets in Afghanistan, 'As both President Bush and the Prime Minister made clear from the outset, the terrain, the weather and the complexity of the targets mean that we can expect no early conclusion to this campaign. It will indeed be a long haul. It may take months, not days or weeks.' Twelve years later, British troops were still there, not leaving until 2014.

Later, Symons was the main cheerleader for Blair in the Lords on Iraq and a fully paid-up member of the 'weapons of mass destruction' club – an odd role for the trade-and-industry spokesperson. On 24 September 2002 she told the Lords, citing what came to be known as the 'dodgy dossier' as evidence, 'As the statement made by my right honourable friend the Prime Minister makes clear, our briefing paper cites example upon example of Iraqi efforts to develop weapons of mass destruction. To an unprecedented extent, the paper draws on intelligence material and leaves no doubt that Iraq's growing arsenal of such weapons can no longer be tolerated. It demonstrates that the Iraqi regime is increasing its capacity to terrorise and intimidate through the amassing of chemical and biological weapons.'

(WMD were, of course, not found in Iraq after the war, despite an extensive search.)

Symons then became minister in the Foreign and Commonwealth Office from 2003 to 2005, where she was Minister of State for the Middle East, and widely known as Tony Blair's 'Middle East envoy'. She was also Minister for Defence Procurement. All of this work as a minister, until standing down in 2005, inevitably gave her excellent contacts and an insider's knowledge and expertise.

By then she and Bassett were on the road to becoming wealthy, though not perhaps on the Blair scale: according to the *Guardian*, in 2003 they were already dividing their time between a country house in Hampshire and a mansion flat overlooking Westminster Cathedral, and their son attended the £20,000-a-year public school St Paul's. But she was about to get a whole lot richer.

As soon as she was no longer a minister, she started to make herself seriously wealthy from consultancy work, although Blair still had two more years as PM and New Labour had five more years in government. She became the Prime Minister's new special envoy to the Middle East, but in the private sector she was also earning around £100,000 a year.

Some of this came from a consultancy with DLA Piper, which earns millions of dollars in the United States by acting as a lobbying firm in Washington for multinational corporations. Documents the company has deposited in the US capital reveal that in the past few years it has earned more than $6 million in lobbying fees from tobacco firms. The firm has also earned $7 million from lobbying for two American defence giants, Lockheed Martin and Raytheon, the company that makes cruise missiles for the US military.

Symons also has a non-executive position in the boardroom of P&O, the subject of a takeover bid from the Middle Eastern firm Dubai Ports World, which is understood to be owned by the Emirates' royal family.

She also took up a boardroom job with British Airways, where she earned £35,000 for fifteen days a year. The lucrative position also provided her with free first-class BA flights for her and her husband. He, in turn, became the special adviser to Lord Falconer, the Lord Chancellor and Secretary of State for Constitutional Affairs.

Since 2010 Baroness Symons has been chairman of the Mayfair-based Arab–British Chamber of Commerce (ABCC). Despite its official-sounding name, this is a private company that specialises in building business and commercial relationships between the UK and the twenty-two member states of the Arab league.

The company promoted Libya during the Gaddafi era as well as many other unsavoury Middle East and North African dictatorships and monarchies including Bahrain, United Arab Emirates, Syria, Sudan and Yemen. Its profile on Iraq is illuminating: 'In its contemporary history, Iraq has been exposed to many wars which have caused large fatalities to the Iraqi people and shattered the economy. The latest war in 2003 and the subsequent violence left the economy severely damaged.' Baroness Symons, of course, was one of the cheerleaders for that war.

The ABCC were promoting trade with Iraq with an event entitled 'Opportunities in Iraq: The Way Forward'. Its website read,

> The Chamber is to organize an event promoting trade relations between Iraq and the United Kingdom. The event will focus on the vast investment opportunities Iraq has to offer, bringing valuable business opportunities to the attention of potential investors to the state. Given Iraq's recent growth statistics, the event will be a significant draw for British investors who have an interest in exploring future business potential in the country.

The ABCC won't say how lucrative her work as chairman is. Nor will Liz Symons. Nor does she stress her role in creating these 'valuable business opportunities' by cheerleading for the war.

She is also 'international consultant' for Blenheim Capital Services Limited, which assists and facilitates, among other things, defence, aerospace, oil, gas and construction contracts and projects, much of that in the Middle East.

It is a subsidiary of Blenheim Capital Partners Ltd, based offshore in Saint Peter Port, Guernsey, and has offices in Washington, DC, Abu Dhabi, the United Arab Emirates, Bahrain and Malaysia. The company says it has worked on projects valued at more than £12 billion. It has recently played a key role in a defence contract with the Malaysian government.

Neither Blenheim nor Liz Symons will say how lucrative her relationship with Blenheim is. But Blenheim also has links with DLA Piper, for which Symons also acts as 'international consultant'. In January 2010 Blenheim Capital Services appointed Sir Nigel Knowles (a member of the LSE Ideas Board, naturally) as chairman and non-executive director. Knowles is also managing partner of DLA Piper.

Again, neither DLA Piper nor Liz Symons will say how lucrative her position as 'international consultant' is or precisely what the role entails.

Symons is also a consultant to Consolidated Contractors Company (CCC), the huge construction company based in the Lebanon with extensive interests across the Middle East, including Iraq and Libya. The company built the notorious Abu Ghraib prison and pops up repeatedly in the Blair story, as we shall see. Symons will not say how much the consultancy work is worth. CCC could not be contacted.

She was also at the centre of a conflict-of-interest row when she accepted a lucrative role with UK investment bank MerchantBridge, which has made millions from contracts in postwar Iraq, after she left government.

The London School of Economics' 'Ideas Board' calls on the university's 'intellectual resources' to study international affairs. The LSE was heavily criticised in 2011 for a 'chapter of failures' in its links with the Gaddafi regime, including accepting a £1.5 million donation from Saif al-Islam Gaddafi six weeks after the institution awarded him a PhD.[18]

Immediately after the fall of Gaddafi, the British firm Heritage Oil bought major shareholdings in Libya. Heritage Oil is owned by Tony Buckingham, who is suspected of links to mercenary operations in Africa and the Middle East. The Libyan National Transitional Council – which ruled from 2011 to 2013 – appointed a new oil minister who, to the dismay of revolutionaries, announced new contracts with international oil firms.

Blair's efforts, with the aid of Rashid, Allen and Symons, in opening Libya's markets to foreign investors during the time of Gaddafi, has deprived the post-revolution government of the national assets needed to rebuild its infrastructure and create a peaceful country. In fact, Gaddafi's fall has left a country at war with itself, warlords fighting for territory and power.

Domestically, as well, old partnerships have not shown their capacity to survive the rigours of Blair's 'private' life. Old friends seeking to build personal wealth find circumstances changing and loyalties shifting.

CHAPTER EIGHT

BLAIR AND MANDELSON: THE PARTING OF THE WAYS

'If you look at Mandelson's known clients a lot of them are close to
"tame oligarchs" – people who might be fearful of [Vladimir] Putin [of Russia]
but support him. This has enabled him to scoop up business in the area
that Blair cannot do business.'
– A FORMER LABOUR CABINET MINISTER.

One of Tony Blair's closest friends was Peter (now Lord) Mandelson. He is credited by Blair himself as one of the three architects of New Labour. As Blair wrote to him when he resigned from his first government over the home-loan scandal in 1998, 'It is no exaggeration to say that without your support and advice, we would never have built New Labour.'

Now, nearly two decades on, the two longstanding friends are no longer that close and it is Mandelson who is distancing himself from Blair, not vice versa. Sources say that Peter is becoming increasingly disillusioned with Tony's pursuit of wealth by advising repugnant dictatorships and corrupt regimes with terrible human-rights records. He is said to believe that these actions are toxic for the New Labour project, since it puts its principal architect in an appalling light.

One source suggested that Mandelson had returned to his old tricks of secretly briefing journalists – but this time against Blair for seeking to advise the new authoritarian Egyptian government of General el-Sisi. Mandelson had previously supported the deposed Egyptian President

Mubarak. A report in the *Telegraph* revealed the connection.[1] It said that he wrote to the Egyptian ambassador in London, Hatem Seif El Nasr, who contacted the then-Minister of Foreign Trade in Cairo, Rachid Mohamed Rachid, on 31 January 2011 outlining Mandelson's offer.

El Nasr's letter, written in Arabic and bearing the Egyptian government seal, stated that Lord Mandelson was

> establishing a new international company of his own for economic advisory to render support and economic consulting for businessmen and enterprise.
>
> The new company aims at renewing and reintroducing the commercial franchises to new communities, and helping grand agencies and organisations to accomplish new goals and make use and adapt with the globalisation consequences on these companies.

The article also points out that

> On Feb 1, Lord Mandelson wrote to the *Financial Times* in support of the Egyptian regime as it clung on to power in the face of mass demonstrations and violent clashes which left at least 846 dead. Mubarak was ousted on Feb 11, 2011.
>
> In the letter, he defended 'reformers' in the regime, including the president's son, Gamal, saying the president was a 'civilian façade' for the security forces while his son was 'the leading voice in favour of change'.

Now Blair is advising el-Sisi, who overthrew the elected Mohamed Morsi and the Muslim Brotherhood as reported in the *Guardian*.[2] The same article quotes a source as saying,

> A former close political associate argued that the ex-prime minister's role in advising the Egyptian regime would cause 'terrible damage

to him, the rest of us and New Labour's legacy'. My source tells me that person was Peter Mandelson, furious that his own plan to aid reformers in Mubarak regime had been upstaged by a deal with Blair three years later.

Others speak of Mandelson resenting that he never got one of the top jobs in a Blair cabinet because he felt he had to sacrifice himself to save the government from embarrassment – particularly with his second resignation over whether he had helped the Hinduja brothers obtain a British passport.

What is officially clear is that the main lobbying and strategic-advice company behind Peter Mandelson's wealth, Global Counsel, wants to distance itself from Tony Blair Associates, the driving force of Blair's business activities. And that is even though it employs some ex-Blairites itself.

Maree Glass, chief operating officer of Global Counsel, put the difference clearly when this question was put to her: 'As you'll see from our research we help our clients understand global political and regulatory trends. You should also note, as has been explained to many journalists, that Global Counsel does not work for governments.'

The big question is whether such a rift is motivated by genuine anger that Blair has moved from his original New Labour project just to make money; jealousy that he has been more successful than Mandelson; or a row generated by rival business strategies clashing like Titans across the globe. What is obvious is that there are similarities in their operations, lifestyles and some of the structures of their different organisations.

Mandelson has also, like Blair, never shied away from wanting to be wealthy. As he said in a famous quote, he was 'intensely relaxed about people getting filthy rich as long as they pay their taxes.'

More recently, in an age of austerity for the masses, he has tried to row back. Speaking on BBC Radio 4's *Today* programme in 2012 after the publication in Davos of a think-tank report on the future of globalisation,

Mandelson said, 'I don't think I would say that now. Why? Because amongst other things we've seen that globalisation has not generated the rising incomes for all.'

Mandelson's Global Counsel does strategic lobbying and is backed by the international communications giant WPP.

'The company will focus on establishing a client base among companies with global ambitions in the new emerging markets, as well as forming partnerships in the developed world with businesses who want to move into the new high-growth economies,' said a WPP press release on 9 December 2012.

WPP was set up by Sir Martin Sorrell in 1985 (its original title was Wired and Plastic Products Ltd) and is now an international marketing company employing 170,000 people worldwide. It includes brand advertising names such as JWT (J. Walter Thompson), Ogilvy and Mather, Young and Rubicon and lesser known ones in Latin America such as Gringo, as well as having a stake in Today Advertising in Burma. Its parent company is now in the offshore tax haven in Jersey, though it moved its HQ back to the UK from Ireland in 2013.

Sorrell is a somewhat controversial businessman who has defended huge salaries for top executives (his was £6.77 million in 2011, up from £4.23m in 2010). His total package, according to 2103 accounts, was worth £29.9 million; this includes his salary, pension, short-term and long-term incentives and benefits including a company car, private health insurance and a housing allowance. This obviously fits in well with Mandelson's definition of being 'relaxed about people getting filthy rich'. His peerage and his only two government posts, ambassador for British business and membership of a government advisory committee on management excellence, all came during Blair's first term of office. He also has a link with Bernie Ecclestone – the man who controversially donated £1 million to New Labour under Tony Blair just at the point when the government was looking at banning tobacco advertising on motorsports –

as he is a non-executive director of Formula One. WPP employed people with long-term links to both Blair and to Mandelson in Whitehall.

Global Counsel was founded by Mandelson. Benjamin Wegg-Prosser (his old special adviser in Whitehall) became its managing partner. He has recruited former senior civil servants from the business department to work with him at the lobbying company and one of them, Stephen Amos, became a partner in March 2013. The company's latest filed accounts for 2013 show that it has assets of just under £1 million.

Mandelson's financial arrangements and his business dealings ape Blair: convoluted, secretive and aimed to avoid public scrutiny. He has two companies – one for his personal finances and another for his business activities. Both hide details of his income. What is interesting is that the structure of his companies, while not as obtuse as the structure set up by Blair to cover his business dealings, still prevents people from finding out his clients and sources of income.

He has also resisted all attempts by the House of Lords to make him disclose his clients in its register of interests, claiming he is providing strategic advice, not acting as a lobbyist, which would require him to declare them. When this was challenged, he said he would still not declare the clients because his business was part of remunerated employment. And so far he has got away with this.

The first company is Willbury. It has two directors, Mandelson himself and his longstanding Brazilian life partner Reinaldo da Silva. But Mandelson is the sole shareholder, suggesting that the money that comes into the firm is entirely from him. The company takes advantage of all the ploys to hide wealth and maintain privacy. It has to file only abbreviated accounts – so none of the details of the fees he receives have to be disclosed, whether it is for his speeches or his book.

His accountants are MHA MacIntyre Hudson. This is an old-established but rapidly growing company acquiring firms through a series of aggressive mergers, with international clients.

Mandelson channels all the money he makes from his speeches and trips he has to declare to Parliament into this company. In 2012, most of his speeches were to bankers and investors such as the London Metal Exchange, Barclays Capital and the Asset Based Finance Association. These have to be declared in the House of Lords register of interests. His latest entry in 2015 does not include payments for any speeches.

The accounts show that his income has been substantial. Over the two years 2010–11 and 2011–12 it was in excess of £1 million. Mandelson seems to have drawn out some £274,000 from the firm. By 2013–14 it was still in excess of £1 million and the accounts show that it made Mandelson a £400,000 advance during that financial year.[3] The purpose of the loan is unclear, but it was not paid back in the year and would, according to tax adviser Richard Murphy, legitimately lessen his tax bill as he does not have to pay tax on the loan if he pays interest at a rate specified by HM Revenue and Customs.

His memoirs, *The Third Man*, are alleged to have netted him £500,000. The accounts suggest that speculation that he may have got £150,000 are nearer to the mark, and, if *The Times* paid £350,000 for the serialisation, it suggests much of the money would have gone back to the publisher against the advance, leaving Mandelson with about £350,000.

The company has one other very interesting member, who links Blair and Mandelson. The company secretary is Maree Gail Glass, who, as we have already seen, is the COO to Global Counsel. Between 2008 and 2010, she worked as personal assistant to Mandelson in the Department of Business. But also significant is that she worked in the private office team for Tony Blair. She could not be a more trusted person to keep details of Mandelson's finances discreet and is another link to Blair.

Mandelson established Global Counsel with his old special adviser and longstanding friend Benjamin Wegg-Prosser. Originally set up as a limited company by both of them with 4,505 shares on 29 May 2010, twenty-three days after Labour's defeat in the 2010 general election, it had, by 23 November that year, been dissolved and transformed into a far more secretive and less disclosing limited-liability partnership.

Its accountants and official registered office were, again, MHA MacIntyre Hudson and, again, both Mandelson and Wegg-Prosser register their official addresses with the company, to avoid disclosing their home addresses. Indeed Wegg-Prosser's Russian wife Yulia, has also registered her address there to avoid people finding out where they live.

As well as Maree Gail Glass, Global Counsel also employs Geoffrey Norris, an adviser with a long track record as a Blair adviser. Norris was both a former government adviser close to Tony Blair and later Gordon Brown when he was PM, and a strident advocate of nuclear power. From 1992 to November 1994 Norris advised Robin Cook when he was Shadow Trade and Industry Secretary and before that he advised Cook on health policy. He then moved to become industry policy adviser to Tony Blair when Blair was still Leader of the Opposition.

In May 1997 Norris was appointed Blair's special adviser responsible for trade, industry, energy, employment and planning. He has stayed close to Blair ever since. On the Global Counsel website Norris describes himself as an expert in energy and industrial policy, who 'has been at the heart of business policy-making in the UK for the last decade' and 'was one of the key architects of Britain and Europe's current approach to energy policy and climate change'.

In 2008 he became a special adviser at the UK Department of Business under Lord Mandelson when Gordon Brown offered the peer a place back in government. When he took up the post at Global Counsel, the Advisory Committee on Business Appointments which approved his move said he could not use any information he had gained inside Whitehall for two years to gain preferential business for his new boss.

Even for Blair's special advisers, Norris was considered extremely close to Blair. The closeness rankled with the former Deputy PM John Prescott, who when once asked by the BBC about Norris said, 'Who's

Norris? Mr Norris is an official in the department. We sometimes call them teenyboppers. You know what I mean?'

Norris was said to be a strong supporter of nuclear power and pushed the nuclear case extremely hard and, along with the government's Chief Scientific Adviser, Sir David King, persuaded Blair to back it.

In March 2005, the *Independent on Sunday* reported: 'Within government, Geoffrey Norris, Tony Blair's special adviser on industry and business, is pressing the nuclear case. It is understood that he was instrumental in the creation of the DTI's Future for Nuclear team.' One Whitehall source told the paper: 'Norris has fought hard to keep nuclear on the agenda.'[4]

By 2008 Norris and his colleagues had held at least nine secret meetings at Downing Street with the bosses of nuclear energy companies while the government was formulating controversial plans for nuclear new build. The *Independent on Sunday* reported that

> no official records were kept of the discussions with the companies, which stand to profit from Gordon Brown's announcement last Thursday [10 January] that he was approving a new generation of nuclear power plants.
>
> The Government initially tried to block details of the meetings requested under the Freedom of Information Act. However, last week it revealed that Geoffrey Norris, Gordon Brown's energy adviser, met bosses from EDF, British Nuclear Fuels (BNFL), E.ON and British Energy at a crucial phase in the Government's deliberations. Confirmation that there are no official records of the meetings adds to concern that certain advisers can operate outside the rules of government accountability.[5]

But, as well as employing true Blairites, Mandelson copied another employment practice by Blair: employing people from Whitehall who were loyal to him in government. Just as Blair employed his trusted aide Ruth Turner from Downing Street in top jobs in the Blair Faith Foundation, Mandelson recruited civil servants who worked closely with him at the

Department of Business and in Europe. An example is Duncan Buchanan, who was hired by Peter Mandelson when Buchanan was the twenty-eight-year-old head of the South Asia unit of UK Trade & Investment (UKTI), a government agency. Buchanan, who was responsible for testing the waters for British companies in India, Pakistan, Sri Lanka, Bangladesh and Afghanistan, left the civil service to take up his new position.

According to the *Guardian*, the decision to hire Buchanan 'suggests that Mandelson plans to target Asia. Any suggestion that he is exploiting business opportunities in Afghanistan would be highly controversial, given his close relationship with Tony Blair, the prime minister who took the UK to war against the Taliban.'[6]

Buchanan, an Oxford graduate, worked for Mandelson as his private secretary in 2008 and 2009, but he spent the following two years in China and then India, the base from which UKTI monitors trade and investment opportunities in the wider region. He is understood to have sent a round-robin email to colleagues announcing his decision to move into the private sector. In the email, Buchanan said he intended to work in 'emerging markets', but refrained from mentioning the name of his new employer.

Buchanan is described by colleagues as 'a good operator' and 'resourceful'. In 2012 he wrote a blog about his first impressions on arriving in China and the difficulties he faced. 'I'm reminded of the old truism – anything worth doing takes effort (or, euphemistically, "the juice is worth the squeeze"),' he wrote.

A source said: 'Peter [Mandelson] is happy with how things are going with Global Counsel and is scooping up civil servants who he rated in government and who have the skills and connections to help him in his business.'

Another is Stephen Adams, now a partner, as previously disclosed. His biographical note on the Global Counsel website says,

Stephen Adams has a decade of experience in European public policy and regulation, chiefly in the field of international economic policy, European integration and multilateralism. Previously, Stephen was a Vice President in the Executive Office of Goldman Sachs International. He was a senior policy adviser at the European Commission, where he was closely involved in the WTO Doha Round trade negotiation and worked on a wide range of bilateral and multilateral economic negotiation. Prior to this, Stephen was a policy adviser to senior politicians in Brussels.

What it doesn't quite say is that Adams was one of the closest people to Mandelson, his speechwriter while he was EU commissioner, and according to a ministry insider one of a group of devoted civil servants to the former Business Secretary. He also tried to set up his own company, Whetstone Partners, from his home address in Reading, which did not come to anything, and then joined Global Counsel.

Mandelson's financial expertise is represented by Dan Conaghan, author of a devastating insider book on the Bank of England and a former *Telegraph* journalist. Neither role is mentioned by Global Counsel. According to its website,

Conaghan has extensive experience in corporate finance and asset management. Previously, he was a director of Glendevon King Asset Management, a London-based investment management company specialising in fixed income funds. Before joining GKAM, he was a director of KC Capital, a corporate finance company focusing on healthcare and leisure transactions. Prior to this, he was a director and member of the investment committee of NewMedia Spark PLC (now Spark Ventures PLC). In addition to his role as a Senior Adviser he is also a Director of Global Counsel Advisory Ltd.

What is particularly interesting is where Mandelson does his business and whom he has recruited to do it. One Labour source, a former cabinet minister, definitely believes that the relationship between Mandelson and Blair is now dominated by rival moneymaking dynasties. He has an interesting explanation.

'When Blair was in government he was close first to Bill Clinton and then George Bush. If you look at Blair's government clients, the vast majority are in the American sphere of influence in the Middle East and the various Stans [e.g. Pakistan, Afghanistan] and Africa. The one area that these people would not want Blair to work for is the Russians.

'If you look at Mandelson's known clients a lot of them are close to "tame oligarchs" – people who might be fearful of [Vladimir] Putin [of Russia] but support him. This has enabled him to scoop up business in the area that Blair cannot do business.'

If you look at Global Counsel and some of its private newsletters, such a thesis stands up. For a start Mandelson has recruited people for their Russian expertise.

One example is Alexander Smotrov who, according to the Global Counsel website, 'has a background in political, international and business journalism, covering energy, EU–Russian relations and Russian businesses across the globe. Previously, he was chief UK correspondent for the leading Russian news agency RIA Novosti between 2003 and 2013. Prior to this, he worked for RIA Novosti in Moscow.'

His LinkedIn profile describes him as responsible for delivery of Russian projects; managing specific Russian clients; monitoring Russian political/business developments; support on major international issues; non-UK media and publicity work.

The other is Miranda Gilbert, who according to the Global Counsel website, 'researches European and Russian media and political trends. She is also responsible for marketing. Previously she has lived and worked in Moscow and has a degree in Russian from Oxford University.'

But the real linchpin in the Russian operation is one of Mandelson's most loyal and longstanding colleagues and friends, Benjamin Wegg-Prosser. Mandelson and Wegg-Prosser have known each other well for nearly twenty years, not long after Wegg-Prosser left Sheffield University in 1995 with a politics degree. Since 1995 Wegg-Prosser has been Mandelson's research assistant in the Labour Party and his special adviser in the Cabinet Office and the Trade and Industry Department until Mandelson's resignation in 1998.

After that he went into publishing, becoming deputy communications director for Pearson. He later purchased Slate, an online US news company from Microsoft and planned an online rival to the *Guardian* to scoop up lucrative education jobs advertising. This led Alan Rusbridger, editor of the *Guardian*, to offer him a commercial publishing job, publishing politics on the Guardian Unlimited website and then *Education Guardian* and *Society Guardian*. In August 2005 he returned to work for Labour, this time for Tony Blair as director of the Strategic Communications Unit until Blair left government in 2007. The latter has been very useful to boost international business.

He then went to Moscow, first working for a pro-democracy charity and then going on to work as director of corporate communications for SUP Media, an influential online media group, now with offices in Moscow, Kiev and San Francisco, which claims to be followed by 50 per cent of Russia's online users for news, blogs and sport. It is co-owned by the Russian oligarch Alexander Mamut, a Putin supporter who now also owns the British bookseller, Waterstones.

Wegg-Prosser also has a second limited-liability partnership with Slate UK – the UK arm of the US online business – called BYF. It uses the same accountants, MHA MacIntyre Hudson, using their address. It had a healthy £500,000 in its account in 2012, which appeared to have been distributed between Wegg-Prosser and Slate.

Wegg-Prosser met his wife, Yulia, in Russia – marrying into the Russian elite – and here the links between Mandelson and Russian oligarchs such as Oleg Deripaska become much closer.

She acts as the main link Mandelson has with the oligarchs and cemented the existing relationship he previously had with them through his longstanding friend, the banker and investor Nat Rothschild, by accompanying Wegg-Prosser when he met Rothschild with Mandelson. Otherwise she has one small company, Peredelkino, which specialises in translation services. The latest accounts for the financial year ending 2014 showed it was a very small business with assets worth around £22,000. Her husband is also a director.

Oleg Deripaska, a Russian billionaire, is pretty central to Mandelson's business in that he has business links with Rothschild. How close they are can be seen in a blog written by Yulia while she was staying with her husband, Mandelson and Rothschild in Klosters, Switzerland, before he set up Global Counsel.

A report in the *Mail on Sunday*[7] described in detail how Mandelson and the Wegg-Prossers stayed in Rothschild's Klosters villa, boasting about the choice of expensive cars owned by the banking tycoon, including a Ferrari, an Alfa Romeo and a Porsche. She blogged in Russian,

Nat is begging us to drive in his smart-looking Porsche, Ferrari and Alfa Romeo, but my boring boys seat me in the Jeep and we drive to the Fluela Pass, the mountain pass which Jeremy Clarkson regards as Europe's most beautiful road.

The pass only functions from April until October. We are overtaken by unbelievably beautiful old timers and I have a feeling that we irritate their eyes with our s*** Jeep.

The blog was hastily withdrawn when the *Mail on Sunday* got hold of it in 2008. It had apparently originally not been thought to have mattered too much, as the original article was in Russian for a Russian audience. Unfortunately, the Wegg-Prossers had forgotten about Google Translate.

Similarly, a libel action brought by Nat Rothschild against the *Daily Mail* revealed Mandelson's close relationship with Deripaska. The libel action came as speculation suggested Mandelson had helped Deripaska obtain favoured tariff deals for his huge aluminium business and to help smooth a £500 million deal with the American company Alcoa for

Deripaska. The EU reduced tariffs on the imports of aluminium while Mandelson was Trade Commissioner in 2005. Mandelson strenuously denied both allegations.

The report[8] described a sauna they attended, along with Rothschild and Mandelson's use of Deripaska's private jet to fly from Moscow to Siberia to visit his estate and later the use of Rothchild's private jet to fly from Davos to Moscow.

The *Telegraph* reports,

> Cross-examining Mr Rothschild, Andrew Caldecott QC, for Associated Newspapers, said: 'We say that to take extensive hospitality from Mr Deripaska, who was not a close personal friend of Lord Mandelson's before he took office, was inappropriate. To put him in a position of accepting hospitality and taking private jet flights exposed him to allegations of inappropriate behaviour.

Rothschild replied, 'I disagree. It was a wonderful weekend and he enjoyed it.' In his witness statement, he added, 'This invitation was to Lord Mandelson as a personal friend. It never occurred to me that it could constitute any kind of declarable gift or that he might be exposed to allegations of impropriety. I took him on the flight to Moscow as a friend and not for any business reason.'

Rothschild lost the case. The *Independent* reported that the judge ruled, 'So far as Lord Mandelson was concerned the benefit was the trip and the hospitality itself. So far as Mr Deripaska was concerned it was a relationship with the EU Trade Commissioner.' The judge rejected the notion that Rothschild and Mandelson had flown out as friends, not business associates, and said Mr Rothschild's behaviour had in part been 'inappropriate'. 'That conduct foreseeably brought Lord Mandelson's public office and personal integrity into disrepute,' the judge said.[9]

The *Telegraph* also reported the judge's ruling, saying, 'Mr Rothschild states that he took Lord Mandelson on the trip as a friend and not for any other business reason. I cannot accept that the position was as simple as that.

I accept that Lord Mandelson had no role in the joint venture, which is what the trip was arranged to promote. But I do not accept that there is a clear line between the business and the personal sides of Mr Rothschild's relationship with Mr Deripaska. They have very extensive business relationships.'[10]

On another occasion, when Mandelson was back as Business Secretary for Gordon Brown in 2008, Mandelson stayed with Nat Rothschild in Corfu and Deripaska's yacht was visiting the island. Both Mandelson and then-shadow Chancellor of the Exchequer George Osborne (also a friend of Deripaska) had also stayed on the super-yacht, *Queen K* – with Osborne revealing Mandelson's close connections to the Russian oligarch while Rothschild accused Osborne of trying to solicit donations to the Tories there (which was subsequently denied).

Rothschild is also thought by the *Financial Times* to have helped Mandelson secure the lucrative post of chairman of Lazard International, a part-time job, for an undisclosed sum. The *FT* reported that the appointment, whereby Mandelson was expected to travel to sort out cross-border issues for its clients, was announced by neither Mandelson nor Lazard.[11]

Probably a better example of Mandelson's connections with Deripaska's companies is the circulation list of people receiving a private newsletter sent out by Wegg-Prosser to more than 350 people, including politicians and clients. The newsletter is said to be a subscriber-only publication, revealing the latest trends and inside information on a variety of political and commercial topics to paying clients. Many of the copies seem to be sent out free of charge, certainly to the people who discussed it with one of the authors, David Hencke.

The list was leaked to the satirical magazine *Private Eye*, and revealed a number of prominent Russian oligarchs, including those close to Deripaska. One was Oleg Mukhamedshin, deputy chief executive of Rusal, Deripaska's aluminium company. Wegg-Prosser declined to disclose to the *Private Eye* if these oligarchs were clients, though was happy to confirm a friendship.

More interesting was the content of some of the private newsletters – which are supposed to give strategic advice – that have been leaked to the authors. Two seem to suggest that Global Counsel has to do a delicate balancing act between not offending Putin and offending British firms they may advise.

One paper was about an oil deal – sanctioned by Putin and between BP and Rosneft – over extracting oil in Russia. The report describes the deal as 'skewed in favour of the Kremlin and its allies' – with the aim of the Russian state having more control over its resources but still having access to BP's technical expertise to extract the oil by having a smaller stake in the oilfield. Given that BP is a subscriber to the newsletter, the analysis highlights the problems facing the company and tries to steer a middle course between Mandelson's Russian oligarch connections and not offending Putin, while being honest about the problems BP faces.

It concludes:

One high profile acquisition in the most prominent sector in the Russian economy cannot be taken as a definitive sign of Mr Putin's vision for the Russian economy, let alone some kind of evidence for a return to Soviet-style control. Like the furore over the jailing of the Pussy Riot singers, his renewed emphasis on orthodox values and the creation of a new agency to inspire patriotism in young people, the move is part of Putin's political balancing of his own instincts, his reading of Russian politics and the factions around him. Whether this assertiveness in the economic and social spheres is a product of Mr Putin's confidence or insecurity is hard to tell.

MANDELSON IN CHINA

Other newsletters are more partisan. One paper, on China's refusal to cut aluminium production, is heavily sympathetic to Deripaska's attempt to enter the market and contains critical coverage of the failure of rival Rio Tinto Zinc in another deal, which ended with the departure in January 2013 of its chief executive Tom Albanese. The briefing on Albanese's sacking is interesting, given Wegg-Prosser's and Mandelson's close connections to Deripaska, Deripaska's own company Rusal, and his interest in the aluminium company Alcoa. Albanese's sacking was widely reported in the press and attributed to a bad deal in Mozambique. The briefing covers and analyses part of the information found in the *Daily Telegraph* and elsewhere.

The new information in the briefing paper talks of how China's heavily state-subsidised aluminium production affects all commercial aluminium companies worldwide – including Russian interests. It provides a lot of detail but is basically a sophisticated rant about China using its nationalist self-sufficiency interests to have overcapacity, preventing 'a new source of demand for western and Russian producers':

By shielding Chinese producers from failure, or even from the sharp capacity cuts that producers in the US, Europe and Russia are undertaking to sustain profitability, the Chinese system is absorbing losses that are falling on private market players elsewhere. All the major global producers including Rusal, Rio Tinto Zinc, Alcoa and BHP Billiton have announced production cuts of between 6–8 per cent of their total aluminium production since mid 2011 and called a halt to or scaled back large capital projects.

A rather similar but more detailed analysis in another newsletter looks at the solar-panel trade wars between China, the US and the European Union. It is highly critical of China. Here again the row between the EU and the US about China subsidising production and China challenging EU subsidies for solar panels has all the makings of a trade war, and the pitch is aimed at European commercial producers fearful of Chinese subsidies.

The report warns,

The European solar industry arguably has bigger problems than China, in the form of its own changing subsidy regime and overcapacity problem. But Europe standing aside to allow Chinese goods to exacerbate the pain will fuel a deep neurosis in the EU about Chinese industrial competition and European policy passivity in the face of it. The fact that the Chinese system is wasteful and unsustainable and that its own internal debate on it is suppressed in an unhealthy way will not console anyone.

Curiously, this savage criticism of China postdates Mandelson's losing one of his key Chinese contacts, the once-rising star, Bo Xilai, now jailed for life for bribery and corruption. Mandelson's connections with Bo Xilai go back to a few weeks after he became EU Commissioner for Trade on 22 November 2004. On 24 February 2005 he arrived in Beijing for a four-day visit to hold talks with Chinese foreign trade officials, including Vice-Premier Wu Yi, Minister Bo Xilai and Chinese businesspeople. It was his first visit to China in his capacity as the Trade Commissioner. This meeting led to a series of detailed negotiations with the Chinese over textiles, and it is clear the two had a good working relationship.

In an interview with a Chinese news website[12] on 25 February 2005 he describes Bo Xilai in glowing terms:

I find him a good interlocutor, a good person to do business with. We both had much more to say than we had planned. We met before during the EU–China Summit at the Hague in December 2004 and there's so much going on internationally in the WTO and the Doha Round where China has an important part to play. I am glad he is exercising China's responsibility as a leading member of the WTO … I regard Bo Xilai as a very able and very conscientious trade minister.

Nowadays, sources say if you ask him about Bo Xilai he says 'Who?'

However, this is not the case with the Russian oligarchs. Mandelson has strengthened his position by joining the board of directors of Sistema, which is controlled by the billionaire tycoon Vladimir Yevtushenkov. The company has invested in major Russian oil firms, telecoms, radars and aerospace, and the mass media and healthcare sectors, among others.

In an interview with the Russian edition of *Forbes*, the oligarch indicated he was happy with the then impending return of Vladimir Putin to the presidency. 'I'm an optimist. I don't see any dramatic scenarios for my business in our country [Russia] whoever is in charge,' he said. 'We have worked with him [Putin] for a long time, we know him well and many of his traits impress us. I don't see any threat to business – be it small, medium or large … I think the combination of wisdom built up over the years with analysis of the mistakes that have been made will allow Putin to make his third term a successful one.'

Yevtushenkov showed little sympathy for Mikhail Khodorkovsky, saying the oil tycoon – who clashed with Putin – fell prey to his 'ambitions' and was too politicised. 'Business should be separate from politics,' he said.

That has not entirely saved him, however, from Putin's wrath. In September 2014 he was under house arrest over alleged money laundering charges. Bloomberg reported: 'The accusations stem from a probe into the alleged theft of shares in oil assets in Russia's Bashkortostan region in which Yevtushenkov's AFK Sistema gained control in 2009, according to the Investigative Committee. Sistema called the accusations groundless and said it would to use [sic] all possible legal means to make their case.'

By November 2014 there were contradictory reports – one saying he had been released and another saying he was still under house arrest.

The list of 350 people who receive the newsletter suggests the Global Counsel has a number of other clients, some of them apparently employing them for specific advice on a particular problem.

One company, Betfair, an international betting firm based in the Gibraltar tax haven, admitted to *Private Eye* that it was a client. And, as the *Eye* commented, the firm was 'facing tricky questions over licences in

European countries such as Italy and Greece and for whom Mandelson's experience as an EU trade commissioner must have looked attractive.'

Once Betfair confirmed its role, Global Counsel obviously made it clear through Benjamin Wegg-Prosser that the list was not all clients, and other firms refused to confirm whether they were.

The list includes a number of companies that seem to have multiple entries – suggesting they may well be clients. They include the banker JP Morgan, for whom Tony Blair acts as a consultant; Glencore, for whom Blair acted as a go-between to settle a dispute with the Qatari royal family; Vodafone; the drug firm Novartis; Nomura; the banker HSBC; the drinks group Diageo; Unilever; the insurer Prudential; the energy firms BP, Shell and E.ON; and the aluminium group Alcoa.

There are also some big players on the list including Sir Martin Sorrell of WPP, who we have seen owns part of Global Counsel; Jeff Tannenbaum, managing director of the Bank of America; and Jeffrey Rosen, managing director of Lazard. Others include Ken Costa, who runs the evangelical Christian Alpha courses and is a former chairman of Lazard International; and Jonathan Kewley, a corporate lawyer with Freshfields and a member of the Business, Innovation and Skills department's professional and business services group.

In Whitehall recipients of the newsletter include Thea Rogers, adviser to Chancellor George Osborne; Martin Donnelly, permanent secretary at the business department; Nick Baird, UKTI chief executive; Sir Kim Darroch, David Cameron's national security adviser; Moscow diplomat Denis Keefe; and the director of the European and global issues secretariat at the Cabinet Office, Angus Lapsley.

The political connections are more interesting, as they span the main two parties. On the list are shadow Chancellor Ed Balls; party chairman Douglas Alexander (twice through his office staff and on a private email); and shadow Education Secretary Tristram Hunt, who in 2013 praised Mandelson in *Total Politics* magazine: 'Peter is … a force for progressive politics in Britain and around the world.'

Right: The Blair family planned a full decade in 10 Downing Street but after leaving Tony Blair began his real quest for wealth.

© *DailyMail/REX and WireImage*

Below: On the same day he resigned as Prime Minister, Blair announced that he had accepted the position as envoy of the Quartet in the Middle East. He is pictured here before a meeting with the Quartet's representatives (from left: Hillary Clinton, Ban Ki-moon, Sergei Lavrov and Catherine Ashton) in 2010.

© *Chris Hondros/Getty Images*

Above: Blair met with President Peres of Israel in July 2014 as efforts were being made to secure a ceasefire between Hamas and Israel to end the military campaign in Gaza. Blair described himself as 'a fully paid-up member of the Peres fan club'.   © *GALI TIBBON/AFP/Getty Imag*

Right: Less than a month before he stepped down as Prime Minister, Blair was all smiles as he visited Libya to meet with his long-time ally Colonel Muammar Gaddafi.It would not be their final meeting.   © *Peter Macdiarmid/Getty Imag*

bove: Now embroiled in a ferocious civil war, during which Blair has advocated mbing campaigns against both sides at different times, Syrian President Bashir -Assad and his wife Asma were welcomed to 10 Downing Street in 2002.

© REX

elow: Although extremely difficult to ascertain an exact figure, one of Blair's ost lucrative contracts is with President Nazarbayev of Kazakhstan – another ad of state whose human-rights record leaves something to be desired.

© PA Images

Above: Since his departure from 10 Downing Street, Blair has spent a great deal of time with oil-rich Middle Eastern leaders, whether it be at global economic conferences, as here, or at less formal events.

© *Fayez Nureldine/AFP/ Getty Images*

Right: Blair returned to 10 Downing Street for a lunch in July 2012.

© *Indigo/Getty Images*

bove: Meeting British troops in Basra in January 2004.

© *STEFAN ROUSSEAU/AFP/Getty Images*

elow: The 'special relationship'.

© *Ron Sachs/REX*

Above: The Iraq War ignites passionate protests among critics. © *Mark Thomas/REX*

Below: Progress, which has been described as a party-within-a-party, is Blair's pressure group within the Labour Party, and the keeper of the Blairite flame.

© *John Stillwell/PA Archive/PA Imag*

The Blairs' appetite for property seems insatiable. Some of the dwellings are
for the gentry, while others are for investment purposes. Blair has connected
s house in Connaught Square (above) with the mews house behind it, and has
created Chequers in Wotton House (below) in Buckinghamshire.

© Martin Rowson 2014 and Steve Bell 20

Also, there are Liam Byrne, shadow Education Minister and a member of Policy Network with Mandelson; and Lord (Andrew) Adonis, shadow Infrastructure Minister. He is also linked via his researcher to former minister Pat McFadden. Former Labour MP and City spokeswoman, now a lobbyist with Portland, Kitty Usher is on the list. And Will Straw, son of Jack Straw and prospective Labour parliamentary candidate for Darwen, is also a recipient. He is linked to Mandelson through a project for the Institute of Public Policy Research and is also working for Ed Balls one day a week.

Jonathan Powell, who, as we have seen, is one of the key Blairite advisers and well connected to Blair's businesses, is also on the list.

Mandelson's list extends to Tories as well. Ed Vaizey, the Culture Minister, is a recipient as well as Zac Goldsmith, through his researcher. And so is Jo Johnson MP, brother of Boris and head of Cameron's policy unit in No. 10.

Among Liberal Democrats who are on the list is Giles Wilkes at BIS, special adviser to Business Secretary Vince Cable. And there is one independent peer, Lord Owen, plus Mandelson's long-term friend Lord Birt. Blair's biographer, Anthony Seldon, the master of Wellington College public school, is there too.

However, checks with some of the people appear to suggest that the list is partly a vanity project – particularly among some politicians, one of whom said the newsletter ended up in his spam queue. None of the politicians contacted appeared to pay for it, while some of the business advisers did not seem to value its content much.

One said, 'Basically, the information is not much more than you could get by an intelligent reading of *The Economist*. It joins up the dots and crosses the *t*'s, but it isn't much more than that.'

Some of the advice also appeared plain wrong.

A document on future developments of the European Union says little more than Peter Mandelson's known pro-EU position says in public with a lot more detail of how it is justified. And, if Global Counsel were so well connected, it would have realised that the strength of Euroscepticism was much more powerful inside the Conservative Party than it suggests in the briefing. This is paralleled by the list of subscribers. It is not going to known Eurosceptics such as Chris Grayling and Theresa May, and therefore has no feedback from them.

Written prior to Cameron's commitment to an in/out referendum on Britain's EU membership and the EU budget settlement, it warns of bad relations between Britain and the EU. It falsely predicts that Britain won't be able to get a budget settlement that limits the growth in EU spending, and talks about the EU wanting a new treaty when in fact it decided to create a stronger eurozone without one.

But Global Counsel's view on the referendum announcement is to quote what must be a minority of Tory ministers, to the effect that a referendum would be 'divisive and suicidal for the Conservative Party'. In fact, the Tories are now committed to one, and this issue has been overtaken by the rise of the United Kingdom Independence Party (UKIP) alongside the issue of whether Cameron should recommend that Britain quit the EU if he does not get what he wants.

It also predicts – and this is still to be settled – that in the end Britain will be disadvantaged if it does not become part of the eurozone for the simple reason that banks that trade in large euro-denominated positions will want to be backed by the European Central Bank as part of the eurozone rather than the Bank of England. Altogether the drift of the argument is that, in the end, London's big banks will decide that it is more logical to be located in the eurozone than in the sterling area and will leave the City.

What is clear from Mandelson's business interests, which may not rival those of Blair, is that, by linking to both pro-Putin oligarchs and getting the financial backing of WPP, he has been able to make himself rich. He has also added a portfolio of clients to tackle specific issues – such as Betfair – and also, as revealed in the *Guardian*, got involved with a dispute over APP and the destruction of the rainforest.[13]

APP is a controversial Chinese–Indonesian company owned by the

Wijayas, a rich dynasty. In 2012, APP had come under growing pressure after it was accused of illegal logging in Indonesia and damaging the habitats of rare animals such as the Sumatran tiger. A year-long Greenpeace investigation, published in March, alleged that endangered trees, known as ramin, have been chopped down and sent to factories to be pulped and turned into paper. The trees grow in peat swamps in Indonesia, where the dwindling number of surviving Sumatran tigers hunt.

Greenpeace alleged that it found ramin logs in a paper mill belonging to APP on nine occasions over a year. Chopping down ramin trees, a protected species under an international treaty, has been illegal under Indonesian law since 2001. Wood from the rainforests is being turned into everyday products around the world, such as photocopying paper, tissues and paper packaging, according to Greenpeace.

APP, part of the Sinar Mas conglomerate, denied any wrongdoing, saying in a statement that it 'maintains a strict zero-tolerance policy for illegal wood entering the supply chain and has comprehensive chain of custody systems to ensure that only legal wood enters its pulp mill operations. APP's chain of custody systems are independently audited on a periodic basis.' It said it welcomed the Greenpeace report, as it would help 'identify and act on any weaknesses in its chain of custody systems.'

Three large companies said that they were going to stop buying paper products from APP, either forever or until they were satisfied that the products were being produced sustainably. At least sixty-seven companies worldwide, such as Tesco, Kraft Foods and the office suppliers Staples, had boycotted APP since 2004, according to a Greenpeace list produced at the time.

In response to the allegations, Global Counsel said, 'Global Counsel are advising APP on how to ensure that the new voluntary partnership agreement on legal and sustainable timber trade between the European Union and Indonesia is a success … As companies in emerging economies grow across the globe meeting high European and American standards is one of their key challenges.'

Since then, Mandelson contacted Zac Goldsmith, the Conservative MP for Richmond, who has high-level connections with environment campaigners, and was able to broker a deal between Greenpeace and APP to protect part of the Indonesian forest. This is still being monitored. But, again, this appeared to be a one-off arrangement.

In 2010 Mandelson moved to an upmarket property inside Regents Park, which he bought for a staggering £7.6 million in his own name. He obtained a mortgage from HSBC Private Bank – a lender favoured by the wealthy; Francis Maude, the Tory Cabinet Office minister and ex-banker, has a similar mortgage. In January 2015, estate agents Zoopla estimated the property to be worth £11.483 million – no wonder Mandelson appeared on BBC *Newsnight* in January 2015 to condemn Labour's new mansion tax, levied on all properties over £2 million.

The home is among an exclusive group of buildings in the park and boasts a wine cellar, a two-storey atrium, elegant reception rooms and views directly onto a park. A conservatory extends into the large, landscaped garden and the master bedroom occupies the entire second floor. There are three bathrooms and two dressing rooms. In 2014, he was able to rent a renovated detached house in Wiltshire from his friend Nat Rothschild so he could enjoy the country life close to Rothschild's estate.

Benjamin Wegg-Prosser has certainly moved up in the world as well. On 5 March 2012 he moved into a Georgian, Grade II-listed, three-bedroom home round the corner from Tony Blair in Connaught Square in London. According to the Land Registry, he paid £1.925 million for the home and took out a mortgage from Barclays. The property had been on the market through Cluttons for £1,999,995. This property's value has risen more modestly, with Zoopla estimating it to be worth £2.64 million in January 2015.

But neither compares to the wealth of the Blairs and neither has quite the scope to rival Blair's business interests – probably because the name Blair still counts in the American sphere of influence for much more than Mandelson does in the world of Vladimir Putin.

CHAPTER NINE

SELLING INFLUENCE TO THE ARAB WORLD

'Emails between McKillen's staff and Tony Blair Associates reveal the ex-Prime Minister's firm was willing to approach leaders in Abu Dhabi, Qatar, Kuwait and Oman in the search for finance. Blair's former chief of staff, Jonathan Powell, was also willing to offer his help.'
– SIMON NEVILLE IN THE *GUARDIAN*, 11 MAY 2012.

Shortly before Blair left office, two of his closest political friends became paid advisers to Consolidated Contractors Company (CCC), the huge Palestinian-owned construction multinational with subsidiary firms in the Middle East, Britain and America, which we have met in connection with several of Blair's activities in Chapters 1 and 7.

Stephen Byers, the former Trade and Industry Secretary, and Baroness Symons, the former Foreign Office Minister responsible for the Middle East, have both been paid as consultants to the company. Byers is also chairman of a British CCC subsidiary, AKWA, which builds sewage works. Symons is 'international consultant' to CCC, which donated large sums to the Conservatives ahead of the 2010 UK general election. By that time neither Byers nor Symons was bothered about this – their friend Tony Blair had been displaced by their enemy Gordon Brown.

In February 2011 contempt-of-court proceedings were brought against CCC for failing to comply with court orders that have frozen its assets in six different countries.[1] On 5 May 2011, Justice Christopher Clarke found two companies in the Consolidated Contractors Group of Companies guilty of contempt of court in ten instances for breaching orders obtained to assist enforcement. A law report noted,

CCC has adopted what has been described as a 'determined and ruthless' strategy of taking every possible point to resist enforcement. Related enforcement proceedings have occupied the High Court, the Court of Appeal and the Supreme Court on almost 100 days since the judgment on liability, resulting in significant clarifications and developments of the law in the field of jurisdiction and enforcement. Enforcement proceedings are also ongoing in ten other countries.

The company faces an anti-suit injunction, three receivership orders, five freezing injunctions and orders requiring the provision of affidavits of assets. CCC was in contempt of these orders on 14 different counts, including by failing to provide information and receiving revenues in breach of the receivership orders. The High Court found the allegations of contempt to be proved on ten counts, describing them as 'serious and deliberate'. The question of sanctions has been adjourned, but the court gave a stark warning to the defendants that if they fail to purge their contempt, they are likely to face significant, continuing, multi-million pound fines.[2]

CCC had been paying Byers as an adviser since 2005, when he was still an MP (he remained in Parliament until 2010). From the time of his election to Parliament in 1992, Byers was one of Blair's most ardent supporters, identifying himself as an outrider for the New Labour project, floating ideas on Blair's behalf to test reaction. So, once Blair became leader in 1994, Byers's rise was rapid, and he joined the cabinet in July 1998, as Chief Secretary to the Treasury. After the sudden resignation of Peter Mandelson, Byers became Trade and Industry Secretary in December 1998, then, after the 2001 general election, Secretary of State for Transport, Local Government & the Regions.

But he ran into serious trouble. It was his adviser, Jo Moore, who sent the infamous email suggesting that the 11 September 2001 attacks on the USA made it 'a very good day to get out anything we want to bury'. A leaked email from the department's head of news, Martin Sixsmith, advised her not to try to bury any more bad news on the day of Princess Margaret's funeral. Moore and Sixsmith both had to resign – but Sixsmith announced that Byers had insisted on his departure as his price to pay for losing Moore. Blair tried to hang on to his old ally, but Byers was doomed, and, after a couple of controversies over policies his colleagues thought far too right-wing, Byers was forced to resign.

Two subsequent incidents made him look unendurably sleazy and greedy. It emerged that he had claimed more than £125,000 in second-home allowances for a London flat owned by his partner, where the MP lived rent-free. Then he was caught out by undercover journalists on the *Dispatches* programme who were posing as lobbyists from an international company. Byers described himself to them as a 'cab for hire' and offered to lobby his parliamentary contacts in support of the fictitious company for a payment of between £3,000 and £5,000 per day. He told them he had helped National Express and Tesco through his relationships with Transport Secretary Lord Adonis and Business Secretary Peter Mandelson. National Express and Tesco denied this. Byers later denied it too. But it was certainly true that he had lobbied Adonis, for Adonis himself later confirmed it.[3]

'I still get a lot of confidential information because I'm still linked to No. 10,' he told the journalists. If necessary, 'we could have a word with Tony'.

Byers the politician was finished, but Byers the businessman was only just getting started. How many words he has had with Tony since he left Parliament in 2010 we do not know, but the extent to which his business interests and those of his old boss overlap is remarkable.

He had worked for CCC since 2005, so the first five years of his association with the company were while he was still a Labour MP. In

2010, the year he left Parliament, he faxed a note of a meeting that he held with a CCC director from his office in the House of Commons.

In this fax, which was leaked to the *Guardian*, he discussed ways of helping the company secure business opportunities in Nigeria, Equatorial Guinea, Kazakhstan and Libya. The document shows how Byers was active in establishing 'good relationships' with the presidents of Nigeria, as well as with Blair's friend and client, the president of Kazakhstan, Nursultan Nazarbayev (see Chapter 5), and establishing 'strategic partnerships' with companies such as RTZ.[4]

In November 2005, Byers flew out to Kazakhstan with his Commons researcher Philippa Menzies at CCC's expense. He paid another parliamentary researcher, Ellen Broome, to work on CCC projects, according to the Register of MPs' Research Assistants.

Byers also became a director of the company set up to promote Ukraine's membership of the EU by Ukrainian oligarch Victor Pinchuk. This happened around the time Pinchuk was donating heavily to the Tony Blair Faith Foundation and Blair was lobbying for Ukrainian entry to the EU. It is a moot point how much Pinchuk is currently donating to Blair's activities. Interpipe, the pipework company that was the origin for much of Pinchuk's fortune, was audited by Ernst & Young in 2013, who revealed that 'the Group's current liabilities exceed its current assets by $649.1 million'. That amount, the auditors warn, is a 'material uncertainty that may cast significant doubt about the Group's ability to continue as a going concern'. We shall meet Mr Pinchuk, and his near-bankrupt business, again in Chapter 12: 'Doing God'.

This is how it happened that, two days before the Scottish referendum in 2014, when every other British political grandee was north of the border, Blair issued his magisterial advice to the Scottish people from Yalta in the Crimea. He was there to speak at YES – the annual Yalta Economic Strategy meeting, promoted by Pinchuk to press the case for Ukraine's EU membership.

Blair's many friends in Qatar have also benefited from Byers's acumen;

we have been told. Blair himself has an ambivalent relationship with Qatar. One wealthy US investor and businessman who used to be close to Blair told us, 'One day he is damning the Qataris but six months before he is getting paid $5 million for one meeting with the Prime Minister. He sort of flops around from one place to another.

'The guy just cannot not be in the press. He cannot stand not to be making news. So he will say anything. He will say the Qataris are terrorists after he had taken a $5 million payment from them. He is all over the place.'

The Qatari regime does not have an enviable human-rights record. On 27 August 2014 Shadow International Development Minister Alison McGovern wrote to University College London (UCL) about labour standards and the possible use of forced labour on its campus in Qatar. McGovern wrote,

> Too many migrant workers in Qatar are subject to forced labour, poverty pay and appalling working and housing conditions under the *kafala* system. Rightly, there has been a lot of attention focused on what is happening to workers building the infrastructure for the 2022 World Cup, but the truth is that this exploitative labour system permeates much of Qatar's economy. All British firms and organisations operating in Qatar need to look carefully at the way the workers they rely on are treated, and universities like UCL can be no exception to that.

Under the *kafala* system, Qatari employers can prevent their foreign workers from leaving the country or changing jobs. The rules surrounding the exit permit that foreign workers need to leave the country were likened to modern-day slavery by human rights groups. Qatar has now promised to reform the system in 2015.

The TUC general secretary Frances O'Grady said in *Union News*, 'Qatar has become a byword for modern slavery, and its disregard for migrant workers' rights should worry any responsible employer. Whether they are builders, footballers or cleaners, Qatar must treat everyone with respect and dignity. UCL can't just wash its hands because the workers aren't directly employed by them. Ethical employment means ensuring decent work at every step in the global supply chain, and the university should respond swiftly and positively to the concerns expressed by so many.'[5]

UCL told the International Trade Union Confederation that the forced labour it had identified concerned people employed by subcontracting firms used by the Qatar Foundation – a client of the Qatari government's favourite lobbyist, Brown Lloyd James (BLJ), whose chief executive for the Middle East and Asia is a former Blair staffer, John Watts. Watts worked for the Labour Party before being recruited into Downing Street to be responsible for 'organizing the Prime Minister's external presentation at government events, public meetings and visits within the UK and globally in front of the British and international media,' according to his CV. In July 2007, when Blair left Downing Street, Watts left too and joined BLJ.

By 2012 BLJ listed among its clients the Tony Blair Faith Foundation, as well as several Qatari clients: the Qatar Foundation, Doha Bank, Education City Qatar, Qatargas, Qatar Chamber of Commerce, Qatar Financial Centre, Qatari Diar, Qatarlum and the State of Qatar.

Other clients frequently have a Blair connection. One of them, a charity called the Loomba Foundation, has Cherie Blair as its president, and asked Tony Blair to make a speech for it after he left Downing Street. The speech never happened. An unconfirmed rumour has it that this is because he demanded a £500,000 fee.

But BLJ's proudest achievement was bringing the FIFA World Cup to Qatar for 2022. We asked Byers if he had helped BLJ to secure the event. He wrote back,

With regard to the Qatar 2022 World Cup, I'm afraid you appear to have been misinformed. I had no involvement in any capacity in the bid from Qatar and have never done any work in any capacity for Brown Lloyd James. I trust this makes the position clear and is helpful. Perhaps you could let me know exactly what it is you have heard about me and I can then give you any further confirmation that you might require about the lack of any role on my part.

So, we asked, was he doing anything at all for Qatar? Had he been advising Qatar on transport or railways? Was he still connected to CCC? Byers replied,

In relation to your further questions I am struggling to identify the public interest. I resigned as Secretary of State for Transport over 12 years ago and stood down from the House of Commons over 4 years ago. Since leaving public office, I and those closest to me have greatly valued the privacy we now have. I know you will respect this.

So why had he given us so emphatic and definite an answer to our earlier question? 'I was happy to reply to your questions concerning the Qatar World Cup bid because the time line was such that it could have been relevant to my membership of the House of Commons.' This means that the timeline on the other matters is such that it clearly cannot relate to his Commons membership.

After he stood down at the 2010 general election, he did not have to declare anything publicly because he was no longer a public figure. But that does not mean that he should expect privacy for all his business dealings. As we have noted, his parliamentary career ended in tatters after he was investigated by John Lyon, the Parliamentary Commissioner for Standards, for boasting he was 'a cab for hire' seeking £3,000 to £5,000 a day for lobbying. The Standards and Privileges Committee concluded in 2010:

We recommend that, for committing a particularly serious breach of the Code of Conduct, Mr Stephen Byers' entitlement to a

Parliamentary photopass be suspended for two years, with effect from 1 January 2011. If Mr Byers had not accepted that his conduct was wrong and had not apologised in such unequivocal terms, we would have recommended that this entitlement be withdrawn for a much longer period.

As for not replying to our question about whether he has still got a role with CCI, Consolidated Contractors International, part of the Consolidated Contractors Company, it is truly relevant. After the 2010 general election he admitted in a letter to the Parliamentary Commissioner, who was finishing his inquiry into Byers's activities, that he was working for CCI, negotiating a dispute between it and BP over the costs of an Azerbaijan–Turkey oil pipeline. And this was while he was an MP, and he did declare his connection, but it has obviously continued.

He had boasted about his role with the company in his undercover conversations with the *Dispatches* programme:

I'm a consultant to a company called Consolidated Contractors International … And they're sort of, it's a family, it's a, that still controls the company, but they're the twelfth biggest construction company in the world. They're bigger than Bechtel, or Balfour Beatty, or whatever, so they're very significant. And particularly … sort of Middle East and the Gulf, and they're growing their influence in the former Soviet States as well, so Kazakhstan, Azerbaijan, those areas … Because what they do is, they do a lot of construction linked with oil and gas, so, I'm doing a fair bit of work with them. I chair a water services company called Aqua, which is based in, in North Yorkshire, but does three-quarters of its work in the Gulf … Desalination, sewage treatment, the big, you know the palm development in Dubai? … We, we do all the sewage for that.

I chair a group in Ukraine, which is a not-for-profit organisation.

I get paid for chairing it, which is to get Ukraine to look towards Europe really … rather than towards Moscow.

…[O]ur, main backers are a couple of oligarchs in Ukraine who've done pretty well, but recognise that, in terms of where their future's going to be, it's not providing steel to Moscow, it's going to be providing, it's going to be getting access to the European market. And having a more open economy, and they see that and so. They, they have made, they're very good, but they just put the money up and they just allow us, there's a, there's a, there's a board of six of us, and they allow us, pretty much, to run it, you know, so.

I've got other opportunities, so I've got, so there's a big railway about to be built in the United Arab Emirates, called Union Railway. They've approached me to go on their sort of international advisory board. Which would be, which would be very interesting, and is remarkably well paid. So I'll do that. Because in reality, I mean, where my strengths have developed has been very much the sort of Middle East and the Gulf.

The real difference seems to be that, while he can tell us, no doubt truthfully, that he did not work for the World Cup bid, he is, like Blair and BLJ, on a Gulf gravy train, advising small oil-rich nations, in this case on transport and other issues. He admits it himself, but has since said he did not get a job with Union Railway.

We are not impressed by the plea for privacy. Consultancy agreements between former cabinet ministers and oil-rich states are not private. It is perfectly reasonable to ask whether he is still doing work in the Middle East and Near East. No businessman would expect privacy over this, otherwise there would no reporting of business deals in the Western world.

As for his family, we have never made and do not intend to make any enquiries about them.

The conversation with the undercover reporters throws an interesting light on Byers's and Blair's first tentative steps in the Middle East, while

Blair was still Prime Minister and Byers still in the government. He said,

> But I mean I'm, even now I'm sort of surprised – and I say this to him – at how much sort of respect, almost affection that people [in the Gulf states] have got [for Blair]. I don't, and I don't quite know why, it seems quite interesting. Because actually he did very little. I, because I remember at the time saying to him, he should visit the Gulf more often, because actually he only went there once as Prime Minister … in the final couple of months of his prime-ministership. Because the first time he was supposed to go, he cancelled and actually sent me instead, for a sort of day trip, overnight there, then a day, then overnight back. And then there's a couple of other reasons. So he, he's been to Saudi a couple of times, but sort of Bahrain, Kuwait, Qatar; and the UAE, he didn't, he didn't go to very often at all.

BLJ clients also included, as it puts it, 'various heads of state and government officials from around the world'. One of these, not mentioned on the BLJ website, was President Assad of Syria. A document published by WikiLeaks offers BLJ's advice to Assad, dated 19 May 2012. It begins by saying,

> It is clear from US government pronouncements since the beginning of the public demonstrations in Syria that the Obama Administration wants the leadership in Syria to survive. Unlike its response to demonstrations in some other countries in the region, there have been no US demands for regime change in Syria nor any calls for military intervention, criticism has been relatively muted and punitive sanctions – by not being aimed directly at President Assad – have been intended more as a caution than as an instrument to hurt the leadership.[6]

It is not clear how BLJ came to this remarkable conclusion. Sometimes a PR company will tell its clients whatever it thinks they wish to hear, but we have no evidence that this was what happened in this case. BLJ had had a lot to do with Syria. The American Foreign Agents Registration Act requires lobbying companies to register the names of foreign principals, and BLJ has registered just one: a Mr Fares Kallas, whose address is given as Office of the First Lady of the Syrian Arab Republic in Damascus. In 2010 it signed a contract with the Syrian government to handle an interview with the First Lady in the American *Vogue* magazine. It charged $5,000 a month plus expenses, and it was worth every dime, judging by the results. The *Vogue* piece, of March 2011, all copies of which seem to have been removed from the Internet, began,

> Asma al-Assad is glamorous, young, and very chic – the freshest and most magnetic of first ladies. Her style is not the couture-and-bling dazzle of Middle Eastern power but a deliberate lack of adornment …
>
> Syria is known as the safest country in the Middle East, possibly because, as the State Department's website says, 'the Syrian government conducts intense physical and electronic surveillance of both Syrian citizens and foreign visitors.' It's a secular country where women earn as much as men and the Muslim veil is forbidden in universities, a place without bombings, unrest, or kidnappings, but its shadow zones are deep and dark. Asma's husband, Bashar al-Assad, was elected president in 2000, after the death of his father, Hafez al-Assad, with a startling 97 percent of the vote. In Syria, power is hereditary. The country's alliances are murky. How close are they to Iran, Hamas, and Hezbollah? There are souvenir Hezbollah ashtrays in the souk, and you can spot the Hamas leadership racing through the bar of the Four Seasons …

Tony Blair yearns for a role in the Syrian business, and attacked his successor as Labour leader, Ed Miliband, for preventing British intervention. It's an odd irony that, if Miliband had followed Blair's advice, Britain would have been bombing Assad's bases, presumably at the same time as it was bombing Assad's enemies, the Islamic State.

Some small consolation came in December 2013 when Pope Francis invited him to come to the Vatican and discuss what might be done about the conflict. It wasn't much. A one-day meeting in January 2014 alongside former Egyptian Vice President Mohamed ElBaradei, US economist Jeffrey Sachs, US religious expert Thomas Walsh, former Russian diplomat Pyotr Stegny, Lebanese Middle East expert Joseph Maila, Spanish diplomat Miguel Angel Moratinos and French economist Thierry de Montbrial. Hardly a stellar line-up. The idea was to discuss ways of promoting a ceasefire in Syria, protecting the Christians there and 'furthering a transitional and unified government'.

John Watts, according to his LinkedIn entry, is now managing director of BLJ Worldwide. He lists his former employers as 10 Downing Street and the Labour Party, and his base as Qatar; his picture shows him on a football field, presumably to emphasise his success in bringing the World Cup to Qatar.

This last was a considerable lobbying achievement. You might have thought someone would have pointed out at the time that the temperature in Qatar when the World Cup is played is likely to be so hot as to pose a real risk to players, and even more to spectators. You might have thought FIFA would take notice of the fact that Qatar was the only one of nine bidders for the 2018 and 2022 tournaments where there was a high risk of a terrorist attack on the competition, according to a report FIFA itself commissioned.[7] It might have concerned it that, as Frances O'Grady of the TUC had pointed out, foreign construction workers on the World Cup site would face working conditions that would make them little more than slaves. It takes lobbying skill of a high order to overcome such weighty objections.

The new FA chairman, Greg Dyke, is trying to unscramble the mess, calling for the competition to be moved either to a time when Qatar's temperature will be tolerable or to somewhere else. As we write, the betting is that it will be moved to January, which will keep faith with Qatar, but will severely disrupt British and European domestic football.

'I don't know how many people have been to Qatar in June. I have,' Dyke told Sky News. 'The one thing I can tell you is you can't play a football tournament in Qatar in June.' How was FIFA persuaded to make this extraordinary decision?

BLJ Worldwide's website disappeared shortly after we began the research for this book, but has now been reinstated. Its Qatar clients include the Qatar 2022 World Cup bid and, on its home page, it hails the achievement thus:

CHANGING A COUNTRY'S DESTINY. BLJ Worldwide led the landmark international communications campaign that helped Qatar win the right to stage the 2022 FIFA World Cup, transforming the future of a country and a region.

How did it do it?

BLJ utilized an array of strategic communications – including public diplomacy, by introducing one country to another in innovative ways – while working on the campaign. We developed messaging that focused on the benefits of hosting the World Cup in the Middle East, and specifically in Qatar. We worked with key journalists in the sports and news sectors in key countries, securing high-profile interviews and story placements in broadcast and trade media.

The present authors are not quite sure how you go about 'introducing one country to another in innovative ways'.

ENTER THE HOTSHOT BANKER

Another key player in Blair's relationship with Qatar is Michael Klein (whom we shall meet again when we discuss Guinea in Chapter 11). Blair's business relationship with Klein goes back to the long-drawn-out merger between Glencore – the world's biggest commodities trading company set up by Marc Rich – and Xstrata, a mining company.

Marc Rich was an American commodities trader, hedge fund manager, financier and businessman, indicted for tax evasion and trading with Iran and controversially pardoned as President Clinton's last act in office. Former President Jimmy Carter said, 'I don't think there is any doubt that some of the factors in his pardon were attributable to his large gifts. In my opinion, that was disgraceful.'[8]

The merger gathered speed in early 2012, but there were frequent stumbling blocks. One was the position of Qatar Holdings, the country's sovereign wealth fund, which wanted to improve the terms. Qatar Holdings had between 11 per cent and 12 per cent of Xstrata and was the largest shareholder in Xstrata after Glencore, which had acquired more than a third of the company. Qatar Holdings eventually agreed to the price.

In September 2012, it was revealed that Blair had helped broker the deal with Qatar Holdings, leading to its acceptance of the offer. The *Daily Telegraph* reported that Blair was advising Glencore, although it also noted that Blair had advised Qatar in the past.[9] The *Financial Times* noted that Blair had brought together Glencore's chief executive, Ivan Glasenberg, and Qatari Prime Minister Hamad bin Jassim bin Jabor Al Thani.[10] Al Thani oversees Qatar Holdings and the oil-and-gas-rich Gulf state's other sovereign wealth fund, the Qatar Investment Authority. According to someone who was then a business associate of Blair's, Michael Klein worked on this with Hamad bin Jassim, and brought Blair into it because Blair had a close relationship with Hamad bin Jassim.

At the foot of a press release (containing the names of bankers and banks involved in the deal) issued on 7 February 2012, was written 'M. Klein and company, LLC and its affiliates Michael Klein Strategic consultant to each of Xstrata and Glencore.' Klein's role was regarded as unusual, as advisers are typically hired by one side of a deal only.

Blair's links with Klein have expanded the former prime minister's banking network at the highest levels. Klein was a Citibanker – one of a group of financiers famous for their international connections – and he had made it to the head of Citi's global corporate investment bank in Europe, the Middle East and Africa. It was reported in the *Wall Street Journal* that Klein had 'built up a reputation as especially close to Middle Eastern billionaires such as Saudi Arabian Prince Alwaleed , a major investor in Citigroup'. The paper also reported that he had arranged Abu Dhabi's $7.5 billion capital infusion into Citi.[11]

Klein, who had been tipped as a possible head of the bank, left Citibank in July 2008, shortly after Vikram Pandit took over its management. Klein quickly found a niche as an independent adviser to big companies, advising Bob Diamond, the head of Barclays, on buying the core assets of Lehman Brothers, after its demise. He also advised Dubai, which was struggling with the debt accumulated by Dubai World. Moreover, it is understood that Klein proffered his banking and financial engineering services to the British government when it was thrashing around and struggling to contain the banking crisis of 2008.

We learn from *Euromoney* that Michael Klein has a 'banking boutique'. Blair is clearly someone he can call on when he needs a door opened or some sweet-talking for a client. The magazine wrote,

> The kiosk is basically a bit of a status symbol. No effort is made to dress the organization up as a corporate entity, espousing team effort and client-focused mission statements. The kiosk is all about the principal and it's obvious that the principal has amazingly strong client relationships because otherwise he wouldn't be appearing on the top line of the deal. In a way, kiosks are doing for star investment bankers what hedge funds did for star traders.[12]

Whether he is a client of Blair or Blair one of his clients may be a moot point.

The *MailOnline* website reported on 15 September 2012, 'Klein and

Blair know each other through their mutual connections to Abu Dhabi, where Blair is on the payroll of Mubadala, the sovereign wealth fund that invests Abu Dhabi's vast oil profits.'[13]

Michael Klein's connections with Blair led to speculation that the two men might merge their interests, although this has been denied by Blair's office. As a master of networking, Blair can draw on Klein's contacts in Middle Eastern financial institutions. That facility chimes well with Blair's political connections. While the partnership may stay *sub rosa*, it also remains powerful.

THE IRISH DIMENSION

Blair's links with Qatar came to light in 2010, when he put the Qatari Prime Minister in touch with the Irish businessman Patrick McKillen. McKillen was seeking £70 million to buy the Maybourne hotel group from the Barclay brothers. The *Guardian* noted, 'Emails between McKillen's staff and Tony Blair Associates reveal the ex-Prime Minister's firm was willing to approach leaders in Abu Dhabi, Qatar, Kuwait and Oman in the search for finance. Blair's former chief of staff, Jonathan Powell, was also willing to offer his help.'

The *Guardian* reported that the High Court in London heard that the colourful Belfast-born businessman met Sheikh Hamed's son Sheikh Jassim in the lobby of Claridge's to discuss a possible investment. McKillen said, 'During the meeting Sheik Jassim said that Tony Blair and his father [Sheikh Hamed] had been doing business in Doha and the issue of Maybourne came up. Tony Blair had suggested that they should make contact with Paddy McKillen.'[14]

He denied the Qatari deal was done by Blair acting as his agent. He said, 'No, it came purely from a discussion in Doha between an ex-head of state and head of state. I'm not sure what business they were doing but the two gentlemen are very close.' As we have seen, Blair's tentacles continue to spread globally, and not least across to the Atlantic, where he has a legacy of support and contacts.

CHAPTER TEN

THE TRANSATLANTIC CONNECTION

'I've had a great friendship with Tony Blair for many years and we both share the ideology of the Third Way.'
– PRESIDENT JUAN MANUEL SANTOS OF COLOMBIA
IN LONDON, JULY 2010.

Tony Blair Associates does much less business on the American continent than in Europe, the Middle East and Asia. But it does have, to our knowledge, two South American public-sector clients and one US commercial client.

At the World Economic Forum Summit in Rio de Janeiro in April 2011, Tony Blair met Erik Camarano, the chief executive of a free-market consultancy, Movimento Brasil Competitivo (MBC), and within months was proposing that they go into business together to seek work in Mr Camarano's home state of São Paulo in Brazil. The previous day, *en route* to Rio, he met his old Colombian chum Juan Manuel Santos, now the president of his country, who was already a client.

It took a year, but Camarano and Blair's partnership eventually landed a contract worth, on Camarano's figures, almost £4 million a year to advise the state government of São Paulo, the economic powerhouse behind Brazil's rapidly growing economy. About £2 million had been earmarked for travel and accommodation costs and Blair's fees, according to Camarano. The sum is disputed by Blair's office, but, as usual, it does not offer an alternative figure.

'We first had contact with Mr Blair at the World Economic Forum last year,' Camarano told the *Daily Telegraph*. 'We were then approached by him and he now has an office in São Paulo. He wanted to bring his expertise to Brazil.

'He saw that Brazil was coming to a state of maturity where we could make use of his experience.

'The situation in São Paulo is very specific. It's different from other states in Brazil where sometimes a lack of money is the crucial question. In São Paulo you do have resources, you have a huge public budget and you have a huge amount of resources to invest from the public sector.'

Blair's South American office is run by Joe Capp, a former senior employee with the consultancy McKinsey, and the project in São Paulo state, an area larger than the UK and with a population of more than 40 million, is costing 12 million Brazilian reals (£3.7 million), according to Camarano, whose company receives only 10 per cent of the fee.

Camarano said that around 40 per cent would go in taxes, because his office would be hiring foreign services. 'I would say that, of the remaining part, which is maybe 6–7 million reals (£1.8–£2.1 million), one part is logistics – which is international travelling, the consulting involved, lodging, accommodations – and then there is a part that is the fee for his office for the consulting work.'

Camarano said that the consulting group would have a large number of experts in fields such as transport, security, education and health.

A São Paulo state spokesman told the newspaper, 'The company of the former British Prime Minister Tony Blair is advising the government of São Paulo in its long-term planning.

'This is being done in partnership with the Movimento Brasil Competitivo, a private organisation that is bearing all the costs of the consultation.'[1]

Erik Camarano's Brazilian Competitiveness Movement (the Movimento

Brasil Competitivo mentioned above) is a Brazilian NGO certified as 'Organization of the Civil Society for the Public Interest', which works to improve competitiveness in the public and private sectors in Brazil.

The other South American client Blair met in the period around the Rio de Janeiro conference in April 2011 was his 'close friend', President Juan Manuel Santos of Colombia. A day before the Rio meeting began, Blair was in Colombia meeting Santos. These two men go back a very long way. In 1999, when Blair had been Prime Minister for only two years and Santos was the hardline right-wing Minister of Foreign Trade in Colombia, they collaborated on a book. It was called, naturally, *The Third Way – An Alternative for Colombia*.

In July 2010 when, as the recently elected president of Colombia, Santos was in London to meet the recently elected British Prime Minister David Cameron, he looked in at Tony Blair's office first. After the twenty-minute meeting Santos told newspapers, 'I've had a great friendship with Tony Blair for many years and we both share the ideology of the Third Way. In my campaign I have said that my government would be close to the Third Way, which is useful not only to Colombia but to the whole world, especially after the financial crisis of 2008.' The Colombian contract came Blair's way just eight months later.

Blair's consultancy business is less active in North America, but the month before that 2010 meeting with Santos he had signed a £700,000-a-year contract to advise Khosla Ventures, founded by Indian-American billionaire Vinod Khosla and based in California's Silicon Valley. Khosla Ventures invests in green technology.

Its mission is to 'assist great entrepreneurs determined to build companies with lasting significance.' Khosla says his goal is 'to be the best assistant there is for anybody trying to build a large, technology-oriented company.'

It is not at all clear what Khosla needs Blair for. The former PM has no expertise in green technology or management consultancy, and it is not immediately obvious what use Khosla might have for his expertise in governance and government relations. In fact, the only area of government relations Khosla seems to be involved in concerns a public beach in California which he has apparently decided to annex.

All California beaches are, by law, public between the ocean and the high-tide mark – but you have to be able to get to them. The previous owners of Martins Beach let people use the road to the beach on payment of a small fee, but Khosla has bought the land and put up a sign that says, 'Private Property: Keep Out'.

People have been coming to Martins Beach for decades. There are public toilets, a café and a car park. The California Coastal Commission has tried to sort the issue out with Khosla, but he is not, apparently, interested in negotiation.[2]

Doing a deal with the state of California is something Blair might have some useful advice on. But, in California, a billionaire can quickly exhaust the legal resources of a small, underfunded state agency without the need for the political sophistication of a former British Prime Minister.

While business in North and South America is not as extensive as it is with the rest of the world, it shows a similar pattern: much of the money for Blair's services comes from old chums.

CHAPTER ELEVEN

AFRICA: MORE COMMERCE THAN CAUSE

'If you DO want to come and invest in Guinea, you will have in the president himself, and in his senior team, partners who can make it happen.'
– TONY BLAIR ADDRESSING A CONFERENCE IN
ABU DHABI, NOVEMBER 2013.

The scene was a crowded conference hall in an upscale hotel in Abu Dhabi in November 2013, where a large number of representatives from Guinea had congregated to hear Tony Blair sing the praises of their much-neglected country to an audience that also contained some very wealthy local sheikhs and financiers. At last, they could see their way to reach out to people who could provide some very greatly needed investment. The audience listened in a reverential hush to Blair as he spoke about the opportunities in one of Africa's poorest countries. Blair's image filled huge TV screens around the platform. The short speech was greeted with acclaim.

Blair was thanked in generous terms by local dignitaries as he descended from the platform. All eyes turned to him as he passed the President of Guinea: how would he celebrate the partnership with President Alpha Condé that Blair had just described so passionately in his speech?

What occurred next could only be described as a calculated letdown, even snub. Blair briefly shook the President's hand and disappeared out of the room in a trice, followed by his entourage, to the President's evident bafflement. (We'll come back to this conference later in the chapter.)

What did those in the audience conclude about Blair's attitude towards Africa? Many in the room questioned Blair's enthusiasm for the subject. Was he just doing it because he was paid? Was he more interested in his local business interests than in Africa's welfare? Whatever the truth, the audience felt short-changed, their expectations of the great British leader dashed.

On one level, the Africa Governance Initiative (AGI) umbrella under which Blair's team works constitutes Blair's bid to bring British 'standards of governance' to Africa. On another, the AGI gives Blair the chance to make contact with and attract the adulation and acclaim of African leaders, reliving the adulation that he has lost at home, said one observer of Africa. 'It is an ego trip for a leader that is history at home.'

It is ironic, and not a coincidence, that Blair is seeking to trespass on the ground that Gordon Brown, his long-term adversary as Chancellor and then Prime Minister, made his own while in government. After leaving power, Brown himself has paid particular attention to Africa as the UN's special envoy for global education.

Blair sought to tap into the growing interest in Africa when he was still Prime Minister. In 2004, during his last government, he set up his Commission for Africa, its board populated by the great and the good, including Bob Geldof, Michel Camdessus (a French banker) and Ethiopia's Meles Zenawi Asres (the President of Ethiopia) and members of NGOs. The Commission published its report 'Our Common Interest' on 11 March 2005. According to the Commission's website, the report 'recognised that everyone would benefit from – and has a role in creating – a strong and prosperous Africa. It put forward a coherent package of measures to achieve this goal.' A report five years later examined how far its goals had been achieved.

Blair created his own African initiative in 2008, after he had left government, and called it the Africa Governance Initiative (AGI). This became a registered UK charity on 5 November 2009. AGI's first chief executive Kate Gross died at the end of 2014. Blair's work in Africa for the AGI is done on a *pro bono* basis; Blair's office insists that Tony Blair Associates has no commercial clients on the continent, so Blair could not be trading advice to governments for a commercial payback. On the other hand, representatives of JP Morgan Chase have been known to accompany him on trips to Africa, for example to Nigeria in 2010. Nigeria is Africa's most dynamic economy and AGI has connections to that country.

How seriously should Blair's commitment to Africa be taken? One observer in a leading African charity is highly sceptical. She told us that Blair sees African leaders through a very simplistic prism. 'He sees good guys and bad guys. John Kufuor, who used to be the President of Ghana, Museveni of Uganda, Meles Zenawi of Ethiopia are all good guys. But a lot of these people didn't turn out so well.' (One might include Colonel Gaddafi in that list.) Blair thinks he can have a unique effect on Africa, going where others have failed, and that was the prompt for the launch of his Commission on Africa, in 2004.

For all Blair's haughtiness on the public stage, as we saw in the investment conference in Abu Dhabi referred to above, the AGI's mission, as expressed on its website, makes every effort to appear unpatronising. The language embodies the rhetoric and clichés of the professional aid donors, replete with largely vacuous jargon.

It goes as follows:

AGI is working for a future in which Africa's development is led by Africans, with governments that are capable of setting and achieving priorities that reflect the rising aspirations and expectations of their citizens. To achieve this vision, we provide practical advice and support to help African leaders to bridge the gap between their vision for a better future and the capacity of their governments to achieve it. We work with countries – currently Sierra Leone, Liberia, Rwanda, Guinea, Nigeria, Ethiopia and Senegal – that are at turning points and where we have had an invitation from the Head of Government to provide capacity development support.

Our model combines the experience of AGI's founder and patron, Mr Blair, with on-the-ground teams of professionals permanently based in our partner countries, working shoulder-to-shoulder with senior leaders in the heart of government to develop capacity and put in place the skills, systems and structures needed to drive the delivery of results on the ground. AGI is a dynamic and fast-growing charity, celebrating its 5th anniversary in 2013.

Elsewhere, the AGI website says,

We work at two levels: At the political leadership level, Tony Blair draws on his ten years as Prime Minister to offer leaders the kind of advice on reform that only someone who has stood in a leader's shoes can give. At the same time our teams, based permanently in each country, work shoulder-to-shoulder with counterparts to put in place the 'nuts and bolts' needed to get things done.

The AGI says it provides the systems for African leaders to build centralised cabinet-style structures around the country's president to give him more power over his fellow ministers. It acts as a form of shadow civil service, discreetly and with a very low public profile. The AGI seeks to impress the President by saying that the same systems enabled Blair to carry out his transformation and modernisation of Britain, for which he is famed.

Critics of the AGI say its mission of 'capacity building' and 'focus on governance' is a euphemism for market liberalisation, making the countries more business-friendly for foreign investors (JP Morgan clients are now more involved in Sierra Leone and Rwanda, for example) at the expense of the infrastructure reform that would make a serious difference to poverty and human rights.

AGI AND THE EBOLA CRISIS

AGI policy towards its activities in Africa shifted sharply with the Ebola outbreak in the middle of 2014. The disease took root at the very heart of the AGI empire, in Sierra Leone, Liberia and Guinea, and the organisation moved staff from the more familiar role of advising ministers of commerce on trading policies and bureaucratic efficiencies to roles more targeted at improving responses to the Ebola outbreak. The well-educated output of top American and British universities brought their technological expertise to the systems used by the local populations to report their suspicions of symptoms of Ebola as well as the deaths of relatives, whose bodies need to be removed for burial.

The AGI staff occupy government offices in Freetown in Sierra Leone and Monrovia in Liberia, isolated from any risk to health, but, as one official told us that 'at last they have found a *raison d'être*. It may not be governance exactly, but the leaders find they are doing good works'. AGI staff are serving as technocrats in a region that is missing many technical skills. Their language is detached from the human tragedy, although that is not to say that these young Westerners whom Blair has put there are not affected by the trauma they see around them.

AGI talks about how it organises 'surveillance operatives' to visit the homes of the sick and dying to ensure they are observing the quarantine requirements. Victoria Parkinson, an AGI executive in Freetown, told us, 'The burial needs to be mobilised. We have to set that up, in conjunction with other partners, through a command-and-control structure. There is a big piece about ensuring that anyone who has died of Ebola is quickly and safely collected and buried in a dignified medical burial.' Parkinson operates a system of whiteboards from her 'command-and-control' centre to check that the response to a report of a case of Ebola is efficient.

Cries for help using the emergency 117 number in Sierra Leone are described by the AGI staff as 'phone data' that needs to be analysed by upgraded communications systems. Call centres are now staffed by ever larger numbers of operators in Freetown. Emily Stanger, a Harvard-educated Texan who works for AGI, told us, 'The number of calls using the 117 hotline has grown sixfold since August.' Stanger, who works out of Freetown, says operators must prioritise the severity of the call. 'We are receiving so many calls a day and there are not enough health workers and beds and community surveillance operators to visit everyone on the same day. We are in the unfortunate circumstance where decisions and priorities need to be made by operators.'

Yet the sick and suffering are happily benefiting from this access to Western expertise. Stanger says, 'We put in a new software system to allow us to track the calls and quickly analyse the data. During the house-to-house campaign in August 2014, the call volume went up to over 1,500 calls Ebola-related a day. It is now 1,200 calls. The response has improved. Before, people might need to call the line four or five times while people waited for a response, to pick up a body or waiting for someone to come to their home after reporting someone sick. Now we are much quicker.'

An incident-management system in Monrovia enables Elizabeth Smith, a UK-educated Blair consultant, to process results using metrics. These are then passed to her political masters in the office of the Liberian Government's chief of staff for action. 'We make sure people are clear about different pillars of our response. These pillars are case management, tracing contacts of the sick and looking at and analysing data. We check that information flows to the incident-management meeting in a form government can understand.'

For all the management speak, Blair's consultants feel torn by the terrible human tragedy. On their way to their government offices, they see bodies on the streets. Parkinson says she feels most pain turning on the television at her Freetown apartment and seeing bodies being removed to morgues. 'There are hard days for us but we need to maintain focus. We need to keep plugging on. It is not just names or numbers on a whiteboard: it is people. I am not as hardened as some people. It can be really tough.'

While the experiences of Blair's teams are clearly traumatic, they are little shared by the patron. He had made just one flying visit to the region by the middle of November that year, when he met the presidents of the affected countries and gave a series of interviews, including one to the BBC, giving some magisterial (and pessimistic) comments on the state of the battle against Ebola.

Curiously, AGI has not been involved in Guinea, leading some to surmise a rift between President Condé and the former British Prime Minister. AGI is seen by Blair (as shown by a passage on the AGI website) as a continuation of the UK's commitment to Sierra Leone following the establishment by Blair of a two-thousand-strong military force in the country, supporting its government when he was Prime Minister. This intervention in the country's civil war was regarded as his most (and only) successful foreign intervention.

Since being PM, I've had a team here in Sierra Leone helping the government, they have been here for 6 to 7 years now. We have a good relationship going back over a long period of time. The tragic thing for the country is that before this Ebola crisis, it was making a lot of progress on the economy. And you can really see the difference in Sierra Leone today from a few years ago. They are going to lose some time because they will have to pick their economy back up and make sure the country goes on a forward path again.

For the most part, Blair prefers to see his African troops as champions of his philosophy of business-oriented reform. Media in African countries have not warmed to the message, complaining that this is another form of colonial exploitation through a local, corrupted elite.

It is a consistent theme of Blair's business that the water is muddied between charity and political intervention. This AGI 'charity' is now bidding for a slice of the UK's £8 billion foreign-aid budget to help rebuild war-torn countries, with African countries among the most needy.

The highly sensitive move has prompted concerns over a possible conflict of interest with Blair's complex business dealings.

In addition, according to a private source, Blair appears to have taken advantage of his relations with Rwanda, Sierra Leone, Liberia and Guinea to create a favourable environment for the introduction of faith schools. Blair talks in terms of 'globalisation of faith' and to this end has established partnerships with universities around the world.

The AGI (for all its protestations) can also appear to be the former Prime Minister's door opener to big and lucrative deals for his commercial organisations. AGI enables Blair to gain an introduction to a country's leaders and power brokers by offering assistance. The payoff for the *pro bono* governmental assistance comes in contracts involving natural-resources projects, major banks and global companies. Here, Blair is the fixer. Nowhere is this more apparent than in the case of Guinea, which we will come to later.

The AGI has twenty employees in London and thirty-eight in Africa, split across seven different countries; the staffing levels in Ebola-hit countries has recently been increased. The latest accounts available, which are for 2013, show that it had an income of £4.79 million, up greatly on the previous year when it received £3.16 million. It has however been criticised by human-rights NGOs for colluding with some of the continent's corrupt and brutal regimes.

AGI receives millions of pounds in donations as a charity, through a complex funding structure. AGI employees are embedded in the governments of at least four African countries – Rwanda, Sierra Leone, Guinea and Liberia – with a significant presence in finance ministries. There are further links between Blair and the leaders of South Sudan and Malawi.

Many of these are countries with presidents who have a close and longstanding personal friendship with Blair. This is not so in Guinea; but, in other respects, Guinea is a perfect example of how Blair operates in Africa.

AGI IN GUINEA

In the often forgotten and desperately poor African country of Guinea, Blair advises President Alpha Condé, whom he met after Condé won the presidential election in November 2010. Guinea borders Mali and Côte d'Ivoire (among other countries) and ranks among Africa's poorest countries, as half the population lives on $1 a day. Dictators took over the running of the country from the French in 1958, and they ran the country into the ground.

Condé is a socialist academic and politician born in 1938. He was the first Guinean leader to espouse democracy and open capitalism that favoured investors, and he was quickly courted by icons of Western capital, such as George Soros, Bernard Kouchner and Tony Blair.

Blair's name is now mentioned in Conakry, the capital of Guinea, in hushed tones. No one knows quite why he takes an interest in Guinea. All suspect that big capital, massive natural resources and mining companies with their global strategies out of reach of their leaders, let alone the ordinary person, are involved.

Guinea's desperate state – now compounded by the Ebola scourge – is as much due to its failure to develop natural resources as it is to its history of naked corruption. Guinea, with its population of 10,600,000, has mines of massive potential, with minerals including iron ore, diamonds, bauxite and rare earth metals. On top of that, it has very fertile agriculture and considerable rainfall. To realise this much-needed value of the commodities buried deep under its ground, much under forests, Guinea needs vast quantities of capital. Blair provides the connections to the wider business and political worlds, where money can be found, albeit at a price.

The President of Guinea is thought to have been introduced to Tony Blair through George Soros – the billionaire hedge fund manager who combines making hundreds of millions of dollars out of currency movements in the global financial markets with political activism on a global scale through his Open Society Foundations. In fact, the original contact may have been made by Bernard Kouchner, a contact of Alpha Condé from his days in Paris. Kouchner is a French politician, and a doctor, and the former French Minister of Foreign and European Affairs in the centre-right François Fillon government under President Nicolas Sarkozy. Kouchner was himself a socialist, but that didn't stop him teaming up with the neo-conservative (and indeed friend of Blair) Sarkozy. Kouchner appeared to share with Blair the capacity to bridge ideologies (while being committed to none), in a French style similar to the Third Way. The Guinean President himself had worked as an academic in law at the Sorbonne in Paris while he was in exile from Guinea.

The relationship between the President, a fiercely independent man greatly respected across Africa, and Blair has not blossomed, according to sources inside the Guinean government. One adviser, who did not wish to be identified, said Blair 'is not that close to Condé and certainly not a friend. He has a limited influence on Condé. He has a lot of partners [other than the AGI] working with him. The President is using Blair primarily to deal with the issue of governance over mining contracts. When the tender is launched for Simandou [Guinea's massive bauxite mine embroiled in a controversial contract], Blair's influence will decrease.' The legal ramifications of this case continue to rumble on, and it has been widely mooted that Blair has a commercial role connected to one of the mineral companies involved in the deal. It is thought that Blair serves as an introducer of global banks to the country – which inevitably includes JP Morgan. The company is bidding to take a role in the development of Guinea's mining industry.

Blair did, however, take the opportunity of a meeting with Condé to propose that he hire Michael Klein, the former senior executive at Citigroup, who, as we have already seen, had been a 'strategic adviser' to both parties in the successful merger of Xstrata and Glencore, a deal in which Blair was a participant. These are two behemoths in the natural-resources field, the former being more of a mining company, the latter a trader of commodities. Blair and Klein assisted in the financial negotiations that created a vastly larger global behemoth.

Curiously, Klein was also on the periphery of the wheeling and dealing that took place in the UK Treasury at the height of the 2008 banking crisis, when City and Wall Street investment banks were being consulted to save the UK's banking system.

Klein's appointment would make sense as part of Guinea's pursuit of investment for its natural-resources sector. But Condé declined to take on Klein, saying he was concerned that such a hiring would bypass local procedures, and it did not go ahead, according to a very close adviser to the President with detailed knowledge of the proposal. The subtext to the rejection is that it came from Blair, whose commercial aspirations in Guinea Condé suspects with a vengeance.

Blair's connections with Michael Klein are well established and described in Chapter 9, where we discuss Qatar, and a merger between Blair's and Klein's operations has been discussed. This has been denied by sources close to Blair.

Blair's operations in the presidential offices of African countries can be separated from those of his foot soldiers in the AGI, whom he can deploy to put down his marker in a country. It would not be unreasonable to imagine that they also give him intelligence on the makeup and positions of government officials and politicians inside the country.

This group of intelligent young men and women, most of whom are only shortly out of university and no doubt enthused by the thought of working in far-flung countries (the connection with the ex-Prime Minister will do no harm on the CV for an application to an investment bank or management consultancy), perform mundane administrative tasks for their governments. One official close to the President, who did not wish to be identified, told us, 'We used to use technical assistance from the World Bank and others like that, right? So what we get from AGI is almost the same thing. Here the goal is to improve governance. That means how to increase efficiency in our presidency, delivery, results related to the President's vision. They are helping to find efficient systems for delivering electricity. One of the Guineans they recruited is assisting different commissions with the process of making sure that the right design is in place.'

The AGI has no brief to rock the boat or deal with a country's tough issues. The same official says that AGI does not get involved in rooting out corruption or other social ills. 'They don't play police. It is purely technical. They are working on behalf of Tony; so they are supposed to be able ... Tony is supposed to be able to report to the President if he sees any wrongdoing. I am certain he does it.'

One adviser, employed by AGI in Guinea, finds such administration difficult, 'yet he builds and controls a centre, to make sure everything is effective. He is getting Condé to control his government. Tony enjoys it. Condé benefits from it as there is a tendency for all government ministers to go off in their own directions. This happens in the West [too]. Why is Blair doing it? That is a question I cannot answer.'

The AGI is very conscious of the danger of ministers pursuing their own private interests and agendas at the expense of the President's. This may explain why the country ranks relatively poorly in the Transparency International Corruption Perceptions Index. The 2014 Index shows the country ranking 145 out of 175 countries listed, an improvement of five places on its 2013 ranking of 150.

Officials from the Guinea government suggest that the AGI has implemented some very rudimentary systems for the presidency. One said that AGI provided furniture for the President's office, which was empty when he first moved in. AGI has brought in a number of expatriates to assist with the administration of the presidency, but it is understood that the NGO is looking for talented Guineans living abroad and with positions in Western companies to replace their own people.

One presidential adviser, who did not wish to be named, told us in the course of the Abu Dhabi investment conference mentioned above that, 'They are now holding open tenders to find Guineans who can replace the people inside the system. We define the profiles [of the people we want to hire] and then publish the announcement. So they are helping in actually replacing themselves.' This does indeed conform with the AGI mission statement appearing on the website, quoted earlier.

Presidential advisers assess that Blair visits Guinea at least twice a year. One said, 'I know from what I hear from his people that he watches closely what is happening.'

Basic bureaucracy has also been introduced by the AGI, to focus the President's resources. So systems to sift and prioritise mail directed to the presidency have been introduced. The Blair team has targeted President Condé's reluctance to delegate minor matters (a habit acquired over long years as an opposition leader with a small team in exile). It sees this as a stumbling block to his efficiency as a leader of a newly composed government. One adviser to the President told us, 'They help us improve the management and coordination systems for the presidency. The Blair people do not get involved in particular dossiers but help improve the efficiency of the overall system.' Such statements indicate the vagueness of AGI's purpose or contribution to the country. This is underlined by Condé's own analysis of the AGI role.

In an interview with the authors, he described Blair's contribution to the country in the following terms:

Mr Blair has enlightened us with the fact that having a vision is important, but it is not enough. It is also very important to have the ways and means to implement the vision.

Mr Blair has learned from his own experience at Downing Street that it is very important for the leadership to drive change and implement the vision. When he took office, he delegated a lot. He had the vision and he counted on others to implement the vision, in ministries. After he saw how things were evolving, he realised it needed to be centralised back into Downing Street and the change had to be forced through from Downing Street.

So he has been helping us by bringing in technical expertise and the human resources that we are lacking. He has helped us to gain the capacity that we are lacking to do the same. We are centralising the implementation of the vision so that the change can be organised from the centre, and driven by the leadership. He has provided us with experts and he has helped us fill some of the capacity gap, and human-resources gap that we had. We are clear about where we want to go, but we probably need some help in implementing it.

The implementation of governance in Guinea is performed by a number of young postgraduates experienced in the fields of development. They work for the Africa Governance Initiative, whose catchline reads 'Five years supporting effective governance in Africa'.

Since November 2011, the organisation has been headed by Shruti Mehrotra, an establishment figure in a number of NGOs. As AGI's projects director, she has the task of organising meetings for President Condé at the World Economic Forum, where she had formerly worked. Mehrotra came up through the ranks of the NGO Global Witness, serving as an independent adviser on resource scarcity, sustainable development and political stability. She started her working life, like so many of Blair's international representatives, at the now-bankrupt Monitor Group in Massachusetts.

According to the website of the World Economic Forum, Mehrotra is 'special adviser to the office of the President of Guinea'. Her biographical entry says,

She worked with the President of Guinea to help achieve the government's vision of inclusive social and economic development for the country. This includes offering support for the country's democratic institutions, mining sector reform, and improvement of energy provision and access, agricultural development and food security for all Guineans.

In 2013, Mehrotra is understood to have handed over the main AGI role in Guinea to Pierrick Judeaux, a former management consultant at Arthur D. Little, who was educated in France – although Judeaux had already left the AGI by the start of 2015. Judeaux is around six foot seven and his large mop of straight black hair towers above even Blair's now silvery mane when the two are seen together. This was the case when Blair attended that conference in Abu Dhabi on 24 and 25 November 2013 on the subject of investment in Guinea, with which we opened this chapter. Guinea was apparently seen as too remote for investors, but perhaps it also lacked the amenities they require. Abu Dhabi is a major investor in the African country's minerals, so there is a logic in the Gulf location.

Alpha Condé and Blair both spoke to the conference but that was where his contribution to a very large and dynamic event ceased. Many suspected he was more interested in the meetings he likely held later with senior officials at Mubadala (and perhaps the ruler of Abu Dhabi himself). That certainly was the impression many would receive from his behaviour at the conference, noted earlier.

Blair's presence at the conference was heralded by the appearance of a bevy of advisers, including Judeaux, accompanied by their leader as they scurried through the hotel's public area in a huddle, absorbed in each other and oblivious of the residents and others on the sidelines. They were in search of a more private space for their high level deliberations.

The Jumeirah at Etihad Towers hotel, where Blair was speaking, had been scouted out by his security attachment as early as the day before the event. Spotted on the sidelines was a watchful, grey-suited British policeman, sporting a Union Flag button in his lapel. He confirmed that he was Blair's security detail from Scotland Yard, working at the taxpayer's expense.

The hotel, with its multiple towers and escalators, is one of Abu Dhabi's largest and most luxurious, 'more Dubai than Abu Dhabi', says the brochure. The conference itself was entitled 'Guinea is Back: Guinea's Development Partners and Investor Conference', and its primary aim was to introduce Condé to international investors and tell them that the country was open to investment ideas and wanted their money to develop his country, one of Africa's poorest. Blair was billed on the conference programme as 'Former Prime Minister of the United Kingdom, Founder and Patron of the Africa Governance Initiative'.

A packed room awaited the speech of the British leader. Blair was seated next to Bernard Kouchner in the front row of the conference and a short way away from Condé. Gestures of affection or even recognition were sparse. Guinea's Minister for International cooperation introduced him with frequent references to 'His Excellency', but Blair did not have headphones to hear the translation. Some were hastily provided.

Dressed in a sombre, almost funereal, black suit, Blair strode to the platform. He made a token effort to speak French (the language of the conference and of most Guineans), for which he apologised, before returning to English and his prepared address. An acknowledgement to his host was formal. 'I was asked a few years ago to help President Condé when he first came to power … We know what happened those past years. The reason I am here today is because I have a profound respect for the President, for his country, and for what he is trying to achieve for his country. And also for apparent optimism about the chances for his success …'

The exaggerated head, hand and arm movements were familiar to those who watched Blair in the House of Commons or on the political stump. This was the inclusivism with which he had persuaded Britain to go to war in Iraq, something much valued by his Gulf sponsors, who approve of his tough rhetoric and actions on the terrorism that rocks their comfortable and well-furnished gilded boat.

The speech reading was word-perfect, carrying with it the appearance of a specious authority. Blair was shown on a large screen to an audience apparently hanging on his every word.

Researchers, perhaps his own, perhaps those in the Ministry of Finance, had laboured long on the economic detail he would present. 'On finances, as you know, the [Guinean] deficit has come down sharply, from 30 per cent of GDP to 1 per cent,' he said. 'Several European countries should be envious of that figure! Inflation has halved, reserves are up …' He reminded the audience of the opportunities in agriculture and in natural resources. He heaped praise on the President as a partner: '… from my experience of the past few years, if you *do* want to come and invest in Guinea, you will have, in the President himself and in his senior team, partners who can help make it happen.'

He nodded in passing to the corruption risk, but he treated it in a coy, roundabout way. All in the Guinean garden was rosy for their British inspiration! 'There is a new mining programme to ensure that things are done in a proper and transparent way.' He also made a claim to understand the investors in the audience. 'Investors need confidence. People know that if they make an investment they will get a proper return. But in Guinea, as elsewhere in Africa, we can see the new Africa rising.'

His sign-off reiterated his friendship and interest in the country, as if any of the audience had doubted it! 'Three years ago I knew very little about this President or his country; today I know a reasonable amount about Guinea. And I can tell you, I am proud to be working there, and I hope you can be part of the story as well.'

The speech lasted no more than ten minutes, before Blair descended from the platform, shook the President's hand and departed the crowded auditorium. President Condé looked slightly bewildered, uncertain if he should follow Blair or stay with the audience. Blair was next seen disappearing down an escalator and out of the hotel, accompanied by Judeaux, Mehrotra, other advisers and the security man.

It is no exaggeration to say that the audience saw this as a slap in the face to their country. After the speech they muttered how disappointed they were that this was the extent of his involvement in the conference, whose importance to Guinea we have already noted. Yet, as far as Blair was concerned, his duty to Guinea had been done. Perhaps the next appointment on his day's crowded agenda included meetings with the government of Abu Dhabi, one of his clients. Would it be too cynical to speculate that the fee he received for appearing at the conference (if indeed he did receive any at all) allowed him no more than an hour or so at the hotel? Whatever the case, the resultant impression was hollow and demeaning.

The impact of the conference was not completely without importance. Links were in fact strengthened between Abu Dhabi and Guinea, with the announcement that Abu Dhabi's Mubadala state company would invest $5 billion in Guinean bauxite. The agreement, said Mohamed Lamine Fofana, Guinea's minister for mines and geology, included $1 billion for extraction and exports of bauxite to the UAE as well as a $4 billion aluminium refinery and a port. It fitted nicely with the UAE's expansion plans for its Emirates Global Aluminium business, set to become the world's fifth largest aluminium company by output by the close of 2015.

AGI IN RWANDA

The AGI has no fewer than ten employees working at the heart of President Paul Kagame's regime, including young executives from JP Morgan. Yet the man they work for is of questionable record and character. Paul Kagame has been accused of human-rights abuses, and Human Rights Watch has said that Blair's support of Kagame has emboldened the leader to continue corrupting elections and suppressing opposition and media.

Kagame is also suspected of involvement in genocide. Kagame's legitimacy is questionable, as the Tutsi leader represents only 12 per cent of the country, with the remainder Hutu; Rwanda is run by the Tutsi elite. One source in the NGO sector, a frequent visitor and commentator on the country, observed that, while Kagame claimed that he was the saviour of the country, his Rwandan Patriotic Front (the ruling party of the President in the country) had killed 200,000 people. This was in the wake of the genocide in 1994 that left 800,000 people dead and ripped apart the country. Western leaders failed to act on the genocide and a residual guilt continues to affect policy.

Blair is part of Kagame's so-called '2020 Vision' for rebuilding the country, whose goal is to create an African Singapore, focused on high technology. The same NGO source notes that 'Kagame pitches this sort of image at foreign leaders visiting the country, like Blair. He knows exactly what foreign donors want to hear, like anti-corruption and transparency, and people like Blair buy it. A lot of the foreign donors have lost patience with the corrupt African dictators.' This source goes on to say that, beyond the capital city of Kigali, the poverty is widespread and untouched. 'People like Blair are swept on rapid tours of these countries, they are swept from one perfect project to the next and they think they've seen the country. They meet the Rwandan elite. They don't ask the questions. They accept what they are shown. I have seen the African laugh when they put the white man back on the plane. The African leaders manipulate the naïveté of Western leaders like Blair, who have a superficial understanding.'

And in 2013 came one of those moments of synergy, quite frequent in Blair's post-prime-ministerial career, when two parts of his life come together. He wants to help Rwanda; he is a consultant and paid to help JP Morgan Chase. It so happened that JP Morgan Chase & Co.'s CEO Jamie Dimon announced an investment in Bridge2Rwanda's Financial Analyst Training Program.

The investment made business sense for CEO Jamie Dimon. He said in 2010 he was 'incredibly impressed' by opportunities in South Africa and the rest of the continent. 'The growth rate of banking in emerging markets is set to be two to three times faster than that of the United States and Western Europe where most of our investment banking is currently focused.' The comment was made after Dimon had visited South Africa with his adviser, none other than Tony Blair.

Blair is an enthusiast for Rwanda as well – repeating data supplied by the government without challenging the fundamentals – although this is an economy largely sourced from overseas aid and from the smuggling of minerals from the Democratic Republic of the Congo. The country's limited indigenous economy is provided by mining and manufacturing; the country's lack of infrastructure and of a literate population impedes the creation of a real economy.

The NGO source quoted earlier doubts the effectiveness of the Blair project in Rwanda. 'The AGI people move into a ministry with people who don't have much experience of Rwanda, and they tell civil servants what to do. Those civil servants say it's a marvellous idea. The moment they leave, everything returns to what it was. There is a mirage of government, but nothing is done. They go along with it, because they know their aid depends on it. They also receive a *per diem* payment for turning up. They pay people for attending a training session. They will also hope for a reciprocal conference in London.' She continued, 'Nobody pretends it is anything other than a cosmetic exercise. We are all playing the game. We pretend to learn, you pretend to teach us.'

Blair is a personal adviser to Kagame, whose Rwandan Patriotic Front is thought to also have been behind brutal killings of opposition politicians and journalists, and Blair has access to a private jet leased by Kagame. AGI has its own office in the capital Kigali, and Blair has visited the President six times since leaving office.

Kagame, like another Blair protégé, Thein Sein of Burma, is a far more sophisticated international operator than most dictators. A private 2010 UN report, leaked to *Le Monde* and the *New York Times*, documented atrocities committed by Rwandan government troops in the neighbouring Democratic Republic of Congo. There were also charges that the Rwandan government is increasingly authoritarian after the opposition was effectively barred from challenging Kagame in the presidential election in August that year – an election he won by a remarkable 93 per cent of the votes. He managed the same sort of majority the time before, in 2003.

Carroll Bogert of Human Rights Watch reported in 2010,

Kagame has denounced the UN report as fabrications from the very institution that stood aside and let the Rwandan genocide happen back in 1994. He's also threatening to pull Rwandan peacekeepers, among the best-trained in Africa, out of Darfur.

The UN Secretary-General paid an emergency visit to Kigali to try to repair the damage, and has delayed formal publication of the report until October 1, when the General Assembly will be safely over and done with.

But that won't stop Kagame from having to face awkward questions while he's in [New York]. The UN report accuses the Rwandan army of systematically murdering tens of thousands of Hutu civilians in Congo following its invasion of Congo in 1996.

Meanwhile, back in Rwanda, tens of thousands of civilians are estimated to have been murdered by Kagame's Rwandan Patriotic Front in its march to power in 1994. Kagame's government has thwarted any attempt by the International Criminal Tribunal for Rwanda, set up by the UN Security Council, to prosecute the crimes of 1994, to prosecute officials of the RPF.

Then there's the steady crushing of political dissent. The *New York Times* has doggedly reported on the lopsided election in August 2010 that gave Kagame 93 per cent of the vote; the exclusion of opposition parties from the race; the shooting of a Rwandan general who has broken with Kagame in broad daylight in South Africa; the fatal shooting of an independent journalist reporting on the South African incident; the grisly murder of an opposition politician; the closure of two opposition newspapers.

Kagame's supporters say the evidence is unscientific, and none of it has stopped Tony Blair praising Kagame's 'visionary leadership' and talking of 'my good friend Paul Kagame' – any more than it has stopped former US president Bill Clinton from calling Kagame 'one of the greatest leaders of our time' who 'freed the hearts and minds of his people to think about the future'.[1]

Kagame's cheerleaders are almost a roll call of Blair's international chums: Blair himself; Clinton; Pastor Rick Warren of America's Saddleback Church, the very conservative and hugely wealthy American evangelist who sits on the religious advisory board of Blair's Faith Foundation; Michael Porter, business guru and founder of the bankrupt Monitor Group. Blair's commitment to Kagame has certainly puzzled the far-from-radical *Economist* magazine. Commenting on an article (published in the *Guardian*) written by Blair about the country on the twentieth anniversary of the start of the Rwandan genocide, *The Economist* said,

> There are only two possible explanations for Mr Blair's one-dimensional appraisal of Rwanda. One is that, despite his mission to bring 'practical change' to the Great Lakes region, he really has only the thinnest understanding of it. Another is that, like most informed Western apologists for Mr Kagame, he considers his abuses an acceptable bill for his successes. That may be right; though it is not a view widely shared among regional experts, who fear Mr Kagame's reluctance to relax his grip is storing up a future explosion in Rwanda. It should also be pointed out that apologists for his regime, including Mr Blair, have a lot of personal credibility invested in Mr Kagame.
>
> Rwanda's progress is a rare and oft-cited case-study in the efficacy of development aid and the new industry in state-building to which Mr Blair is an enthusiastic entrant. That is because of how impressive it is, for any poor country, let alone one recovering from an appalling conflict. So development wonks are inordinately attached to Mr Kagame, and correspondingly forgiving of his abuses. This does not mean they are cynical or wrong. It does make them partial witnesses to his regime.[2]

In fact, there are signs the US may be losing patience with Kagame (as indeed it is with Blair). It is cutting aid to Rwanda and warning Kagame that he could face criminal prosecution over meddling in the neighbouring

Democratic Republic of the Congo. The White House has criticised Kagame for the suppression of political activity and made clear that it does not regard Rwanda as democratic.

But Kagame has one high-profile international friend he can rely upon. Tony Blair is willing to defend the Rwandan president regardless of allegations of human-rights abuses, political oppression and rigged elections. He told a Rwandan press conference in 2009, 'Our consultancy is not to tell the people of Rwanda what to do, but to help get done what the President wants.'

However, many large Western banks have yet to seriously consider Rwanda a dollar destination. 'For the most part, big banks don't have a presence in Rwanda,' said Bridge2Rwanda's managing director Clay Parker. 'This was a good way to involve JP Morgan. They are sponsoring an educational program for finance – something where they can see their impact.'[3]

Blair's AGI operation is so fraught with political and commercial undertones that much of its evident positive import is lost. While the work his willing team of highly competent young staff in combating the Ebola epidemic makes a worthy, if limited, contribution to the international effort, the patron's apology for the Rwandan dictator Paul Kagame is highly damaging. Kagame has arguably more blood on his hands from the killing of Hutus than Ebola will ever claim. Blair will argue he is backing a 'moderniser', while quietly forgetting the means he used to obtain power.

Pragmatism infuses the former Prime Minister's thinking as he trumpets the good deeds his AGI organisation does in Africa. Africans are too canny to see Blair as more than fellow traveller who forever mingles opportunity with promotion, self-enrichment with self-righteousness. They do not make comfortable companions.[4]

CHAPTER TWELVE

DOING GOD

'The Tony Blair Faith Foundation communications team and
the top brass spend a long time trying to second-guess what
might be embarassing for Tony Blair.'
– MARTIN BRIGHT, FORMER EDITOR FOR THE
TBFF WEBSITE 'FAITH AND GLOBALISATION'.

Tony Blair launched the Tony Blair Faith Foundation on 30 May 2008 to 'educate, inform and develop understanding' about different religions. His first major speech about it, nearly two months before the launch, was on 3 April 2008 at Westminster Cathedral. Blair said he wanted his new Foundation to organise a global campaign to mobilise young people, across religious divides, to work together towards achieving the Millennium Development Goals, 'Faith and Globalisation'.[1]

Several years on, it is still hard to understand exactly what it is for, and what good it hopes to do. The confusion seems to extend to the Foundation itself. Early in 2014 the website had this to say: 'We aim to demonstrate the vital importance of interfaith collaboration and showcase how faith communities can be huge assets to government and international policy.' So it is not just about improving relationships between faiths, but making the influence of religion in the world stronger. It is followed by one of those meaningless feel-good sentences in which the Foundation appears to specialise: 'We inform, educate and inspire how religion motivates the world today.' How can you inspire how religion motivates the world?

By December the same year, all that had gone, to be replaced by, 'We provide the practical support required to counter religious prejudice, conflict and extremism in order to promote open-minded and stable societies.'

What is happening here is that, throughout its life, the TBFF has two goals, and they fight each other. One is to improve the relationship between faith communities: the TBFF aims to counter extremism in the world's six leading religions, which it identifies as Buddhism, Christianity, Islam, Hinduism, Judaism, and Sikhism. The other seems to be to make religion a stronger force in the world.

No one would argue with the first – if you could stop Muslims, Christians, Buddhists, Hindus, Sikhs, Jews and the rest from killing each other, you would certainly have helped towards making a better world. The second is of course far more controversial, and the website also says, 'The TBFF aims to promote respect and understanding about the world's major religions and show how faith can be a powerful force for good in the modern world.'

So is it promoting peace between religions, or is it promoting religion? It seems often to want to do the second while looking as though it is only doing the first.

In an interview with *Time* magazine at the time of the launch, Blair said the Foundation was 'how I want to spend the rest of my life', though most of his life now seems to be going into some of the other things described in this book.

The TBFF denies that there is, or even could be, any conflict of interest with Blair's other activities:

Mr Blair's charities are independent entities with their own governance structures – including chief executives who are accountable to a board of trustees. The charities are subject to Charity Commission regulation, and completely separate from Mr Blair's commercial operation or any of his other organisations. The Trustees and the Patron have agreed a memorandum to confirm the regulations governing the relationship, and it is the board of trustees that make decisions about the charity's activities, and it has a legal obligation to do so.

This is an ambitious claim: that there is no conflict of interest because Blair does not control (or perhaps even influence) his charities. It seems, on the face of it, far-fetched. Insiders, speaking to us anonymously, say that while Blair seldom comes into the building – because his presence disrupts the work – it is his perceived wishes that inform pretty well every decision. Any suggested course of action must pass the test of: 'Are we sure this will not embarrass Tony?'

The chief executive is Charlotte Keenan, a banker who is married to a Conservative MP. She came to the TBFF in 2008 after a career in corporate finance, partly spent working for Blair's client JP Morgan Cazenove. She is an Oxford theology graduate, was President of the Oxford Union, and studied International Relations and Public Policy at Harvard and international affairs at Columbia. The TBFF website says she 'has extensive experience in international capital markets and M&A advisory work. Her sector focus was in industrials, mining and energy.'

She is in regular and frequent contact with Blair, and they often travel abroad together. While Blair seldom goes to the TBFF's Marble Arch offices, the top brass at the Foundation are frequent visitors to Blair's headquarters in Grosvenor Square for formal meetings with him. A fairly typical meeting in Blair's office in early 2014 consisted of Blair, Keenan, PR consultant Kate Bearman, editor of the Faith and Globalisation website Martin Bright, and Blair's chief of staff Catherine Rimmer, a former BBC journalist.

Keenan's deputy, also director of programmes, Matthew Lawrence, is another former JP Morgan Cazenove banker. He, say insiders, spends most of his time travelling the world, fundraising and visiting

TBFF projects. The TBFF website says Lawrence spent fifteen years in investment banking. So both the director and her deputy are bankers by profession.

Other senior staff include Peter Welby, son of Archbishop of Canterbury Justin Welby, and the operations manager, Emma Selwood. According to Martin Bright, the fact that Blair often employs old friends or the children of old friends or the children of important people such as the Archbishop of Canterbury is partly explained by the fact that the security service briefed him to be careful about whom he appoints because of the risk of accidentally employing a terrorist risk.

Peter Welby, a York University graduate who studied Arabic in Egypt, warned about Vladimir Putin's Russia after its annexation of Crimea. 'I fear the Government would be wise to consider reversing some defence cuts, just in case,' he wrote in an article published on the Faith Foundation website. One of Welby's 2014 contributions to the website is a piece entitled, 'What is ISIS?' He declares with the authority of a gloom-laden Middle East analyst, 'Buoyed by its advance, the group declared a Caliphate, a move that has split the jihadi world despite long being the aspiration of such organisations. What is more shocking is that over one month since these events, the Iraqi government is yet to make any significant gains in its counter-attack.'

Faith Foundation communications are run on Blairite lines. There are no fewer than seven communications staff, which seems excessive given the size of the organisation and how averse it is to communicating. Heading it up is communications director Parna Taylor, and a key figure is PR consultant Kate Bearman, who, like most of the leadership of the Blairite pressure group Progress, cut her political teeth in Labour Friends of Israel. Press officer is William Neal, who worked in Parliament and is a pillar of the Blairite pressure group Progress. New in 2014, Neal is not quite as averse to talking to journalists as his predecessor, but that is a low bar to jump.

They spend, we are told, a lot of time in meetings talking about strategic communications, which they call 'strat comms'. They once spent a full half-day with four or five staff talking about Twitter protocols for members of staff on their individual Twitter accounts – a dreadful waste of time and money, but also an indication, says Martin Bright, of the perceived need to control everything. Discussions about whether to issue a press release are lengthy and tormented, and generally end up with the decision that it will be safer not to.

Over and over again, they return to worrying about the need to avoid anything which might embarrass the distinguished founder of the Foundation.

There is no overt role in its governance for the charity's founder and patron, Tony Blair, but his seems to be the principal influence on key decisions, even when he does not specify precise wishes. When the TBFF appointed a journalist to edit its Faith and Globalisation website, a monthly hour-long meeting with Blair was arranged.

Yet, in the few on-the-record conversations we were able to have with them, officials of the TBFF were at pains to stress that they were quite apart from the rest of Tony Blair's activities, and took their decisions with no reference at all to what went on anywhere else in the Blair empire.

Given the TBFF's sensitivity to embarrassing Blair, we understand there was great concern in the office when the *Daily Telegraph* ran a story which suggested sympathy with the Muslim Brotherhood, because of Blair's known strong hostility to the Brotherhood. Senior officials at the TBFF felt that references to the Brotherhood on the Faith and Globalisation website might not be to the patron's taste. The editor of the website, Martin Bright, left after five months, feeling that he had not had the freedom he was promised and he points out that, as a matter of fact, the website never did run an article about the Muslim Brotherhood. 'Draw your own conclusions,' he told us. How decisions were made on the website's contents, we do not know, but it is a matter of fact that, since then and at the time of writing, there have been no articles about the Muslim Brotherhood on the Faith and Globalisation website.

The TBFF communications team and the top brass 'spend a long time trying to second-guess what might be embarrassing for Tony Blair', we were told by Bright, whose claim that Blair exerts a lot of influence over the charity sparked a Charity Commission investigation. 'The atmosphere is dominated by underlings worried about saving Blair from embarrassment in the media.'

Bright continues: 'The Faith Foundation is an independent charity with Tony Blair as its patron. He is not supposed to have any executive role. But it was clear from the outset [of Bright's employment] that [Blair's] reputation was to be protected at all costs.

'Tony's private office began to treat my website as its own think tank or government department, with regular calls for briefings on the Middle East, radical Islam or particular conflicts. He once asked me for a worldwide map of madrassas in the world, ranked according to how radical they are, which is an impossible request.

'There's a huge communications department aimed at not publishing anything,' he says. He adds that long meetings are held to work out positions on such matters as Iraq, Kazakhstan and the Gulf states that will not cause embarrassment for the charity's patron, who took Britain to war in Iraq and has important clients in Kazakhstan and the Gulf states.

It is playing with words to say that Blair has nothing to do with the running of his Faith Foundation. He is in daily touch with it; his needs are at the forefront of the minds of its top staff all the time; and it reflects Blair's beliefs and personality in every aspect of its activities. Even if we believed that he seldom or never instructed its top brass what to do, his needs, interests and wishes would remain their first thought when any decision needed to be made. It is like the claim that Rupert Murdoch has nothing to do with the political attitude of the *Sun*.

Seven months after launching the Foundation, in December 2008, Blair announced a partnership with the Canadian businesswoman, philanthropist, politician and billionaire Belinda Stronach. They were going to join forces, and to collaborate with what they called 'representatives of a broad cross-section of the communities of faith and spiritual belief in Canada' in 'a new proposed interfaith initiative'.

Ms Stronach herself said, 'We are looking to work with Canadians of faith and belief to build a secure and neutral public space in which to encourage and facilitate inter-faith cooperation on practical humanitarian matters where there is a large degree of consensus, starting with the MDGs. And the process of the interfaith collaboration itself is also an important endeavour.'[2]

This sounds rather like a meaningless collection of feel-good jargon, but Stronach specialises in sentences that sound as though they were taken from a management textbook. The Belinda Stronach Foundation, according to its own publicity, 'builds partnerships with individuals, non-governmental organizations, business large and small, as well as other foundations who work in Canada and around the world to develop and incubate innovative programs confronting global challenges.'

The Stronach Foundation website says that Blair and Stronach set up Faiths Act and the Faiths Act Fellowship in Canada as an opportunity for people around the world to work together across faith divides in pursuit of the Millennium Development Goals.

On 24 April 2009, speaking to a Canadian audience, Blair said, 'Out there, in those remote parts of Africa, a health clinic or hospital is a rarity. People have to travel miles, sometimes a hundred miles or more to get there, but, for obvious reasons, they don't get there and they die. But every one of those communities, no matter how remote, has a place of worship in it. And they could be the means of distributing the bed nets and medicine. The infrastructure of faith could be the answer to this problem.'

Put at its kindest, the TBFF's objective is to maximise the good that faith does in the world, and minimise the harm, which sounds like a perfectly respectable and indeed laudable, if rather limited, objective. However, when we examine what it actually does we wonder whether we have understood TBFF's purpose correctly.

MR VARKEY AND THE FAITH FOUNDATION

TBFF's activities include what it calls a 'strategic partnership' with GEMS Education, founded by Sunny Varkey, who is a member of its strategic advisory board. Launching it, Blair said, 'It is rather unique, this organisation that Mr Varkey and his family has put together. The fact is they are providing really high-quality education and they are doing it in a way that I think is very interesting, very innovative and actually very exciting and there's lots of education systems worldwide can learn from this.'

The admiration is mutual if you believe the Varkey GEMS Foundation website. Varkey states,

> The Tony Blair Faith Foundation is an organisation that shares our belief in the fundamental importance of high-quality teaching. Like the Varkey GEMS Foundation, it understands the importance of investment in a strong support network for teachers: via its Country Co-ordinators and teachers' workshops both on and offline, the Tony Blair Faith Foundation provides ongoing support for teachers the world over.

GEMS – Global Education Management Systems – is an international chain of fee-charging and profit-making schools, set up as a commercial enterprise, and these schools have made a very great deal of money for Mr Varkey. There's nothing especially wrong with that. It's entirely legal, and Varkey is doing only what several perfectly respectable chains of private schools are doing. But how does it tie in with TBFF's stated objectives, and how can it be suitable work for a charity? What makes Sunny Varkey a role model for a faith organisation?

Varkey is an extremely rich Dubai businessman. His fortune is based on education and healthcare in the Gulf; he owns the top private hospital in Dubai. Starting with eighteen fee-charging schools in Dubai, mostly for expats, Varkey pioneered thirteen cut-price (he prefers the term 'affordable') fee-charging schools in Britain in 2004. Then he signed a deal that gave him a launch pad to bid for academies in association with 3Es, a company that manages a clutch of state schools.

3Es was Prime Minister Tony Blair's favourite education company. Opening one of its schools, he said its name 'apparently stands for "education, education, education". I've heard that phrase before, and wonder if they should be paying me royalties.' They could certainly afford to. The company's wealth began with Kingshurst, near Birmingham, the first of the city technology colleges created in the late 1980s by the then Tory Education Secretary, Kenneth Baker. The colleges got a huge state handout, supplemented by a much smaller sum from business.

Kingshurst's then principal, Valerie Bragg, teamed up with her husband, Berkshire's former chief education officer Stanley Goodchild, to create a company to manage other state schools. The company flourished. It won the management contract for two Surrey schools, provided services for many more and ran academies under the Blair government. Though Kingshurst had been almost entirely paid for by the taxpayer, Bragg and Goodchild ran 3Es entirely as a private company.

In 2005, Prime Minister Tony Blair tried to put some of his academies Varkey's way. Academies were a new sort of school, pioneered by the Blair government, and run by sponsors, which were often commercial organisations. Sponsors need to be approved by the Education Secretary. For a while it looked as though Varkey might get his hands on two academies in Milton Keynes, but he was forced to pull out after protests from local parents.

But he still, of course, had his thirteen private fee-charging schools in the UK. These, he says, work by taking advantage of economies of scale in a similar way to a supermarket, with centralised purchasing and teachers shared among schools. The aim was to open up a new market by charging fees that started at about £6,000 a year – less than half the normal cost at that time. The product is less luxurious, with a narrower curriculum, perhaps teaching only core subjects, and class sizes similar to those in state schools. But, in a market-driven education system, you get what you pay for. And at least it would keep out the very poor, which may have been an important selling point for the punters.

That is why, in 2004, Varkey envisaged perhaps doubling the number of children whose parents paid for their education, with two hundred new schools. His target market was the 50 per cent who, according to a poll, would send their children to a fee-charging school if they could afford it. Since he is offering little that a state school can't offer, the extra pupils would have to come from families who do not want their children mixing with the sort you get at local comprehensives. Private schools would not be available to all, but they would move down a class.

If he succeeded, this would be a hammer blow to British state education, because it would take into private schools the children of the motivated parents – those willing to pay as much as they could afford for their children's education – and leave in state schools two categories: the children of the very poorest and the children of those to whom education does not seem important. Anyone who knows anything about schools will tell you that, unless you have some pupils who are motivated to learn, you are destined to become a sink school.

It would pave the way for state education to become the refuge of those who cannot or will not afford anything better. It would mark the end of the road for the 1944 Education Act and for good universal schooling for all children of school age.

So far this remains a dream – the proportion of children going to fee-charging schools has remained constant at 7–8 per cent for many years. But we are left wondering what on earth a 'strategic partnership' with Mr Varkey has to do with any of the TBFF's stated aims; and why a former Labour Prime Minister would be anxious to collaborate with a project that, if it succeeded, would destroy state education in Britain.

Whatever the reason, Mr Blair likes to keep in touch with Mr Varkey and underline his support for what Varkey is doing. When he was in Britain in January 2010 he found time to visit a GEMS school. One of his former senior staffers told us that GEMS liked to have a political celebrity from every country on board. Tony is its Brit. Its American is Bill Clinton, though he seems much less active in its support than Blair.

The TBFF's alliance with World Jewish Relief (WJR) 'to raise awareness of and funds for both organisations' vital work in Africa', according to the publicity,[3] is an example of the Foundation engaging in some real and useful work.

In Sierra Leone, the two organisations have put money into training priests and imams to give health education as part of the war on malaria. In even the smallest village there is either a mosque or a church, so that is the best way of reaching the population. Here the Tony Blair Faith Foundation seems to have found a job that is well worth doing by anyone's standards, and the link with faith is one that obviously helps the work. There is a lot of criticism of the Foundation, and there's a lot to criticise, but here we find it doing genuinely good and worthwhile charitable work, and it would be churlish not to acknowledge that.

Less tangible, and more suspect, is its work to train the leaders of tomorrow. It has carefully selected ten 'exceptional young people' to take part in its 'young leadership programme'. This again is supposed to be part of the fight against malaria, though it looks more like an attempt to choose tomorrow's leaders, and to make sure they are people of faith – of the TBFF's ten young leaders, there are five Christians, three Muslims and two religious Jews, all from the UK.[4]

Then there is the 'Face to Faith' initiative which apparently 'engages students across the world in discussion of global issues through different faith, belief and cultural lenses.' This focuses on the teaching of religion in universities, which Blair, and hence the TBFF, seem very interested in. They think there isn't enough of it. Hence the TBFF's partnership with Durham University, announced in July 2009, designed 'to create a global network of twelve leading research universities teaching Faith and Globalisation over the next two years.' Tom McLeish, Durham's pro-vice-chancellor, in launching the TBFF link to Durham said, 'The suggestion by the Tony Blair Faith Foundation that Durham take the UK lead in the topical international network becomes natural.'

Durham was the third partner university, following Yale and the National University of Singapore (which has apparently been persuaded to run a course called 'Religion and Technology'). The Durham course 'will develop greater understanding of the impact of faiths and cultures on the world and the inter-relationship between faith and globalisation.' Blair said that the TBFF 'will focus on building and developing the Faith and Globalisation course which started at Yale – creating a tight network between the twelve partner universities, and ensuring that this is recognised globally as a leading teaching, research, and social action orientated initiative.'[5]

In fact, it all started at Yale. A year after founding the TBFF, in 2009 Blair was appointed to teach a course on issues of faith and globalisation at the Yale Schools of Management and Divinity. He was paid what Yale has said was a 'not insubstantial' sum for ten two-and-half-hour seminars a year – the figure of £680,000 has been reported by the *Daily Telegraph* and never denied. But, more importantly, while he was there he was introduced to Yale's major benefactors, and he could tap them up for donations to the TBFF.

While teaching at Yale, Blair graced the launch of a healthcare research partnership between Yale and University College London in New Haven, Connecticut. He said that, while at Yale, 'I have witnessed first-hand Yale's increasing international reach, under President Richard Levin's visionary leadership.'[6]

Yale's then dean of divinity, Professor Harold Attridge, told the *Sunday Telegraph*: 'Whatever exchanges hands on the money side is done above my pay grade. I believe there is some contribution to the Foundation in lieu of salary to him. This is all done at the [Yale] president's level so it doesn't affect my budget.'

Attridge went on: '[Fundraising] development is always implicated in everything we do. But we don't raise money for them [the TBFF] and they don't raise money for us. But there is a symbiotic relationship between the two and people are interested in both, and, if those things happen, that is all well and good. We might have a dinner for our benefactors and alumni. Our intent is to get them excited about Yale, but, if they want to get excited about the Faith Foundation, that is their call. That's the way it works.'

When it was suggested Blair had an ability to attract 'big money', Attridge replied, 'That's true.'[7]

The TBFF has an office on the Yale campus run by Scott Macdonald, an experienced American fundraiser who for the 2012–13 academic year advertised to take on a Yale student on an internship in the TBFF Yale office.

Professor Attridge, like Blair, is a Roman Catholic, but the relationship between Blair and Yale owed much to one of Attridge's colleagues, Professor Denys Turner, who lectured in theology at Cambridge University before going to Yale. Turner joined Opus Dei, the secretive Roman Catholic cult organisation, in 1961. He left it in 1969. He now believes that Opus Dei traded on the instinct that Catholics then had for obedience, exercised a kind of mind control and cultivated a psychology of dependence on the organisation.

All the same, he has described leaving Opus Dei as a catastrophic experience, and he says he was told that he would lose his soul over it. He became a Catholic Marxist close to the radical Slant group, which included the academics Adrian Cunningham and Terry Eagleton, and the late Dominican Laurence Bright.[8]

But the key fact is that Professor Turner's daughter is Ruth Turner, like her father a devout Roman Catholic, who was Blair's head of government relations when he was PM, later becoming the TBFF's first chief executive, and, according to Professor Attridge, who did all the staff work on Blair's side to close the deal with Yale. She was arrested in the 'cash for honours' investigation but not charged with any offence.

Turner left the TBFF job to have a baby, but Blair is understood to have made a very favourable financial settlement which included allowing her to return to the TBFF in a part-time capacity as soon as she was ready to do so. So she is now back, working part time as the TBFF's director of policy.

After Yale, other universities joined, and since Durham signed up four more universities have been persuaded to teach more religion and ally it to globalisation. Monterrey Technical University in Mexico will teach 'Globalisation and Belief Systems'; the University of Western Australia will teach 'Religion and Globalisation'; and Peking University in China will teach 'Interfaith Relations in a Globalised World'. The University of Sierra Leone, Foyrah Bay College, will teach 'Faith and Globalisation'.

BLAIR AND CHARLES CLARKE

The idea that the world can be made a better place by creating university courses that link all the important subjects to religion is something that Blair and his old friend Charles Clarke share, and Clarke is playing his part in achieving it.

Blair and Clarke go back a long way. As the 1970s turned into the 1980s, when they were young and ambitious Labour politicians, neither of them yet in Parliament, they fought the Bennites in Islington together. Blair's first decision as an MP in 1983 was to vote for Neil Kinnock for leader, on the advice of Kinnock's adviser and Blair's friend Clarke.

A decade later, they spearheaded the post-Kinnock 'modernisers' and Clarke served as Blair's Education Secretary and then his Home Secretary. Later, when he knew he would soon have to stand down, Blair planned to make Clarke Foreign Secretary in order to give him a fighting chance to frustrate Gordon Brown and become Blair's successor as Prime Minister. He confided this plan only to Clarke, who shared his loathing of Gordon Brown, and then only after the plan fell apart because Clarke was forced to take the rap for a Home Office failure and resign as Home Secretary. Blair says in his autobiography that he regrets not giving Clarke the Foreign

Office anyway, but he could hardly give him a promotion when he was forcing him to resign because of an error.

It was Clarke who, in those dreadful weeks before Blair finally resigned as PM, said all the things Blair was thought to believe about Gordon Brown but could hardly say himself, because he was supposed to preserve the fiction that he wanted Brown to succeed him. Clarke said that Brown was a deluded control freak, and would lead Labour to disaster. He urged Blair not to hurry out. He still harboured hopes of being the Blairite candidate for the succession.[9]

In short, Clarke, though he dislikes the word, is among the purest of the Blairites.

Now Clarke, who the last time we discussed it with him did not believe in God, is running a £12 million Religion and Society programme at Lancaster University, which has close ties with the TBFF. Clarke, like Blair, thinks that faith is a good thing for society, though apparently without feeling the need of it for himself. 'I went along with the view of many on the Left that religion was essentially a diversion and a destructive thing, until it became clear that almost all the people involved in positive community action were men and women of faith of some kind,' he told the *Daily Telegraph*. This assertion is, to say the least, unproven.[10]

THE FAILED HARVARD UNIVERSITY PROJECT

In 2014 came a collaboration with another great university, and before the year was out it had gone horribly wrong. The TBFF teamed up with Harvard University's Faculty of Divinity to create a website about faith and globalisation. To edit the new website, at the start of 2014 the TBFF appointed journalist Martin Bright.

After less than a year, the project collapsed, having lost both its editor and its partner. Harvard pulled out after the TBFF and the Harvard Divinity School (HDS) fell out badly. The issue, we are authoritatively told,[11] was the article Blair wrote for the *Observer* in January 2014 announcing the collaboration between the two organisations.[12] Reading it, HDS realised suddenly that it and Blair had very different ideas of what the new initiative would do, and it was furious with Blair.

The article identified abuse of religion (and by religion he was understood to mean Islam) as the chief likely source of conflict in the twenty-first century. Blair said he wanted the world 'to start to treat this issue of religious extremism as an issue that is about religion as well as politics, to go to the roots of where a false view of religion is being promulgated and to make it a major item on the agenda of world leaders to combine effectively to combat it.'

HDS felt it had unwittingly been shackled to what might be seen as an anti-Islam agenda – and, worse, that its new initiative had been shackled to Blair's defence of the Iraq War, for in the same article he wrote of Iraq that 'exactly the same sectarianism threatens the right of the people to a democratic future … It is one reason why the Middle East matters so much and why any attempt to disengage is so wrong and short-sighted.'

The divinity school told us tersely, 'HDS was engaged in discussions on a working relationship with the TBFF team but decided not to pursue a formal collaboration after realizing that the aims of both organizations would be better served independently.'

As for Martin Bright, he lasted just five months. On the face of it, he was a surprising choice in the first place, because he had been political editor of the *New Statesman* in the days when the Blairites saw the magazine as being under the control of the hated Brownites. However, he was widely known to have fallen out of love with the Brown camp, and he felt badly treated by the Brownite owner of the *New Statesman*, Geoffrey Robinson, after Bright had been forced to leave the magazine in circumstances that are hotly disputed to this day, with Bright describing political reasons and our *New Statesman* sources quoting professional ones. In recent years he has been, pretty reliably, an opponent of the Brown camp, and this alone ensures him a welcome in Blairite circles, as a sinner who repenteth. It also helps that he went from the *New Statesman* to be political editor of the *Jewish Chronicle*, and he is, from Blair's point of view, sound on Islam – British Muslims see him as an unrelenting opponent.

Bright was approached about the job by two Blair emissaries, one of whom was a recruitment consultant who had cut her political teeth in Labour Friends of Israel, which has become a kind of nursery for Blairites. He started the job in late January 2014 with an hour-long meeting with Blair himself, and was promised a similar meeting with Blair every month.

Though not a religious man himself, Bright is interested in religion, and wrote in the *Jewish Chronicle* in the week he took up the appointment in late January 2014 that he and Blair 'share a conviction that the role of religion in the geopolitics of the 21st century remains poorly understood. At the same time, we know there are academics, intellectuals and journalists out there who can bring a profound knowledge of this field to those of us who crave a more comprehensive and nuanced approach.'

He had come to admire Blair, he wrote. 'As might be expected with anything involving Tony Blair, the scope and ambition of this project is vast. The intention is to make this site the first port of call for anyone wishing to grasp the nature of conflicts where religion plays a part.'[13]

The website, launched in April, was to contain analyses of religious conflict and contribution in various parts of the world. So what would happen, we asked Bright on his appointment, when he wanted to run an analysis of a country that is one of the clients of Tony Blair Associates – Kazakhstan, for example, where there is plenty of religious conflict, and the role of Blair's client, the President, might not stand too much scrutiny? What would happen when he was told that, in order not to embarrass the patron, the website should not run such-and-such a story? Bright said he'd cross that bridge when and if he came to it.

As we have seen, five months after he arrived, Martin Bright left. In the aftermath of his departure, the experiment of getting a journalist to run the website and trying to run it on newspaper lines was not judged a success. Bright knew that his replacement would not be a journalist and would run a more tightly controlled operation. In the event, there was no operation to run. The communications department has taken over his website, he says, and there is no longer any pretence of independence.

After leaving, and after talking to us, Bright wrote an article for the *Daily Mail* about his experiences, and Blair's friends and loyalists were beside themselves with fury and rushed to say that he was talking rubbish.[14] One of the authors happened to meet Matthew Taylor, still a Blair friend and the partner of TBFF founder and director Ruth Turner, the morning the piece appeared. He said, 'Bright says the office is full of bean bags. I've been there many times, I can tell you there are no bean bags.' We pass this on because it's the only firm information we have ever been given on the record (or, at least, not *off* the record) by anyone as close to Blair as Taylor. There are no bean bags in Blair's office. We hope Taylor does not get into too much trouble for telling us this.

THE RELIGIOUS ADVISERS TO THE TONY BLAIR FAITH FOUNDATION

Company accounts show that senior employees at the Foundation received six-figure salaries in 2009–10.[15] The Foundation then employed twelve staff and managed to raise £3.5 million in the twelve months to April 2009. In February 2013 its accounts showed that it had almost £3 million in the bank, and employed twenty-eight people with annual staffing costs of £1.3 million, and was operating in twenty countries. A year later, it was still employing twenty-eight staff, we are told.

The formal governance structure includes a Religious Advisory Council. To what extent this is purely ornamental is hard to fathom, but presumably it has some influence, if only because, should a member of this council dislike what is going on, he or she could create great embarrassment.

This council includes top international figures from most main religions, but until 2013 no Catholic at all – although the Blairs are themselves Catholics – and no Muslim cleric or theologian. The only Muslim on the board was a politician – the adviser to the Prime Minister of Kuwait, who is, of course, the biggest client of Tony Blair Associates.

Outside these two faiths, the board is a pretty impressive array of the great and good in world religions. Blair has recruited the Rev. David Coffey, president of the Baptist World Alliance, and Roshi Joan Halifax, Abbot of the Upaya Zen Center. Its Jewish representatives could hardly be more distinguished: not only Rabbi David Rosen, chairman of the International Jewish Committee on Interreligious Consultations, but also the former British Chief Rabbi, Sir Jonathan Sacks.

The Anglican church is represented by the Rt Rev. Richard Chartres, Lord Bishop of London, and some of the biggest figures in evangelical Christianity are there: from the West Indies, the Reverend Joel Edwards, director of Micah Challenge International and former general director of the Evangelical Alliance, a famous West Indian evangelical Christian; from America, the Rev. Dr Rick Warren, founding and senior pastor of the hugely wealthy and important Saddleback Church; and, from Africa, the Rt Rev. Josiah Idowu-Fearon, Bishop of Kaduna, who campaigned for laws in Nigeria that would send gay people to prison.

Sikhs and Hindus are also represented by distinguished scholars and theologians. For the Sikhs there is Professor Jagtar Singh Grewal, former chairman of the India Institute of Advanced Study and former vice-chancellor of Guru Nanak Dev University; and, for the Hindus, Anantanand Rambachan, professor and chair of the Religion Department at St Olaf College, Minnesota.

Against this glittering array, the presence as the sole Muslim representative of Dr Ismail Khudr Al-Shatti, adviser in Diwan of the Prime Minister of Kuwait and former president of the Gulf Institute for Futures and Strategic Studies, seemed incongruous, for he is a politician, not a religious figure at all. Dr Abdul Wahid, chairman of Hizb ut-Tahrir UK, told us that he had never heard of Ismail Khudr Al-Shatti, and added, 'The single Muslim name will be unknown to most Muslims across the world. Whereas several of the members of this advisory council are prominent people – for example, Lord Sacks, Bishop Chartres, Joel Edwards – the Tony Blair Faith Foundation appears to have been unable to recruit a single person from the UK's two-million-strong Muslim community, nor anyone from a much larger European Muslim community, nor anyone of any global prominence across the Muslim world.'

Blair was already popular in Kuwait for bringing an end to Saddam Hussein's regime in neighbouring Iraq, which could by itself have been sufficient reason for Al-Shatti's willingness to cast himself in the role of fig leaf. But Al-Shatti must also be fully aware of, if not actually a party to, the lucrative contract between TBA and the Kuwaiti government. It is the usual problem with Blair: too many hats.

The lack of a credible Muslim figure is the direct result of Blair being seen as anti-Islam. It is the same problem that has shackled his effectiveness as Middle East envoy. The architect of the war in Iraq is now seen as the man who wants to bomb Muslims in both Iran and Syria, having called first for a bombing campaign against President Assad, and then for a bombing campaign against ISIS (or the Islamic State) in Iraq.

The English-language *Arab News*, a moderate and respected news source across the Arab world, has an explanation for all this:

Unlike George W. Bush, Tony Blair persists in crossing continents, portraying himself as a man of peace – apparently blind to his toxic image throughout the Muslim world as a pro-US, pro-Israel war-monger. Perhaps Blair is so ethnocentric as to be incapable of viewing the world through Muslim eyes. It may also be that he simply does not care what people think about him. Certainly, there is an impression of bone-headed insensitivity about the efforts of the Tony Blair Faith Foundation to counter 'extremism', to 'deradicalize' British Muslims who have been to Syria, or who might be thinking of going there, to enlist as jihadists ... Many are bound to feel that the deradicalizing endeavors of this latter-day British crusader, this unrepentant instigator of bloody interventions in Muslim lands, cannot be other than counterproductive.[16]

Following the killing in London of Fusilier Lee Rigby on 22 May 2013, as Muslim leaders queued up to condemn the murder in the strongest possible terms, Blair announced that the act was a symptom of 'a problem within Islam'. He dismissed the argument that religiously motivated terrorist attacks are the work of a fringe few. There is, he said, an 'exclusivist and reactionary world view' throughout the Muslim world.

The 'problem within Islam', he said, came from 'the adherents of an ideology that is a strain within Islam. And we have to put it on the table and be honest about it.

> Of course there are Christian extremists and Jewish, Buddhist and Hindu ones. But I am afraid this strain is not the province of a few extremists. It has at its heart a view about religion and about the interaction between religion and politics that is not compatible with pluralistic, liberal, open-minded societies …
>
> I understand the desire to look at this world and explain it by reference to local grievances, economic alienation and of course 'crazy people'. But are we really going to examine it and find no common thread, nothing that joins these dots, no sense of an ideology driving or at least exacerbating it all?

He was saying that murderous extremists of other religions are just individual murderous extremists – but in Islam they are something like the mainstream. He's not the only person to say this. But he is the only person to say it who is at the same time claiming to bring faiths together and work for better understanding between them.[17]

It was hugely harmful to the TBFF's reputation in the Muslim world – so much so that TBFF chief executive Charlotte Keenan tried to limit the damage with a blog post called 'What Tony Blair meant about Islam'. According to her, he was 'characteristically clear in his view that when the perpetrators cloak their crimes in such language it is ludicrous to say that these terrorist attacks are nothing to do with religion'.

He was actually saying much more than that. He was drawing a clear distinction between Islam and the world's other religions.

His words, no doubt, represented Blair's honest opinion. But, if he is serious about having an organisation that bears his name, and that has credibility with all faiths, that is an opinion he would avoid giving public expression to. For he has a lot of ground to make up in the Muslim world. Muslims will find it hard to forgive him for Iraq, even if he had not followed this in July 2005, after the 7/7 London bombings, with a speech at Labour's national conference in which he said,

> The greatest danger is that we fail to face up to the nature of the threat we are dealing with. What we witnessed in London last Thursday week was not an aberrant act. It was not random. It was not a product of particular local circumstances in West Yorkshire ... What we are confronting here is an evil ideology ...
>
> This ideology and the violence that is inherent in it did not start a few years ago in response to a particular policy. Over the past twelve years, al-Qaeda and its associates have attacked twenty-six countries, killed thousands of people, many of them Muslims. They have networks in virtually every major country and thousands of fellow travellers. They are well financed. Look at their websites ...
>
> Neither is it true that they have no demands. They do. It is just that no sane person would negotiate on them. They demand the elimination of Israel; the withdrawal of all Westerners from Muslim countries, irrespective of the wishes of people and government; the establishment of effectively Taliban states and sharia law in the Arab world *en route* to one caliphate of all Muslim nations ...
>
> Its roots are not superficial, but deep, in the madrassas of Pakistan, in the extreme forms of Wahabi doctrine in Saudi Arabia, in the former training camps of al-Qaeda in Afghanistan, in the cauldron of Chechnya, in parts of the politics of most countries of the Middle East and many in Asia, in the extremist minority that

236

now in every European city preach hatred of the West and our way of life.

This is what we are up against. It cannot be beaten except by confronting it, symptoms and causes, head-on. Without compromise and without delusion. Their cause is not founded on an injustice. It is founded on a belief, one whose fanaticism is such it can't be moderated. It can't be remedied. It has to be stood up to. And, of course, they will use any issue that is a matter of dissent within our democracy.

But we should lay bare the almost devilish logic behind such manipulation. We must pull this up by its roots ...

Thirty-seven Muslim organisations signed a statement protesting about this speech, saying, 'To equate "extremism" with the aspirations of Muslims for Sharia laws in the Muslim world or the desire to see unification towards a Caliphate in the Muslim lands, as seemed to be misrepresented by the prime minister, is inaccurate and disingenuous.'

Hizb ut-Tahrir said, 'He was propagating a narrative that was born out of right-wing US think tanks that certain orthodox ideas from Islam are somehow a precursor to terrorist violence.' Dr Abdul Wahid, chairman of Hizb ut-Tahrir UK, told us, 'Tony Blair conflates the bombing of 7/7 with orthodox and peaceful things. The TBFF just wants to find like-minded people. He has a certain narrative on Islam.' Blair has a long way to go before his Faith Foundation will have credibility among Muslims.

Even odder than the absence of a credible Muslim was the complete absence of a Catholic representative, even though Blair was received into the Catholic Church in 2007 shortly after leaving office, as we predicted in our 2005 book *Tony Blair in Peace and War* – a prediction widely dismissed at the time. In June 2009, three months after Cardinal Cormac Murphy-O'Connor resigned as Archbishop of Westminster and leader of Catholics in England and Wales, the TBFF announced that he had agreed to be a member of its Religious Advisory Council – and the Cardinal then rather pointedly said that he had not agreed to this, and had no intention of agreeing to it.

This is because neither the Foundation nor the Blairs have gone down well in Rome following the former PM's demands for wholesale changes in Catholic belief and practice. The Blairs managed to annoy Pope Benedict by disagreeing with the Vatican's hard line on homosexuality and abortion, while acting as ambassadors for Catholicism.[18]

But this is unlikely to be the full story. We know that the Catholic Church, which only a few years ago was proud and excited about its high-profile recruit and was telling us Blair intended to convert long before Blair himself admitted it, has gone distinctly cold on the man. The Blairs have always been mystics, which is why Blair did so badly in his debate against the late Christopher Hitchens on theism versus atheism. He has never believed his religion requires arguing for: it's just true, and that's all there is to it.

So far, so good: the Catholic Church is based on authority, on a set of beliefs laid down by Christ and by popes who are infallible in matters of faith and dogma, beliefs that are simply true, and that's that. The trouble is that Blair wants the bulwark of the authority, but does not always want to accept the authority of the Pope.

As long ago as 2001, the Blairs were introduced to spiritualism by Carole Caplin's spiritualist mother Sylvia. Cherie took to wearing a 'magic pendant' known as a bio-electric shield. Catholics purse their lips in disapproval at this sort of behaviour.

It's also suggested in Catholic circles that Blair's current activities may bring discredit on the Church if it is too closely associated with him. The relentless moneymaking does not accord well with Christ's teaching, they say, though there are, of course, many very wealthy Catholics.

Whatever the reason, the Church has moved to distance itself from the Blairs, which is why Cardinal Cormac Murphy-O'Connor pointedly contradicted the TBFF statement that he had agreed to join the Religious Advisory Council. This was an acute embarrassment for the TBFF.

Worse was to follow. The Blairs were equally pointedly not invited to the installation of the new Archbishop of Westminster, the Most Rev. Vincent Nichols, who said Catholic thinking was 'rather different' from the kind promoted by Blair.

Nichols was furious because, among other things, Blair had used an interview with the gay publication *Attitude* to criticise the approach of the Pope towards gay rights. He argued that religious leaders must start 'rethinking' the issue.

Blair's falling-out with the Catholic Church was serious. According to the *Tablet*, the Catholic weekly, Stephen Pound, Labour MP for Ealing North and a Catholic, said that Blair's 'hubristic' attitude was 'extremely counterproductive. Entrance to the Vatican is only gained through a series of iron-clad, hermetically sealed, heavily padlocked and bolted doors, and I can hear them creaking shut as we speak.' Pound warned Blair against 'dictating to the Pope through the media.' Meanwhile, Catholic theologians queued up to condemn the former Prime Minister and all his works. Professor Michel Schooyans of the Catholic University of Louvain spearheaded the attack with a sarcastic speech in which he said, 'The fresh "convert" does not hesitate to explain to the Pope not only what he must do, but also what he must believe! Is he a Catholic? ... So now we are back in the time of Hobbes, if not of Cromwell: it's civil power that defines what one must believe.'[19]

Catholic Action UK, a ginger group that seeks to ensure that the Church does not grow lax on its fundamental beliefs, spits fury about the Blairs, and Cherie in particular. A 1,300-word 'dossier' on Cherie Blair accuses her of heinous crimes. She apparently 'visited the exhibition stand of the International Planned Parenthood Federation, Population Concern and Marie Stopes International' at the Commonwealth Heads of Government meeting in November 1999. Not content with this wickedness, she 'endorsed CEDAW [the Convention on the Elimination of Discrimination against Women], specifically mentioning CEDAW's affirmation of women's so-called "reproductive rights"'. And then, in

2004, horror of horrors, 'in a lecture to students at Harvard university, Mrs Blair described the US Supreme Court's striking-down of the Texas law against sodomy as "a model of judicial reasoning".'

There was more. As a lawyer, Mrs Blair once represented a lesbian against South West Trains, who had refused to grant travel concessions to her same-sex partner. She has said that the Catholic Church is not ideal, therefore implying that it is not infallible, a dreadful heresy. She 'accepted an invitation to the gay wedding [same-sex civil partnership ceremony] of anti-life [code for pro-abortion] MEP Michael Cashman'. She supports Human Rights Watch, which is pro-abortion. The charge sheet goes on and on.

The dossier ends: 'Why is she still being invited to speak at Catholic institutions? This must stop.'[20]

It is easy to laugh – and comparatively safe, since these people no longer have the power to burn you at the stake – but the zealots of Catholic Action UK do represent something, just as the Muslim extremists Blair denounces represent something. They can make it awkward politically for the princes of the church to cooperate with the Tony Blair Faith Foundation.

Nonetheless, a TBFF spokesperson told us, 'The Foundation works side by side with anyone committed to practically supporting preventing religious prejudice, conflict and extremism. Given that context and our mission, it would be totally counterproductive to favour one religious or non-religious group, and we would never do that.'

The relationship between Blair and the Catholic Church has not been eased by Blair's close relationship with the remarkable Father Michael Seed. Seed was the Blairs' confessor and confidant when they were in Downing Street, as secretary for ecumenical affairs at Westminster Cathedral, and he celebrated masses for the Blairs. As late as September 2014 the Catholic newspaper *The Universe* was still describing him as 'The priest who converted Tony Blair to Catholicism.'[21] He proved to be very good at getting celebrities into the Roman Catholic Church: in addition to

Blair, he helped in the conversion of Ann Widdecombe and John Selwyn Gummer. Seed confidently told us, while Blair was still Prime Minister, that Blair would convert to Catholicism as soon as he left Downing Street. He was right, but people who thought they were close to Blair told us he was wrong.

Seed was closer to Blair than they were. Seed was very close. Close enough to become a fundraiser for Blair's pet education project, his academy schools, introducing wealthy businessmen of his acquaintance to Blair's people. Close enough for Cherie Blair to call him a man who turned 'the great into the good'. Close enough to know the Blair family's deepest secrets.

Close enough, after Cardinal Basil Hume died in 1999, for the relationship to become an irritant to Seed's new boss, Cardinal Cormac Murphy-O'Connor, who does not seem to have appreciated Father Seed's talking about the famous new convert whose arrival he was expecting; nor did he think much of Father Seed's seeming endorsement of Blair's controversial policy of academy schools.

Murphy-O'Connor's irritation was reported in the *Daily Telegraph* just as Blair was resigning as Prime Minister, and this may have played a part in the Cardinal's refusal to join the TBFF Religious Advisory Council the following year. But Seed continued to be a player, increasingly moving in the rarefied world of the American and Middle Eastern megarich, which Blair was getting to know so well, until the wheels conclusively fell off the Michael Seed bandwagon in 2012, when a *Mail on Sunday* investigation found that he was trying to sell papal honours as well as introductions to clients for arms dealers, for cash.[22]

Papal honours are given on the authority of the Pope, and several prominent Catholics have one, as well as a few people judged by the Catholic Church to be exceptionally deserving. Jimmy Savile was awarded a papal knighthood, and there is no procedure for withdrawing it posthumously.

Father Seed, an apparently humble little priest who seemed to us to model himself, or at least his image, on G. K. Chesterton's Father Brown, was suddenly an embarrassment to the Catholic hierarchy. And, in a different way, so was Tony Blair, who had the same aura of Middle Eastern money about him. The past association between Blair and Seed, in addition to Blair's theological unreliability, seems to have fed the Church's desire not to be too closely associated with Blair.

So Britain's important Catholics wanted nothing to do with the TBFF. But, from Blair's point of view, not having any Catholic prelate on the Religious Advisory Council who could match the Chief Rabbi, or the Bishop of London, or the world's top Christians, Sikhs and Buddhists was clearly a weakness that had to be addressed.

That may be why we have not heard much from Cherie Blair since 2009 on abortion, or homosexuality, or ordination of women, or any of those matters on which her deeply held views are heretical. She has confined herself to safe subjects, such as women entrepreneurs.

In 2013 the problem was partially resolved, aided no doubt by the arrival of a new and more liberal Pope: Francis. An important Catholic finally joined the council, though not a member of the British Catholic hierarchy. This was Archbishop Diarmuid Martin, Roman Catholic Archbishop of Dublin and the second most important bishop in Ireland. Martin is the leading voice for reform in the Catholic Church in Ireland. He has called for a full independent inquiry into the Irish Catholic Church's child-sex-abuse scandal, a call resisted and resented by many of his colleagues, among whom he is therefore quite unpopular.

A not wholly successful attempt has been made to address the lack of a credible Muslim figure. In 2013 the TBFF Religious Advisory Council recruited Imam Umer Ahmed Ilyasi, chief imam of the All India Organisation of Imams and Mosques. The website of this organisation says of Ilyasi,

He is well versed in Islamic Jurisprudence and his opinions in relevant circles are regarded as being authentic and trustworthy.

He is one of the few Islamic scholars who hold very candid and vocal position [sic] on extremism and terrorism in whatever form it exists. By nature he is a rationalist and is being guided by reason and wisdom even in the most provocative situations.[23]

But Abdul Wahid of Hizb ut-Tahrir tells us, 'I'm afraid I had never heard of Umer Ahmed Ilyasi or this organisation before receiving your email. I checked with a close friend of mine, an Indian Muslim, who had also never heard of him or the organisation – and was frankly stunned by the claim on his website that he is the spiritual leader of half a million imams in India. He in turn checked with friends and relatives in India, who had also never heard of him or the organisation. I further checked with an Indian Muslim businessman I know who had heard of him some years ago, but did not know much.'

The American and African evangelical Christians on the Council hold deeply conservative views, and, like the Catholics, represent another good reason for the Blairs to soft-peddle their liberal views about homosexuality, abortion and the place of women.

The Rev. Rick Warren founded Saddleback Church in Lake Forest in 1980 with one other family. Today, it is one of America's most influential churches, with about 20,000 people attending the weekend services. He is the author of *Purpose Driven Life*, and built the Purpose Driven Network, a global alliance of pastors from 162 countries and hundreds of denominations who have been trained to be what he calls purpose-driven churches. He founded Pastors.com, an online interactive community that provides sermons, forums, and other practical resources for pastors.

Warren is strongly against abortion, same-sex marriage and stem-cell research, and could be expected to disapprove of any move by the TBFF to support any of these things.

But even stronger disapproval would come from the Rt Rev. Josiah Idowu-Fearon, Bishop of Kaduna. Although the Bishop preaches an end to religious violence in his country, Nigeria, he has also said, 'Unfortunately, some Anglican leaders do not embrace the official positions of the Church, making dumb comments such as "Muslims do not have a monopoly on violence."[24]

And, although he has said that corruption is even worse than homosexuality, he thinks the latter is pretty bad and ought to be punished: 'The church in Nigeria is, however, grateful to the National Assembly for passing a law against same-sex marriage,' he told an internet newspaper for young Nigerians.[25]

Legally, the TBFF is run by its trustees. For the first five years of the trust's existence, there were just the three of them: a lawyer, an investment banker and an advertising executive.

Robert Clinton is a lawyer at Farrer and Co., and also a director of the Cherie Blair Foundation for Women. Farrer and Co. are TBFF's lawyers, and this company's Lincoln's Inn address is the only address given out for the Foundation – its real Marble Arch address is kept as secret as possible.

Robert Coke is the co-head of absolute return and buyouts at the Wellcome Trust, chairman of the British Private Equity and Venture Capital Association's advisory board and director of the Private Equity Investors' Association.

But the advertising man is the most interesting, for Jeremy Sinclair created the infamous, but unsuccessful, 'Demon Eyes' advertising campaign against Blair for the Conservatives in the 1997 election. 'It is nasty, it is vicious, it is negative. It is all the things that you would expect from the Conservative party,' said Blair at the time.

That campaign reinforced M&C Saatchi's reputation as the Rottweiler of political advertising. But it was far from being Sinclair's first campaign for the Conservatives, nor his last. He was responsible for the famous, and devastatingly successful, 'Labour Isn't Working' poster in 1978, which helped ensure Margaret Thatcher's election victory the following year. He was back working for the Conservatives in 2010, scrapping the planned positive campaign about the virtues of David Cameron for a ruthlessly negative one demonising Gordon Brown, so he has a reasonable claim to being the man who won the 2010 election for the Conservatives.

He lists his interests as 'spiritualism, architecture and Conservative politics', which gives him a lot in common with Blair, though Blair is not thought to be especially interested in architecture.

Sinclair took a copywriting diploma from Watford School of Art and went straight on to work for Saatchi & Saatchi in 1968. He has never worked anywhere that is not owned by the Saatchi brothers. He rose rapidly within the agency, creating campaigns for major clients such as Silk Cut cigarettes and British Airways.

He had reached the post of deputy chairman when, in 1994, a board rebellion secured the ousting of Maurice and Charles Saatchi. Sinclair opted to stay with the Saatchis, who had made his career, and to whom he was a perfect foil, adding a calmness that they lacked. So he was the founding director of the new firm created by the Saatchis, M&C Saatchi.

In 2013 Blair brought in two old friends to add to his trustees: Dame Gail Rebuck and Sir Michael Barber. Rebuck is chairwoman and chief executive of the huge publishing empire Random House, which published Blair's autobiography. She was married to Blair's pollster and friend, the late Philip Gould. Barber was chief adviser to the Secretary of State for Education on school standards during Blair's first term as Prime Minister, and the real architect, along with Andrew Adonis, of Blair's education policy. During Blair's second term he worked as Blair's chief adviser on delivery, reporting directly to the Prime Minister.

After Blair resigned as PM, Barber worked as global head of education for McKinsey, then chief education adviser for Pearson.

The Tony Blair Faith Foundation is also a registered charity in the USA, where its five directors, apart from Blair and the first TBFF chief executive, Ruth Turner, included Tim Collins, the billionaire businessman who accompanied Blair on a trip to Libya to meet Gaddafi. As previously discussed, Collins claimed that Blair asked him to make that trip in his capacity as a Trustee of the TBFF, though no one has established any link between the work of the TBFF and Blair's dealings with the Libyan dictator Colonel Gaddafi. Gaddafi certainly saw none – he apparently thought Collins was there to advise on building beach resorts. Collins was obliged to disabuse him of this notion.

Collins is deeply involved with the Yale Divinity School. It was precisely the opportunity to meet its super-rich donors such as Collins that made the Yale Divinity School so useful for the TBFF after Blair ran a course there.

Collins was one of the early donors to the TBFF, but has now stopped both donating and giving his time to it. His defection removes a key figure from the early days. Collins had helped set up Blair's link with Yale, had provided money to help start the TBFF, put him in touch with other wealthy donors, imagining that Blair would make his priority doing reconciliation work around the globe.

Our sources tell us that Collins has become thoroughly disillusioned with Blair; that the visit to Libya was a turning point for him; that he was willing to go on supporting the TBFF as long as Ruth Turner was there, because he had a lively admiration for her. But, after her departure, he felt it was no longer a good use of his time.

Collins himself avoids talking about Blair publicly, and apparently still thinks Blair is an entertaining character, but has no interest in supporting the Faith Foundation without Ruth Turner.

He feels there is too much crossover between Blair's businesses and his public and charitable work. Bill Clinton, he believes, has handled this a lot better.

Collins was also puzzled by Blair's conversion to Catholicism, and asked for a robust theological explanation, which he never felt he got. He fears being tainted by Blair's reputation.

Another director of TBFF in the USA is Alfred E. Smith IV, who ticks two key boxes for Blair: he's a Catholic and he's fabulously wealthy, having spent thirty-five years on Wall Street. There is also Linda Lader, wife of former US ambassador to London, Philip Lader. Philip Lader is chairman of WPP, the global media and communications firm that bankrolls Peter Mandelson's commercial activities.

In 2014, the hole left by the departure of Tim Collins was filled by Rabbi Peter Rubinstein. Rubinstein is Rabbi Emeritus at the Central Synagogue in New York, and, according to its website, oversees the Bronfman Center for Jewish Life as the director of Jewish community at 92nd Street Y. 'He is recognized as a leader in the changing face of the Jewish community and was ranked number 3 in *Newsweek*'s 2012 list of "America's 50 Most Influential Rabbis". He has been on the list ever since its inception.'[26]

There is every sign that America is where Blair sees the long-term future of the TBFF.[27] He is far more comfortable these days in the USA than in Britain, for at home he is now widely disliked, whereas in the US, where faith and power are more closely linked, he is still a hero. Unlike in the UK, Blair's religious fervour is seen as a strength in the US. Blair's status there is such that he is now called on to sprinkle stardust at religious gatherings, such as the National Prayer Breakfast in Washington. He regularly crops up in Washington society diaries.

That, insiders have told us, is the justification for continuing to have the sponsor's name in the title of the organisation. TBFF leaders recognise that the name 'Tony Blair' in the title weakens the organisation in Britain. But it strengthens it in the USA, they say, which is why it's there and why it stays.

In March 2010 the *Observer* reported that the former Prime Minister was preparing to launch a 'faith offensive' across the USA, after building up relationships with a network of influential religious leaders and faith organisations. It noted the growing TBFF activity in the USA, the relationship with Belinda Stronach, and also a relationship with what the TBFF described as 'the Washington-based Center for Interfaith Action'. This centre, which has now changed its name to Religions for Peace following a merger, supported a meeting of major international organisations active in faith-based approaches to combating malaria, in collaboration with the TBFF.[28]

Another of the TBFF's charitable activities is the sponsorship of an annual film competition under the title Faith Shorts. In 2012, the winners of this competition were announced in London on 26 November. Charles Andrew Flamiano, a sixteen-year-old Catholic filmmaker from General Santos City, Philippines, won the first prize in the 14–17 age category for a film titled *Letting Go, Letting God*. We first learned of this from the TBFF website but for some reason all reference to it has now been removed from the site, though you can still find newspaper coverage.[29]

Letting Go, Letting God is a three-minute tale, acted to mournful music, of a young woman who is told she has terminal cancer. As she walks along the hospital corridor, understandably depressed, she drops her notes containing her diagnosis in front of another young woman in a wheelchair, who picks them up, reads them, and hands her a small crucifix. She hugs the crucifix to her bosom and feels better. That's it, except for three little slogans that pop up on the screen afterwards, the last of which is 'Love out your faith, you'll never know whose life you'll touch.'

Of course it's the work of someone very young, but, if it's the sort of work the TBFF tries to encourage, then it seems reasonable to conclude that TBFF is, to some extent at least, a proselytising organisation on behalf of religious belief generally, and Christianity in particular.

In a 2013 advertisement for a new head of communications, the TBFF sums up its work alliteratively (Blair has always been addicted to alliteration):

Leadership: we seek to ensure that current and future leaders understand the role religion plays in the modern, globalising world.

Literacy: we educate and support young people to help them become global citizens.

Lives: we help religious communities in 140+ countries work together to save lives.

It also organises events, often in the House of Commons. We attended a 'debate' on 'How faith can help deliver global health' in one of the modern committee rooms there. It wasn't a debate at all. The whole platform of speakers seemed to agree entirely with each other and with the views of the TBFF. Those expecting a glimpse of the former PM himself were to be disappointed. We had to make do with the Shadow Development Secretary Ivan Lewis and Shadow Health Secretary Andy Burnham. Burnham suggested that the Ten Commandments might be amended to include eating five pieces of fruit and vegetable per day.

The message from the TBFF at this meeting was that faith-based organisations were being used to deliver aid on the ground but not being given any say in how development policy is made. Its purpose seemed to be to argue that churches should be able to influence national aid and development policy. This was strange, because getting more say for religions in public policy is not at all what we thought the TBFF was founded for – and is arguably not a charitable objective, but a political one.

The audience was rather partisan. One member of the audience conducted his own straw poll: did anyone disagree with the notion that faith-based organisations should have a say over government policy on international aid? No one did. And what about domestic policy? Labour MP Ivan Lewis put the essential message in a nutshell, and this was what the TBFF chose to pull out for its website: 'Faith communities should not be at the periphery of health development policy. They need to be at the centre if we are to make real progress in this area.'

Jeremy LeFroy, Conservative MP for Stafford, offered a reassuring thought: 'Not everyone in government is a pagan – I've met many ministers who agree with the idea of faith playing a greater role in development.' The director of Charles Clarke's Religion and Society programme at Lancaster University, Professor Linda Woodhead, was there to argue that government officials need to be better informed about which channels to go through in faith communities.

There was, says the TBFF, 'general consensus that faith communities have reach, authority and are cost-effective. But, the efficiency of health development could be improved further if governments consulted with faith communities at the point of policy development rather than delivery.'

So here we have an organisation that refuses to declare who funds it, yet argues for certain groups – religious ones – to have a greater influence over government policy, to be consulted when policy is formulated. These religious organisations to which the TBFF wants to give greater influence in International Development Policy are all represented on the TBFF's Religious Advisory Council. Some of them support marginalisation and imprisonment of homosexuals in, say, Uganda and Nigeria. Mr LeFroy did not think that was a problem, because 'we gave them most of these laws during the age of Empire'.

The suggestion that faiths and churches should have more say in public policy on matters such as aid, development and health policy may have achieved 'general consensus' on a panel hand-picked by Tony Blair's Faith Foundation, but it remains contentious outside that room. It is, of course, an arguable view, but arguing for it might not be appropriate work for a registered charity.

It's also a controversial view. There are many who would argue that religions should not have a say in public policy on such matters. If they are to do so, which religions get a say will become even more controversial. Is Islam to have a say along with the rest, and, if so, will those evil strands in Islam identified by Blair be excluded?

When Tony Blair's Faith Foundation takes a stand on such matters, the question of who funds it becomes acute. No charity can ignore the views of major funders if it is to take a view on controversial matters, and the TBFF must take more notice than most because it has only major funders. A collecting tin being shaken in the street for the TBFF would not attract much money, which is probably why you never see one.

THE BIG DONORS

If the TBFF is going to take stands on such contentious issues, it ought to say where it gets its money. Otherwise there will always be the suspicion that it is funded by organisations that stand to benefit, in terms either of money or of power, from the policies it advocates.

The TBFF not only refuses to say who any of its funders are, but also refuses even to say whether Blair himself is among them. We asked for information on donors and got this:

Re the Tony Blair Faith Foundation's finances, all information can be found in our annual report which can be found here: http://www.tonyblairfaithfoundation.org/news/2012/01/30-0 and is also available on the Charity Commission's website. If you do have any questions relating to our work on the ground or indeed need any further details on the themes discussed at the event you attended please do let me know.

We pointed out that this gave no information on donors, and got this: 'As is the case with many charities, we don't disclose information about our donors.' This is entirely legal – the Charity Commission demands only that accounts reveal the full amount donated, not where it comes from. It is, however, fairly unusual. Most charities reveal the names of their major donors.

In the TBFF's case, it almost certainly has only major donors. The TBFF claims that some of its income 'could be described as grassroots giving, smaller donations from people motivated to support a specific campaign or area of work', but refuses to say how much.

If we were entirely reliant on the TBFF itself for our information, we would know nothing at all about its donors. In fact there are some sources of money we do know about.

Newspaper tycoon Rupert Murdoch is one, to the tune of $100,000, according to a US tax return quoted by the *Daily Mirror*. Blair used to be very careful of his relationship with Murdoch and his newspaper empire News Corp. When former *News of the World* editor Rebekah Brooks was arrested on a charge of phone hacking (she was subsequently cleared), Blair got in touch with News Corp to offer her, Murdoch and Murdoch's son James advice on a 'between us' basis. He advised Brooks to 'keep strong' and 'take sleeping pills'.[30]

It was *Guardian* editor Alan Rusbridger who drew attention to the timing of the Blair offer, in a tweet on 21 February 2014. 'Blair's advice to Rebekah 7 days after Milly Dowler, 3 days after Coulson arrested & as Ed Miliband attacking Murdoch,' he wrote.

Another major funder we know of – as we saw in Chapter 1 – is Haim Saban, creator of the Power Rangers (and one of the richest people in America, according to *Forbes* magazine), along with his wife Cheryl. His Saban Entertainment merged with News Corp's Fox Children's Productions to form Fox Kids Worldwide Inc. in 1996. It was renamed Fox Family Worldwide Inc. in 2001, then acquired by Disney and renamed Disney XD.

Saban's political agenda is clear and straightforward, and he makes no secret of it. He says, 'I'm a one-issue guy and my issue is Israel.' He has also said, 'I used to be a leftie but am now very much on the right. The reason for the switch is Israel.'

In addition to funding the TBFF, Saban contributed heavily to George W. Bush's re-election campaign, mainly, if not entirely, because he approved of Bush's stance on the Middle East. The other American politician Saban admires is Joe Lieberman, who has been described by an authoritative Washington-watcher as 'among the strongest backers of Israel on Capitol Hill.'[31] Lieberman was Democrat Al Gore's running mate in the 2000 presidential election, but he split with the Democratic Party mainly over his support for the Iraq War, and now quarrels with it over Iran. By 2008 he was supporting Republican candidate John McCain against Barack Obama – and he almost became McCain's running mate.

In 2010 he was widely quoted as saying that the Obama administration, may want to consider the fact that their relationship with their Israeli wife is more valuable than their newfound relationship with their Arab mistress. Obama was asked the same question Hillary was asked: 'If Iran nukes Israel, what would be your reaction?' Hillary said, 'We will obliterate them.' We . . . will . . . obliterate . . . them. Four words, it's simple to understand. Obama said only three words. He would 'take appropriate action.' I don't know what that means. A rogue state that is supporting killing our men and women in Iraq; that is a supporter of Hezbollah, which killed more Americans than any other terrorist organization; that is a supporter of Hamas, which shot twelve thousand rockets at Israel – that rogue state nukes a member of the United Nations, and we're going to 'take appropriate action'![32]

An Israeli television interviewer once told him, 'You really are our rich uncle in America, and we can rely on you.' He told Israeli television of the Obama administration, 'They are leftists, really left leftists, so far to the left there's not much space left between them and the wall.'[33]

Tony Blair is publicly signed up to Saban's view about Iran and Israel. If that were not the case, it is most unlikely that Saban would be funding his Faith Foundation. We do not, of course, suggest that Blair took this position in order to get his hands on Saban's money – we are sure Blair sincerely holds the opinion he expresses. But it is a reminder that money comes with strings attached. Tony Blair would have to be very careful not even to appear to criticise the government in Tel Aviv, should he ever wish to do so, if he wants his Faith Foundation to keep receiving Saban's money. If this can be said to be relatively harmless for the patron of the TBFF, it is crippling for the Quartet Representative. We are told by TBFF insiders that Saban is one of a large number of very wealthy strongly pro-Israel Jewish donors, and that there are no Muslim donors at all. Even within the organisation this is seen to be a problem Our sources also say that the senior management of the organisation are concerned about this, and anxious for it not to become public knowledge, for fear of embarrassing their patron, who, not for the first time, is wearing more hats than are entirely comfortable.

Another big funder is a Ukrainian oligarch, son-in-law of Ukraine's former President. The scale of Victor Pinchuk's funding of Blair's charity emerged at a meeting he hosted at the Davos World Economic Forum in Switzerland in January 2013. He has given the TBFF $500,000 (£320,000) – a fifth of all the donations declared in its 2013 accounts.[34]

Pinchuk, like Saban – and, if our sources are to be believed, like a very large number of TBFF donors – is fiercely pro-Israeli, this view fuelled, in Pinchuk's case, by bitter experience of anti-Semitism in his childhood in Dnipropetrovsk, Ukraine's fourth-largest city, 280 miles from the capital Kiev.

Pinchuk, whom *Forbes* ranked 255th on the list of the wealthiest people in the world, with a fortune of $4.2 billion, is a steel magnate and philanthropist who made his fortune after marrying the daughter of Leonid Kuchma, Ukraine's former President. He is also an old friend of Blair's.

Blair's choice of priorities may have nothing at all to do with donations to the TBFF, but it is a matter of record that, in October 2012, Blair undertook an official tour of Pinchuk's new Interpipe Steel Works in Dnipropetrovsk. Unusually, Blair did not charge for the visit. Photographs of Blair touring the factory with his host were posted on Pinchuk's company website. They showed a grinning Blair signing a hard hat and presenting it to a grateful Pinchuk. 'The public figure [Blair] has managed to see live the modernisation and development of the Ukrainian metallurgy,' says the website.

Blair apparently, according to the company's website, said while he was there, 'I have visited a huge number of Great Britain mills. Interpipe Steel is undoubtedly an outstanding creation. This is one of the best and most modern mills in the world. I am greatly impressed with the spectacular and almost fantastic design of the facility. It is a real pleasure for me to come to Dnipropetrovsk and see the true personification of the twenty-first-century industry. It is extremely essential for Ukraine to have such a state-of-the-art production facility as Interpipe Steel. The most up-to-date technologies, the brand-new approaches to the work – all these things are an enormous success for the country. The mill should become a platform for development – a symbol of what the modern industry must be like.'[35]

While he was there, Blair also gave a lecture to university students and staff from Pinchuk's factory entitled 'Modernising Countries in [the] 21st Century'.

TBFF priorities may have nothing to do with who gives it money, but it is also a matter of record that its activities now include an educational programme in Ukraine, launched in June 2011 in collaboration with the Victor Pinchuk Foundation.[36]

The visit to Pinchuk's factory was at least the third time Blair had visited Ukraine since he left Downing Street in 2007. In 2008 the former Prime Minister was a guest speaker at a conference held in the Black Sea resort of Yalta and organised by Pinchuk, at which Blair pushed Ukraine's case to join the European Union, the presidency of whose commission Blair was then widely tipped to take.

Pinchuk has been a keen advocate of EU membership, setting up a firm to promote Ukraine's EU credentials. Its directors included, until 2010, Stephen Byers, Blair's former Trade Secretary, who, as we have seen, has also been active with Blair in the Middle East.[37]

Blair and Pinchuk seem to have been introduced by Bill Clinton and senior staff at the Clinton Foundation, which has also received money from Pinchuk.

Pinchuk has been accused of exploiting his relationship with the daughter of the president of Ukraine to grab state privatisations on the cheap, and of swindling two Ukrainian business associates out of hundreds of millions of dollars amid a mass sell-off of state-owned industry by the country's leader at the time, Leonid Kuchma.[38]

Born in Kiev in 1960, Pinchuk grew up in Dnipropetrovsk and studied at the city's metallurgical institute before beginning a career as a research engineer in pipe production. He founded Interpipe in 1990, just as the Soviet Union was breaking up.

He met his second wife, Elena Franchuk, in 1997, and they both left their spouses to marry in 2002. Elena's father was Ukraine's president from 1994 to 2005 – the years when Pinchuk turned himself from a successful businessman into a billionaire. Interpipe bought a 50 per cent stake in the Nikopol steel plant in 2003 for $80 million.

Like many of those who became suddenly wealthy when the Soviet Union collapsed, Pinchuk faced the threat that a new government might want a share in his wealth, and the sale was contested two years later, following a change in government. Viktor Yushchenko, the president who came to power after the Orange Revolution, said, 'Despite all of Pinchuk's sniffles and groans, the factory will be returned to the state.' In fact, Yushchenko was still in power when the privatisation was confirmed as lawful.

The Pinchuks bought a house in Kensington in central London for £80 million in 2008, a then-world record price. The house has an underground swimming pool, gym, sauna and cinema, and now probably houses some of his contemporary art collection, reckoned to be one of the best collections in private hands.

Pinchuk, who also has an office in Mayfair, is a major collector of Damien Hirst's work but refuses to say which of the British artist's creations he owns. He has also spent large sums on work by Jeff Koons, and in 2006 he opened the Pinchuk Art Centre in Kiev, where some of his collection is housed and where Hirsts have been exhibited.

'To spend money is much more exciting than to make it,' he once said.[39]

Pinchuk was very much a player in the troubles in Ukraine at the start of 2014. Former President Viktor Yanukovych, now in exile, used to worry about the attitude of the oligarchs, of whom Pinchuk is one of the three most important, because they control much of the Ukrainian economy, and Yanukovych had not managed to place them under control, as Putin has done in Russia.

Pinchuk's television stations have covered the troubles extensively, and they were not sympathetic to Yanukovych's switch away from the EU and towards Russia. Yanukovych's enforced departure made way for a pro-EU government, and new president Petro Poroshenko is more to Pinchuk's taste.

Ukraine is now moving towards much the same position as the existing clients of Tony Blair Associates in that part of the world, as we have seen in an earlier chapter. Blair's interest in the country could then include not just the TBFF taking money from the oligarch, but also Tony Blair Associates taking money from the government.

We also know of a $1 million donation from a reformed Junk Bond King, Michael Milken. According to Andy MacSmith in the *Independent*,

He was the 1980s Junk Bond King, who piled up untold wealth in the boom years, but came to grief at the end of that decade when he copped a 10-year jail sentence, a $200 million fine and a permanent ban on dealing in securities, after pleading guilty to six felonies, in what was then the biggest fraud case in the history of the US securities industry. The jail sentence was later reduced to two years. Since his release, he has reinvented himself as a philanthropist, contributing huge sums to medical research.

The *Wall Street Journal* reports that the star guest at the annual Milken Institute Global Conference in Beverly Hills this week was Tony Blair. The former Prime Minister was asked about a number of topics, including his time as a wannabe rock star, at Oxford University, when he was lead singer for a band called Ugly Rumours.

When the session ended, Mr Milken informed his 'visibly shocked' guest that he was donating $1 million to the Tony Blair Faith Foundation.

So who else is there? We don't know, and rumours are rife. One journalist who has done a lot of work on Blair's activities told us confidently that the TBFF was funded by orthodox Zionists. But another journalist, Melanie McDonagh, wrote, 'Tony Blair's Faith Foundation [is] handsomely supported by Arab donors.'[40]

Our sources tell us there are no Muslim donors, but do the government of Kuwait and oil-rich sheikhs associated with the government give money to the TBFF? If so, why? Is the government merely continuing to pay the debt it appears to feel it owes to the architect of the Iraq War, or is it expecting a return for its money, in terms either of the policy of the TBFF or in the statements made by Tony Blair?

It is certainly the case that a very large proportion of its income comes from wealthy and uncompromising supporters of Israel.

Defending its refusal to give the names of its big-money donors, a spokesperson told us, 'The public absolutely has a right to know that any funding received by the charity has been used solely in furtherance of the charity's aims. Company law and charity law set out a series of regulations and reporting requirements on charities precisely so that the public can have confidence in how registered charities are run. The Foundation complies with all its obligations under company and charitable law.'

He went on to explain what these are, and added, 'There is no requirement for a charity to list individual donors. We, like many other charities, don't name individual donors in our accounts as many people prefer for their donations to charitable causes not to be made public. Individuals can of course make known their support of the Foundation if they wish.'

It is the trustees, not the donors, who decide what the TBFF will do, he said, though it does accept donations for specific purposes. 'But a restricted donation may not be accepted if the trustees are not confident that it will be spent in the interests of furthering the charity's aims.'

However, the TBFF will go a long way to please its big-money donors. In a 2013 advertisement for a head of communications, TBFF says, 'TBFF is seen as a pioneering and innovative thought leader, and funder-friendly organisation.'

And what of Mr Blair himself? It seems likely that he is giving the TBFF some money from his own enormous earnings, though we cannot know this for certain. We remember what an old friend and colleague of Blair's said to us in an unguarded moment: 'He says he gives money to his charities, but I don't think he gives enough to his charities.'

This is borne out by the fact that in 2012 the TBFF's income started to fall off slightly, but Blair's own income continued to grow. The TBFF reported an income of £3.66 million, down slightly on the £3.75 million that it received in 2010.

Perhaps this is why, in July 2012, the TBFF advertised for a head of major gifts to join a four-strong fundraising team and report to the head of fundraising:

> We are looking to recruit an exceptional individual for this new post, who will help develop our international portfolio of Major Donors. Working at the most senior of levels, this individual will need to have at least 5 years professional fundraising experience with a proven track record of securing six and seven figure major gifts.

The team, said the advertisement, 'oversees all donor solicitation, engagement, donor events and donor management, from an increasing number of international sources that include high net-worth individuals, trusts, foundations, corporations and statutory bodies.'

The long – very long – advertisement gave something of an insight into how fundraising for something like the TBFF works. It is not the sort of organisation that could go onto the streets and expect ordinary people to throw in the sums of money that ordinary people can afford. A charity chugger for the Tony Blair Faith Foundation would have a very hard sell indeed. Ordinary people might want to give comparatively small amounts of money to Oxfam, or Save the Children, or Crisis, but that sort of money does not go to the TBFF, and neither is the TBFF interested in sums of that size. It is interested in big money from very rich people.

So, says the advertisement, the successful candidate will 'manage a range of international donors and prospects, and will work ... to ensure that each donor has the most appropriate and stimulating engagement strategy.' Required attributes include 'experience of creative cultivation, solicitation and stewardship techniques' and 'a track record of working with major gift prospects to secure six and seven figure gifts'.

The culture of secrecy endemic in all Tony Blair's operations must be retained. The post holder would 'work alongside people from the other Tony Blair organisations, and will have access to confidential information ... They will be required to sign a confidentiality agreement.'

However, no appointment was made, and there are no plans to reopen the appointment.

Interns are taken on, unpaid, for three months. Even they have to sign a confidentiality agreement. They are told, 'Your Volunteer Internship Agreement will contain a confidentiality clause. During your internship you may be exposed to sensitive data, and therefore confidentiality is extremely important.'

The *Liberal Conspiracy* blog reported TBFF posting advertisements for an external-affairs intern and an education intern, both lasting for a period of three months.

Making use of unpaid interns is controversial. Blair's office told *Liberal Conspiracy* that the Office of Tony Blair does have interns, but it pays them the London living wage. However, the office says, the Blair charities, such as the TBFF, have their own policies and, 'as charitable organisations, they have volunteers'.

It goes on:

Like all charities who rely on those motivated to help their cause, the Tony Blair Faith Foundation values the contribution of those who volunteer for us. By volunteering our interns are giving practical support to help prevent religious prejudice, conflict and extremism, helping current leaders and the next generation understand the impact and complexity of religion in the world.[41]

This confuses the words *volunteer* and *intern*. A volunteer is not an unpaid intern. What TBFF and the other charities have is not volunteers, but unpaid interns. The TBFF justifies this on the grounds that it is a charity, but it is hardly the sort of charity to which a young person might wish to donate their time for charitable reasons – in other words, to volunteer. For the TBFF, taking on unpaid labour is not the same as for, say, Oxfam or Amnesty.

If they go to work for the TBFF as an intern, they are probably doing so in the same spirit as they might if they were an intern in a commercial organisation. They are hoping for good experience, exposure to exciting work and the possibility of a job at the end of it. And the TBFF knows that, for its statement goes on: 'In return, participants get all we can offer in terms of a structured programme of professional development.'

Our information is that the TBFF does not deliver this. Its interns, in at least some cases, are simply unpaid labour, doing the boring work for nothing. We are aware of people who already have a decade or so of relevant experience applying for paid work, and being offered unpaid work in their field of expertise instead.

One such person was told that paid data-input work was available; that it might well be repetitive and boring, but would require a high degree of accuracy; that it would be commercially confidential and the person would need to sign a confidentiality agreement; that it would be based in a satellite office in Stanmore; and that the person would need to agree with the core proposition of the project.

The offer, when it came, was all these things – but as an unpaid intern, doing boring data-input work for which the person had earned a living doing for some years, and in Stanmore, way out of reach of the heart of the TBFF's operations in Marble Arch and well away from anything interesting.

THE MINOR PARTNER: THE TONY BLAIR
SPORTS FOUNDATION

The Tony Blair Sports Foundation was launched in 2007 for Blair to 'give something back to the North East.'[42] It aims to encourage more people in the region to take part in sports. What figures and anecdotal evidence we have suggests that it is struggling, and not making a huge contribution to the region. It appears not even to have its own website, just a very uninformative page on the website of the Office of Tony Blair.

After working its way up to an income of £348,233 in the year ending 31 March 2010, it brought in only £37,576 the following year, less than half what it spent on staff.

It does not sound as though Blair is making the same effort with his rich contacts for his Sports Foundation as he is for his Faith Foundation. He has told the staff, and any volunteers the charity may have, to go out and raise money, and he will match everything they raise, pound for pound.[43] This is quite a common method for a very rich man to donate money to a charity – but extremely odd when it is his own charity and bears his name. Further, it requires the staff and volunteers to go out and combat the hostility that the mention of his name will arouse in many circles in order to bring in money.

CONCLUSION

If the Faith Foundation was what Tony Blair wanted to work on for the rest of his life, just what was it that he thought he wanted to do? Its objectives seem ill-defined and contradictory. Its work is mostly not what we associate with charity, and it is certainly not charitable towards Islam. Sometimes it feels like a recruiting sergeant for faith – almost any faith, so long as it's not Islam.

Its secret donors' list will one day make fascinating reading, but we know enough already to be sure of two things. Firstly, most of them, if not all of them, would cease to donate if Blair ever fell out with Israel, surely an awkward position for the Middle East envoy to be in. And secondly, they are all very seriously rich. The well-intentioned person with a modest income and a bit of money to spare for a good cause is not the sort of donor the Tony Blair Faith Foundation has any interest in. Its advisers and funders are the wealthy and the well-connected. It is staffed by more than its fair share of bankers, and they occupy both top positions.

Perhaps Tony Blair has forgotten the quote from Jesus in the Gospel according to St Matthew: 'And again I say unto you, it is easier for a camel to go through the eye of a needle, than for a rich man to enter into the kingdom of God.'

CHAPTER THIRTEEN

FAMILY FORTUNES

*'While this venture is a commercial one, it is not
about replacing the NHS or profiteering.'*
– CHERIE BLAIR ON HER PRIVATE
HEALTHCARE BUSINESS.

After Tony Blair's last appearance in Parliament, the Blair family came out of 10 Downing Street, and Blair, smiling, got into the back of the waiting Daimler, on the side nearer the home he was vacating. Cherie came round the other side, stunning in purple, and turned for a moment to wave at the world's media; and she said, 'Bye. I don't think I'll miss you.'

Blair was furious, as Cherie records in her autobiography:

> Sitting there in the back of the Daimler, Tony stony-faced beside me, I stared out of the window as we passed the Cenotaph. He was right to be angry … leaving was to be done on his terms and was to be done with dignity and grace, and what I had just done was neither gracious nor dignified … I sat beside him feeling both foolish and small.

And so, with Cherie's help, the incident contributed to the general impression of Blair as the charming, socially adept man, and Cherie as the gauche and accident-prone female partner. This fiction would not have survived if the world's media had been in Hampshire a week later, in the magnificent garden of Charles Powell's Hampshire home. In fact, this story is made public here for the first time.

The very upper-crust Charles Powell, Baron Powell of Bayswater, had acted as Prime Minister Blair's special envoy to Brunei – controversially, because Powell was also on the payroll of BAE Systems, and the company was in dispute with Brunei over the purchase of three warships. One of his brothers is Chris Powell, once Labour's favourite advertising man, and another is Jonathan Powell, Blair's chief of staff in Downing Street, who became the chief consultant of Tony Blair Associates. Charles pronounces his surname to rhyme with *hole*, but Chris and Jonathan pronounce it to rhyme with *towel*.

The occasion was a party to celebrate Jonathan's marriage to the journalist Sarah Helm, and Sarah made a speech containing a graceful and witty reference to her presence on the anti-Iraq War march. Then, with Cherie seated at the table nearby finishing her dessert, Blair rose.

'Hi, everybody,' he said. 'So now you all know why I decided to resign as Prime Minister. I thought it was time to give Jonathan back to Sarah.' Then, turning to the happy couple, he added, 'Anyway, Jonathan was never any good in bed.'

'There was a kind of nervous semi-silence,' one of the guests told us. 'It was so wrong on so many levels. We all tried not to look at Cherie, or Jonathan, or Sarah.'

CHERIE

Cherie Blair is much more socially and politically adept, and much faster on her feet, than people give her credit for – perhaps more than she gives herself credit for. One of us (Beckett) once asked her to sign his copy of her book on prime ministers' wives. It happened at the same time as our book on Tony Blair's premiership was out, and the Blairs, with some justice, considered it hostile. She wrote on the cover sheet, 'To Francis. I promise this is not fiction. Cherie Blair.' She had barely a second to think. It was quick, witty and clever.

Today the Blairs live very separate lives. As the two stories at the start of this chapter illustrate, by the time they left Downing Street they had lost that instinctive feel for each other that they must once have had. The business empires of Tony and Cherie Blair are separate, and the couple do not work together. They are seldom seen together.

Middle East sources have told us that, during the two to three days a month Tony spends in the region, Cherie is never there. She does go to the region herself, for her own business, always at times when he is not there. None of the Middle East correspondents we spoke to had seen the Blairs together.

Neighbours in Connaught Square report the same thing. Cherie is seen a lot in the square, wandering around the huge house, going to the odd community event, and looking depressed. Tony is seldom seen, and the two are never seen together. People who have worked for the Blair organisation, including Martin Bright, confirmed for us that the Blairs are seldom seen together.

What is going on, we understand, is the disintegration of their once very close marriage. When we heard that lawyers may have been consulted with a view to a divorce, we put it to two people who know the Blairs very well. The first paused for a very long time, refused the option of denying the story, and said, 'I can only say that, if Cherie were contemplating that, Tony would do everything he possibly could to dissuade her.' The other said, 'There has been talk of a divorce for a long time but she'll never do it. Her hatred of the media would be greater than her hatred of his affairs.' This person assumed that the rumours of affairs are true, though Blair never personally comments on them except to deny them.

There is also, of course, the fact that they are both Catholics and their church forbids divorce, but their Catholicism is sufficiently flexible for him to overcome that obstacle.

How has it come to this?

The Downing Street years took their toll on the marriage. Many politicians and friends of the Blairs have told us that, in Downing Street, she had a thoroughly raw deal, pilloried by the press as a surrogate for her husband and not protected by his spin doctors, who gave priority to protecting the PM.

She was persuaded against her better judgement to take a prominent role in Blair's public life. She would rather have concentrated on her legal career, but she was forced into the role of consort, for which she was not at all suited.

Perhaps she was all the things the media said she was: a bit too greedy for the trappings of power, for the access to freebies. But it was not just the media that turned on her. It was the relentless Downing Street New Labour machine as well. She was used as a lightning rod for Blair.

The rumours of Tony Blair having affairs with other women have not helped, although Blair's office has consistently denied them.

Media magnate Rupert Murdoch, to whom Blair has been close ever since 1994, filed for divorce from his very much younger wife Wendi Deng in June 2013, and believes that Blair alienated her affections. Murdoch is thought to have confided in his daughter Elisabeth Murdoch and her husband, PR man Matthew Freud. The one thing we know for certain is that the once close relationship between Murdoch and Blair has broken down completely.

Blair telephoned an old business associate in the US in 2014 and assured him that he was not having an affair with Wendy Deng. But the business associate, who also knows Murdoch well, told him that Murdoch thought it was true, and that Murdoch did not believe the denials. That much, at least, is certain. Whether or not Blair has been having an affair with his wife, Murdoch *believes* he has.

This matters terribly to Blair. It will not affect how the British perceive him, but he has pretty well given up hope of salvaging his reputation here. It does affect how the Americans see him, partly because extramarital affairs are more damaging there, but principally because it will destroy his relationship with Murdoch and NewsCorp, which he has nurtured so carefully ever since 1994. His reputation in America is desperately important to him.

CHERIE AND LAUREN BOOTH

Cherie is also now much taken up with the tangled affairs of her own family, stemming mostly from the untidy life lived by her father, the actor Tony Booth. They are a turbulent family – one of her ancestors was John Wilkes Booth, who assassinated President Lincoln. Tony Booth has eight daughters who have three different mothers, and the poverty of Cherie's childhood was harder to bear because she knew her father was making money as an actor. Nonetheless, Cherie takes a lot of trouble with her now elderly and frail father, and he for his part was quoted in October 2010 as saying that he would do anything for Cherie.

In the same *Daily Mail* interview, he said he did not love Cherie's half-sister Lauren Booth.[1] 'I don't know if we'll ever speak again. I suspect not,' the actor told the paper. He sneered at her conversion to Islam, and attacked 'the things she said about Cherie and Tony, which were unforgiveable'. She had been sent a belated email to tell her of his 2010 stroke, but she had not been in touch, he said.

Few things are as simple as they look. When we spoke to Lauren, two years later, she had never seen the email and did not know her father had had a stroke until we told her.

Lauren had certainly embarrassed Prime Minister Blair by her outspoken attacks on his policies, but so had Tony Booth himself. He made no secret of the fact that he considered that Blair's government was damaging the welfare state.

When Lauren was a journalist in London, regularly attacking Prime Minister Blair's policies from the left and finally irretrievably falling out with him over Iraq, there were newspaper stories saying that she was trading on her relationship with Cherie, a relationship which they said had never been close. None of this was true, and the stories were often under the bylines of journalists known to be close to the New Labour spin machine.

In fact, Lauren was a good writer and broadcast performer, quite capable of making her own way in journalism, though the relationship with Cherie did her career no harm. And she and Cherie were close. Right up to 1997, when he became Prime Minister, she was very close to Blair as well – she says she 'loved him to bits' in those days.

When Tony Booth nearly burned to death in 1979 by falling into a drum of paraffin during a drunken attempt to get into his locked flat, Tony Blair was a great support to the family, says Lauren.

But Lauren Booth and Tony Blair have not spoken for more than a decade now. Lauren has become a Muslim and a Palestinian activist. Tony Booth suggests in his *Mail* interview that she did this only to embarrass Blair, but this is not at all likely: she defends her position with detailed knowledge and genuine passion, and is very much on the side of the moderate, tolerant Muslims.

Before all that, in 2000 she and her actor husband Craig Darby and their two daughters went to live in France. After a few years, she told Darby she was going to leave him. The next day he received serious head injuries in a motorbike accident. In the years since then, she has moved back to Britain, become a Muslim, watched her husband recover with agonising slowness, and fought a long and bitter battle with him over custody of their two daughters. At one stage she was taken to court and accused of kidnapping her children. She won, and kept the children, but it cost her £50,000, and the custody battle was still going on when we spoke to her in 2014.

Desperate to raise the money, she turned to Cherie, who lent her £15,000. But Cherie was insistent that it was a loan, and Lauren ultimately could not repay it in time. She petitioned for her own bankruptcy, and the order was made on 10 December 2010.

Lauren found asking Cherie for money very hard. Cherie's childhood has left her very careful about money. She is very wealthy now of course, but, however much she has, it never seems to be enough to bring her peace.

She feels, we're told, that she made her life, she went through hardship to put herself through grammar school, that 'she'll always be that grammar school girl toiling over her homework.'

The struggle to get by intensified when she studied for the bar, as she recalls in her autobiography:

> While everyone else took a break at lunchtime, I stayed in [Lincoln's Inn library]: reading, making notes and eating my sandwiches … Every week I would buy a loaf and a little round box of Kraft Dairylea with its six triangles of processed cheese wrapped in silver foil. I would keep them on the windowsill and make up one sandwich every day, the cheese getting softer and softer as the summer built up to a heat wave. It was all I could afford.

Greg Dyke tells a story of how, when he was a director of Manchester United in the late 1990s, Cherie telephoned him from Downing Street to ask if he could get her discounted United shirts for her children. Dyke said she could have them free. She replied that she could not take them without payment as they would have to be declared as a gift – but she would like a discount, please.

Lauren still has a high regard for her half-sister, though the business of the loan put a strain on their relationship. She calls her 'a woman of great integrity and loyalty'. When Lauren came across a case of a sixteen-year-old Afghan girl in Britain facing a forced marriage, she told Cherie and 'Cherie got on with it straightaway – I left it with her.'

Cherie communicates with her family in terse text messages: 'RU OK God bless.' 'She's not mean, she's not hard-hearted. She might be a bit brusque,' says Lauren, and adds, 'It's good that she still cares about me – I've given her a lot of grief over the years.'

Lauren told us she admires the work of Cherie's Foundation for Women, though regretting its strong focus on Israel – 'There are a lot of poorer areas around the world.' The Cherie Blair Foundation for Women, set up in 2008, claims to provide women entrepreneurs with access to business development support, networks, finance and technology. At the top of its website is the stern motto, 'Empowering women, driving growth'.

But that doesn't mean that just because you're a woman entrepreneur you can apply to it for help. The Foundation told us, 'We do not accept unsolicited grant applications. Instead, we work together with our local partners to develop projects in line with our mission statement. We work within a global community of organisations aiming to economically empower women and we welcome new knowledge partners.'

The biggest donor is media tycoon Haim Saban, the billionaire who made his fortune from the children's television programme *Mighty Morphin Power Rangers*, and his wife, Cheryl.

This is the same American Israeli billionaire who funds the Tony Blair Faith Foundation and, as we have seen, says, 'I'm a one-issue guy and my issue is Israel.'

So it is hardly surprising to find Cherie's Foundation to be very active in Israel, nor to find Cherie herself going there with Cheryl Saban to talk up their funding of places at Western Galilee College for women to study economics, accounting and business administration, and providing women in Israeli business with capital and mentors.

Compared with her husband's charities, Cherie's charity is an open book. It does list donors in its annual report, but it does not put amounts, so that the reader does not know who the big money donors are. The list, naturally, includes JP Morgan. It also includes big commercial names such as Exxon Mobil. Perhaps surprisingly, it also includes USAID, whose purpose is to 'provide economic, development and humanitarian assistance around the world in support of the foreign policy goals of the United States.'[2]

The Foundation's income in the year ending 31 October 2012 was £1,818,151 and at that time it employed eleven staff.

Cherie Blair is dedicated to building businesses and making money. Her accent has gone from Liverpool to London, her style from political wife to lead business partner. Today the language is that of profits, whether it is funding private healthcare clinics in the poorer parts of the UK or guiding businesses through the world's riskiest markets,

To achieve this, Cherie has two routes. One is through developing and commercialising her legal expertise. The other is through financial investment. She is at the same time a hard-nosed consultant to countries and companies and a businesswoman and manager.

Cherie Blair tries to operate beneath the radar. Business people in emerging markets have their enemies in the marketplace but high-profile political folk in business have double the trouble: business competitors and ideological foes.

PRIVATE SECURITY AND PRIVATE HEALTH

One vehicle that Cherie Blair uses is Omnia Strategy, a consultancy she founded in 2011, which makes its money from her claim to have deep intelligence knowhow and plugged-in intelligence sources. Another vehicle is Mee Healthcare, a firm that sets up a one-shop-suits-all medical, optical and dental service in British supermarkets.

Through Omnia Strategy, Cherie has advised governments including Albania and Bahrain, a pressure group in Nigeria and a company in Egypt. Omnia bears comparison to groups like Control Risks and Kroll, which help companies manage political and security risks, but with a legal rather than straightforwardly security emphasis. Synergies between Omnia and Tony Blair's political and security apparatus are inevitable, although the principals are careful to discount such suggestions.

Yet office location provides some support for such a proposition. Omnia Strategy occupies anonymous offices at 1 Great Cumberland Place, near Marble Arch in Central London, alongside Tony Blair's Faith Foundation, Cherie's Foundation for Women, her son Nicky Blair's company (we'll come to that) and (bizarrely) the London office of her son Euan Blair's employer (we'll come to that, too). This is a fortress-like building, overlooking Hyde Park, where security is tight and no one enters without codes and prearranged meetings. The Omnia Strategy website, like Tony Blair's various organisations, provides no postal address or phone number.

The medical end of the Cherie Blair portfolio took off in January 2012, when she was reported to be seeking £65 million to help fund a chain of private health clinics. She had joined forces with an American fund manager to raise $100 million from investors on both sides of the Atlantic. She was working with the Allele Fund, a private-equity outfit founded by Dr Gail Lese, a Republican-supporting businesswoman. Cherie and Lese are said to be close partners. The business is based in the Cayman Islands and in Delaware, a notorious US onshore tax haven.

Lese's skill in business management was demonstrated during a brief stint at Fidelity, where she made record returns in record times. Lese, an American, is a qualified doctor and the Allele Fund website says,

> Dr. Lese has a deep commitment to public service and volunteerism. Her extensive volunteer service has included serving on the Board of Directors of the Mass Mentoring Partnership, the American Red Cross of Cape Cod and Big Brothers/Big Sisters of Cape Cod; tutoring and mentoring students in the Boston, Los Angeles, and New York public school systems; founding multiple community service programs including a scholarship program to help economically disadvantaged students attend college; service as a volunteer physician at the L.A. Free Clinic; and helping to procure and grant wishes for terminally ill children with the Make a Wish Foundation. Dr. Lese has received numerous recognitions for her distinguished leadership and impact in public service.

The company's motto is, 'Your one-stop connection for quality health, wellness and life'. Its strapline states, 'we will serve you with integrity in all we do'.

The company's brand name is Mee Healthcare and its website proudly proclaims, 'Mee provides a range of premium healthcare and wellbeing services at accessible prices.' Mee's innovative centres offer GPs, dentists, hearing and eye experts and even pampering services such as manicures and pedicures, all under one roof. Cherie Blair told the *Financial Times*, 'While this venture is a commercial one, it is not about replacing the NHS or profiteering, but complementing the services it already offers.'[3]

Maybe. But it is private medicine, and it will, whatever way you look at it, benefit from moves towards NHS privatisation.

Allele says its aim is to 'invest in, build, and grow, a variety of leading international businesses which are committed to making a difference and helping people globally. The Fund's team takes significant operational roles within fund portfolio companies to steward them to success.' One investor in Mee Healthcare is Brooks Newmark, a member of the Treasury Select Committee and the Conservative MP for Braintree since the 2005 general election.

While Mee puts Cherie Blair in a very visible position on the high street, Omnia stays firmly out of sight. Its 'advisory panel' includes Peter Wilson, a director at Protection Group International (PGI), and he gives Cherie access to 'experience and expertise from UK government, intelligence, military personnel and commercial organisations'. Wilson tells us his role as a member of Omnia's advisory panel is unpaid, and he has ceased to be a director of the firm.

Wilson, who worked in the Foreign Office and McKinsey, has investments in a number of hi-tech companies. He describes himself as an adviser to the British government on political reform in developing countries. Wilson wrote a very right-wing book called *Make Poverty Business*, which claims to construct 'a rigorous profit-making argument for multinational corporations to do more business with the poor. It takes economic development out of the corporate social responsibility ghetto and places it firmly in the core business interests of the corporation.' Wilson said that PGI had 'no business connections' with Omnia.

Cherie Booth QC, described on the company's website as Cherie Blair CBE, is the chair of Omnia, whose website says it is a

Pioneering international law firm that provides strategic counsel to governments, corporate and private clients. We tackle complex problems that require an innovative and multi-disciplinary approach … we provide a bespoke service and carefully select a tailored project team which may include solicitors, barristers, corporate general counsel, former CEOs, strategy consultants, diplomats, economists, investment bankers and communications specialists from across the globe.

In fact, Omnia Strategy has a rather wider remit of advisers and this includes 'private investigators', who are hired to provide intelligence expertise on countries, markets and individuals. Wilson's profile says,

We [Omnia] are a legal strategy consultancy that helps you achieve your international goals through our integrated expertise in law, governance and economics. We work with you to translate and embed global standards throughout your organisation. We help governments to attract international support and investment by strengthening laws, institutions and practices. We help businesses from emerging markets to become internationally respected, successful companies by strengthening governance, structures and practices.

Cherie's colleagues at Omnia include Sofia Wellesley, who worked at the Libyan Investment Authority, which Tony Blair and his client JP Morgan got to know very well in the days of the late Colonel Gaddafi. There, she 'project managed a team to start up the operations of the sovereign wealth fund and to oversee assignments that formulated governance, human resource and asset allocation strategies.' Wellesley is quite young – still only thirty-one in 2014 – but definitely out of the top drawer: she is descended from the Duke of Wellington and married James Blunt in 2014.

Another partner in Omnia is Julia Yun Hulme, a former lawyer for Tamoil Group – the brand name of Dutch oil company Oilinvest – where she was 'in charge of all legal aspects of the company including corporate governance, mergers and acquisitions, arbitration, compliance and restructuring.' Oilinvest itself was controlled by a Libyan holding company until civil unrest led to the holding company being wound up in March 2011. This appeared to leave the company without an ultimate owner.

Cementing the company's Middle Eastern links, Cherie recruited Laura Edwards, a recent Cambridge law graduate, as an analyst to Omnia in August 2013. Edwards is listed as an editor for the 'Proposed Constitutional Framework for the Republic of Tunisia', a document put together by Cambridge University's Wilberforce Society, a think tank that aims to connect students and 'leading policy makers'.[4]

Omnia is known to use former intelligence officers and investigative companies to conduct due diligence.

Among its clients is the government of Bahrain. The *Sunday Times* reported in February 2012:

> Cherie Blair is offering her services as a legal and human rights consultant to the Bahraini regime, which cracked down on protests last year. Blair, who visited the country in November, is promoting her services through Omnia Strategy, her consultancy. Other Middle East regimes facing the threat of revolution are being offered her services as an adviser on legal reforms … The consultancy said in a statement that its work was intended to help Bahrain implement reforms which will help safeguard human rights. However, opposition groups are sceptical about the regime's commitment to reform.[5]

So they might be. Her husband says the same thing about his Kazakhstan client.

According to a Human Rights Watch report published on 21 January 2014, Bahrain has

> increased restrictions on the exercise of core human rights like freedom of speech, assembly, and association. Security forces arbitrarily arrested

scores of people and authorities detained and prosecuted activists. There were continuing credible reports of torture and ill-treatment in detention. The government failed to carry out key recommendations of the Bahrain Independent Commission of Inquiry, which at the government's request examined the government's and security forces' response to mass protests in 2011.[6]

It seems sad that a distinguished, able and passionate human-rights lawyer should end up shilling for the likes of the government of Bahrain, which, during the Arab Spring, relied on imported Saudi troops to keep democracy at bay.

Other Middle Eastern clients include the Egyptian construction company Orascom Construction Industries and its London operation called OCI (UK), based at Cork Street, in London's Mayfair. OCI says on its website that it targets large industrial and infrastructure projects, principally in Egypt and North Africa. It does major commercial, industrial and infrastructure projects throughout Europe and the Middle East and it pursues institutional projects in the Middle East and Central Asia.

Omnia advised the government of Albania in 2012 and 2013 when it was facing a claim from a firm of oil developers called Sky Petroleum. Sky, which is based in Texas, was claiming that the country had illegally stopped a licence it had been granted to explore for oil. Omnia Strategy won the case and Sky had to pay Albania's costs.

Africa is another marketplace for Omnia. The Bakassi Support Group reportedly hired Omnia in 2012 to prepare a legal brief to review the International Court of Justice's judgments in a hearing in Nigeria's capital Abuja on its claim for lost territory, whose sovereignty had been ceded to Cameroon.

Cherie Blair is the founder of Matrix Chambers, but Omnia Strategy takes her closer to the commercial and security application of law, especially in insecure jurisdictions. Matrix Chambers' website says she is a high-profile expert in discrimination, public law, media and information law and employment law. She has appeared in the European Court of Justice and in Commonwealth jurisdictions, and also lectures internationally on human rights. Appointed QC in 1995, she is a Recorder in the County Court and Crown Court, a Bencher of Lincoln's Inn and an Honorary Bencher of King's Inn, Dublin. She is also an accredited Advanced Mediator under the ADR Chambers/Harvard Law Project and an Elite Mediator with Clerksroom.

Cherie Blair sees the law and enterprise as her route to business leadership. These businesses, it seems to us, tell us two things about Cherie Blair. First, she is, as she has always been, her own woman. She never fitted into the traditional pattern of the prime-ministerial wife. A seriously clever and independent-minded woman, she has chosen to do her own thing. And Omnia is nothing at all like Tony Blair Associates. It utilises her skills and knowledge – and, although it clearly benefits from the contacts she has made as the wife of the PM, it is the sort of work she might well have done if she had not been married to a prime minister (except that she would probably have become a judge).

The second is less comfortable. Why on earth is this woman, always more left-wing than her husband and more committed to the welfare state, hawking private healthcare products around the globe? And why is she helping the dictators who run Bahrain with their repressive policies?

EUAN AND NICKY BLAIR

Cherie is actively involved in the careers of her sons Euan and Nicky, both of whom have offices in the concrete tower at 1 Great Cumberland Place, overlooking Hyde Park – an office building that may yet become known as the Blair Tower.

If you look on the plate at the entrance, you would have no idea that this was what went on inside. Other occupants of the building have their company names on the plate – Gherson Solicitors and Michael Berg and Partners, chartered surveyors, on Floor 2, Oil Spill Response Ltd on Floor 1, and so on – but there is no mention at all of the Tony Blair Faith Foundation, and the occupants of Floor 7 are given simply as 'CBFW' and 'CBO'. The first must be the Cherie Blair Foundation for Women, and the second, probably, the Cherie Blair Organisation.

Cherie Blair's eldest son Euan, born in 1984, started by working in merchant banking with Morgan Stanley, but then took a job with the huge Australian employment agency Sarina Russo Job Access, which started business as an academy in 1979 and has made Sarina Russo a multimillionaire. He started as an adviser, but he is listed at the time of writing as acting CEO UK, in which post he works in the company's London office.

His profile on their website reads: 'Before joining Sarina Russo Job Access, Euan worked at Morgan Stanley where he helped raise funding of more than $60Bn for UK companies including Marks & Spencer, National Grid, Vodafone, and Unilever. He has also advised on funding strategies for a number of public sector and charitable clients including Transport for London, Network Rail and the Wellcome Trust.'

Sarina Russo herself is now part of the Blair inner circle – a guest at Cherie's sixtieth-birthday party in 2014 and at Euan's wedding, and a friend of both Tony and Cherie. She told an Australian radio station all about it, in a rather cringe-making interview down the line from London:[7] 'It's really extraordinary – the Blairs are just like the royal family here in the UK.'

As for Euan, she seemed to suggest he takes after his father in being driven by a desire to help the less fortunate: 'He actually gave up merchant banking … and he was really searching to get a feel of, you know, the people in this country, the homeless, the drug addicts, you know, the disadvantaged. It's obvious it's in his blood and he really wants to make a difference, and he's got the beautiful wife, Suzanne, who's very much into social finance, and she helps prisoners to get finance so that when they leave jail they've got some sort of financial stability.'

How did he get the job?

'Well, what happened was, he came to me for career advice ... and a couple of days, a week later he says, I'd like to work for your company, and he's told everyone it's the happiest job he's ever had.'

The truth is a little more complicated. Euan Blair has had a meteoric rise in Russo's company: as has been noted, a few months after joining to do business development, he is now the acting UK CEO. This company is very big in Australia but only started working on the English market in 2009. It has five offices in the West Midlands, including its head office in Coventry.

It is its London office from which Euan works though. Russo's nephew, Michael Pennisi, is one of his colleagues in that office. It is, presumably, not a mere coincidence that Euan Blair's employer's office is on the same floor of same office block as his mother's and his brother's companies. But what exactly is the connection between Sarina Russo and the Blairs?

There is also an office in Wembley, where surprisingly the Tony Blair Faith Foundation also has an office.

Euan's company owes its meteoric rise in Britain – it now has eight offices and employs almost one hundred people – to one contract, and that is a government contract. It is to do with the welfare-to-work programme. The government sends unemployed young people to the company, and the company trains them in such matters as how to write a CV, employability skills and how to dress for interviews. It does so as a subcontractor of Serco, the enormous government outsourcing company.

The company's 'vision' is, according to its website, 'to constantly innovate and excel at the delivery of exceptional recruitment, education and training services to all clients, candidates and students. This is achieved by the delivery of superior services to all of our customers and fellow staff.'

Euan Blair was at first based in the Coventry office, and was attending meetings of the local constituency Labour Party.[8] There was speculation that his ambition was to be a Labour MP, and that working for Ms Russo might look better to a local Labour Party than working for a merchant bank. However, the Coventry connection is now a little academic, since Geoffrey Robinson (born in 1938), whose Coventry North West seat Euan is thought to have had his eye on, announced that he intended to stand again in the 2015 general election. Euan no longer works in Coventry, and his parliamentary ambitions were then thought to rest in Bootle. However, if Euan ever intended to be a Labour parliamentary candidate, he had given the idea up by 2014.

Cherie is also helping her second son, Nicky, develop a sports-management business called Magnitude. She has taken a 20 per cent stake in the company and is a director, and management meetings are held at the Blairs' Buckinghamshire home. Nicky has a desk and dedicated phone line at the Omnia Strategy headquarters, which is in what we have affectionately termed the Blair Tower, and the Blair Tower is the business address.

Magnitude is a so-called 'e-sports business', which manages teams competing on computer games online for prize money. The firm posted an £8,200 loss and according to its accounts, is almost £17,000 in the red. Nicky owns 40 per cent of the business and another 40 per cent is owned by his business partner Gabriel Moraes.

The company came under scrutiny from Westminster Council after Nicky moved it from his home to his mother's office – and there was concern that Cherie Blair might be breaking council-tax rules by using an office for her two charities and allowing a commercial undertaking to be based there; she gets an 80 per cent discount on business rates because she runs charities.

But the phone line and desk were found by visiting Westminster Council officials to be in Omnia Strategy's offices, which paid full business rates for the area they occupied.

A council spokesman confirmed that Mrs Blair's offices, next to Hyde

Park in Central London, had been the subject of an unannounced check by officers, who found the space was occupied by three different entities – the two charities and Omnia. Westminster Council decided not to take any further action.

It began as a limited company and in 2013 was turned into a partnership. The last public files at the end of 2012 show that the limited company was dissolved and the directors state that they can cover all their debts. But it meant the end of the gaming business. The decision meant that it no longer filed full accounts with Companies House.

Cherie Blair takes an active interest in the new business, managing foreign football players, which has now been rebranded with an office in Rio in Brazil. Cherie took time out of her busy schedule to meet an unknown Mexican footballer, then seventeen-year-old prodigy Raúl Mendiola, in a Los Angeles hotel. Mendiola is signed to Magnitude, which is acting as his football agent.

So, according to an article in the *Mirror*, are a number of promising Brazilian stars.[9] It reported: "Magnitude Brazil Sports Ltd opened its office in a glass and marble-fronted skyscraper in Rio in 2011 … It now exists solely in South America.'

Over the past two years, Blair and Moraes, with their South American business partners Rafael Fraga and Vinicius Marques, have been signing up talent from Brazil's biggest clubs. Highly rated players with Magnitude include defender Marlon Santos da Silva Barbosa, 18, who plays for Fluminense, and midfielder Leandro Alves de Carvalho, 17, of Botafogo.

Magnitude Brazil are also said to have an arrangement with Desportivo Brasil, a Sao Paulo club which develops players for top sides.

Effectively Nicky is now working outside the UK with a business solely based in South America and no longer regularly scrutinized in the British media. He is predicted to do very well with his new talent when Brazil and Mexico take part in the World Cup in Russia in 2018 and in Qatar in 2022.

While Cherie's empire cannot be compared to Tony's worldwide moneymaking in either scale or content, it does exhibit a similar determination to maximise her wealth by every means possible. There is now far less emphasis on her campaigns for human rights, and much more on her determination to make money from private health and private security. Just like Tony, she has good connections with billionaires, and her sons, Nicky and Euan, are budding entrepreneurs. Both Cherie and Euan look set to benefit enormously from the further privatisation of public services and the NHS.

CHAPTER FOURTEEN

THE PROPERTY PORTFOLIO

'We took out a mortgage the size of Mount Snowdon.'
– CHERIE BLAIR IN HER AUTOBIOGRAPHY
SPEAKING FOR MYSELF

Tony and Cherie Blair have created a property empire for themselves and their immediate family that replicates his lifestyle when he was Prime Minister. His central hub in London's Connaught Square is an even more luxurious version of No. 10, including a mews house for an office and security protection. Their Grade I-listed country pile, South Pavilion in Buckinghamshire, is the equivalent of Chequers – down to having a modern sports pavilion and tennis courts.

Their offices at Marble Arch Towers and Cherie's and Euan's offices at 1 Cumberland Place are the equivalent of Whitehall ministries and departments.

The entire family are also colonising Marylebone in multimillion-pound properties, each within easy walking distance. And one of Blair's closest confidants, Lord Mandelson, lives within walking distance in Regents Park, alongside his former bag carrier, Benjamin Wegg-Prosser, who has a house a few hundred yards from Blair's HQ at Connaught Square.

The property empire of Tony and Cherie Blair and their immediate family is nothing if not extensive. The Blairs now own a staggering thirty-six properties – including two blocks of flats – worth tens of millions of pounds. Thirty-one are in the UK, and another five are abroad. They buy their children expensive homes and their relations more modest properties.

Nothing is too grand for the Blairs. As well as buying the homes they have also spent a fortune modernising, extending and adapting them and landscaping their gardens to meet their tastes.

Tony and Cherie seem never to have got over the time he was Prime Minister and he could entertain in Chequers and live in Downing Street. 'He runs his office like No. 10, with ladies keeping his diary,' says a former staffer. When interviewing prospective staff, he is normally dressed in jeans, drinking coffee from a Starbucks cup.

It was not always like this. Until Tony Blair became PM their lifestyle was comfortable rather than grand. They first lived in an up-and-coming area of Hackney called Mapledene. This was Hackney's equivalent of a poor man's Islington – a convenient berth for thrusting middle-class professionals such as lawyers and journalists who didn't want to commute to work from the boring suburbs. They bought up neglected but rather fine-looking properties that would go for a fortune in Chelsea but went for a comparative song because of their location in rundown Hackney.

As they became more prosperous they moved to the more fashionable and expensive Islington, and, once Blair became MP for the safe Labour seat of Sedgefield, they purchased a modest but scruffy property, Myrobella in Trimdon for £30,000 in 1983 as a constituency home. They also purchased two flats for Euan Blair in Bristol in 2002 in a very controversial deal through a blind trust advised by Peter Foster, an Australian conman. They paid £525,000 for both and sold one in 2008 for £260,000. The second is still owned by Cherie Blair and has no mortgage but can be rented out for at least £1,200 a month. They originally had a mortgage costing £2,000 a month for both flats but derived a rental income of £2,400 a month when the Blairs owned both.

The turning point for the Blairs, once they had acquired the taste for more gracious millionaire-style living, took place in 2004 when they purchased 29 Connaught Square – and the transition to the private lifestyle of the billionaire jet set when he left office in 2007.

CONNAUGHT SQUARE

The purchase of Connaught Square certainly stretched their pockets at the time and the PM's salary was lower than the deposit. The cost was an eye-watering £3.65 million and they had a deposit of only £182,500, relying on a 95 per cent mortgage of £3,467,500 from the Cheltenham and Gloucester (now part of state-owned Lloyds) over twenty-five years.

Cherie said her in memoirs, *Speaking for Myself*, that they took out a mortgage 'the size of Mount Snowdon', adding, 'Yes that was very scary. Particularly since I was the person who had to support it. Because whatever else happened, we had to meet the monthly payment and it was down to me. Because no one else was going to meet it, were they?'

At the time there was speculation that the Blairs had overpaid, but, with an estimated value at the time of writing of over £8.3 million[1] in the present property boom, no one is going to say that now.

The Blairs bought the property from wealthy art historian Roger Bevan, who had led a residents' campaign to buy the freehold of the property and others in the square from the Church Commissioners. The Old Etonian and Cambridge graduate also encouraged the residents to restore the square and reinstate the original railings, which had been destroyed by an IRA bomb attack in the seventies.

The Blairs had different ideas, which became very clear when they also purchased a small mews cottage at the back of the square, 5 Archery Close, for between £600,000 and £800,000 in February 2007 with a mortgage from Lloyds TSB.

The mortgage was discharged by 2008 – showing the Blairs' change in fortunes – and the former PM bought the freehold so he owned both properties.

What happened next, as the *Daily Mail* reported in June 2007,[2] was to cause consternation with the neighbours and has never really been resolved. The *Mail* said a

huge tarpaulin covers scaffolding used by workmen linking the three-storey house with a mews cottage.

The entire rear of the Grade II listed building, which the Blairs bought in 2004 for £3.6 million, has been ripped off so the two houses can be joined, providing a massive living area for the former Prime Minister and his family.

A bulging skip stands outside, and the west side of the square is now little more than an eyesore. A vast new kitchen is being built, as well as accommodation for security staff and a suite of offices from which Mr Blair will run his new career. There will also be a sun terrace and four solar panels to provide green energy …

The once-peaceful square, just north of Hyde Park, has never seen anything like it. Tony and Cherie recently attended a residents' garden party to try to soothe ruffled feelings, but there is still resentment at the disruption the new neighbours are causing.

Police have drawn up plans to seal off the area in the event of demonstrations and have asked residents to consider carrying utility bills to prove their identity to officers manning security cordons around the square.

A petition circulated among residents has suggested that to protect the Blairs, part of the square could be turned into 'a gated community policed by armed guards [with] a police helicopter hovering above'. It added that, if the risk to the family was so great, they should not be living in a residential square.

A community police officer told worried neighbours last week: 'We are in a new situation and we are not going to know how it will affect everyone until the family is here.'

The reason cited for all these changes was that the Blairs claimed that MI5 and Special Branch told them it would make their main home safer. Panic alarms, motion detectors and CCTV cameras were fitted as part of an extensive security system. The mews house was also thought to be used as a nanny flat.

The project was overseen by one of Cherie Blair's close confidants Martha Greene, an American restaurateur and film producer, who seems to have taken over the role once performed by Carole Caplin in Downing Street, when Blair was PM, as an adviser to Cherie.

Greene came to Britain from America in the 1980s and joined Saatchi & Saatchi, rising from 'gofer' to apprentice producer in just three years. In 1990 – the year her first marriage to sound engineer Robin Saunders ended – she set up the independent production company Stark Films.

One of her most notable successes in a wide-ranging career was taking over the popular upmarket Villandry restaurant in Great Portland Street.

She seems to be a very feisty character and was highly praised by people in the advertising industry. Tim Mellors, now president and chief creative officer of the agency Grey Worldwide North America, provides a graphic description of her presence of mind when producing a film for BP in Martinique when everything went wrong. In a blog[3] he described the situation:

There are times when doing a runner is the wisest call a producer can make. On a BP underwater shoot in Martinique, some of the crew turned out to be inter-island drug runners making a bit of spare cash. They were authentic badasses, and although they didn't like us, they really hated the gay French art director. So much so that they chopped the head off his Old English Sheepdog to teach him a lesson. Feisty Martha went up to them to remonstrate and they replied by (literally) taking a crap in her handbag.

Within 20 minutes Ms Greene had us on a light plane out of

there. I remember making a mental note: when the shit really hits the fan (or the handbag), make sure you have a good producer.

An article in the *Daily Mail* [4] in 2006 describes her as 'the sensibly attired New Yorker who has, with measured steps, effectively replaced Carole Caplin in Cherie's affections and confidence.'

According to the article, so close was she to the Blairs that when she split with her former partner Ivan Ruggeri, a former Italian tour operator, she engaged a high-flying family lawyer, Maggie Rae, to thrash out the acrimonious details of their separation.

According to the *Mail*, 'Key among her demands is a confidentiality agreement under which Ruggeri promises not to divulge any of the details of their relationship, or anything she may have told him about her friendship and business dealings with the Blairs.'

Her new partner would also have been useful to the Blairs. He is Jonathan Metliss, a corporate lawyer, a Tory donor, a member of the Westminster Conservative Association and on the executive of the campaign group Conservative Friends of Israel. His entry in *Debrett's People of Today* shows extensive links with Israel. On 7 September 2010 the annual publication listed him not just as a member of Conservative Friends of Israel, but also as an executive of the Britain Israel Communications and Research Centre, a joint secretary and executive member of the Parliamentary Committee Against Anti-Semitism and a member of the Inter-Parliamentary Committee Against Anti-Semitism (which perhaps should refer to the Inter-Parliamentary Coalition for Combating Anti-Semitism).

Debrett's also lists Metliss as a member of the executive of the Israeli British Business Council, a director and member of the executive of the British–Israel Chamber of Commerce, a director of the Weizmann Institute Foundation and a vice-chairman of the Friends of the Weizmann Institute (UK) – the last two of which are connected to the Weizmann Institute of Science in Israel – a chairman of the British Friends of Haifa

University and a member of the Advisory Board of Tel Aviv University Business School and the Board of Governors of Haifa University.

Greene seems to have been involved in brokering the deal to buy Connaught Square while Tony and Cherie were still in Downing Street, and, according to people living in the square, her reward was the use of the building for offices while she was in London.

According to the *Mail* she also gave Cherie other advice. 'When Cherie doubted the wisdom of giving her first solo television interview, it was Greene who convinced her that going on *Richard [&] Judy* was a splendid idea.'

And, when Cherie wanted to boost her fitness regime, it was Greene's advice that led her to train with Steve Agyei – himself a former protégé of Carole Caplin.

On a lecture tour in 2005 it was Greene who flew first-class to Dubai with Cherie and stayed in adjoining hotel rooms. Press coverage was, according to Greene, a necessary evil: 'If we could exclude [the British press] we would.'

She also organised the domain name for Cherie Blair's charitable foundation and organised the catering for the Blairs' twentieth-wedding-anniversary meal.

SOUTH PAVILION

The rise in the Blairs' fortunes once they had left office can also be seen from the fact that, a year later, they were able to buy their own 'Chequers' – South Pavilion, Wotton Underwood, in leafy Buckinghamshire – then on the market for £5.75 million.

According to the Land Registry they paid the full price, having fallen in love with the former home of actor Sir John Gielgud, who lived there until his death in 2000. They bought the place from Effie Lecky, wife of budget Canadian airline boss John, with what is thought to be a £4 million mortgage from Lloyds TSB, before the owners put it on the market.

The grand, seven-bedroom, Grade I-listed mansion is next door to

Wotton House, a stately home that opens its doors to the public in the summer. The two houses are located at the end of a secluded country road, with rolling meadows on either side. There are no more than ten detached houses dotted along the road, separated from one another by wraparound gardens and tree borders.

It's an affluent area: Robin Gibb, Rowan Atkinson, David Jason – they all have houses round here. If you want to be out of the public eye, it's ideal, just like Chequers with its tree-lined drive off a public road except, of course, that the road to the house is a public highway.

Wotton House was restored to its former glory by the actress Elaine Brunner in the 1950s. It had been built at the beginning of the eighteenth century and was almost identical in design to Buckingham House in London – now integrated into Buckingham Palace. In October 1820, the main house was gutted by a great fire, and all that survived intact were the two pavilions, linked to the house by low screen walls.

In the rebuild that followed, the external appearance of Wotton remained the same – although Sir John Soane, the architect, did persuade his reluctant client, the Marquis of Buckingham, to let him reduce the overall height by 8 to 10 feet.

Now occupied by David and April Gladstone – David being a direct descendent of Liberal Prime Minister William Gladstone – it was designed as the original Buckingham Palace. A residence fit for a queen occupied by a scion of a PM therefore lies next door – separated now by only a six-foot-high steel fence.

The Blairs though were not satisfied with the existing building and applied for no fewer than nine separate applications for developments in the next four years. This is despite its having ornamental gardens, a tennis court and a swimming pool already.

They started with a relatively uncontroversial application reviving a proposal by the previous owners to build a garden studio and a proposal to build a mess room. There were no objections in March 2008 and both went ahead.

They then moved in July 2009 to extend and refurbish the gardener's pavilion in the grounds, leading to six objections and one letter supporting the proposal. Enquiries for this book found at least five could be suspect – they all came from the same computer IP address and gave false postal addresses.

The main objections were that it would set a precedent, could be used as a separate dwelling and shouldn't be adapted, as it is in the grounds of a listed building. There was also concern expressed that part of the existing kitchen garden would be built over and that the size and nature of the existing building should be preserved. But they were overruled and consent was given after some modifications to the plan.

The next proposals were more contentious. A scheme to build a new sports pavilion and retain the fencing round the tennis courts in September 2011 led to a condition imposed by the county's archaeological officer. He warned, 'This development could cause some harm to the asset's archaeological interests, but not such substantial harm as to justify refusal of planning permission if the development is otherwise acceptable.'

They requested that a condition be imposed that no development shall take place 'until the applicant … has secured the implementation of a programme of archaeological work in accordance with a written scheme of investigation which has been submitted by the applicant and approved by the planning authority.'

Buckinghamshire Gardens Trust objected to the original plans on the grounds of the impact of the tennis-court fencing, the size of the sports pavilion, its design and how it is proposed it will adjoin the existing historic wall. But this also went ahead after it was modified.

The Blairs also took advantage of the government's green-energy scheme by fitting discreet solar tiles to the building, both saving them energy and allowing them to benefit from the Coalition government's green 'feed-in tariff' by selling surplus energy to the National Grid.

More serious objections rose over plans to chop down a hundred trees and prune others and erect a 6-foot-high, 300-foot-long, modern steel boundary fence between the property and its neighbour Wotton Hall.

A Mrs Evans of Lower Green, Westcott, objected to the tree felling, saying, 'There is no need for the trees to be felled, and the works could destroy the atmosphere surrounding the South Pavilion and could be detrimental to the village.[5]

Buckinghamshire Gardens Trust, the Georgian Group and English Heritage also objected to the boundary fencing.

Buckinghamshire Gardens Trust expressed concern about the utilitarian modern design. 'They said they hope the fence could be screened by planting but do not see how it could be guaranteed. They consider a pattern to stimulate historic ornamental. Fencing within the mansion grounds would be more appropriate.'[6]

The *Telegraph* reported that the Trust wrote a letter to the council saying, 'We are concerned that the severely utilitarian modern style of the proposed fence damages the historic character of this area of designed landscape.'[7]

The Georgian Group said that a condition should be applied requiring the removal of the railings when the current occupant no longer occupies the building.[8]

English Heritage was concerned too, saying Blair's plans, which included chopping down a hundred trees, would damage the special character of the house. In particular, English Heritage disliked Blair's plan to put roof lights in the sports pavilion.

However the new railings went ahead in 2012 after concerns, agreed by English Heritage, that the then-boundary fences were not secure, a council report describing them as 'too weak and too low' to 'prevent trespass' on Blair's private property. In return, two trees had to be protected and a large number of laurel and holly bushes were planted to obscure the boundary fence and add to the privacy of the Blairs.

BLAIR'S CHILDREN'S HOMES AND CHERIE AND
EUAN'S BUDDING PROPERTY EMPIRE

The go-ahead in 2012 for all these schemes marked the end of the Blairs' 'improvements' to the property. They had now turned to providing homes for their children and family.

Euan, their eldest son, had bought his first property in May 2008 for £462,501 from Patrick Boyle, a Paris-based trademark lawyer. The spacious two-bedroomed garden flat in Liverpool Road was in upmarket Barnsbury not far from the Angel and Upper Street, Islington. It was, however, on a busy road, used by traffic to avoid the jams on the main road between the Holloway road and the Angel. He got a mortgage from Lloyds and sold it nearly two and half years later, in September 2010, for £496,000, making a £33,499 profit.

Cherie Blair stepped in to allow him to move to a much grander property in Shouldham Street in May 2010 in the coveted W1 postal district and within walking distance of the Blairs' London home in Connaught Square. So, with Cherie's help he jumped from a £500,000 flat to a £1.29 million home jointly owned by him and his mother. The property was also secured with a Lloyds TSB mortgage.

The estate agents, York Estates at the time, waxed lyrically about the attractiveness of the property, though they have since, we suspect after representations from the Blairs, removed details of the property from the Internet. At the time they emphasised that it was a rarely available freehold in central London. 'This 4-storey Georgian house has planning permission to extend at lower ground and ground floor levels. Alternatively the house can be occupied in its current condition. It has three bedrooms, a study, two bathrooms, a garden, and both a drawing room and a reception room.'

The property became the centre of a planning row after a neighbour suggested that Euan was subletting the property, and the Blairs were forced to change some alterations they had made to the Georgian home. Euan was helped again by his mother months before he married his longstanding girlfriend Suzanne Ashman. She is the daughter of motor-racing entrepreneur Jonathan Ashman and was educated at the private St Paul's Girls' School in west London. She later read philosophy, politics and economics at Trinity College, Oxford, and went on to work at the Tony Blair Faith Foundation.

The grand, six-bedroom Georgian townhouse in Marylebone, purchased in September 2013, shows that Euan intends to follow his father's lifestyle. Months afterwards, in March 2014, the one-bedroom mews house that backs on to the property was also purchased so the two properties could be amalgamated in a replica of Tony and Cherie Blair's Connaught Square home – enough for both a home and an office.

The entire cost of purchasing both properties came to £4.825 million but neither of them is owned by his wife Suzanne Blair. Instead the main home is jointly owned by Cherie and Euan and the house that backs onto it by Cherie alone. Both properties have a mortgage from Lloyds Bank.

The six-bedroom property was put on the market for £3.695 million – and was sold to Cherie and Euan for £3.625 million. Estate agents described it as a 'bright, modernised property [that] benefits from beautiful high ceilings, floor to ceiling windows and wooden floors. The accommodation comprises of a master bedroom with en-suite bathroom, five further bedrooms, two further bathrooms, two spacious reception rooms, kitchen, utility room and guest cloakroom.'

No sooner had they bought it than they applied for planning permission and listed-building consent (it is Grade II-listed) to both improve and repair it.

Among the problems they discovered was a large crack in the West flank wall. Their architects commented,

We understand from neighbours that this West flank wall has always caused concern to the previous owners, with a large vertical crack mid length extending as far as the second floor. The previous owners had cosmetically restored (render only) before the sale of the property, and it is only now that we are aware of the situation, and we seek to remedy the recurring problem.

It shows you that, even at the luxury end of the market, it is still *caveat emptor*: buyer beware.

The biggest changes involved developing the basement or old vaults below the ground floor. This included swapping the kitchen and utility room and creating a bedroom and a playroom for a future Blair generation. The plan for a mega £100,000 kitchen on the ground floor did not meet with Westminster Council approval and had to be substantially reduced in size. Other proposals met with more approval from Westminster as Euan has sympathetically restored some lost features.

More gigantic works were needed for the £1.2 million, one-bedroom mews house that backs onto the main house, which at the time of going to press had not yet been approved by Westminster Council. These included digging out a basement and creating a courtyard between the two homes.

It is described by estate agents as,

A unique period cottage laid out over two floors and located in this charming mews off Marylebone High Street … The accommodation features open plan ground floor space refurbished in a 'Cape Cod Style' with light timber flooring and large skylight. A gentle spiral feature staircase leads up to the upper floor which comprises of a spacious and light double bedroom with exposed beams and a recently fitted shower room with skylight.

Cherie has more ambitious plans for her son with outline planning proposals submitted in August to substantially enlarge the property. Work is going ahead in January 2015 to build the basement, as this did not require planning permission.

It was probably only fair that the Blairs helped Euan buy a grand house. Only the year before, they had bought expensive properties for both daughter Kathryn and son Nicky, both within walking distance of each other and not far from Connaught Square.

Kathryn had a £975,000 upper-floor maisonette just off Regents Park and very close to Baker Street. She owns it jointly with Cherie and there is no mortgage.

Nicky was bought a very nice mews house – again, jointly owned with Cherie – in Marylebone, close to the station and near to a private hospital. This, too, was bought for cash. It was a three-storey freehold home with three bedrooms, two bathrooms, a very useful garage and a sun terrace, and cost £1.13 million. It is now owned by a wealthy Punjabi politician and orthopaedic surgeon.

Nicky moved in 2012 – to a new home bought for £1.35 million – a stone's throw from his sister near Baker Street and Regents Park and within easy walking distance of Peter Mandelson's home inside Regents Park. The estate agent's pictures of the home show it has been extensively modernised with a sunny patio garden, expensive kitchen and bathroom. It has three bedrooms and a superb 24-foot reception room with views to the front and back of the house.

That leaves just one other family property purchased by the Blairs, purchased for Tony Blair's sister for £600,000 in the village of Wotton Underwood in Buckinghamshire, a walk away from the Blairs' home, South Pavilion. Again this is jointly owned by Cherie Blair and bought for cash.

Cherie and Euan Blair have also obtained a new role as private landlords. Two blocks of flats have recently been purchased in the Manchester area. One – 31 and 33 Gloucester Road, Urmston – was bought for £650,000. They have set up a new company, Oldbury Residential Ltd, based at Cherie's offices in Great Cumberland Place, London. The ten flats are within two adjoining double-fronted Victorian houses that had been on sale for some time. Described by the estate agent as an 'excellent buy-to-let investment', the property was originally on the market for £850,000.

The *Daily Mail* reported in October 2014, 'Sources close to the Blair family said they plan to renovate the flats and rent them out to young professionals.' The estate agent's blurb said, 'This prestigious development consists of nine luxury apartments and a simply spectacular and utterly unique luxury penthouse apartment. These apartments are currently tenanted, achieving a rental return of £4,650 per month.'[9]

Since then they have purchased another block of 14 flats: 2–8 Higher Hillgate, Stockport SK1 3ER.

All this leaves the increasingly wealthy Blairs with a formidable property empire for themselves and their family. They have all three of their children within walking distance of their London home and both Peter Mandelson and Benjamin Wegg-Prosser live nearby. It can only be a matter of time before Leo Blair, born in Downing Street, also acquires a £1 million home.

The Blairs' ever-expanding property empire

£265,000, BRISTOL: Two flats bought in 2003 by Cherie with help of conman Peter Foster. One since sold for £260,000. The other was up for sale but in January 2015 appeared to have been withdrawn from the market. It is worth £265,000 as of January 2015.

£3.65 MILLION, LONDON: Five-storey Grade II-listed Georgian townhouse bought in 2004. Original mortgage £3.47 million. Thought to be worth £8.4 million as of January 2015.

£5.75 MILLION, BUCKINGHAMSHIRE: Grade I-listed manor house bought in 2008. Original mortgage estimate £4 million. Thought to be worth around £8 million as of January 2015.

£800,000, LONDON: Mews house immediately behind townhouse, bought in 2007 with mortgage, since paid off. Mews houses were selling for £1.8 million in that street as of January 2015.

£1.29 MILLION, LONDON: Four-storey Grade II-listed townhouse bought for Euan Blair in 2010 with mortgage. Now sold.

£975,000, LONDON: Three-bedroom maisonette in Georgian house bought for Kathryn Blair in 2010 for cash. Said to be sold for £1.45 million in 2014.

£1.35 MILLION, LONDON: Four-storey Georgian townhouse bought for cash for Nicky Blair in 2012. Worth £1.8 million as of January 2015.

£600,000, BUCKINGHAMSHIRE: Three-bedroom cottage bought for cash for Sarah Blair (Tony's sister) in February 2013.

£3.625 MILLION, LONDON: Six-bedroom townhouse jointly owned by Cherie and Euan for him and his wife Suzanne with a mortgage in September 2013. Worth over £4 million as of January 2015.

£1.2 MILLION, LONDON: One-bedroom mews house backing onto the six-bedroom townhouse bought by Cherie Blair with a mortgage for Euan and Suzanne in March 2014.

£650,000, MANCHESTER. Ten flats, purchased in 2014, owned by a new company set up by Cherie and Euan Blair.

£1.3 MILLION (ESTIMATE), STOCKPORT: 14 flats, purchased in 2014, owned by a new company set up by Cherie and Euan Blair.

CHAPTER FIFTEEN

A ROUTE BACK TO BRITISH POLITICS

'The party people, exiled for years in the Siberia of Party drudgery far from the centre of government, suddenly re-emerge in the halls of the Kremlin with renewed self-importance.'

– TONY BLAIR ON THE LABOUR PARTY IN HIS AUTOBIOGRAPHY, *A JOURNEY.*

Tony Blair felt the party forced him out to make room for Gordon Brown. Nonetheless, Labour was the political vehicle that had taken him to the top, and, if he wished to continue to be involved in British politics, it was the only vehicle he could credibly use.

But it was awkward. His autobiography, *A Journey*, records that he once wrote to the then Liberal leader Paddy Ashdown of 'our cavalier attitude towards our parties'. It also records that, in order 'to circumvent' his party, 'what I had done was construct an alliance between myself and the public.' He claimed a direct emotional attachment with the people, which declined towards the end of his premiership: 'For me and for the people, this was sad. My relationship with them had always been more intense, more emotional, if that's the right word, than the normal relationship between leader and nation.' And he summed up his view of the party workers who had made his premiership possible in these words: 'The party people, exiled for years in the Siberia of Party drudgery far from the centre of government, suddenly re-emerge in the halls of the Kremlin with renewed self-importance.'[1]

And he was by then a very divisive figure in Labour Party politics. There are those who almost idolise him, whom we will call the Blairites, and there are those who loathe him; and there are not many in between. In 2007 the supporters of the new Prime Minister, Gordon Brown, mostly came into the category of those who loathe Blair, for that year the Blair–Brown wars reached their crescendo.

However bad you think the Blair–Brown wars were, they were probably worse, and they are still going on. In 2013 Brown's one-time spin doctor Damien McBride published his memoirs, and it was remarkable to see how quickly they could be reignited, with Blair and Brown supporters using the occasion to fight their old battles in public one more time.

Blair himself hasn't forgotten or forgiven. There's a brief sentence – blink and you could miss it – in his autobiography that speaks eloquently of his still-burning fury and resentment. Writing of the very early 1980s, before he became an MP, he says he wrote occasional articles for the *New Statesman*, 'then a serious political magazine.'[2] Why that intrusive, sneering little word 'then'? Because when Blair was leader, the *NS* was bought by Geoffrey Robinson, and was said to have moved into the Brown camp (though it wasn't obvious from its content). That one little word that he couldn't resist tells you that his resentment at the magazine's apostasy is still red and raw.

Blair privately hoped that a Blairite might stand successfully against Brown in 2007; his old ally Peter Mandelson, then European Trade Commissioner, made it publicly clear that he considered Brown unfit to be Prime Minister. Charles Clarke and John Reid were telling Blair not to hurry out. Both saw themselves as possible challengers to Brown.

But Blair's premiership was doomed. His alienation from his party was complete. He told the chat-show host Michael Parkinson on television that God and history would judge him over Iraq, which infuriated Labour people who thought the electorate and his party ought to be the judges to whom a prime minister defers. He was no longer even an electoral asset; in fact the polls indicated that he had become an electoral liability.

He and Brown were constantly sniping at each other, retreating, withdrawing, publicly telling the world that all was peace and privately encouraging their lieutenants to say damaging things about each other. There was a stream of non-attributable venom directed at Brown the Chancellor from 'ministers close to Tony Blair' and 'longstanding friends of the Prime Minister' and 'former cabinet ministers' appearing under the bylines of journalists whom insiders knew to have particularly good contacts in Blairite circles, such as Patrick Wintour of the *Guardian* and Andrew Grice of the *Independent*.

Ministers started to resign, and more resignations were threatened. Labour MPs were panicking about the polling evidence, which showed that a Blair-led Labour Party was electorally doomed next time.

The Blairites mounted a restless search for a candidate called Notgordon Brown. (Ask 'a cabinet minister close to the Prime Minister' whom he wanted to see as leader and he'd reply, 'Notgordon Brown.') As we mentioned earlier, at one point Blair was grooming Charles Clarke for the role – he told Clarke this, according to Clarke's interview with the *Daily Telegraph*'s Charles Moore – but the plan fell apart when Clarke was forced to resign as Home Secretary. In 2007 the mantle seemed to have fallen on David Miliband, but he, after a few days' indecision, decided not to run against Brown.

So, as long as Brown led his party, Blair's only option was to stay right out of domestic politics – and he did. But Brown resigned after losing the 2010 election. Blairite hopes then rested on David Miliband getting the job, but Miliband lost, narrowly and surprisingly, to his brother Ed – partly because David was seen as too close to Blair. Ed had been close to Brown, and was thought to hold views that were more traditionally Labour than Blair could stomach; even worse, he was thought to be close to the unions.

Blair's hoped-for smooth passage back under a David Miliband leadership was no longer possible. He had a number of options, none of them very attractive. He could stay right out of domestic politics, as he had done under Brown, which was probably what Ed Miliband would have liked best. He could throw in his lot wholeheartedly with the new leadership, supporting it to the hilt and biting his tongue when it did something of which he disapproved, which is what former party leaders are supposed to do, and what Neil Kinnock had done for Blair himself. He has not been able to bring himself to do this, presumably because he feels sure that the Blairite flame is not safe in Ed Miliband's hands.

He could fight openly, hoping to force Miliband out before the 2015 general election, or force him out after electoral defeat, giving the Blairites another chance to install a leader in whose hands the legacy would be safe. Or, if Miliband seemed likely to survive and perhaps lead Labour to victory in 2015, he could work to ensure that the new Prime Minister would be tethered by a Parliamentary Labour Party consisting overwhelmingly of Blair loyalists.

The great untold story of the Ed Miliband years is that Blair chose to fight. The battle is mostly discreetly hidden from view, but there is war on the ground, carefully shielded from public gaze. Just occasionally – as in Falkirk in 2013 – it explodes into the media; and just occasionally the two men have a public row, no less spectacular because of the careful, emollient-sounding words in which it is clothed.

September 2013 was a month of coded warfare between Blair and Miliband. At the start of September 2013 Ed Miliband did something few opposition leaders ever get to do: he changed the course of events. If Miliband had not decided unexpectedly to oppose David Cameron's proposed military action over the use of chemical weapons in Syria, Britain and the USA would have begun a bombing campaign against Assad, and there is a good chance that this would have escalated into boots on the ground. By the time it became apparent that ISIS was a far greater threat than Assad, we would have been committed to destroying Assad.

Blair's criticism, though expressed in weary, more-in-sorrow-than-in-anger tones, was clear, unambiguous and intended to be damaging. When, a couple of days later, negotiations that had the potential to prevent the use of chemical weapons in Syria started to look as though they might succeed, Blair's voice was not heard.

When, towards the end of September 2013, Miliband called for the government to stand up to the energy companies, who were imposing huge price rises at the start of the winter, the former Conservative Prime Minister John Major supported him, telling a parliamentary press gallery lunch, 'Governments should exist to protect people, not institutions. We'll probably have a very cold winter, and it is not acceptable to me, and ought not to be acceptable to anyone, that many people are going to have to choose between keeping warm and eating.'[3]

For Miliband, it must to some extent have made up for the fact that his own former party leader and Prime Minister, Tony Blair, was a great deal less helpful to him than Major. Blair could easily have declined to comment. Instead, he went out of his way to make it clear he thought that Miliband was being irresponsible, silkily implying to journalists that it would be unhelpful to Miliband if he spoke his mind.

Blair told Sky News, 'I'm not going to comment on the policy. He's got the job of being leader of the Opposition. I did that job for three years. I know how tough it is. I'm not going to get in his way.' He could very easily not have spoken, had he wanted not to damage Miliband.[4]

And, as so often happened when they were in government together, Peter Mandelson came out and said the things that Blair wished it to be understood that he thought. He said, 'I believe that perceptions of Labour policy are in danger of being taken backwards.'

Blair may not have said these words, but the same week as Mandelson said them, Blair wrote in the *New Statesman* as a more general comment on Miliband:

Parts of the political landscape that had been cast in shadow for some years, at least under New Labour and the first years of coalition government, are illuminated in sharp relief. The Conservative Party is back clothing itself in the mantle of fiscal responsibility, buttressed by moves against 'benefit scroungers', immigrants squeezing out British workers and – of course – Labour profligacy. The Labour Party is back as the party opposing 'Tory cuts', highlighting the cruel consequences of the Conservative policies on welfare and representing the disadvantaged and vulnerable … The ease with which it can settle back into its old territory of defending the status quo, allying itself, even anchoring itself, to the interests that will passionately and often justly oppose what the government is doing, is so apparently rewarding, that the exercise of political will lies not in going there, but in resisting the temptation to go there.[5]

For once, Miliband was goaded into a reply:

As he was the first to recognise, politics always has to move on to cope with new challenges and different circumstances. For example, on immigration, Labour is learning lessons about the mistakes in office and crafting an immigration policy that will make Britain's diversity work for all not just a few. It is by challenging old ways of doing things, showing we have understood what we did right and wrong during our time in office that One Nation Labour will win back people's trust.

As September closed, Blair got in a last dig, before an invited audience of movers and shakers at the influential Mile End Group at Queen Mary College, London, in the presence of a number of spies, including the old Libyan hand Sir Mark Allen. In the chair was John Rentoul of the *Independent*. Rentoul once wrote a fairly good biography of Blair, but in recent years his approach to the former Prime Minister has become almost fawning.

Here Blair mused that it was a mistake for people to rise to the top having spent their lives in politics, with no experience of the 'wider world'. He did not mention Ed Miliband by name, but no one was in any doubt whom this was aimed at.

These examples, Blair might argue, are all occasions when he felt very strongly that Labour's leader had got it wrong, and felt he must say so. What happens, therefore, when he has the chance to give Ed Miliband a little support in a tight spot on a matter where he actually *does* support the Labour leader? Just such a chance turned up towards the end of 2013, when the *Daily Mail* launched its bitter attack on Miliband's father Ralph, calling him – untruthfully – 'The man who hated Britain'.[6]

Miliband took the unusual, and brave, decision to counterattack, rather than do what most politicians do in the face of unfair media onslaughts, which is lie low and hope not too much of the dirt sticks to them. He was widely supported across the political spectrum, including by Prime Minister David Cameron.

This was an area where Blair could have given Miliband much-needed support with a good conscience. But nothing was heard from Tony Blair. Was this simply an oversight? One journalist, Ian Hernon of *Tribune*, thought he would find out; he asked Blair's press office if *Tribune* could get a statement from him about the *Mail*'s slur on Miliband's dad. He was told that the former Prime Minister had no comment to make.

As often happens, the Blairites said the things Blair only implied. Charles Clarke says that 'some people find Ed Miliband weird and geeky' and that he has failed to express clear policies. It's code for 'He's not a proper Blairite'.

When Blair was giving his support and encouragement to former *News of the World* editor Rebekah Brooks in her hour of need during the phone hacking trial, Ed Miliband was calling for her resignation.

Mostly, however, the battleground is the selection conferences up and down the country where the men and women who will be Labour MPs after 2015 are chosen. On one side are the Blairites, working mainly through the New Labour pressure group Progress. On the other side are Miliband's friends as well as the trade unions and the Left.

Every stage of these selections is a battle. First you have to get the data – the names and addresses of the local party activists who will make the choice. Those with good connections get the data first, and give themselves a head start. Then you have to use it effectively. And all the time you have to be watchful lest your enemies are getting or using the data in a way that might be illegal, against party rules or capable of being made to look grubby.

Progress has proved itself a tactical master in these battles. 'We're doing it too, but Progress is well ahead of us,' we were told by one of the left's most prominent fixers. 'In this Parliament so far [to December 2013] Progress has won 35 to 40 per cent of the winnable seats that have selected a candidate. The trade unions and the left have been less successful. We are not organised in the same way. Progress have staff and contacts and money and a very effective network.'

THE POWER OF PROGRESS

One of Progress's great assets is that it controls Labour Students – a Labour-affiliated body. But its biggest asset by far is money. 'If you are well-funded and have some young supporters with time and energy, you can make the most of the three leaflets you are allowed, for example targeting them carefully and producing different ones for each ward,' we were told. 'Progress leaflets are beautifully produced by PR consultancies.'

Getting a local party membership list in advance often provides a crucial advantage, and being connected to Progress delivers this advantage in many constituencies.

Progress is easily the most effective of the organisations seeking to influence Labour, and the main reason for this is that it is, by a very long way, the richest. David Sainsbury is funding it at the rate of about £260,000 a year. The next-biggest donors – a long way down – are the British Private Equity and Venture Capital Association (BVCA), the Advertising Association, the Childcare Voucher Providers Association, Facebook, PricewaterhouseCoopers and Sovereign Strategy. Smaller sums – less than £5,000 a year – come from Labour Friends of Israel and the European Azerbaijan Society. Azerbaijan is a major Tony Blair Associates client, and the money from the society was spent on a rally praising Azerbaijan and its oil business at Labour's 2012 conference.

Other donors include Bell Pottinger, a lobbying firm that has worked on behalf of the government of Bahrain. After seven people died following a police clampdown early in 2011, protesters gathered outside Bell Pottinger's London office with placards reading, 'You can't spin the unspinnable'. Bahrain isn't the only authoritarian regime Bell Pottinger has represented in recent years. Its clients include Yemen, Sri Lanka and Belarus.

According to the Bureau of Investigative Journalism, 'Bell Pottinger boasted to undercover Bureau journalists that it helped engineer the lifting of an EU travel ban on the man dubbed "Europe's last dictator"' – the dictator of Belarus. In recent years, Labour Ministers and MPs, including Douglas Alexander, have condemned the dictatorship in Minsk.

The European Azerbaijan Society is London-based and is one of the slickest and best-funded lobbying operations anywhere in Europe. It works for a brutal dictatorship that has little concern for freedom of expression or human rights, according to the freedom-of-speech organisation Index on Censorship and Human Rights Watch.

For example, Azerbaijan investigative reporter Khadija Ismayilova received a collection of photographs through the post that appeared to show her having sex with a man. Attached was a note warning her to 'behave' or she would be 'defamed'.

Her crime was to use the Right to Obtain Information law to get documents about corruption in Azerbaijan, and expose the business interests of President Aliyev's daughter.

They assumed – Ismayilova told journalists in London at the Frontline Club – that, like some other journalists who have suffered similar blackmail campaigns, she would temper her reports. But Ismayilova went public with her story. Days later, on 14 March 2012, an intimate video of Ismayilova filmed by a hidden camera was posted to the Internet. Honour killings still take place in Azerbaijan and the authorities knew that Ismayilova's life could be in serious danger.

'The current state of freedom of expression in Azerbaijan is alarming, as the cycle of violence against journalists and impunity for their attackers continues,' says a report from the London-based human-rights organisation Article 19. 'Journalists, bloggers, human rights defenders and political and civic activists face increasing pressure, harassment and interference from the authorities; and many who express opinions critical of the authorities – whether through traditional media, online, or by taking to the streets in protest – find themselves imprisoned or otherwise targeted in retaliation.'

Azerbaijan works hard to present itself as a modern, democratic country with excellent business opportunities for multinational corporations, and Tony Blair can undoubtedly help with this. But recent attacks against journalists and activists reveal a government unwilling to hear the voices of its people, and there are about sixty political prisoners, according to the former head of advocacy at Index on Censorship, Mike Harris.[7]

Another major former donor was a trust created by the late Lord (Michael) Montague, in his lifetime a Progress supporter; this has given a total of £875,500. Pharmacia and Pfizer also gave £52,287.

Progress's total income in the fifteen months from 1 October 2011 to 1 January 2013 was £489,654. In the previous twelve months it was £368,598, and that is approximately its annual income.[8]

By the start of 2012, Progress had raised more money than the Green Party, Scottish Labour or Plaid Cymru. It had raised significantly more than any members' association in the Tory Party or Liberal Democrats and 122 times more than the next highest in the Labour Party. It had the organisation and funding of a minor political party.

The money would have made a huge difference to the cash-strapped Labour Party, if it could have had it. But it can't. Lord Sainsbury doesn't think Ed Miliband is sound; Sainsbury supported David Miliband's campaign to the tune of £200,000 and has been alienated by Ed Miliband's clear wish to draw a line under New Labour. Progress is a safe home for Sainsbury's money, because there it cannot be used to help Ed into Downing Street.

David Sainsbury's £260,000 a year and four- and five-figure sums from finance companies and the like account for nearly the whole income. The exact figures are impossible to work out because Progress does not reveal smaller sums, or the income from early capital sums received from, for example, Lord Montague's trust. But put all we do know together, and you are already getting close to the total income of about £370,000 a year.

So there is not much for the ordinary Labour Party member to make up. Progress's claim that it is 'funded by Labour Party members who support our aims and values' is presumably based mainly on the fact that Lord Sainsbury is a Labour Party member. We know that individual membership costs £25 a year but we do not know how many members there are. It can't be very many, even though membership is boosted by opponents such as Jon Lansman – veteran Bennite and political adviser to Michael Meacher MP – who likes to keep in touch with what the other side is doing.

Most political organisations, including Progress's Labour Party rivals, make it as easy as possible for people to get in touch with them, because they are always on the scrounge. They need money. They are run on a shoestring.

Progress is just the opposite. It has a sophisticated website on which it is easy to find things that the organisation wishes you to find, such as a picture of Ed Miliband speaking against a backdrop of the Progress logo or a message from Tony Blair. But it is like all the Blair organisations – it makes it hard for the reader to get in touch. There are no contact telephone numbers or email addresses on the website. You can choose to follow director Robert Philpot or deputy director Richard Angell on Twitter, or on LinkedIn, but you cannot write to them.

Actually, the first time we looked, at the end of November 2013, we discovered eventually that it was possible to navigate one's way, by a very circuitous and time-consuming route, through to a page that had on it an email address for Mr Angell, so we sent him an email. When no reply had been received by 11 December, we went back to the website. Angell's email address had disappeared.

Simply, other political pressure groups make it very easy to get in touch because they need your money. Progress doesn't need your money.

For a political organisation, Progress's structure and process of decision-making is remarkably opaque. It does not seem to spend a lot of time asking its members what they want. In January 2012, Lord Adonis, a close Blair adviser, was made its chairman, but there is no record of an election being held for the post, and no one seems to know exactly who made the decision.

Its rivals for the soul of the Labour Party are both less well-organised and far less well off, and they all rely to a greater or lesser extent on trade-union funding.

The old right, the trade-union right wing, which had for decades been the right wing of the Labour Party until Blair arrived in 1994 and moved the frontier, is represented by Labour First, run by the vastly experienced Labour and trade-union fixer John Spellar MP. The left is represented by Labour Futures, and the key figure is Jon Lansman. Neither of these organisations employs any staff of its own. Only Progress does that.

The four directors of Progress Ltd include Jennifer Gerber, the director of Labour Friends of Israel, and lobbyist Jon Mendelsohn, former chairman of Labour Friends of Israel, who in 2013 was created a life peer as Baron Mendelsohn. In 1998 Mendelsohn was caught on tape along with Derek Draper boasting to Greg Palast, an undercover reporter posing as a businessman, that Progress could sell access to government ministers and create tax breaks for Palast's supposed clients. He also advised an undercover journalist posing as a representative of American energy companies to rephrase their plans into language that sounded 'Earth-friendly' since 'Tony [Blair] is very anxious to be seen as green. Everything has to be couched in environmental language – even if it's slightly Orwellian.'

The other two directors are Robert Philpot, the full-time executive director, and Stephen Twigg MP.

Progress was founded in 1996, two years after Blair became Labour leader, and describes itself as 'the New Labour pressure group which aims to promote a radical and progressive politics for the 21st century.' The twenty-first century is mentioned in this message presumably so as to underline Progress's commitment to being 'modern', since it is hard to see what other century it might be promoting anything for.

Its first director was Jon Mendelsohn's friend and colleague Derek Draper, then research assistant to Peter Mandelson. For the first thirteen years of its existence, Progress mainly provided support and cheerleaders for everything Tony Blair did. Then, in 2007, Blair resigned as PM and the game changed. It provided a platform for those who were critical of Gordon Brown. It was a convenient way for Blair to attack Brown without having to put his own name to anything. He could appear to be above the fray.

In addition, and crucially, it supported reliably Blairite candidates in selections for parliamentary seats. During that parliament it held six parliamentary candidate workshops, to train its people in how to win selection battles. Candidates it boasts having helped get selected in that period include Stephen Twigg in Liverpool and Emma Reynolds in Wolverhampton.

After Brown resigned as Prime Minister it supported David Miliband for the leadership. His brother Ed's election was a nasty shock, and the organisation stepped up its work of training parliamentary candidates, to equip them for selection battles, and to protest about trade-union influence in these selections.

These two activities went together. No doubt Progress supporters believe as a matter of principle that unions should have less say in the selections; but it is also the case that the unions were often the only obstacle to Progress's ability to dictate them. The only serious opposition to a Progress-supported candidate was often a union-supported candidate, and the only machine capable of matching Progress was that of the unions.

One of the trainers for these selection battles was Matthew Doyle, former Blair spin doctor in Downing Street and by then the director of communications for the Office of Tony Blair – whose services were presumably provided free as a donation in kind from Tony Blair. Training in speechwriting was supplied by Paul Richards, former chair of Labour Students and the Fabian Society, adviser to Blairites Patricia Hewitt and then Hazel Blears.

Weekend seminars at splendid country houses were provided at the expense of generous commercial sponsors, including Bell Pottinger, which was founded by Margaret Thatcher's favourite advertising man.

Those candidates it chooses to help through the selection process can expect a lot of support on the ground: a team to canvass local party members, introductions to influential people, even lists of the contact details for local party members.

Its many successes include placing its former deputy director, Jessica Asato, as the prospective parliamentary candidate for Norwich North, a seat Labour should win back from the Conservatives in 2015 – it is essentially a Labour seat, thrown away by the Labour high command's ham-fisted handling of expenses issues surrounding its then-Labour MP Ian Gibson in 2009.

It is no wonder that, by 2011, the left was describing Progress as a 'party within a party' in a deliberate echo of the charge mainstream Labour Party people used to level at Militant in the eighties. It is not an entirely accurate parallel. Militant, after all, had a policy of 'entryism' – of getting into the Labour Party in order to turn it into a different sort of party – whereas Progress seeks to continue the policies and legacy of a former Labour Prime Minister.

Nonetheless, there was a shred of truth in Jon Lansman's March 2011 attack: 'Progress operates at several levels, of course, like the Militant Tendency in the 1980s: the politics (and the surroundings) may be very different, but the methods are surprisingly similar. They even have "readers' meetings" … It is only someone who is regarded as politically reliable, truly "one of us", who is introduced to the covert layers of operation, and only as necessary, though many more are aware of the kind of activities that Progress is engaged in than are themselves involved – the way any secret organisation sustains and protects itself.'[9]

But, Lansman told us in 2014, that was then, and this is now. It had by then become less of a party within a party, and less committed to the overthrow of Ed Miliband. The change, he says, was detected by Labour political fixers in January 2012, and the reason, he believes, is that it proved impossible to get a consensus around an alternative to Ed Miliband. David Miliband had ruled himself out, and the Blairites cannot stand Ed Balls, the shadow Chancellor.

That did not prevent a trade-union move at the 2012 Labour Party conference to expel the organisation for being a party within a party. Progress hastily promised reform, and has become more open about its finances and the names of those who control it.

The heart of its activities remained the continuation of New Labour policies and protecting the legacy of Tony Blair. An email to its members in July 2012 was headed 'New Labour's unfinished business'.[10]

But the methods were, for the time being at least, becoming less aggressive. Tony Blair himself started, early in 2012, to have meetings with small groups of Labour MPs. A 'source close to Mr Blair' told *Public Affairs News* magazine, 'He wants to re-engage in the UK. He has things to say and he thinks it's the right time. The question is how he re-enters the UK scene without re-entering domestic politics and interfering with the Labour Party.' The pious wish not to interfere with the Labour Party evoked a hollow laugh from those who knew what Progress had been up to.

The news was too much for Richard Heller, once adviser to Denis Healey and a stalwart of the old right in the Labour Party, who relieved his feelings with a furious, passionate blog post:

In 1956 Britain's prime minister took this country into an unlawful and unprofitable war in the Middle East, and misled its parliament and people about its origins and purpose ... Once an international icon, Anthony Eden disappeared into political oblivion ... He did not hawk himself round the world for money. Although a vastly more experienced diplomat than Tony Blair he was never offered any international appointment. He did not set up any foundations in his name. He did not have a spin doctor or a retinue of any kind. Above all, he abandoned any hope of a political comeback.

Eden's afterlife was a sign of a Britain with high standards in political life. Politicians were penalised for error, failure and dishonesty. If Tony Blair returns to a frontline role in British politics, it will show that those standards have finally collapsed.

Blair seriously believes that he is entitled to such a role and that the British people should be grateful for his wisdom. Once again, he has demonstrated one of his terrifying strengths as a politician – he is never embarrassed by himself ...

Blair now thinks that the time is right for him to 're-engage with the British people' ... Clearly Blair is seeking some special and personal avenue for this re-engagement, because he has always had the option of standing as an MP, as ex-premiers used to do routinely. Sir Alec Douglas-Home fought two general elections after being defeated as prime minister, and loyally served his successor, Ted Heath, in opposition and government. Standing again at a by-election would 're-engage' Blair automatically with a selection committee and local voters and guarantee the maximum exposure for his current views. Blair could also ask for a life peerage and contribute in the House of Lords without the risks of facing a voter.

There is one major problem with either of these comeback routes: he would undergo scrutiny about his murky finances.

Tony Blair has let it be known that he has 'things to say' to the British people. He may have to say some of them to the Leveson inquiry, on his relationship with Rupert Murdoch. Eventually the endless Chilcot Inquiry will have 'things to say' about him and Iraq.

It would have been seemly for Blair to await the judgment of Chilcot and Leveson before seeking a comeback, but perhaps he knows already that he will get an easy ride.

For millions of British people the one thing that they want to hear from Tony Blair is 'I'm sorry' and it's the one thing he never can bring himself to say. Of course, he is not alone in this attitude. No one with authority or status in modern Britain ever apologises for their conduct – whether bankers or bosses or footballers. No matter how badly they mess up or offend people or even wreck lives they still expect admiration and money. Even in this depressing context, Blair's return to a frontline role would represent a very special nadir.[11]

You can agree or disagree with Heller, but he's right to point up the key importance of the Chilcot Inquiry in all this. If Chilcot goes half as far in its criticism of Blair as Blair's enemies hope, it will be very damaging to Blair's attempts to re-enter British politics.

A journalist who is close to Blair, Matthew d'Ancona, reports that Blair himself understands this, and is very apprehensive about Chilcot. D'Ancona quotes a 'close ally' of Blair as saying, 'He is deeply concerned about it. It could define his legacy.'[12]

The report of this investigation, launched by Gordon Brown in 2009, has been delayed over and over again. The last witness gave evidence in 2011, and the report will not now appear until sometime after the general election on 7 May 2015 – and maybe a long time after that.

One of the factors holding it up is a row over whether up to 200 cabinet-level discussions on the Iraq war, notes sent between Blair and George W. Bush, and more than 130 records of conversations between either Blair or Brown and the White House may be published. The Cabinet Office has blocked publication of most of them, almost certainly at Blair's insistence. Blair, who, as we have discovered many times, never lets any information into the public domain that he can keep secret, told the inquiry that it was important 'that the British Prime Minister and the American President are able to communicate in confidence.' He said he would give the inquiry the gist of what was said. Not everyone will be satisfied that Tony Blair's summary will give them the full picture.

In November 2014, after several deadlines for publication had passed, Blair was reported to have seen the draft report. In January 2015 Sir John Chilcot told the Prime Minister that publication must be held up by 'the process of giving individuals an opportunity to respond to provisional criticism in the Inquiry's draft report.'[13] We may safely assume that one of these individuals, perhaps the main one, is Tony Blair.

So what is he worried about? Not, presumably, that it might damage Labour's chances if it appears before the election, since it emerged in December 2014, via leaks and interviews with people close to the former PM, that he had written off Labour's chances anyway; he saw the most likely election outcome as a defeat for Ed Miliband, after which he had hopes that Progress candidate Chukka Umunna would oust Miliband and return Labour to pure Blairite principles. And on the penultimate day of 2014, Blair himself broke cover with an interview in the *Economist* where he claimed that the 2015 election would be a return to the old pre-Blair sort, 'In which a traditional leftwing party competes with a traditional rightwing party, with the traditional result.' Asked if he meant a Tory win, Blair said: 'Yes, that is what happens.' He said he saw no evidence of a shift to the left in public thinking after the financial crisis – a move that Miliband thinks has occurred – and added: 'I am still very much New Labour and Ed would not describe himself in that way, so there is obviously a difference there. I am convinced the Labour party succeeds best when it is in the centre ground.'[14]

The next day he tweeted that these remarks had been misinterpreted: he wanted and expected Miliband to win.[15]

Seeing that all this needed clarification, he gave the BBC's Nick Robinson an interview on 12 January 2015 during which he said that the public must decide whether Ed Miliband 'has a problem', he said, and they were crying out for 'clear leadership and direction'. Asked to endorse Miliband, he said it 'will be for the people to choose.'[16] Just a week later, Peter Mandelson was on television calling Ed Miliband confused and unconvincing, denouncing the mansion tax, and talking up the Liberal Democrat alternative.[17] On 7 February the *Observer* had Blair saying blandly that he would do whatever the Labour Party wanted him to do to help win the election.[18] Miliband might have been tempted to reply with what Clement Attlee once wrote to Harold Laski: 'A period of silence from you would be welcome.' But a period of silence is one thing he is unlikely to get.

The war is well under way, no less vicious because everyone concerned politely denies that it has ever been declared.

THE BATTLE OF FALKIRK

At the 2013 Progress conference there was much complaint that Progress candidates had not been selected in certain constituencies, and accusations that the trade unions had been too successful. The closing session of the conference saw the battle between Progress and the unions suddenly burst into the open.

The session featured a panel discussion with Peter Mandelson, *Times* columnist and Blair loyalist David Aaronovitch and Blairite former MP Oona King, and they were asked what could unite Progress and the trade union Unite. It appeared that nothing at all could achieve this.

Aaronovitch spoke first, laying into the new Unite general secretary Len McCluskey with a vehemence and ferocity that seemed to startle his audience. He attacked the validity of McCluskey's election, which McCluskey won by 2–1, because there was a poor turnout, though this is probably at least partly explained by the fact that most people saw the election as a foregone conclusion. The attack echoed, in its arguments and its ferocity, the bitter attacks made on unions by Conservative ministers such as Lord (Norman) Tebbit over the years.

Then Mandelson took up the story, as though on cue, and said that

McCluskey had been responsible for manipulating the selection battle for a new Labour candidate for Falkirk. That was the first most of the audience had heard of the battle, which was quickly to become headline news. Aaronovitch came back at once and said, 'I think all the media here have their headline for tomorrow.' Indeed they did. They probably arrived expecting it.

It was a carefully staged media event, and successfully laid the groundwork for the Progress narrative about the selection of a Labour parliamentary candidate for Falkirk: that the unions manipulated the selection and tried to steal the candidature. The real story is rather different, and shines at least as much light on the Progress *modus operandi* as those of the trade unions.

The Falkirk selection issue was one of the most divisive affecting Labour in 2013. The sitting MP Eric Joyce was deselected by Labour after being involved in a drunken brawl in a House of Commons bar. This was followed by another incident at Edinburgh Airport, where he was accused of abusive and threatening behaviour over a mobile phone and racist comments after being arrested by police. He admitted a breach-of-the-peace charge at Edinburgh Sheriff Court in March 2014, was fined £1,500 and ordered to pay compensation. He pleaded not guilty to two charges relating to obstruction and making offensive remarks, and his plea was accepted without trial.

For the media, what followed after his deselection was a gift, but it was seriously misrepresented. The media and Progress saw it as an opportunity to attack trade-union power in general, and Unite in particular, over the manipulation of a Labour candidate selection in a Scottish town.

In fact it was a battle for the heart and soul of Labour between the unions on the one hand and Progress and the Blairite modernising wing of the party on the other. What was little more than the normal rivalry of various groups fighting to get their candidate selected as an MP was turned into a national battle for the future of the party.

That it was really a battle of ideas was publicly confirmed by the

Blairite former cabinet minister John Reid, who told the BBC, 'It is at heart an ideological battle, a political battle between those who want to take Labour back to the seventies and eighties, as Len McCluskey does, where we represented the sectional voice, the weak echo of every industrial demand of the trade unions, and those like Ed Miliband, who want to see us move increasingly towards an open party which reaches across class, across geography, across gender in which ordinary trade unionists can play their part, along with many others.'[19]

Of course every commander draws battle lines where he would like them to be, not where they necessarily are. Reid's description of the two sides is a partisan one, and his assumption that Ed Miliband is a fully paid-up Blairite moderniser is more what he hopes than what he believes. But the statement is useful as confirmation that Progress and the Blairites are at least as much engaged in the battle as the unions.

The scandal – such as it was – seems to have arisen out of two separate incidents. One involved the union Unite, and the other the local chairman of the Labour constituency party, Stevie Deans, who is also a Unite convener at Grangemouth Oil Refinery. Stevie Deans took two decisions. As chairman of the local party he decided to recruit some of his relations as members, particularly the Kane family. This is hardly a criminal offence, as the police would later realise. The problem arose because some of the family members hadn't realised they had been signed up.

Also, Unite decided to copy a very successful campaign run by the shop workers' union USDAW to recruit new Labour members free of charge for a year so long as they also signed a direct debit to start paying in a year's time. The problem was that they didn't get them to sign direct-debit mandates, and, when they realised their mistake after they submitted the new members to Labour HQ, they hurriedly went round and got people to sign the mandates. These arrived at Labour HQ in a big plastic bag; but some of the direct debits were signed by partners.

All this got Labour HQ worried – particularly as the leading candidate for the constituency was Kari Murphy, office manager for Tom Watson

MP, Labour's campaign director for the general election, a prominent member of Unite and a close friend of Len McCluskey, the union's general secretary.

So a very experienced constitutional officer, Eric Wilson, based in the north of England, investigated the state of affairs and sent a memorandum to HQ.

At the same time – though this was not reported until well after the event by Rajeev Syal of the *Guardian* – Progress was doing the same thing, or rather worse. As Syal reported,[20] Gregor Poynton, who wanted to challenge Unite from the right, paid the membership fees of eleven new members.

'Gregor Poynton told the *Guardian* that he paid for the new recruits with a single cheque of £137 in July last year [2012] – a move which raised concerns with Labour officials. Two new members say their joining fees were paid for by Poynton or members of his family in the expectation they would vote for him at a future selection meeting.'

Poynton, like Kari Murphy, is a well-connected young Labour Party member. He is a former party election-strategy manager and Scottish Labour Party organiser who is married to the MP and shadow Defence Minister Gemma Doyle. He is from Falkirk and his parents still live in the town. Gemma Doyle is connected to Jim Murphy, who was later moved by Ed Miliband from the role of shadow Defence Secretary, and is also on the Blairite wing of the party.

The *Guardian* reported:

One of those recruited last July, who asked to remain anonymous, joined because of a long-standing friendship with the Poynton family. 'I wanted to help them and ensure the town is represented by someone local,' the source said.

The source said the joining fees were paid by Poynton or a member of his family from July 2012 until sometime in 2013.

Now all of this, we understand, was conveyed to Labour HQ with a recommendation that it should be sorted out locally by long-serving official Eric Wilson.

But Labour HQ rejected this and decided to set up a high-level investigation under Jane Shaw, an experienced compliance officer. This move appeared to be backed by Iain McNicol, the party's general secretary. But more importantly, figures close to Ed Miliband wanted firm action. They are said to have included Torsten Bell and Bob Roberts, the former *Mirror* journalist who is now the Labour Party's executive director of communications.

So a separate report was prepared but, before it could be published, some of its contents were leaked to the *Mail on Sunday*, concentrating entirely on the role of the Unite union. Ed Miliband put the local party under special measures.

The party, not knowing whether the paper had the report, acted by calling in the police after a Tory MP, Henry Smith, had also reported them. Unite retaliated by bringing in its own lawyers, who interviewed all the families involved and produced their own twelve-page report, saying that there had been no fraud, only some mistakes, and Miliband backed down over the charges against Unite. The police also found no evidence of fraud.

But it was not without cost. Campaign director Tom Watson, who had been implicated by the press in the scandal, resigned from the shadow cabinet. His office manager, Kari Murphy, withdrew as candidate and the party decided on an all-women shortlist and said none of the members recruited from the day Joyce was deselected could vote for a successor, reducing the constituency party to a rump of about 120 members.

General Secretary Iain McNicol was moved sideways. Never Miliband's choice, this former GMB union official lost any major say in the general election campaign to Spencer Livermore, a former head of strategy to Gordon Brown, under the chairmanship of another Blairite, Douglas Alexander, as Labour Party chairman.

More significantly, and despite Miliband's agreeing that Unite had not committed electoral fraud, the way was opened for a special conference to discuss whether to change the whole relationship between the unions and the party, reducing further the trade union link. And one leading official at a barbecue in Miliband's private north London home in July called for Unite to be disaffiliated.

In context, the whole issue was blown up for other purposes. It was used as a catalyst to reform union-party relations and power and to allow reform of party funding. Miliband agreed to limit union contributions, which would inevitably lead to his committing himself to funding political parties from the taxpayer if he wins the 2015 general election.

One idea being studied by Labour is to end taxpayer funding for free election addresses – which costs £63 million for Westminster and European elections – and transfer the cash directly to the political parties. That way, Miliband can claim that in an age of austerity no extra taxpayer funding is being given to political parties.

But the Progress agenda in the whole affair was clear: further reforms along Blairite lines with the aim of separating the unions from major decision-making inside the Labour Party, as well as more Labour MPs from Progress and fewer from the unions. It's the agenda that was laid down clearly by Peter Mandelson, carefully prompted by David Aaronovitch, on the last day of the 2013 Progress conference.

Miliband badly wants to avoid another Unite-versus-Progress bloodletting, Falkirk style. He almost got one, in Bootle on Merseyside, but it was averted by the local Labour Party. This one centred on the man who once, as Blair's head of communications, trained candidates for selection battles, Matthew Doyle – once head of communications and broadcasting for the Labour Party and for five years, until 2012, political director at the Office of Tony Blair.

In 2014 he tried to get selected for the safe Labour seat of Bootle when veteran Labour MP Joe Benton announced he was standing down at the 2015 general election. Doyle entered a field that included Peter Dowd, Labour leader of Sefton Council and also Bootle born-and-bred Alex Flynn, Unite's director of communications.

The stage was set for another bruising battle between Unite and Progress, but Bootle Labour Party tried to take matters into their own hands. By September 2014 Dowd was way ahead, with Flynn as his most likely challenger. Doyle failed to get a single nomination from a Labour ward. He was hoping for support from USDAW, the shop workers' union, which ultimately mainly supported Dowd.

In desperation, he tried to enlist support from Angela Eagle, Labour MP for Wallasey and shadow Leader of the Commons. But she told him that he didn't stand a chance and it wasn't worth her trying to get him support. She says, 'If you are not from Bootle, the fiercely independent constituency Labour Party is not even interested. He should have known this before he stood.'

Bootle Labour Party compiled a shortlist that included neither Doyle nor Flynn. A complaint was made to the National Executive Committee, which instructed Bootle Labour Party to include both Flynn and Doyle on the shortlist. But in the end the formidable local party machine made sure that by hook or by crook Peter Dowd, the favoured son, got the nomination. Alex Flynn came second while Matthew Doyle, despite his work for Progress in advising how their candidates could win seats, came nowhere – as Angela Eagle had earlier predicted.

The Blairites normally operate within the Labour Party under the camouflage of Progress. But Blair's occasional public interventions are carefully timed.

BLAIR'S SPEAKING INCOME

Normally, of course, Blair speaks in public for money, not for political ends. Public speaking has earned him £9 million,[21] as he charges up to £200,000 per lecture, mostly through the Washington Speakers Bureau, of which George W. Bush is also a client. He signed with the bureau in October 2007, four months after ceasing to be PM, taking a $600,000 signing bonus. He has also signed up with the All American Speakers Bureau, whose website gives his fee as $200,000 upwards.

Yet, for a man once considered an orator, he has turned into a stiflingly boring speaker, frequently appearing to do little more than read out his host's PR handout, but sometimes producing a breathtakingly banal observation of his own. 'When things are in the balance, when you cannot be sure, when others are uncertain or hesitate, when the very point is that the outcome is in doubt – that is when a leader steps forward,' was the insight he shared with a Beijing audience in 2008. At a conference on Africa in 2013 he said that there was 'something wonderful, vibrant and exciting' about the continent's culture and traditions; and, speaking of economic development, helpfully pointed out, 'With electricity, given the technology we now have at our fingertips, everything is possible. Without it, progress will be depressingly slow. Likewise with roads and often ports.' At Ateneo de Manila University in the Philippines he said that the main problems President Obama faces 'are essentially global in nature'.[22]

The All American Speakers Bureau is one of several agencies that have also represented Blair, and they listed his minimum fee as $200,000 – twice the rate of Donald Trump.

However, the huge sums that he commands are something of a mystery, given the content of his private-sector lectures. 'The reason I am in Dongguan now is because I was told that everything that was happening here was amazing,' Blair said during a 2007 speech at a VIP banquet in China, for which his fee was in the region of $200,000. 'Dongguan's future is immeasurable.' Actually, the future is always immeasurable, in Dongguan as everywhere else; the title of the speech was 'From Greatness to Brilliance'. Such twaddle infuriated Chinese newspapers, which said Blair's empty remarks showed he was interested only in 'digging for gold' and 'money-sucking'. Deng Qingbo wrote in the *China Youth Daily*, 'Why pay such a high price to hear the same thing? Is it worth the money? Do these thoughts multiply in value because they come from the mouth of a retired prime minister?'[23]

Dongguan is a city of 1.7 million permanent residents and 10 million migrant labourers, mostly living eight or more to a room in the workers' dormitories that are attached to the city's industrial estates. Typical wages range from £40 to £100 per month.

In 2010 Blair published his autobiography, *A Journey*. He took three years to write it and donated the £4.6 million advance and all royalties to a sports centre for injured soldiers. The donation was dubbed 'blood money' by some of Blair's critics, who said he gave the sum to assuage his guilt for taking the UK to war against Iraq in 2003.

Even this autobiography appears to be aimed at the US market. 'Tony Blair is an extremely popular figure in North America,' said Sonny Mehta, his publisher. 'His memoir is refreshing, both for its candour and vivid portrayal of political life.'[24]

But, from time to time, Tony Blair speaks about British politics to a British audience, and is not paid for doing so. Almost always it is because an opportunity has arisen to undermine Ed Miliband.

CHAPTER SIXTEEN

A GOLD-PLATED PRISON

'I think Blair is now a very sad man. Rich, but [he]
betrayed everything the Labour Party was about.'
– GREG DYKE, SPEAKING TO AUTHORS.

Tony Blair was an energetic Prime Minister. When the lights dim and the public attention moves on to other stars, where will the fallen hero turn for adulation and thrills? Blair still doesn't have an answer that satisfies him. He doubtless receives a kick from being paid very large sums for very small tasks.

A speech to a remote country will pay him handsomely, much more than he was paid for a year's work as Prime Minister and twice as much as a Member of Parliament earns in a year. Then there are the huge sums of money for a casual introduction, for picking up the telephone. He likes it, of course. But he can live in only one house at a time.

And, though money buys power, he is finding that there are limits to that, just as there are limits to political power. He was never happier than when making decisions that affected the lives of others, having colleagues in politics and the media hanging on his every word and gesture. His money doesn't buy this buzz. The more money he acquires, the less likely it is that he will ever regain or even come close to the power that once was.

Money made by a businessperson is different from money made by an ex-politician. The former, if made legally, is regarded as an achievement; he pulled himself up by his bootstraps, or he had a clever idea. The latter is seen as the fruit of compromises of principle and the milking of contacts.

When Blair left power, he was told that the public expects politicians, in whom it has placed its trust, to pursue good causes before self-enrichment. The latter is allowed with discretion, but the former enables them to retain their credibility. Blair has paid the price for failing to heed this sage advice from a savvy and religious American businessman.

By pursuing money for its own sake, the arch image maker has tainted his image beyond redemption. Many in the British public – and increasing numbers of foreign politicians – hold Blair in contempt.

Blair and his dwindling band of admirers blame the media, which they say will never give him a fair hearing. Years ago, when Blair was fighting the Old Labour types he so despises, they used to say that they would never get a fair hearing from the media. Blair despised them for their defeatism. His first act as Labour leader was to fly halfway across the world to pay homage at the court of King Rupert Murdoch, and he tailored Labour's policies so that they did not alienate the media. Now, in a wrenching irony, he bemoans media bias against him and seems unable to accept that he has done anything to deserve it. And he has alienated Rupert Murdoch utterly and, as far as we can see, irretrievably.

He will keep his money and make more, but, in Britain at least, it will leave him isolated, surrounded by no more than bevies of flattering acolytes and corrupt dictators. They will give him the wealth and adulation he craves. But those who count morality as a value will cast him aside.

He does not want only money: he wants influence, and power, and respect. That is why his international work is structured as it is.

Mike Harris, lobbyist, former Blairite, and former head of advocacy at Index on Censorship, has made a close study of Blair's international work. There's a growing move, he says, to privatise diplomacy, and Blair is at the cutting edge. If you watch Blair at work, whether as Middle East envoy or as a paid consultant, or as the patron of international charities, you can see that he's aiming to be an alternative to conventional public-sector diplomacy.

Just in the way that the British government likes to outsource other functions to private-sector suppliers, so increasingly governments all over the world are outsourcing their diplomacy, and their relationships with other governments, to him. Sir Malcolm Rifkind, in fact, described him to us as someone who 'operates a public/private partnership in diplomacy.'

This is making him immensely rich and immensely powerful. He has now made more money than any ex-prime minister in history. The contrast between Blair and Labour's most successful prime minister, Clement Attlee, who died leaving just £7,295, is stark.

Many former prime ministers have inherited a lot of money, as Harold Macmillan did, but no former prime minister has made anything like the sort of money Blair has made. And no former prime minister has built his or her wealth so directly on his or her former office.

Through various business initiatives Blair has amassed a fortune, which we believe, from the information we can put together, to be at least £60 million, before we even begin to consider his vast property empire.

It's not a sin to make money. In recent years, other former prime ministers have done it. Blair's immediate predecessor, John Major, took a senior position with the American private equity firm Carlyle Group. Margaret Thatcher, among other things, made $500,000 a year as a consultant with Philip Morris. That did not stop Thatcher being widely admired, or Major continuing to be regarded as an honourable man. Blair, in Britain at least, is increasingly reviled. Why is this? And does he deserve it? There are several differences between Blair and all his predecessors.

First, their earnings are dwarfed by Blair's – he has turned himself into what the *Daily Telegraph* has called 'a human cash register'.

Second, they were far more discreet and restrained than Blair in their business dealings, and by Blair's standards they were easily satisfied.

Third, Blair, while making his money, has also sought to create an international political profile: becoming Middle East envoy, launching an unsuccessful bid for the presidency of the European Council, attempting unsuccessfully to be a sort of elder statesman in the Labour Party. And he has set up charities, to many of which he has given his name – the Tony Blair Faith Foundation and the Tony Blair Sports Foundation.

Fourth, they were more discriminating about the sort of people they were prepared to endorse.

Last, and most important, they did not try to mix a public-service career with their commercial activities. It was always clear whom they were working for at any given time. Malcolm Rifkind attempts to explain this away thus: 'I am no fan of Blair but I am not going to join a witch-hunt. I think he is wasting a lot of his life being a Flying Dutchman wandering round the world; it shows how restless he is. There is something almost manic in it. I don't admire him, but he is free to choose whatever way of life suits him as long as it is within the law.'

The problem with this view, though, is that like Pooh-Bah in *The Mikado*: he is Lord High Everything Else. You never know what role he is playing today: the Middle East peace envoy, the principal of Tony Blair Associates, the patron of the Tony Blair Faith Foundation – and often he is more than one of these distinguished people. That's what has made Blair's business dealings appear so suspect, and has opened him to charges of conflicts of interest.

The appearance that – for example – his role as Quartet Representative in the Middle East assists the expansion of his business empire is utterly toxic, and has helped to destroy his usefulness in the Middle East. That's what has ensured that the respect in which he is held has plummeted since he left Downing Street.

We have found that the same people and the same companies keep cropping up again and again in different contexts, and it has not always been easy to know in which section they ought to go. They include:

332

- MOHAMMED RASHID, former financial adviser to Colonel Gaddafi's eldest son and to Palestine's Yasser Arafat – he is now in hiding after being sentenced in absentia to five years in jail for fraud;
- BARONESS SYMONS, whose services to Gaddafi's Libya continued almost until the day the Colonel himself faced his grisly death;
- MARK ALLEN, the British spy whose secret deals with Colonel Gaddafi and his son Saif al-Islam paved the way for Symons and Blair in Libya;
- MICHAEL KLEIN, a former banker from Citigroup, fixer and expert in Middle East financial institutions.

Then there are the institutions and companies that have joined the gravy train:

- MONITOR GROUP, the now bankrupt American management consultancy from which Blair draws much of his talent.
- BROWN LLOYD JAMES, the consultancy run by a former Blair aide, which was commissioned to burnish the image of Syria's President Assad, as well as that of the Tony Blair Faith Foundation;
- CONSOLIDATED CONTRACTORS COMPANY, a huge Palestinian-owned construction multinational.

The names of these and other businesses keep recurring, whether we are writing about Kuwait, Palestine, the USA or anywhere else.

Blair's massive earnings are supplemented by pension and other benefits that cost taxpayers more than £250,000 per year.

'Blair is transfixed by money,' Peter Oborne, chief political commentator for the *Daily Telegraph*, told us, and we have been driven to the conclusion that, in this at least, Oborne is right. Blair has sacrificed everything else he had and appeared to value – his reputation and his ability to do good in the world – in pursuit of wealth. Conservative MP Sir Malcolm Rifkind is rather succinct with his thoughts on this matter: 'Any good he might have done is long since dissipated.' He seems the living embodiment of Hilaire Belloc's famous couplet:

> I'm tired of Love; I'm still more tired of Rhyme;
> But money gives me pleasure all the time.

Even his desire to make the world a more religious place, with more understanding between faiths, suffers. Any influence the Tony Blair Faith Foundation might have, in Britain and Europe at any rate, is crippled by the toxic name of the former Prime Minister in the title. The calculation, we are told, is that it does the organisation good elsewhere, particularly in the USA. Now some are doubting that Blair can sustain that, as Rupert Murdoch uses his formidable firepower in the US media to respond to disclosures – denied by Blair – of a relationship with Wendi Deng, Murdoch's ex-wife.

According to John Kampfner, a former editor of the *New Statesman*, 'Blair loved being on the world stage and then he was forced out of office against his will. His business deals allow him to remain on the stage and continue to hobnob with the rich and powerful.'

His best friends now admit that he is damaged goods. Charles Clarke told the *Huffington Post*: 'There is no question that he has damaged his reputation. The money has damaged his reputation, some of his contacts have damaged the reputation, some aspects of the way he's spent his life have damaged his reputation.'

If that's a friend, imagine what his enemies are saying! Here are some examples.

'I think Blair now is a very sad man, rich, but [he] betrayed everything the Labour party was about,' says Greg Dyke. Simon Kuper of the *Financial Times* writes of what he calls 'Blair's disease' – the disease of former national leaders monetising their years at the top. He wrote, 'If you are super-rich, you probably have an ex-leader working for you, like an overpaid tennis coach. Blair, for instance, has shilled for JP Morgan Chase, Qatar and Kazakhstan's cuddly regime.'

Kuper thinks Blair (and to a lesser extent former President Nicolas Sarkozy in France and former Chancellor Gerhard Schröder in Germany) planned it from the start. 'Most ex-leaders link up with the plutocratic class while still in office. These people have been planning their careers since kindergarten,' he wrote.[1]

There was certainly a time when he was not quite sure about his post Prime Ministerial career, and perhaps that is still true. A former senior employee told us, 'I think he went through a period when he wasn't entirely sure what he wanted to do. One thing about Tony wanting to make money, quite honestly, is that he is so persuasive and charismatic and kind of marketable, that he has made only 10 per cent of what he could make. I think he was feeling uncertain as to how much money he wanted to make and how he wanted to make it.'

Indeed, this source suggests that at a certain point, Blair wanted to set up an investment bank (called 'Blair Bank', perhaps). But he stepped back from the brink, though we don't know why.

Blair was always criticised in the Labour Party for his readiness to leap to the defence of the mega-rich. Now that he is one of them, this is more true than ever. So he told Charles Moore in July 2012, 'We must not start thinking that society will be better off if we hang 20 bankers at the end of the street … Don't take 30 years of liberalisation, beginning under Mrs Thatcher, and say this is what caused the financial crisis … Wrong!'

This is a caricature of the criticisms of the financial community, whose culpability for the financial crisis of 2008 is not in doubt. No one has suggested hanging twenty bankers at the end of the street, but it has been suggested that we cap their bonuses and limit their ability to gamble with our money.

The lesson of the previous thirty years, Blair claimed, was that, in a globally interdependent economy, 'We didn't understand properly the true implications of the financial instruments involved, and so we didn't supervise and regulate them properly. But we mustn't go back to the state running everything.' Given that one of the most serious failings of the government he led was its failure to supervise and regulate finance, this is a startling admission.

The need to find a role in the world is Moore's analysis of the 'Blair disease'.

I detect in him something like Britain's famous problem of having lost an empire, but not yet found a role. At 59, he's still young for a man in his position. He has been out of the game for five years. You can see, he wants to get back in, when he says, 'Since I left office, I have learnt a huge amount, especially about what is happening in Europe and the world. Sometimes it's quite shocking to me: how useful would this knowledge have been!'

Yet this is part of the sacrifice he made for money. He could have got back in the game and made good use of all that knowledge, but he would have had to make that – and not the pursuit of wealth – his top priority. He could, for example, have made a real contribution to Middle East peace – enough, you would have thought, to satisfy the most demanding ambition. But he would have had to give up other ambitions, most notably the accumulation of money, in order to do that.

Moore goes on:

He thinks, I suspect, that he'd be a better prime minister now than he was before. Blair tells us, 'I'd like to find a form of intervening in debates.' How? By getting elected again? 'I don't think that's possible.' A peerage? A wonderful look of amused contempt suffuses his tanned face. Something in Europe, perhaps? 'I would have taken the job [the presidency of the European Council] if they had offered it to me, but they didn't.'

Long before he ceased to be prime minister, the Blairs had acquired a worldwide reputation for being money-hungry. Their property portfolio began when Blair was still in office (see Chapter 14 for details of the Blairs' acquisition of properties).

Cherie's precarious childhood seems to have left her with a pretty well insatiable need for financial security. Blair, too, suffered childhood insecurity – though not on the same scale as his wife – when his father had a stroke. How far do these personal factors explain their apparent need to build wealth way beyond their needs? And to what extent is it due to the fact that Blair admires, and is dazzled by, the very rich?

Blair's relentless quest for financial enrichment has been dogged by accusations of conflicts of interest and suspicions that he is benefiting from the most controversial decision of his premiership – to go to war against Iraq. Readers will by now have seen what we have said about oilfields and the Middle East, and will have made up their own minds on this question.

It's certainly the case that during Blair's time in office he was able to make contacts and cultivate relationships that would later make him rich, and that some of these came about as a result of the Iraq War. The demise of Saddam Hussein made him popular in Kuwait, where he has made millions as an adviser to the Emir and where he even has his own office inside the Kuwaiti parliament buildings.

And apart from the Iraq War, there's no doubt that just being prime minister helps his cause. Malcolm Rifkind told us,

Once you have ceased to be prime minister and you don't have public responsibilities, your added value ... does relate to your international experience and people you know. It doesn't just mean other presidents or PMs, but someone like Blair would be of enormous value to someone who wanted to get access to another company. If someone wants to see the CEO of a company and part of the delegation is Mr T Blair, you can guess what the answer would be.

There are serious questions to ask about conflicts of interests between his public role as Special Envoy to the Middle East and his private business activities, as well as how much he has benefited financially from relationships he cultivated and decisions he made while in office – in particular the Iraq adventure.

When he left office Tony Blair felt a sense of bitterness, which went much wider than his famously antagonistic relationship with Gordon Brown. It was the Labour Party, and not just Brown, that forced him into resignation, and his view about the party he led, never very complimentary, became tinged with resentment.

He was, as Charles Moore notes, a relatively young man for a former prime minister. Just as he had been the youngest PM since Lord Liverpool in 1812, he was now the youngest *former* PM, still full of energy and ambition. There were several courses he could have chosen. He could easily have had a career in international politics, which would probably have brought him the Presidency of the European Council (which, as we have seen, in the event he failed to get) if he had devoted himself to it and placed a lower priority on making money.[2]

He could have thrown himself into his work as Middle East peace envoy, in which case he might now have more to show for it, and he would have avoided the increasingly strident accusations that he does not work hard enough at the job, that he has not taken the time to brief himself properly, and that he seems to see it mainly as a way to meet oil-rich folk in the region.

He could have devoted himself to his charity work, or to campaigning on matters about which he feels strongly, such as climate change and religious faith. He could have devoted himself to business, and he would have done very well indeed, making himself quietly very wealthy, away from the public gaze. Few people would have complained, and he would not have had to tolerate the constant carping criticism that he appears to find so irksome.

It seems that, in effect, he chose to do a little of all of these, but all of them overshadowed and controlled by a determination to become seriously rich. And that is what has been so toxic for his reputation in Britain. He was for a long time able to comfort himself that his reputation in the USA, which matters much more to him than his reputation in Britain, was still strong, but that is now in serious danger, and not just from the breach with Rupert Murdoch. The speech he gave in 2014 saying that what is happening in Iraq has nothing to do with him has also damaged his reputation there, we hear from Washington sources.

One Blair loyalist and former staffer, who does not want to be named – he would be permanently exiled from the court if it was known he had said this to us – told the authors privately that he was surprised at the huge amounts of money his old master appears to be amassing. 'He says he gives money to his charities, but I don't think he gives enough to his charities,' he said, so we asked, 'How much is he giving to his charities?' 'I've no idea,' said our informant hastily. Blair's spokeswoman Rachel Grant told writer Ken Silverstein, 'In the past few years Mr Blair has given significant amounts of his income to the charities.' But just what are 'significant amounts'?

We do have some idea how he funds his charities. He treats some of them at least in the way that the mega-rich often treat charities, by trying to incentivise them to raise money elsewhere. Thus, he gives the Tony Blair Sports Foundation matching funds.

When hard times come, it is the charities, not the business, that suffer. While income appears to be stagnant and starting to drop off at his charities, his own earnings go from strength to strength.

It is important to remember that, despite all this, not everything Blair does is worthless. Some of the work of the Tony Blair Faith Foundation and the Africa Governance Initiative is excellent. The work combating malaria and the interventions in the Ebola crisis are just two examples of Tony Blair's organisations, backed by his wealth and that of his contacts, indisputably doing good in the world.

THE GQ AND SAVE THE
CHILDREN AWARDS

All of that is why Tony Blair's reputation has plummeted – and why attempts to revive it often end up making things worse. In 2014, in quick succession, he was first named *GQ* magazine's Philanthropist of the Year, and then went to New York to accept the Global Legacy Award from Save the Children.

The first was greeted mainly by cynical laughter: there was a feeling that *GQ* and Tony Blair were made for each other. The TV presenter and former footballer Gary Lineker tweeted, 'Apparently, Tony Blair has won *GQ*'s philanthropist of the year award. Finally these awards have grasped irony!' Even Blair himself seemed to join in the mirth – or perhaps he was being serious when he accepted the award with the words, 'I feel the pulse of progress beating a little harder.' Did he remember that on the day of the Good Friday agreement he had said, 'This is no time for soundbites, but I feel the hand of history on my shoulder'?

But the second was more serious, and led to a speedy backlash. Critics were swift to point out that Justin Forsyth, formerly a special adviser to Blair, is the head of Save the Children UK, and Jonathan Powell, Blair's former chief of staff, is on the board. Did they have anything to do with the decision to give Blair the charity's Global Legacy Award?[3]

The award was made on 14 November, and within a week the charity realised it had blundered into a PR disaster, as this internal email, which was leaked to the *Guardian*'s Harriet Sherwood, shows:

Colleagues in the Middle East, SCUK [Save the Children UK] and at SCI [Save the Children International] have started to receive a high volume of complaints and negative reactions regarding the award given by SC US to Tony Blair, who is a hugely controversial and divisive figure in many parts of the world.

The reactive line below was developed by SCUK, but this will also need to highlight how this award is not a recognition of other aspects of Blair's controversial foreign policy, nor of his role as Peace Envoy with the Quartet, and focuses purely on this achievement in terms of international development.[4]

The 'reactive line below' said that the award was only about 'Tony Blair's leadership on International Development' as PM. He established the Department for International Development and hosted two G8 summits, in 1998 in Birmingham and in 2005 in Gleneagles, which STC considered to be key events in the battle against world poverty. 'The UK's achievement of 0.7% of GNI to international aid in 2014 is the culmination of work started under his leadership,' it added, though both his successors, Gordon Brown and David Cameron, might claim their share of the credit for meeting the target in rather more challenging economic circumstances than Blair faced.

The email also revealed that the charity was getting hostile questions from all over the world, and asked for some answers.

'We have also been asked to provide answers to the questions below … A reactive on Blair's role in Iraq would not go amiss, either,' the email continued.

One of the questions, mostly asked by supporters in the UK, was, 'Is Save the Children a pro-Israeli organisation?' Another was, 'How much money did you raise for this Gala?'

There were also some questions specifically from supporters in the occupied Palestinian territories:

- 'As a non-governmental, non-partisan charity working in the oPt [occupied Palestinian territories] since 1973, how do you see the role of the Quartet and Mr Blair as a mediator for the peace negotiations in the region?'
- 'Following the offensive on Gaza and the settler violence against Palestinians in East Jerusalem as well as other areas of the West Bank, and in light of the failure of the Quartet to stop these

violations against civilians in Palestine, how do you justify awarding the chairman of the Quartet?'
- 'You as Save the Children are considering yourself the voice of Palestinian children, do you think that the Quartet has played its role to protect and stop violations to children's rights in the oPt?'

Meanwhile Jasmine Whitbread, chief executive of Save the Children International, was writing to the charity's staff worldwide a letter that showed something near panic at the top, and that was also leaked to Sherwood at the *Guardian*:

I wanted to write to you directly about the concerns over the recent award given to Tony Blair by Save the Children US at their annual gala dinner in NY. In the scheme of all the critical work we are doing for children around the world some of you might ask why I am focusing on this issue, but it has touched a nerve close to our sense of identity and as such I think it's important that we have a shared understanding of how this happened, what we are doing about it, and how we will come out of this together …

We are all frustrated and disappointed about the situation we are in, but I think we can understand how this happened: In our current structure, members make their own decisions about their marketing and fundraising as long as these are in line with our brand and other agreed guidelines. If there is a sensitive question then they consult, and this does increasingly happen. In this case, SC US simply did not anticipate anything sensitive – in the USA Tony Blair is widely seen very positively for his contribution to international aid … I first heard about this when it became public and was immediately in touch with Justin [head of STC UK] and Carolyn [head of STC US], who agreed with me that there should have been a better process of consultation and risk assessment and that we must learn from this …

Now, this is very odd. That STC US did not understand the negative reaction to be expected from other countries is believable. But Blair's former adviser Justin Forsyth, head of STC UK, was asked to convey the invitation to Blair before it became public. If the Americans did not realise the likely reaction, he must have done. Why did he not warn his American colleagues? Was he keen for his old boss to have an honour that might restore Blair's reputation? Or did he warn them, and see his warning ignored?

The email continues:

> Urgently, right now, a team is trying hard to contain the situation and stop things escalating further, detracting from our wider work for children ... Importantly, we must safeguard and rebuild the trust and commitment to our shared values that we have worked so hard on over the last few years. This will take time and effort ...
>
> While I can't pretend I'm not very concerned about this situation, I'm confident that we can pull together to come out of it in a better place. There is so much that is amazing about what we are doing together for children ... Let's use this experience, painful as it is, to inform our next strategy ...

The next day, Whitbread was handed a letter from 500 STC staff, which said, 'We consider this award inappropriate and a betrayal to Save the Children's founding principles and values. Management staff in the region were not communicated with nor consulted about the award and were caught by surprise with this decision.' The executive director of Human Rights Watch, Kenneth Roth, tweeted, 'As this man defends any dictator who'll pay him, @SaveChildren inexplicably gives him award.'

A petition to the charity to withdraw the award mustered more than 125,000 signatures.[5] Save the Children's Director of Policy and Advocacy Brendan Cox later responded to the petition:

'As you know, this was a decision made by Save the Children US and although we (STC UK) were made aware of the decision, and we passed on the invite to his office at their request, we weren't part of the decision making process. In retrospect we should have foreseen the controversy this might generate.

For a number of reasons this is not a decision Save UK would have taken...'[6]

The response from Blair's office screams of an organisation that feels it's under siege. It accused the *Guardian* of bias, saying that it 'conveniently disregards the facts that support the award as well as quotes from African presidents, the head of USAID and indeed anything which would give a more balanced view than the one presented.'

Julie Crowley of Blair's communications team wrote to the *Guardian*'s Harriet Sherwood,

Your piece is a complete distortion of the truth, it is not impartial, balanced or fair, and is simply an exercise in muck-raking. You chose to ignore the support received by Tony Blair for his work in Africa, given by those who should matter most and know best, the people who have witnessed the impact made by the AGI in delivering better lives for their people, let alone the legacy from his time in office.

And it beggars belief that you quote George Galloway, who is not only biased but is making a film about the killing of Tony Blair, how is he best placed to make any sort of judgement on Tony Blair's work in Africa.

You did not make any attempt at all to provide a balanced picture and simply sought to smear and denigrate. I am frankly appalled.

Harriet Sherwood's piece seemed to us to be moderate, careful and accurate (you can judge for yourself: it's at http://www.theguardian.

com/politics/2014/nov/28/save-the-children-tony-blair-award-row).
She didn't use the quotes Ms Crowley supplied from President Ellen
Johnson Sirleaf of Liberia and President Ernest Bai Koroma of Sierra
Leone about what a good chap Blair is, which were neither interesting
nor relevant to her story. And when George Galloway, in the title of his
film, uses the word 'killing' he makes it perfectly clear that he's talking
of a financial killing. His producer has also told us that she has made
this distinction clear to Blair's office.

A similarly over-the-top letter went from Blair's head of communications
Rachel Grant to the *New Republic* after a piece by American investigative
journalist Ken Silverstein.[8] Our notes are in square brackets.

> Dear Sir,
>
> It's with huge disappointment that I read Ken Silverstein's unbalanced
> and vindictive article. [We thought it was well researched and
> thoughtful. Judge for yourself – it's at http://www.newrepublic.com/
> article/politics/magazine/107248/buckraking-around-the-world-
> tony-blair.]
>
> It is one thing to disagree with Mr Blair's views but it is something
> entirely different to not reflect our side of the argument simply
> because the facts don't fit the story.
>
> I spent a considerable amount of time explaining Mr Blair's
> work, the work of his charities and the fact that much of his work
> is done pro-bono – none of this has been reflected in the article.
> This is poor by any standard of journalism and unacceptable for a
> publication like the *New Republic*. [If Silverstein's conversations with
> Blair's spokespeople were like ours, they answered the questions they
> thought he should have asked, rather than the questions he did ask.]
>
> So to set the record straight again:
>
> Around two thirds of Mr Blair's time is spent doing pro-bono
> work. [We have asked for this figure and not been given it. In fact,

Blair goes to so many places wearing more than one hat that the figure cannot be worked out. For example, his meeting with the Emir of Kuwait described in Chapter 4 no doubt counts towards the two-thirds, because he was supposedly there as Middle East envoy. But the product was a contract for Tony Blair Associates.]

His commercial interests fund his philanthropic work. [We've asked for figures on this, which of course we've not been given. The Blair charities are largely funded by Blair's mega-rich friends – the likes of Haim Saban, Rupert Murdoch and Victor Pinchuk. No doubt Blair gives them some money too, but we do not know how much.]

The work in Kazakhstan is entirely in line with the international community's agenda for change, and many Western governments as well as international organizations, including the EU, OSCE and World Bank also work with Kazakhstan on this agenda. [It's one thing for governments to deal with a brutal dictator because he's there, he's the government, and he's containable. It's quite another for a company to take the man's money to go out into the world and burnish his image.]

The signs of progress in Kazakhstan, again which are not cited but which I gave to Mr Silverstein, are facts such as GDP reaching double digit growth in the last 20 years; Kazakhstan's renouncing of its nuclear weapons (something President Obama praised in his press conference recently with President Nazarbayev), it is a majority Muslim country of religious tolerance, and one of the few to have built a synagogue in recent years and that it has played a key role in supporting the allied effort in Afghanistan. [Silverstein was writing – properly, in our view, not about the economic growth of Kazakhstan, or its attitude to religion or nuclear weapons, but about human rights in the country.]

There is not space to list everything that is wrong in this article but you should not take that as any indication of its accuracy.

Yours faithfully
Rachel Grant
Director of Communications
The Office of Tony Blair

The last sentence of Grant's letter is a Blair classic, and is echoed in another exchange we have seen. The *Liberal Conspiracy* blog said, 'Blair currently receives £63,468 as part of his pension package following his exit from office, on top of an allowance of £84,000 a year. In case he felt this was an insufficient amount to live from, the variety of positions he has taken on led to an estimation that he had earned £80 million since leaving office in 2007.'

Blair's office replied, 'It's always best to check the facts before running a story. Firstly, the figures you quote on Mr Blair's earnings are completely wrong.' It did not say what the correct figures were.

There really is, among Blair and the Blairites, a feeling that they are under siege. Folk like Charles Clarke and journalist John Rentoul, still Blair's main cheerleader in national newspapers, feel genuinely affronted that anyone should be asking unwelcome questions about his activities.

His staff, even down to the humblest intern, have to sign ferocious confidentiality agreements – we have had several pained conversations with people who wanted to talk to us but had just re-read their agreements, which suggest all sorts of appalling consequences if they give us any information at all.

One of these, who worked in banking, thought the confidentiality agreement he had to sign in banks was ferocious – until he saw the one he had to sign before working for Tony Blair Associates. A bank's confidentiality agreement could be two or three pages long; this was more than twenty. One source required to sign such a document questioned whether it would pass current legal tests. But he does not care to find out.

Blair and the Blairites are genuinely baffled by why Blair is so reviled in Britain, hence the fury of Charles Clarke and the bafflement of John Rentoul, when we start asking questions; the instinct to close ranks against any intruder, to clam up and say nothing.

A former senior member of his staff says, 'My opinion is that his PR is rubbish because he feels so beleaguered; he thinks he'll never get a fair hearing in the British press. There are a few journalists that he knows and trusts, like John Rentoul, but he feels that the press is out to get him in a way.

'So he thinks, Even if I'm really cooperative with them, they'll still write bad things about me, so I'm not going to bother, I'm just not going to talk to any of them. People think there is something to hide when there isn't.'

That may be the reason, or part of the reason. But it is also true that treating any and every bit of hard information like gold bullion, never to be given away, enables Blair's spokespeople to throw dust in the faces of their pursuers. If you mention a figure – if you say, 'Is this the amount Blair receives annually from the government of Kazakhstan?' or, 'Is this the proportion of his income that Tony Blair gives to his charities?' – they will say, in a well-rehearsed phrase, that there has 'been a lot of inaccuracy' reported about his earnings.

They will tell you that your figure is wrong, but not give you an alternative figure. So everyone who writes about them has to make the best estimates possible, from the information that is available, and then they can then tell you that you have failed to check the facts.

His spokeswoman says the amount of money Blair gives to his charities is 'substantial', which tells us nothing. Why not tell us, and let us judge whether, against his earnings, it really is substantial? Why not do what the former member of his staff quoted above thinks he ought to be doing? 'I would stick the charities and the commercial activities in the same organisation and show figures,' says the former staff member. 'His charities employ large numbers of people, who have to be paid, so he's being phenomenally successful financially and, of course, he's made his family wealthy, which John Major has set out to do as well.'

A GOLD-PLATED PRISON

If Tony Blair were a private individual, out in the world enriching himself the best he can – as his immediate predecessor John Major is – he could get away with this sort of thing. Rightly or wrongly, we demand lower standards of transparency from private companies.

But most of Blair's money comes from the public sector in different countries, and most of his time is spent doing public-sector work. It is as though Capita were to take over government or local authority functions, but then say that, as a private company, it did not have to tell the public anything about them.

Tony Blair has turned himself into an international outsourcing company, very like Capita, but on a global scale. He will be, and should be, held to account for it in the international media. This book is an attempt to do just that.

NOTES

Chapter One

[1] www.jonathan-cook.net, 23 April 2013: http://www.jonathan-cook.net/2013-04-23/tony-blairs-tangled-web-the-quartet-representative-and-the-peace-process/

[2] www.bruxelles.blogs.liberation.fr, 22 October 2009: http://bruxelles.blogs.liberation.fr/coulisses/2009/10/conseil-europ%C3%A9en-comment-blair-a-fait-pschiiiiiiiiit.html

[3] *Daily Mail*, 28 September 2011: http://www.dailymail.co.uk/debate/article-2042775/Tony-Blairs-Middle-East-adventures.html

[4] Alvaro de Soto's report to the UN after his Middle East mission, 'End of Mission Report,' May 2007: http://image.guardian.co.uk/sys-files/Guardian/documents/2007/06/12/DeSotoReport.pdf

[5] *Ha'Aretz*, 19 July 2007: http://www.haaretz.com/weekend/magazine/all-the-dreams-we-had-are-now-gone-1.225828

[6] www.jonathan-cook.net, 23 April 2013: http://www.jonathan-cook.net/2013-04-23/tony-blairs-tangled-web-the-quartet-representative-and-the-peace-process/

[7] *The Guardian*, 21 June 2013: http://www.theguardian.com/politics/2013/jun/21/tony-blair-six-years-middle-east-envoy

[8] *Daily Mail*, 28 September 2011: http://www.dailymail.co.uk/debate/article-2042775/Tony-Blairs-Middle-East-adventures.html

[9] *Independent*, 16 December 2012: http://www.independent.co.uk/news/world/middle-east/useless-useless-useless-the-palestinian-verdict-on-tony-blairs-job-8421163.html

[10] http://www.tonyblairoffice.org/quartet/pages/how-we-work1/

[11] *The Guardian*, 13 May 2009: http://www.theguardian.com/commentisfree/belief/2009/may/13/tony-blair-faith-foundation

[12] Toby Greene, *Blair, Labour and Palestine* (Bloomsbury, 2013)

[13] *The New York Times*, 5 September 2004: http://www.nytimes.com/2004/09/05/business/yourmoney/05sab.html?_r=1&

[14] www.project-syndicate.org, 10 June 2013: http://www.project-syndicate.org/commentary/lee-rigby-and-the-struggle-to-contain-violent-islamists-by-tony-blair#i02z3GXBCdjblch4.99

[15] *Daily Telegraph*, 4 July 2010: http://www.telegraph.co.uk/news/politics/labour/7870784/Tony-Blairs-security-team-cost-the-taxpayer-250000-a-year.html

[16] *The Guardian*, 25 September 2011: http://www.theguardian.com/politics/2011/sep/25/tony-blair-middle-east-deals

[17] http://www.palestine-studies.org/files/pdf/jps/11844.pdf [document no longer available]

[18] *Financial Times Magazine*, 29 June 2012: http://www.ft.com/cms/s/2/b2ec4fd6-c0af-11e1-9372-00144feabdc0.html

[19] *The Times*, 24 May 2007: http://www.thetimes.co.uk/tto/business/industries/naturalresources/article2180803.ece

[20] *Ha'Aretz*, 8 June 2012: http://www.haaretz.com/news/middle-east/palestinian-court-sentences-arafat-aide-in-absentia-1.435118

[21] *Financial Times*, 21 December 2009: http://www.ft.com/cms/s/0/d375ca6c-edcf-11de-ba12-00144feab49a.html#axzz3PdBxIRoI.

[22] *Daily Mail*, 14 December 2010: http://www.dailymail.co.uk/news/article-1338368/Tony-Blairs-company-make-27m-advising-Kuwait-govern-itself.html#ixzz2iRbEO7wm

[23] www.mondoweiss.net, 31 May 2013: http://mondoweiss.net/2013/05/billion-palestine-capitalism.html

[24] *Times of Israel*, 27 May 2013: http://www.timesofisrael.com/memo-to-kerry-its-not-the-economy-stupid/

[25] Ibid.

[26] *Le Monde*, 28 September 2013

[27] http://www.quartetrep.org/quartet/pages/the-initiative-for-the-palestinian-economy

[28] *The National Interest*, 25 September 2011: http://nationalinterest.org/blog/jacob-heilbrunn/tony-blairs-closest-business-partner-col-gadaffi-5931

Chapter Two

[1] http://www.tonyblairoffice.org

[2] *The Sunday Times*, 22 February 2009: http://www.thesundaytimes.co.uk/sto/Test/politics/article151975.ece

NOTES

[3] Ken Silverstein, *The Secret World of Oil* (Verso Books, 2014)

[4] *The Guardian*, 1 December 2009: http://www.guardian.co.uk/politics/2009/dec/01/mystery-tony-blair-finances

[5] *New Republic*, 4 October 2012: http://www.tnr.com/article/politics/magazine/107248/buckraking-around-the-world-tony-blair

[6] *Sunday Telegraph*, 13 January 2013: http://www.telegraph.co.uk/news/politics/tony-blair/9797837/Tony-Blair-widens-his-web-via-the-stock-markets.html

[7] Ibid.

[8] *Daily Telegraph*, 13 January 2013: http://www.telegraph.co.uk/news/politics/tony-blair/9797837/Tony-Blair-widens-his-web-via-the-stock-markets.html

[9] *The Guardian*, 24 September 2011: http://www.theguardian.com/politics/2011/sep/24/tony-blair-mark-labovitch-resignation

[10] www.taxresearch.org.uk/Blog/, 1 December 2009: http://www.taxresearch.org.uk/Blog/2009/12/01/what-has-blair-got-to-hide-because-thats-the-riddle-at-the-heart-of-the-conundrum/#sthash.7H6qLB6Y.dpuf

[11] Nicholas Shaxson, *Treasure Islands: Tax Havens and the Men who Stole the World* (Vintage, 2012)

[12] Accounts from Windrush Ventures, 2013

[13] *The Guardian*, 17 March 2010: http://www.theguardian.com/politics/2010/mar/17/tony-blair-cash-south-korea-oil

[14] www.oneindia.com, 8 November 2010: http://news.oneindia.in/2010/11/08/toiletroll-talk-fetches-tony-blair-50kpounds.html

[15] *Daily Telegraph*, 9 June 2013: http://www.telegraph.co.uk/news/politics/tony-blair/10108005/Tony-Blair-strikes-gold-in-Mongolia.html

[16] *Daily Mail*, 9 September 2012: http://www.dailymail.co.uk/news/article-2200655/The-million-dollar-man-How-Tony-Blair-wafted-Claridges-secure-massive-pay-day-just-hours-work.html

[17] *Daily Telegraph*, 18 November 2012: http://www.telegraph.co.uk/news/politics/tony-blair/9685253/Tony-Blair-strikes-business-deals-in-Brazil-and-Colombia.html

[18] *Daily Telegraph*, 4 January 2014: http://www.telegraph.co.uk/news/politics/tony-blair/10551183/Tony-Blairs-fortune-boosted-13m-by-bumper-year.html

Chapter Three

[1] www.bruxelles.blogs.liberation.fr, 22 October 2009: http://bruxelles.blogs.liberation.fr/coulisses/2009/10/conseil-europ%C3%A9en-comment-blair-a-fait-pschiiiiiiiiit.html

[2] *The Times*, 10 July 2014.

[3] *The Economist*, 22 October 2009: http://www.economist.com/blogs/charlemagne/2009/10/tony_blair_s_eu_hopes_go_pschi

[4] *Süddeutsche Zeitung*, 17 May 2010: http://www.sueddeutsche.de/politik/

einigung-auf-neues-spitzenduo-europas-kleiner-nenner-1.133484

[5] www.bruxelles.blogs.liberation.fr, 22 October 2009: http://bruxelles.blogs.liberation.fr/coulisses/2009/10/conseil-europ%C3%A9en-comment-blair-a-fait-pschiiiiiiiiit.html

[6] *Le Monde*, 3 June 2014

[7] *Financial Times*, 29 January 2008: http://www.ft.com/cms/s/0/9ccda392-cdea-11dc-9e4e-000077b07658.html#axzz3PdeFazIc

[8] www.bloomberg.com, 28 January 2008: http://www.bloomberg.com/apps/news?pid=newsarchive&sid=atrJFZT2p9Kc&refer=uk

[9] *Daily Telegraph*, 9 January 2010: http://www.telegraph.co.uk/news/politics/6950815/Tony-Blairs-new-job-with-luxury-goods-firm.html

[10] http://www.bornrich.com/bernard-arnault.html

Chapter Four

[1] *Forbes*, 20 November 2012: http://www.forbes.com/sites/stevedenning/2012/11/20/what-killed-michael-porters-monitor-group-the-one-force-that-really-matters/3/

[2] *Daily Telegraph*, 23 September 2011: http://www.telegraph.co.uk/news/politics/tony-blair/8784596/On-the-desert-trail-of-Tony-Blairs-millions.html

[3] http://www.american.edu/soc/success/haneen-communication.cfm

[4] http://www.freedomhouse.org/template.cfm?page=251&year=2010

[5] Trade Arabia, 23 October 2009: http://beta.tradearabia.net/news/OGN_169308.html

[6] *The Sunday Times*, 3 January 2010: http://www.timesonline.co.uk/tol/news/world/iraq/article6973974.ece

[7] http://en.wikipedia.org/wiki/Khaldoon_Al_Mubarak (as of 1 February 2015)

[8] *The Sunday Times*, 3 January 2010: http://www.timesonline.co.uk/tol/news/world/iraq/article6973974.ece

[9] *Gulf News*, 26 July 2007: http://gulfnews.com/news/gulf/uae/government/mohammad-bin-zayed-makes-short-visit-to-qatar-1.191313

[10] *Gulf News*, 23 November 2007: http://gulfnews.com/news/gulf/uae/government/abdullah-stresses-joint-efforts-for-peace-1.213572

[11] *Gulf News*, 21 March 2009: http://gulfnews.com/only-two-state-solution-to-middle-east-issue-says-blair-1.58709

[12] *Gulf News*, 15 April 2008: http://gulfnews.com/news/gulf/uae/government/uaes-shaikh-abdullah-receives-middle-east-special-envoy-tony-blair-1.98099

[13] http://www.tonyblairfaithfoundation.org/newsroom/entry/hct-links-arms-with-tony-blair-faith-foundation-to-develop-new-multi-f/ [page since removed]

Chapter Five

[1] *New Republic*, 4 October 2012: http://www.tnr.com/article/politics/
magazine/107248/buckraking-around-the-world-tony-blair

[2] Ken Silverstein, *The Secret World of Oil* (Verso, 2014)

[3] https://www.youtube.com/watch?v=xaWWw1lwwpE

[4] Authors' interview with Ken Olisa, 2014

[5] Jonathan Aitken, *Nazarbayev and the Making of Kazakhstan* (Continuum, 2009)

[6] *Independent*, 31 October 2011: http://www.independent.co.uk/news/people/
profiles/the-two-faces-of-tony-blair-6255021.html

[7] *Independent*, 12 March 2011: http://www.independent.co.uk/news/people/
profiles/goga-ashkenazi-by-royal-ascent-2239797.html

[8] *Daily Mail*, 15 December 2011: http://www.dailymail.co.uk/news/
article-2074374/Goga-Ashkenazi-Prince-Andrews-pal-joy-killing-wolf.html

[9] http://www.tap-ag.com/the-pipeline/the-big-picture/southern-gas-corridor

[10] www.bbc.co.uk, 9 October 2013: http://www.bbc.co.uk/news/world-
europe-24450227

[11] *Washington Post*, 9 October 2013: http://www.washingtonpost.com/blogs/
worldviews/wp/2013/10/09/oops-azerbaijan-released-election-results-before-voting-
had-even-started/

Chapter Six

[1] www.asiancorrespondent.com, 22 October 2012: http://asiancorrespondent.
com/91064/tony-blair-adds-burma-to-se-asia-good-governance-tour/

[2] Ibid.

[3] Ibid.

[4] *New Republic*, 21 January 2014: http://www.newrepublic.com/article/116241/
burma-2014-countryside-concentration-camps?b&utm_campaign=tnr-daily-
newsletter&utm_source=hs_email&utm_medium=email&utm_content=11717587

[5] Ibid.

[6] Ibid.

[7] Ibid.

[8] *Daily Mail*, 19 March 2010: http://www.dailymail.co.uk/news/article-1259030/
Tony-Blairs-secret-dealings-South-Korean-oil-firm-UI-Energy-Corp.
html#ixzz1XrL59Pgo

[9] *The Guardian*, 17 March 2010: http://www.guardian.co.uk/politics/2010/
mar/17/tony-blair-cash-south-korea-oil

[10] *Daily Mail*, 19 March 2010: http://www.dailymail.co.uk/news/article-1259030/
Tony-Blairs-secret-dealings-South-Korean-oil-firm-UI-Energy-Corp.
html#ixzz1XrL59Pgo

[11] *Daily Mail*, 20 March 2010: http://www.dailymail.co.uk/news/article-1259496/

Boss-Korean-firm-gave-Tony-Blair-secret-cash-jailed-bribery.html#ixzz1ibrZ6APW
[12] *Daily Mail*, 11 June 2013: http://www.dailymail.co.uk/news/article-2339864/
ALEX-BRUMMER-Sewer-rats-The-greedy-foreign-owners-water-firms-squeeze-
customers-dry-Thames-Water-avoiding-tax-final-insult.html#ixzz2r2o0MVeX
[13] *Independent*, 11 June 2013: http://www.independent.co.uk/news/uk/home-
news/sold-down-the-river-how-thames-water-diverts-its-tax-liability-via-the-
caribbean-despite-549m-profit-and-67-price-hike-8652305.html
[14] Ibid.
[15] Ibid.

Chapter Seven
[1] Ken Silverstein, *The Secret World of Oil* (Verso, 2014)
[2] Ibid.
[3] *Daily Telegraph*, 1 October 2011: http://www.telegraph.co.uk/news/politics/tony-
blair/8801699/Libyan-link-oligarch-funded-Blair-initiative.html
[4] *Daily Telegraph*, 4 August 2013: http://www.telegraph.co.uk/news/politics/tony-
blair/10220684/Tony-Blair-helped-Colonel-Gaddafi-in-1bn-legal-row.html
[5] www.politico.com, 21 February 2011: http://www.politico.com/blogs/
laurarozen/0211/Among_Libyas_lobbyists.html?showall
[6] *Time*, 18 May 2006: http://www.time.com/time/world/
article/0,8599,1195852,00.html#ixzz2Zl24q2Jq
[7] *Daily Mail*, 6 September 2009: http://www.dailymail.co.uk/news/
article-1211483/Ex-spy-BPs-Lawrence-Arabia.html#ixzz1EtrE0VMc
[8] http://www.lse.ac.uk/IDEAS/people/bios/allenMark.aspx
[9] *Independent*, 6 September 2011: http://www.independent.co.uk/news/world/
africa/libyan-rebel-leader-says-mi6-knew-he-was-tortured-2349778.html
[10] *The Guardian*, 23 October 2013: http://www.theguardian.com/global/2013/
oct/23/abdel-hakim-belhaj-justice-llibyan-dissident
[11] *The Guardian*, 4 September 2011: http://www.theguardian.com/world/2011/
sep/04/mark-allen-mi6-libya-profile; *Daily Telegraph*, 22 July 2010: http://www.
telegraph.co.uk/news/worldnews/northamerica/usa/7905061/BPs-MI6-adviser-
called-before-Senate-over-Libya-deal.html; *Independent*, 6 September 2011: http://
www.independent.co.uk/news/world/africa/libyan-rebel-leader-says-mi6-knew-he-
was-tortured-2349778.html
[12] *Daily Mail*, 6 September 2009: http://www.dailymail.co.uk/news/
article-1211483/Ex-spy-BPs-Lawrence-Arabia.html#ixzz2khf2wBBc
[13] *Daily Telegraph*, 4 August 2013: http://www.telegraph.co.uk/news/politics/tony-
blair/10220684/Tony-Blair-helped-Colonel-Gaddafi-in-1bn-legal-row.html
[14] *Daily Telegraph*, 29 January 2010: http://www.telegraph.co.uk/news/earth/
environment/climatechange/7054986/Tony-Blairs-climate-change-project-paid-

for-by-Oleg-Deripaska-oligarch-who-entertained-Lord-Mandelson-and-George-Osborne.html

[15] *Daily Telegraph*, 24 September 2011: http://www.telegraph.co.uk/news/politics/tony-blair/8787074/Tony-Blairs-six-secret-visits-to-Col-Gaddafi.html

[16] *The Week*, 1 December 2011: http://www.theweek.co.uk/uk-news/saif-gaddafi/43196/blair-government-pressured-oxford-admit-saif-gaddafi; *Daily Telegraph*, 30 November 2011: http://www.telegraph.co.uk/education/universityeducation/8926790/Blairs-government-tried-to-get-Oxford-place-for-Saif-Gaddafi.html; www.narkive.com, http://uk.politics.misc.narkive.com/SoJRL3QZ/education-education-education-tony-blair-tried-to-get-saif-gaddafi-into-oxford

[17] *Time*, 18 May 2006: http://www.time.com/time/world/article/0,8599,1195852,00.html

[18] www.bbc.co.uk, http://www.bbc.co.uk/news/education-15966132

Chapter Eight
[1] *Daily Telegraph*, 17 December 2011: http://www.telegraph.co.uk/news/politics/8963427/Lord-Mandelson-courted-Mubaraks-dying-regime.html

[2] *The Guardian*, 2 July 2014: http://www.theguardian.com/politics/2014/jul/02/tony-blair-advise-egypt-president-sisi-economic-reform

[3] *The Guardian*, 2 October 2011: http://www.theguardian.com/politics/2011/oct/02/peter-mandelson-asia-business

[4] *Independent on Sunday*, 13 January 2008: http://www.independent.co.uk/news/uk/politics/secret-nuclear-talks-held-at-no-10-769989.html

[5] *The Guardian*, 2 October 2011: http://www.theguardian.com/politics/2011/oct/02/peter-mandelson-asia-business

[6] Ibid.

[7] *Mail on Sunday*, 26 October 2008: http://www.dailymail.co.uk/news/article-1080660/Use-Ferrari-Mandy-told-Rothschild-Klosters-holiday.html

[8] *Daily Telegraph*, 25 January 2012: http://www.telegraph.co.uk/news/politics/9036927/Nathaniel-Rothschild-says-sauna-with-Lord-Mandelson-was-purely-pleasure-not-business.html

[9] *Independent*, 11 February 2012: http://www.independent.co.uk/news/uk/home-news/rothschild-loses-libel-case-and-reveals-secret-world-of-money-and-politics-6720015.html

[10] *Daily Telegraph*, 10 February 2012: http://www.telegraph.co.uk/news/politics/9073717/Nathaniel-Rothschild-loses-High-Court-libel-battle.html

[11] *Financial Times*, 18 November 2012: http://www.ft.com/cms/s/0/6a7f9d88-3180-11e2-92f0-00144feabdc0.html#axzz2d43qGI3p

[12] www.caijing.com.cn, 22 June 2005: http://english.caijing.com.cn/2005-06-22/100013763.html

[13] *The Guardian*, 10 May 2012: http://www.theguardian.com/politics/2012/may/10/mandelson-advises-company-rainforest

Chapter Nine
[1] *The Guardian*, 2 February 2011: http://www.guardian.co.uk/politics/2011/feb/02/ccc-construction-high-court-contempt
[2] www.uk.practicallaw.com, 26 May 2011: http://uk.practicallaw.com/5-506-1731?sd=plc
[3] *Independent*, 24 March 2010: http://www.independent.co.uk/news/uk/politics/so-is-there-any-truth-in-stephen-byers-claims-that-he-was-able-to-alter-policy-1926156.html
[4] *The Guardian*, 2 February 2011: http://www.guardian.co.uk/politics/2011/feb/02/ccc-construction-high-court-contempt
[5] *Union News*, 28 August 2014: http://union-news.co.uk/2014/08/forced-labour-university-college-london-campus/
[6] http://wikileaks.org/syria-files/docs/2089956_political-communications.html
[7] *Sunday Times*, 15 June 2014
[8] *Los Angeles Times*, 21 February 2001: http://articles.latimes.com/2001/feb/21/news/mn-28265
[9] *Daily Telegraph*, 8 September 2012: http://www.telegraph.co.uk/finance/newsbysector/industry/mining/9527478/Glencore-and-Xstrata-merger-descends-into-acrimony.html
[10] *Financial Times*, 4 July 2013: http://www.ft.com/cms/s/2/dc99ef1e-de45-11e2-9b47-00144feab7de.html#slide0
[11] *Wall Street Journal*, 7 February 2012: http://blogs.wsj.com/deals/2012/02/07/one-banker-stood-on-both-sides-of-glencore-xstrata/
[12] *Euromoney*, September 2013 http://www.euromoney.com/Article/3256868/Abigail-with-attitude-Phone-chargerVerizon-flexes-its.html
[13] *Mailonline*, 15 September 2012: http://www.dailymail.co.uk/news/article-2203546/Tony-Blair--1m-hour-mediator-lives-opulent-country-estate.html
[14] *The Guardian*, 11 May 2012: http://www.theguardian.com/business/2012/may/11/court-tony-blair-hotels-bid

Chapter Ten
[1] *Daily Telegraph*, 18 November 2012: http://www.telegraph.co.uk/news/politics/tony-blair/9685253/Tony-Blair-strikes-business-deals-in-Brazil-and-Colombia.html
[2] www.npr.org, 27 January 2014: http://www.npr.org/2014/01/27/264901370/california-fights-billionaire-s-keep-out-sign-for-beach-access

NOTES

Chapter Eleven

[1] www.hrw.org, 19 September 2010: http://www.hrw.org/news/2010/09/21/rwanda-president-crisis

[2] *The Economist*, 7 April 2014: http://www.economist.com/blogs/blighty/2014/04/tony-blair-s-latest-intervention

[3] www.bloomberg.com, 30 November 2010: http://www.bloomberg.com/news/2010-11-30/jpmorgan-s-ceo-jamie-dimon-incredibly-impressed-by-africa-opportunity.html

[4] www.hrw.org, 19 September 2010: http://www.hrw.org/news/2010/09/21/rwanda-president-crisis

Chapter Twelve

[1] www.tonyblairoffice.org, 3 April 2008: http://www.tonyblairoffice.org/news/entry/millennium-development-goals-are-litmus-test-of-worlds-values/

[2] www.tonyblairoffice.org, 5 December 2008: http://www.tonyblairoffice.org/news/entry/tony-blair-and-belinda-stronach-join-together-to-support-faiths-act-fellows/

[3] www.tonyblairoffice.org, 30 March 2009: http://www.tonyblairoffice.org/news/entry/bringing-people-together-across-faith-communities-for-action-in-africa/

[4] www.tonyblairoffice.org, 15 April 2009: http://www.tonyblairoffice.org/news/entry/ten-uk-faith-fellows-announced-to-help-deliver-millennium-development-goals/

[5] www.tonyblairoffice.org, 8 July 2009: http://www.tonyblairoffice.org/news/entry/tony-blair-announces-durham-university-partnership-as-faith-and-globalisati/

[6] www.tonyblairoffice.org, 8 October 2009: http://www.tonyblairoffice.org/news/entry/tony-blair-attends-launch-of-transatlantic-healthcare-alliance-between-yale/

[7] *Daily Telegraph*, 19 December 2012: http://www.telegraph.co.uk/news/politics/6844763/Tony-Blair-earned-680000-for-his-foundation-for-50-hours-work.html

[8] http://www.thetablet.co.uk/article/4774 [page no longer available]

[9] Francis Beckett, *Gordon Brown: Past, Present and Future* (Haus Publishing, 2007)

[10] *Daily Telegraph*, 26 February 2012: http://www.telegraph.co.uk/news/politics/labour/9105663/Charles-Clarke-Thanks-to-religion-Ive-found-life-after-politics.html

[11] Authors' interview with Martin Bright

[12] *The Guardian*, 25 January 2014: http://www.theguardian.com/politics/2014/jan/25/extremist-religion-wars-tony-blair

[13] *Jewish Chronicle*, 24 January 2014: http://www.thejc.com/comment-and-debate/columnists/115017/finding-nuance-religious-debate-i%E2%80%99ve-got-quite-a-job

[14] *Daily Mail*, 2 August 2014: http://www.dailymail.co.uk/news/article-2714316/Inside-Blair-s-lair-Five-spin-doctors-ministerial-red-box-town-hall-meetings-doughnuts-deals-dictators-After-THAT-party-Cherie-former-ex-PM-employee-reveals-really-happens.html

[15] *Daily Telegraph*, 13 February 2010: http://www.telegraph.co.uk/news/religion/7229874/Tony-Blairs-faith-charity-pays-six-figure-salaries-to-top-officials.html

[16] *Arab News*, 31 October 2014: http://www.arabnews.com/news/652761

[17] *Daily Mail*, 2 June 2013: http://www.dailymail.co.uk/debate/article-2334560/The-ideology-Lee-Rigbys-murder-profound-dangerous-Why-dont-admit--Tony-Blair-launches-brave-assault-Muslim-extremism-Woolwich-attack.html

[18] *Independent*, 8 April 2009: http://www.independent.co.uk/news/world/politics/blair-pope-is-wrong-about-gays-ndash-and-most-catholics-think-so-too-1665363.html

[19] *The Guardian*, 13 May 2009: http://www.theguardian.com/commentisfree/belief/2009/may/13/tony-blair-faith-foundation

[20] www.catholicactionuk.blogspot.co.uk, 5 December 2008: http://catholicactionuk.blogspot.co.uk/2008/12/dossier-on-cherie-blair.html

[21] *The Catholic Universe*, 18 September 2014: http://www.thecatholicuniverse.com/priest-tells-rochdale-inquiry-horrific-abuse-school-4174

[22] *Independent*, 8 April 2009: http://www.dailymail.co.uk/news/article-1370323/Tony-Blairs-priest-fixed-papal-knighthoods-cash.html

[23] http://www.allindiaimamorganization.org/about-umer-ilyasi.html [page no longer available]

[24] www.berkleycenter.georgetown.edu, 1 July 2010: http://berkleycenter.georgetown.edu/interviews/a-discussion-with-bishop-josiah-fearon-of-kaduna

[25] www.ynaija.com, 22 December 2013: http://www.ynaija.com/corruption-worse-than-homosexuality-bishop-of-kaduna-speaks/

[26] http://www.centralsynagogue.org/about_us/our_clergy/rubinstein

[27] *Observer*, 14 March 2010: http://www.theguardian.com/politics/2010/mar/14/tony-blair-faith-foundation-america

[28] Ibid.

[28] www.huffingtonpost.com, 5 November 2012: http://www.huffingtonpost.com/charles-andrew-flamiano/letting-go-letting-god-faith-shorts-finalist_b_2134803.html

[29] *Daily Mirror*, 28 February 2014: http://www.mirror.co.uk/news/uk-news/rupert-murdoch-donated-100000-tony-3190828#ixzz3CGpWUzlk

[30] http://www.washingtonindependent.com/86305/but-really-would-joe-lieberman-ever-criticize-israel

[31] *New Yorker*, 10 May 2010: http://www.newyorker.com/magazine/2010/05/10/the-influencer

[32] www.tabletmag.com, 14 May 2010: http://www.tabletmag.com/scroll/33826/will-israel%E2%80%99s-%E2%80%98rich-uncle%E2%80%99-buy-%E2%80%98newsweek%E2%80%99

[33] *Sunday Telegraph*, 10 February 2013: http://www.telegraph.co.uk/news/politics/to-ny-blair/9859780/Revealed-Tony-Blair-and-the-oligarch-bankrolling-his-charity.html

[34] www.interpipe.biz, 24 October 2012: http://www.interpipe.biz/en/media/newsone/58S

[35] http://tonyblairfaithfoundation.org/foundation/news/tony-blair-announces-new-education-projects-ukraine [page no longer available]

[36] *Daily Telegraph*, 10 February 2013: http://www.telegraph.co.uk/news/politics/tony-blair/9859780/Revealed-Tony-Blair-and-the-oligarch-bankrolling-his-charity.html

[37] *The Times*, 12 October 2013: http://www.thetimes.co.uk/tto/law/article3892816.ece

[38] *Daily Telegraph*, 10 February 2013: http://www.telegraph.co.uk/news/politics/tony-blair/9859780/Revealed-Tony-Blair-and-the-oligarch-bankrolling-his-charity.html

[39] *Spectator*, 17 September 2012: http://blogs.spectator.co.uk/coffeehouse/2012/09/britain-should-call-for-reform-of-existing-blasphemy-laws/

[40] www.liberalconspiracy.org, 3 July 2013: http://liberalconspiracy.org/2013/07/03/excl-tony-blairs-office-once-agains-caught-not-paying-interns/

[41] http://www.tonyblairoffice.org/sports/

[42] www.tonyblairoffice.org, 18 March 2011: http://www.tonyblairoffice.org/news/entry/join-team-tbsf-in-running-jogging-or-even-walking-the-great-north-run-and-h/

Chapter Thirteen

[1] *Daily Mail*, 30 October 2010: http://www.dailymail.co.uk/news/article-1324985/Cherie-Blairs-father-Tony-reveals-doesnt-love-daughter-Lauren-Booth.html

[2] http://freetown.usembassy.gov/usaid.html

[3] *Financial Times*, 30 March 2012: http://www.ft.com/cms/s/0/dff5c3a0-7a63-11e1-839f-00144feab49a.html#axzz3CjApK9Gr

[4] http://thewilberforcesociety.co.uk/proposed-constitutional-framework-for-the-republic-of-tunisia/

[5] *The Sunday Times*, 5 February 2012: http://www.thesundaytimes.co.uk/sto/news/uk_news/People/article867909.ece

[6] www.hrw.org, 1 September 2014: http://www.hrw.org/news/2014/09/01/dispatches-time-stand-bahrain-s-dissidents

[7] https://www.youtube.com/watch?v=8bOeLWxL87M

[8] www.order-order.com, 22 September 2012

[9] *Daily Mirror*, 14 June 2014: http://www.mirror.co.uk/sport/football/news/tony-blairs-son-nicky-set-3695781

Chapter Fourteen
[1] http://www.zoopla.co.uk/property/29-connaught-square/london/w2-2hl/25001801
[2] *Daily Mail*, 30 June 2007: http://www.dailymail.co.uk/news/article-465370/The-ghostly-history-Blairs-new-home-Connaught-Square.html#ixzz2hd5nU8oM
[3] http://beakstreetbugle.com/articles/view/31/unsung-heroes-the-agency-producer
[4] *Daily Mail*, 25 June 2006: http://www.dailymail.co.uk/femail/article-392345/Cheries-fixer-dumps-lover-married-lawyer-whos-Tory.html
[5] http://publicaccess.aylesburyvaledc.gov.uk/online-applications/files/8BFBB735D306045106EC07166D67D550/pdf/11_00928_ATP-DELEGATED-1009746.pdf [page no longer available]
[6] http://publicaccess.aylesburyvaledc.gov.uk/online-applications/files/81DA36B7B7977843311C38E10C82F48C/pdf/11_02700_APP-DELEGATED-1058069.pdf [page no longer available]
[7] *Daily Telegraph*, 14 January 2012: http://www.telegraph.co.uk/news/politics/9013969/Tony-Blair-is-accused-of-damaging-character-of-his-country-estate.html
[8] http://publicaccess.aylesburyvaledc.gov.uk/online-applications/files/81DA36B7B7977843311C38E10C82F48C/pdf/11_02700_APP-DELEGATED-1058069.pdf [page no longer available]
[9] *Daily Mail*, 3 October 2014: http://www.dailymail.co.uk/news/article-2779244/Cherie-Blair-son-Euan-landlords-block-650-000-Victorian-era-block-flats-rubbish-hasn-t-collected-weeks.html

Chapter Fifteen
[1] Tony Blair, *A Journey* (Arrow, 2011)
[2] *Ibid*
[3] *The Guardian*, 22 October 2013: http://www.theguardian.com/politics/2013/oct/22/john-major-windfall-tax-energy
[4] *London Evening Standard*, 27 September 2013: http://www.standard.co.uk/news/politics/tony-blair-refuses-to-back-ed-miliband-on-energy-price-freeze-8841475.html
[5] *Daily Mail*, 27 September 2013: http://www.dailymail.co.uk/news/article-2435751/Red-Eds-pledge-bring-socialism-homage-Marxist-father-Ralph-Miliband-says-GEOFFREY-LEVY.html
[6] http://www.mjrharris.co.uk/?s=azerbaijan
[7] www.socialistunity.com, 14 March 2012: http://socialistunity.com/progress-a-

party-within-a-party/; www.progressonline.co.uk, 21 February 2012: http://www.progressonline.org.uk/2012/02/21/response-to-the-recent-document-concerning-progress/; http://www.progressonline.org.uk/about-progress/how-progress-is-funded/

[8] www.leftfutures.org, 13 March 2011: http://www.leftfutures.org/2011/03/welcome-to-the-blairite-party-within-a-party/

[9] *Tribune*, 27 July 2012

[10] www.politics.co.uk, 7 May 2012: http://www.politics.co.uk/news/2012/05/07/comment-leave-us-alone-tony-blair

[11] *London Evening Standard*, 22 January 2014: http://www.standard.co.uk/comment/matthew-dancona-tony-blairs-instincts-on-iraq-were-right--and-syria-proves-it-9077015.html

[12] http://www.iraqinquiry.org.uk/

[13] *The Economist*, 30 December 2014: http://www.economist.com/news/britain/21637431-former-labour-leader-casts-doubt-his-partys-chances-winning-next-election-dont-go

[14] *The Guardian*, 31 December 2014: http://www.theguardian.com/politics/2014/dec/31/tony-blair-denies-report-saying-ed-miliband-cant-win-2015-election

[15] *Daily Telegraph*, 13 January 2015. http://www.telegraph.co.uk/news/politics/ed-miliband/11341667/Voters-must-decide-if-Ed-Miliband-has-a-problem-says-Tony-Blair.html

[16] *Daily Telegraph*, 19 June 2014: http://www.telegraph.co.uk/news/politics/ed-miliband/10911015/Ed-Miliband-is-confused-and-unconvincing-Lord-Mandelson-says.html

[17] *Daily Telegraph*, 13 January 2015: http://www.telegraph.co.uk/news/politics/ed-miliband/11341667/Voters-must-decide-if-Ed-Miliband-has-a-problem-says-Tony-Blair.html

[18] *The Guardian*, 7 February 2015: http://www.theguardian.com/politics/2015/feb/07/tony-blair-ed-miliband-labour-general-election

[19] *The Guardian*, 13 November 2013: http://www.theguardian.com/politics/2013/nov/13/falkirk-labour-gregor-poynton-paid-recruits

[20] *Daily Telegraph*, 23 September 2011: http://www.telegraph.co.uk/news/politics/tony-blair/8784596/On-the-desert-trail-of-Tony-Blairs-millions.html; *The Guardian*, 10 April 2009: http://www.guardian.co.uk/politics/blog/2009/apr/10/tony-blair-speaking-fees;
Daily Mail, 6 April 2009: http://www.dailymail.co.uk/news/article-1167682/Blair-worlds-best-paid-speaker-pocketing-364-000-just-hours-work.html

[21] Ken Silverstein, *The Secret World of Oil* (Verso, 2014)

[22] *Daily Telegraph*, 9 November 2007: http://www.telegraph.co.uk/news/worldnews/1568845/Chinese-turn-on-Tony-Blair-over-speech.html; *New Republic*,

4 October 2012: http://www.newrepublic.com/article/politics/magazine/107248/
buckraking-around-the-world-tony-blair

[23] *Observer*, 14 March 2010: http://www.theguardian.com/politics/2010/mar/14/
tony-blair-faith-foundation-america

Chapter Sixteen

[1] *Financial Times*, 21 March 2014: http://www.ft.com/cms/s/2/c1fc1f6a-afc3-
11e3-9cd1-00144feab7de.html#axzz3RcyFtS69

[2] *Daily Telegraph*, 23 July 2012: http://www.telegraph.co.uk/news/politics/tony-
blair/9420909/Tony-Blair-The-West-is-asleep-on-the-issue-of-Islamist-extremism.
html

[3] *Nonprofit Quarterly*, 1 December 2014: https://nonprofitquarterly.org/
policysocial-context/25241-save-the-children-s-own-staff-deem-tony-blair-s-
humanitarian-award-reprehensible.html

[4] *The Guardian*, 28 November 2014: http://www.theguardian.com/politics/2014/
nov/28/save-the-children-tony-blair-award-row

[5] *Washington Post*, 26 November 2014: http://www.washingtonpost.com/blogs/
worldviews/wp/2014/11/26/what-is-tony-blairs-global-legacy/

[6] http://www.38degrees.org.uk/, 27 January 2015: http://blog.38degrees.org.
uk/2015/01/27/tony-blair-global-legacy-award-campaign/

[7] *New Republic*, 4 October 2012: http://www.newrepublic.com/article/politics/
magazine/107248/buckraking-around-the-world-tony-blair

INDEX